Without Apology

Without Apology

Writings on Abortion in Canada

EDITED BY SHANNON STETTNER

AU PRESS

Copyright © 2016 Shannon Stettner

Published by AU Press, Athabasca University
1200, 10011 – 109 Street, Edmonton, AB T5J 3S8

ISBN 978-1-77199-159-9 (pbk.)   978-1-77199-160-5 (PDF)   978-1-77199-161-2 (epub)
doi: 10.15215/aupress/9781771991599.01

Cover design by Marvin Harder, marvinharder.com.
Interior design by Sergiy Kozakov.
Printed and bound in Canada by Friesens.

Library and Archives Canada Cataloguing in Publication

Without apology : writings on abortion in Canada / edited by Shannon Stettner.

Includes bibliographical references.
Issued in print and electronic formats.

    1. Abortion—Canada. 2. Abortion—Canada—History. 3. Abortion—Canada—
Anecdotes. I. Stettner, Shannon, editor

HQ767.5.C2W58 2016   362.1988'80971   C2016-902290-0
                                                 C2016-902291-9

We acknowledge the support of the Canada Council for the Arts, which last year
invested $153 million to bring the arts to Canadians throughout the country.

 Canada Council   Conseil des arts
for the Arts   du Canada

We acknowledge the financial support of the Government of Canada through the
Canada Book Fund (CFB) for our publishing activities.

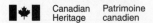 Canadian   Patrimoine
Heritage   canadien

Assistance provided by the Government of Alberta, Alberta Media Fund.

Government

Contents

Acknowledgements

The first acknowledgment belongs to my friend and colleague Kristin Burnett, who encouraged me to pursue this project. She has generously reviewed several chapters, and I appreciate her support, advice, and friendship throughout.

I extend my deepest gratitude to all of the contributors who have shared their stories, experiences, ideas, and research. I'm thankful that they have entrusted me with their words. Their voices are brave, powerful, intelligent, compassionate, and inspiring.

I am indebted to the wonderful people at Athabasca University Press; their commitment to this collection has made for a rewarding relationship. In particular, I am grateful to Megan Hall, for her direction and support, and, especially, to Pamela Holway, who has been a thoughtful guide, pushing my analysis and prose, helping the book achieve greater clarity and sense of purpose. Thanks as well to the anonymous reviewers who were as excited about the project as I am.

My works builds on the wonderful scholarship and activism of many historians, feminists, and social commentators. Their commitment to this issue and to social justice is inspiring.

Finally, I am grateful for my family and friends and for their love and support over the several years of this project. How lucky am I that I get to spend each day with my favourite two and four-legged beings: I am blessed beyond measure.

Without Apology

Without Apology

An Introduction

SHANNON STETTNER

For a very long time, the voices that spoke publicly about abortion were mostly those of men—politicians, clergy, lawyers, physicians, all of whom had an interest in regulating women's bodies. Even today, when women speak openly about abortion, the voices are of those who are professionally or politically invested in the topic. We hear most frequently from journalists and leaders of women's and abortion rights organizations, sometimes from women who hold political office, and, on occasion, from female physicians. We also hear quite frequently from spokeswomen for anti-abortion groups. Rarely, however, do we hear the voices of women who have made the decision to terminate a pregnancy. Yet without hearing from these women—without giving them a place to speak about their experiences and to share their ideas on abortion—we run the risk of thinking and talking about the issue only in the abstract.

This collection was inspired in part by some of my earlier research, which focused on the politics of abortion in English Canada during the 1960s, a decade marked by public pressure to decriminalize abortion.[1] Perhaps unsurprisingly, women's voices were often muted in historical accounts of the period—a familiar form of discursive erasure. As I discovered, however, women *were* speaking up and in fact took an active part in the debates surrounding the need for abortion law reform. What was lacking, and to some extent still is, was not merely public space for their voices but the will to hear them. As Arundhati Roy argues, "There's really no such thing as the 'voiceless.' There are only the deliberately silenced, or the preferably unheard."[2] Despite a subsequent lack of recognition, the sharing of women's experiences with and ideas on abortion was integral to the political change that occurred during the 1960s. Such sharing is, in my view, essential to the struggle to ensure that abortion is not only legal but also safe and accessible in Canada and elsewhere in the world. Only by speaking openly and honestly to one another and attending closely to the situations and thoughts of those who have had an abortion will women, and men, be able to move beyond the polarizing rhetoric that has characterized the issue for so long.

Invisible Stigmata

In 1992, two scholars, Carolyn Ellis and Arthur Bochner, wrote as a couple about their unplanned pregnancy and decision to opt for abortion. They chose to share their experience in part because they firmly believed that the "act of telling a personal story is a way of giving voice to experiences that are shrouded in secrecy."[3] Commenting on the limited scope of narratives about abortion, they wrote: "We know little about the details of the emotional and cognitive processes that are associated with living through this experience. The stories that are told are primarily about illegal abortions performed in back rooms or dark alleys, couched in generalities, and disclosed many years after they occur."[4] These often harrowing tales seek to portray women in as sympathetic a light as possible—typically as victims of circumstances beyond their control.[5] While such narratives were crucial to the fight to decriminalize abortion, and while they serve as an important reminder of why that fight was so important, they are easily perceived as having little contemporary relevance. They sensationalize abortion, at a time when we need, instead, to make efforts to normalize this very common procedure. In addition, these stories rarely reveal the thought processes behind women's decisions or otherwise describe situations to which women today can easily relate. Women do not see themselves reflected in these stories, and the lack of contemporary narratives that speak to their own experiences could contribute to the perpetuation of silence surrounding abortion.

Although there have been some published accounts of Canadian women's abortion experiences, few women speak publicly about their abortions. In 1998, the Childbirth by Choice Trust published *No Choice: Canadian Women Tell Their Stories of Illegal Abortion*. The appearance of this collection was a notable step forward, but because it focuses on the experience of abortion before the procedure was decriminalized, the narratives in it tend to share much with disturbing tales of "back alley" abortions. Despite the welcome publication, in 2014, of Martha Solomon and Kathryn Palmateer's collection *One Kind Word: Women Share Their Abortion Stories*, modern accounts of abortion in Canada remain sparse, revealing the strength of the stigma that continues to surround the subject. As Solomon points out in her contribution to this collection, "Secrets are invariably tinged with a fear of discovery. Secrets can leave people feeling muzzled, fearful, and ashamed." The desire for privacy should not be born of a fear of exposure. While no woman should feel compelled to share her abortion story, in a just world she should not be afraid to do so.

Yet the stigma persists. As the authors of one study note, "in public discourse and from the perspective of women having abortions . . . the idea that there are 'good abortions' and 'bad abortions,' stemming from 'good' and 'bad' reasons for having them, is prevalent."[6] Indeed, the motives for abortion are often divided into "hard" and "soft" categories. Abortions performed for so-called hard reasons are those done in cases where the pregnancy resulted from rape or incest or where concerns exist about maternal health or fetal abnormality. The soft reasons are related to socioeconomic or lifestyle considerations such as career aspirations or the timing of the pregnancy.[7] As Janine Brodie observes, "The public is more likely to favour free access to abortion when a woman is cast in terms of the victim than when abortion is associated with decisions relating to women's self-determination."[8]

Anti-abortion activism has also contributed to the stigma attaching to abortion. Women have internalized anti-abortion messages that refer to them as "selfish," as "baby killers," and by a host of other epithets. Ironically, they have at times been encouraged in this endeavour by the abortion rights movement itself. In "Rethinking the Mantra That Abortion Should be 'Safe, Legal, and Rare,'" sociologist Tracy Weitz traces the history of the oft-quoted comment, showing how it was adopted as a conciliatory approach to a contentious issue, first by American politicians and then by abortion rights organizers themselves. However, every time we add a qualifier, a "but," to the statement "I'm pro-choice," we draw a line of separation between ourselves and women who have abortions. How often, for example, do we hear individuals who identify as pro-choice say things like, "I'm pro-choice, but I'm glad I never had to make the decision," or "I'm pro-choice, but I think it's best to prevent the pregnancy in the first place," or "I'm pro-choice, but I would never have an abortion myself"? These statements distance the speaker from those women who were not "lucky" enough to escape their fertile years without needing to have recourse to abortion. The comments (especially the second) also imply that women who become pregnant unintentionally are cavalier about their fertility and have failed to assume adequate responsibility for birth control. The last of the three statements, and possibly the most familiar, is arguably the most damaging because it perpetuates the shame felt by some women who have chosen to have an abortion. There is smugness in this statement, which, consciously or not, makes a value judgment—"Abortion may be okay for you, but not for me." Moreover, such statements are a public proclamation that the speaker has not had an abortion, as though having had one is somehow bad, which can inadvertently silence women who have had one.[9] By participating in the act of creating distance between women who have had an abortion and those who have not, we reinforce the stigmatization that surrounds the procedure. In other words, the act of supporting abortion on a conditional basis silences women.

We have recently witnessed a marked increase of women in North America talking publicly about their abortions. Much of this sharing seems to have been prompted by efforts across the continent to attack the legal basis of women's reproductive rights. In the United States, Republican victories in the 2010 midterm election set the stage for renewed anti-abortion efforts, with states all across the country introducing literally hundreds of abortion bills that sought, in various ways, to limit access to the procedure.[10] In 2012, we in Canada saw an attempt to reopen the abortion debate at the federal level via Motion 312, which sought a formal discussion of when fetal life begins. The motion was defeated by a large majority, but the fact that it was brought forward at all was alarming.[11] Although women responded to these threats by speaking up, their stories primarily appeared online and were often posted anonymously.[12] In other words, as long as many people feel that this remarkably common medical procedure is not an appropriate topic of conversation, we are still a long way from a world in which women will not feel obliged to conceal the fact that they had an abortion.

The Politics of Language: Problematizing "Choice"

In addition to the desire to create space for women to share abortion experiences, this book stems in part from my own dissatisfaction with how we talk about abortion and from the lack of public discussion within the Canadian women's movement about how to move forward discursively and strategically as advocates for reproductive rights and freedoms. Although, historically, "pro-choice" has been the term most often associated with support for a woman's right to control her own reproduction, it has been criticized for the assumptions implicit in it, which potentially limit the reach of the movement for reproductive rights. In 1982, writer and feminist Kathleen McDonnell called abortion "the forgotten issue of the women's movement."[13] She followed this pronouncement with her book *Not an Easy Choice* (1984), in which she argues that the notion of personal choice is legitimate only "if a woman seeks to end a pregnancy for reasons other than financial ones." As she went on to point out, "Many of the constraints on choice, such as economic factors, are embedded in our social structure and can only be eradicated by wider social and economic change that creates conditions more amenable to having children."[14]

McDonnell's focus on social and economic change makes sense given the history of socialist feminist organizing in Canada.[15] While certainly not all, or even most, of the early Canadian proponents of women's rights were inspired by a socialist perspective, many of the women involved in the 1970 Abortion Caravan, for example, identified themselves as socialist feminists.[16] Similarly, the Ontario Coalition for Abortion Clinics (OCAC), founded in 1982, is a socialist feminist organization. Carolyn Egan, a founding member of OCAC, explains in this collection how, by situating its organizing within a socialist feminist framework, the coalition recognized that "choice" is always circumscribed by women's social and economic conditions. This conceptualization has meant that OCAC has purposefully collaborated with activist groups, labour unions, and NGOs such as the Immigrant Women's Health Centre that address a myriad of issues affecting women's lives.

It has not only been socialist feminists, however, who have been critical of framing of abortion in terms of individual choice. Rather, a range of feminists, many from the United States, have voiced similar concerns. Writing in 1984, roughly a decade after the US Supreme Court's decision in *Roe v. Wade*, the American political scientist Rosalind Petchesky drew a connection between arguments based on individual choice, according to which decisions about abortion are a "matter of conscience," and arguments based on an individual's right to privacy, which likewise have the effect of removing the issue of abortion from the public sphere. In *Roe*, the Supreme Court placed limits on state intervention in abortion, on the grounds that such intervention violates a woman's right to privacy, stipulating that, during the first trimester of pregnancy, only a woman's physician should be involved in her choice regarding abortion.[17] In Petchesky's view, an individual's legal right to privacy therefore provides only "a 'shaky' constitutional basis for women's abortion rights insofar as it lends itself to interpretations favouring the professional and proprietary claims of doctors."[18] Petchesky was also critical of building the case for abortion on the concept of a woman's right to privacy because doing so "asserts the personal and individual character of pregnancy and childbearing" and thus offers no ground on which to argue that "women, as a 'class,' are entitled to abortion services."[19] Such a denial, she argued, perpetuates the class divisions between women, as it leaves those individuals with fewer means to fend for themselves.

American historian Rickie Solinger has been similarly critical of the notion of "choice." As she points out, in the 1960s and early 1970s, the discussion around abortion was usually framed in terms of "rights." In the wake of *Roe v. Wade* (1973), however, feminists eager to consolidate gains embraced the language of "choice"—a term that allowed them to talk about abortion without actually using the word. "Many people," she writes, "believed that 'choice'—a term that evoked women shoppers selecting among options in the marketplace—would be an easier sell; it offered 'rights lite,' a package less threatening or disturbing than unadulterated rights."[20] As Solinger further argues, the notion of choice "became a symbol of middle-class women's arrival as independent consumers," consumers who "had earned the right to choose motherhood, if they liked." Women of colour, however, had earned no similar right and did not enjoy a similar choice.[21] Adding to the critique, Andrea Smith has questioned the narrow focus of both the pro-life and pro-choice movements on the legal status of abortion. She argues that the decriminalization of abortion does nothing to address, much less to resolve, what are really social justice issues and that only broad economic, social, and political change will ameliorate inequities in reproductive rights.[22]

These were not the only criticisms of the language of "choice," and some women abandoned the notion entirely in favour of "reproductive justice." The term can be traced to 1994, when a group of black women met in Chicago to address the health issues facing women of colour. In an effort to forge a link between reproductive rights and social justice, the group chose to call itself Women of African Descent for Reproductive Justice.[23] The concept gained organizational strength in 1997, with the founding of the SisterSong Women of Color Reproductive Health Collective in the United States. Using a human rights framework, SisterSong sought to build a coalition of groups that were interested in moving beyond what they perceived as the polarizing language used by both the pro-choice and pro-life sides. Those who founded SisterSong chose to speak of "reproductive justice," rather than "choice," because they felt many women do not have the luxury of choice—that a fundamental transformation of society will be required before all women are in a position to control their reproductive lives. Loretta Ross, one of the founders and a long-time national coordinator of SisterSong, defines "reproductive justice" as

> the complete physical, mental, spiritual, political, social and economic well-being of women and girls, based on the full achievement and protection of women's human rights. It offers a new perspective on reproductive issue advocacy, pointing out that for Indigenous women and women of color it is important to fight equally for (1) the right to have a child; (2) the right not to have a child; and (3) the right to parent the children we have, as well as to control our birthing options, such as midwifery. We also fight for the necessary enabling conditions to realize these rights. This is in contrast to the singular focus on abortion by the pro-choice movement.[24]

Miriam Pérez, a Cuban American reproductive justice activist, distills the tenets of the movement to the simplest definition: "working to build a world where everyone has what they need to create the family they want to create."[25] The reproductive justice framework became increasingly visible in the United States following SisterSong's coplanning of the April 2004 March for Women's Lives held in Washington, DC.[26] And, increasingly, it informs the organizing of the traditionally pro-choice organizations. For example, at the start of 2013, Planned Parenthood announced its decision to abandon the dichotomous pro-life/pro-choice framework, and in 2014 Choice USA renamed itself URGE: Unite for Reproductive and Gender Equity.[27]

Reproductive justice advocates acknowledge the limits of the discourse of "choice," including what Marlene Fried and Susan Yanow describe as "the failure to disassociate abortion politics from population control, and reducing reproductive rights to the issue of abortion." They argue that a reproductive justice framework is capable of "rejuvenating the meaning and practice of reproductive rights with an expansive multi-issue perspective and agenda for action. This provides an opportunity to create new alliances internationally and joins the abortion rights struggle to other health and social justice movements."[28] The Asian Communities for Reproductive Justice have outlined three main frameworks within which to fight reproductive oppression: reproductive health, which focuses on the delivery of health services; reproductive rights, which focuses on protecting women's legal right to reproductive health care; and reproductive justice, which focuses on addressing structural inequalities through organizing and movement building.[29]

In Canada, the conversation about the adoption of "reproductive justice" developed more recently. In 2010, activist Jessica Yee (now Jessica Danforth), the founder and executive director of the Native Youth Sexual Health Network, observed a resistance to the concept of reproductive justice (RJ) on the part of the pro-choice movement in Canada. She noted both a "deeply entrenched reluctance to adopt RJ at all" and the tendency toward a purely nominal adoption of the term: "RJ appears to be this 'add-on' of 'it looks good to have it' so even if it's included in an organization's mandate, their policies, procedures, and practices don't change."[30] A year later, in June 2011, the Aboriginal Health Initiatives Committee of the Society of Obstetricians and Gynaecologists of Canada issued a joint policy statement in tandem with a wide array of Indigenous organizations and mainstream Canadian medical associations outlining the need to adopt a reproductive justice framework in order "to reduce the inequity in the availability and accessibility of sexual and reproductive services" for Canada's Indigenous peoples.[31]

I would argue that, in the years since Danforth wrote her critique, women's rights organizations in Canada have shown increasing enthusiasm for reproductive justice as a conceptual framework. Even if, at this stage, the embrace is sometimes more nominal than real, many organizations have either formed around or adopted a RJ framework. The period has, for example, seen the founding of Reproductive Justice New Brunswick and the Vancouver-based Reproductive Justice League of Canada, as well as the Centre for Gender

Advocacy at Concordia University in Montréal. In addition, the Abortion Rights Coalition of Canada has declared its support for RJ, recognizing that "the sexual and reproductive health and rights of people from many diverse communities are disproportionately affected by marginalization and oppression."[32] All the same, as I discuss in the conclusion to this volume, the actualization of reproductive justice as an organizing principle is very much a work in progress in Canada. As we move forward, we must heed critiques by long-term reproductive justice activists, such as Danforth and Loretta Ross, and not lose sight of the origins of the concept.

Engaging in dialogue about terminology is critical to the growth and effectiveness of any movement. Those who advocate for women's reproductive freedom and autonomy must be cognizant that some abortion rights supporters (especially those who are not activists) are not entirely comfortable with the terms in which abortion is publicly discussed in Canada. Andrea Smith cautions us against "simplistic analyses of who our political friends and enemies are in the area of reproductive rights," while Pérez astutely observes: "Language matters. It can invite people in, or discourage people from joining. It can allow people to feel seen."[33] For this reason, an absence of open dialogue about the framing of abortion rights and how that framing affects movement strategy can have the effect of alienating potential allies. In her discussion of the history of the language used to talk about abortion in the United States, American feminist Jennifer Baumgardner argues that "the U.S. can't remain in the same rhetorical place it was in the '70s, or even the '80s."[34] Her observation holds true for Canada, too. Canadians are, it seems, beginning to engage in conversation about the framing of abortion rights, and, while this is a very welcome development, it is an ongoing and imperfect process that involves growing, learning, sharing, and listening.

Bridging Divides: The Origins of This Collection

This anthology, a combination of personal reflections and analytical essays, aims to create space for voices that often go unheard—a space for women who have had an abortion to speak openly about their experiences and for those who deliver abortion services or who advocate for abortion rights to share their thoughts. At the same time, it seeks to explore some of the many issues that surround abortion and to discuss new strategies for debating reproductive rights. Together, these voices challenge us to think about the complexities surrounding abortion without losing sight of concrete realities.

While researching and writing my dissertation, I was involved with the Ontario Coalition for Abortion Clinics (OCAC). Two important observations emerged from my involvement with this organization. First, I became aware of the depth of the historical memory of front-line work carried out by abortion rights activists, whose knowledge and experience has not been adequately recorded.[35] This potential loss is linked to my second observation, namely, of the need for closer collaboration between academic feminists and front-line activists. At various activist events that I attended in Toronto over the years, I often overheard academic feminism dismissed as irrelevant or out of touch.[36] Although no doubt some of it warrants this criticism, important discussions of language and strategy do take place in the academy, and stronger alliances among all involved in advocating for access to abortion can benefit the movement as a whole. Of course, this must be a reciprocal relationship, with academics learning much from the ideas and experiences of activists.

Conversely, the academic world continues to be suspicious of scholars whose work is overtly linked to political objectives. While scholars accept that we all bring our experiences, identities, and biases to our work, there remains an expectation that we will make every effort to banish them from our work—that scholarship must be clearly separated from personal values and agendas. Similarly, scholars are not supposed to rely on their own experience as evidence. Work that contains an autoethnographic or narrative element—politically engaged writing in which the scholar maintains an explicit presence, essentially becoming a character in the story—makes many academics uncomfortable.[37] This volume was prompted in part by my struggle to reconcile these two identities, academic and activist, and by my belief that it is not only possible but important to be both; my education is a privilege that necessitates social and political engagement. Some of the pieces in this collection demonstrate the potential of bridging the gap between front-line and academic feminisms. I think, especially, of Colleen MacQuarrie's explanation of her activist research methods, which have breathed new life into the reproductive rights movement on Prince Edward Island.

This collection does not seek to debate the pros and cons of abortion. Rather, it aims to integrate thought and action and to explore the topic of abortion from a variety of experiential perspectives. Therefore, when I circulated a call for contributors to this collection, I solicited narrative pieces grounded in personal experience as well as analytical reflections on issues currently confronting the reproductive rights movement in Canada. The call was sent to an array of women's rights groups, some broadly based and others that focus on abortion. I also extended invitations to individual activists, academics, journalists, politicians, and authors of online pieces, all of whom had previously addressed the topic of abortion.

Despite my earnest desire to include the voices of women who are neither activists nor academics, this did not prove easy. After all, these women had to be willing to share a deeply personal experience and to trust me not to reveal their identity if they wished to remain anonymous. Indeed, some of those who contacted me, wanting to share their stories, were unwilling to share their names at all, which attests to the power of the stigma that continues to surround abortion. So, of course, there are voices missing here—those of women who are still safeguarding their secret, perhaps after a whole lifetime of having done so. Responses also tended to come from women who have activist connections, an online presence, and relatively high literacy and education levels. So there are other missing voices. Their absence signals the degree to which solidarity remains to be achieved. It suggests that abandoning the rhetoric of choice is not enough—that the quest for social and reproductive justice has only just begun.

Without Apology: An Overview

While the essays in this anthology work together in a myriad of ways, I have chosen to group them into five parts. Part 1, "Speaking from Experience," consists of contributions from seven women who write about their encounters with abortion. The first of these, by Judith Mintz, begins with a quotation from Kristi Siegel: "Women's autobiography is distinguished by its uneasy relationship to the body and maternity." The authors in this section explore their relationships with their reproductive bodies, sharing their thoughts on abortion through narrative and autoethnography. These pieces begin to illuminate the divergent ways in which women experience "choice," raising questions for future discussion about issues of isolation and inadequate support and about the social attitudes that provoke judgment, stigmatization, and, by extension, feelings of shame.

With the exception of Wagner's piece about her search for an abortion provider before abortion was decriminalized in Canada, these narratives are not about the issue of access. Most of these women were able to take for granted their ability to access abortion services, and we need to acknowledge the element of privilege associated with their experiences. Even though, in theory, all women in Canada are entitled to make the decision to have an abortion, women are not equally empowered to act on it. Purely in practical terms, women who live in remote and rural areas, especially in the North, do not have ready access to abortion services. In addition, women who are poor or who lack the education on which our capacity to operationalize our rights so often depends face barriers to abortion access that the women in this collection generally did not confront. Indigenous women and women who belong to racialized minorities, who must already contend with racism and glaring social and economic inequities, also face additional barriers not represented by the narratives in this collection. These are among the missing voices. Also missing are the voices of transgendered and non-binary people. At the time I issued the call for papers, I had not yet considered their reproductive experiences. This is an erasure that I regret and would not reproduce if I were to reissue the call today.

The narratives in part 1 illustrate the importance of recognizing the diversity of women's abortion experiences. Some women struggle to decide whether to continue a pregnancy. Other women don't agonize over their decision but know with certainty what is right for them in that moment of their reproductive lives. At other times, the difficulty lies not in the decision itself but in the circumstances surrounding the abortion. One striking feature in these narratives, for example, is the differing levels of support that the women received. The pieces by Mackenzie and E.K. Hornbeck are noteworthy because of the abundant support that these two women enjoyed: all women should be so well supported through their abortion journeys. But, as the other narratives reveal, women often are not well supported, for a variety of reasons. One key issue remains the feelings of isolation and shame that women experience, which gives rise to the need to keep their abortions secret. As long as abortion is something that women feel they must hide, this lack of support will continue.

The complexity of women's feelings about abortion is an issue worthy of serious attention, and yet it has received relatively little discussion in Canada, whether in academic or public forums. Increasingly, especially in the United States, pro-choice supporters have acknowledged the need to move away from "the oversimplified dualism of good/bad, black/white, easy/hard, trauma/relief" and to recognize the multiplicity of women's experiences with, and feelings about, their abortions.[38] In 2008, Nancy Keenan, then president of the National Abortion Rights Action League (now called NARAL Pro-Choice America), acknowledged, "Our community tends to run away every time somebody talks about the many emotions that come with this choice. . . . We have not done enough to make people who are 'pro-choice but struggling' feel like they are part of this community."[39] The decision to have an abortion can be a complicated one, and women who are contemplating that decision often negotiate a range of emotions. Similarly, in addition to a sense of relief, women who have had an abortion may experience feelings of guilt or regret, even when the advantages of terminating the pregnancy were clear. The experience of an unwanted pregnancy may also crystallize other difficulties in a woman's life, such as a bad relationship (or the lack of a serious relationship) or an impending financial crisis. Abortion ends the unwanted pregnancy, but it does not end ongoing sources of stress, which a woman may now be obliged to confront.[40] For all these reasons, women may require, or at least benefit from, some form of supportive counselling, especially after the fact. Clearly, this support needs to come from people who are sympathetic to a woman's situation, rather than those who may sit in judgment, thereby exacerbating emotional distress.

One of the concerns that discourage dialogue about the need for access to post-abortion counselling is a fear of playing into the hands of abortion opponents, who have recently adopted a new "pro-woman" stance. They argue that if women who have had an abortion need counselling, then abortion must be harmful; therefore, it should either be outlawed completely or, at the very least, be prefaced by mandatory counselling.[41] We know that such arguments are false. The American Psychological Association's Task Force on Mental Health and Abortion surveyed the existing literature on abortion and women's mental health and found that "the relative risk of mental health problems among adult women who have a single, legal, first-trimester abortion of an unwanted pregnancy for nontherapeutic reasons is no greater than the risk among women who deliver an unwanted pregnancy." As the authors acknowledged, while "some women feel confident they made the right choice and feel no regret; others experience sadness, grief, guilt, and feelings of loss following the elective termination of a pregnancy," including, in some cases, "clinically significant outcomes, such as depression and anxiety."[42] If even one woman feels that she needs to be better supported post-abortion, then it is incumbent on those of us who are pro-choice to support her. If we fail to fill that void, we cede this ground to the anti-abortion movement.[43] Witness, for example, the proliferation of explicitly anti-abortion sites such as Canada Silent No More and Project Rachel, which purport to offer support to women who are struggling with the "physical, emotional or spiritual pain" and other "harmful after-effects" of abortion.[44] Such blatantly ideological sites must be countered by spaces that validate all responses to abortion, positive and negative, in a supportive and nonjudgmental environment. As long as abortion remains something secretive and shameful, women will not be free. If we remove the atmosphere of judgment, talking openly about abortion will not require the same sort of courage that it currently does.

In part 2, "Abortion Rights Activism," we hear from women who, in a variety of ways, are working to transform the social attitudes and institutional structures that give rise to secrecy and shame. In June 1970, Prime Minister Pierre Trudeau met with women from the Vancouver Women's Caucus—the women who had planned and participated in the Abortion Caravan of May 1970. In response to their request that abortion be further decriminalized, Trudeau told them: "It is your job to change public morality. The public is not ready for this."[45] In the decades that followed, women's groups responded to challenge, although not with a view to changing public morality as much as changing public awareness and understanding. The five essays in part 2, written by both front-line and academic activists, document different approaches to activism—street protests, photographic exhibits, empowerment through education—across several generations.

Together, these pieces illustrate a critical point, namely, that abortion rights activism does not occur in a vacuum. As Aalya Ahmad, writing for the Radical Handmaids, points out, "Too often, abortion rights are isolated from their intrinsic connection with the other rights that feminists have fought for," rights that include "access to education, affordable child care, freedom from stifling poverty, and the ability to leave abusive partners." In other words, women's reproductive life does not occur in a vacuum either. As these pieces explain, the right not to be pregnant, as well as the right to expect the quality of support that makes it possible to continue a pregnancy, depend on a broader set of rights and freedoms. Accordingly, even though they may come together around a specific concern, activists must understand the systemic relationships and inequities that undergird that concern, and it is in this larger context that they must situate their work.

The third part, "Challenging Opposing Positions," contains seven essays that address the Canadian anti-abortion movement, providing observations from both long-term and more recent reproductive rights activists. These authors describe their perceptions of the opposition, including its affiliation with Christian fundamentalism—an understudied aspect of the abortion debate in Canada.[46] They suggest strategies for responding to anti-abortionists, as well as ways to reframe the abortion debate.

In Canada, as elsewhere, most anti-abortion activism has taken the form of demonstrations, picketing, petitions, and media and public "education" campaigns. Canada has, however, witnessed several instances of anti-abortion terrorism. Other incidences of illegal protest, generally involving the arrest of protesters for breaking clinic injunctions, continue to occur.[47] The anti-abortion movement also continues to try to recriminalize abortion: since the 1988 *Morgentaler* court decision that saw the abortion law overthrown, more than forty private members' bills that contain at least some anti-abortion measures have been introduced in the House of Commons.[48] Fortunately, all attempts to date have failed. Most recently, the Canadian anti-abortion movement, much more media and message savvy than in the past, has attempted to rebrand itself as moderate. To this end, anti-abortion organizations have developed an extensive arsenal of new strategies, many of which rely not on moralizing and appeals to emotion but on persuasion through reasoned argument. One is to attack abortion from the "taxpayer" perspective by arguing that abortion is not a medically necessary service and therefore should not be funded by public monies.[49] Another is to adopt what appears to be a "pro-women" stance by arguing, for example, that abortion harms women. More broadly, the movement seeks what anti-choice blogger Andrea Mrozek calls "cultural change," the goal of which is to transform the way that Canadians view abortion to the point that choosing abortion would become unthinkable.[50] These new anti-abortion strategies demand new responses.

Part 4, "Practitioners and Clinic Support," comprises six reflections about the abortion experience from the perspective of abortion providers and clinic support staff. These pieces offer insight into the relationship between women who are seeking an abortion and the counsellors and physicians whose job it is to guide them through the experience. We hear from three abortion counsellors, who speak of the harassment to which pregnant women are subjected at the hands of anti-abortion protestors standing guard outside abortion clinics. They also emphasize the need to normalize abortion, in part by the sharing of stories, so that women are spared the sense of isolation and shame that too often surround the experience. This theme is echoed by one of the three physicians from whom we also hear, who suggests that those of us who support reproductive rights—whether as medical practitioners, counsellors, and activists or simply on principle—need to think further about how we approach both the topic and the experience of abortion.

These authors also underscore the need to keep abortion legal. Today, doctors no longer routinely confront the sometimes horrific consequences of "hotel-room" abortions—an experience that one of three physicians recalls from the early days of his practice. However, in the era of legalized abortion, violence of another sort still hovers in the air. While it has been some time since abortion clinics were bombed and doctors shot, the threat to personal safety remains very real. In Canada, a handful of physicians are well known for their efforts to make abortions available; unfortunately, they became known because they became victims of anti-abortion violence. We need to remember the experience and words of Garson Romalis, who was shot and stabbed in two separate attacks on his life. Romalis, reflecting many years later on his experience as an abortion provider, wrote, "After an abortion operation, patients frequently say 'Thank You Doctor.' But abortion is the only operation I know of where they also sometimes say 'Thank you for what you do.'"[51]

The final part, "Sites of Struggle," consists of four critical reflections that seek to complicate the dialogue on abortion. Drawing on intersectional approaches, the authors suggest possible avenues forward that are less about access per se and more about justice and equity. Indigenous women, who have repeatedly been the target of what Karen Stote aptly describes as "reproductive violence," are among the racialized groups for whom the narrative of choice holds little meaning. Freedom is always constrained by circumstance, and the right to access abortion becomes a mockery when women are coerced into having one or are encouraged to ingest long-acting, and potentially harmful, contraceptives on the grounds that they are too poor to have any further children. Stote's chapter makes clear that until those of us who claim to support social justice commit to changing current conditions—conditions that do not merely produce poverty, racism, and political oppression but in fact depend for their very existence upon such systemic inequalities—reproductive "rights" will remain out of reach for all but the socially and economically privileged.

Women's reproductive rights and oppressions are also connected to advances in medical technology. Both Bindy Kang and Jen Rinaldi explore how such developments, often presented in a positive light, can actually constrain and coerce women's options. The visibility of the fetus has altered social perceptions surrounding pregnancy and, by extension, the place of abortion in the story. As Kang's essay illustrates, dominant values ironically provide a "moral" justification for racism: pregnant women whose ethnic roots lie in cultures that historically have favoured male children are assumed to be more likely to abort a female child. Kang examines such assumptions, demonstrating powerful connections between them and the long history of racism in Canada. Rinaldi in turn points out that fetal imaging means that the mother now shares the stage with the fetus, images of which play into the hands of those who oppose abortion. She argues that the narrative surrounding prenatal testing is premised on a happy outcome; when "abnormalities" are discovered in the fetus, however, the story goes awry, and women may accordingly be encouraged to terminate the pregnancy. Prenatal diagnostic technology can thus have the effect of limiting a woman's capacity to choose.[52] Rinaldi's piece encourages us to consider the implications of abortion for those of us who also advocate for disability rights. Disability scholar Tom Shakespeare describes the issue this way: "At the heart of the debate around pre-natal genetic testing are contested choices and rights: a woman's right to choose, the civil rights of disabled people, the postulated rights of the unborn child, the rights of the individual versus the rights of the collective."[53]

Kang and Rinaldi's pieces complicate the dialogue but leave us no closer to a resolution (if, indeed, we seek one). The final chapter, by Shannon Dea, suggests that, rather than continuing to focus on points of conflict, the two sides could search for common ground and, by adopting a harm-reduction model, work together to minimize the need for abortion. In this way, it may be possible to reconceptualize the binary framework—"pro-life" versus "pro-choice"—to move beyond the impasse. Her argument reminds us of Andrea Smith's suggestion that we reject simplistic definitions of political allies and political enemies lest we sacrifice possibilities to work toward common goals—a position echoed by Nick Van der Graaf, in his contribution to this volume.

Just as there is no one abortion experience, there is no right or wrong way to feel about one's abortion. Relief, happiness, grief, sadness, ambivalence: all these emotions are normal reactions to terminating a pregnancy. The only emotions that are not natural are shame and feelings of isolation. Those emotions are forced on us by external sources, whether they be anti-abortion activists who want us to feel bad about our choices or pro-choice advocates who try to avoid the complicated emotions that can accompany an abortion. My hope is that this collection will help to normalize the experience of abortion—that is, to make visible this extremely common procedure—and, in so doing, help to dispel the sense of shame with which women who have had an abortion still struggle and that prevents them from talking their feelings through. I also hope that the collection will encourage new and more experientially informed discussion among those of us concerned with safeguarding abortion rights.

Notes

1 See Shannon Stettner, "Women and Abortion in English Canada: Public Debates and Political Participation, 1959–1970."

2 Arundhati Roy, "The 2004 Sydney Peace Prize Lecture: Peace and the New Corporate Liberation Theology," *University of Sydney: News*, 4 November 2004, http://sydney.edu.au/news/84.html?newsstoryid=279.

3 Carolyn Ellis and Arthur P. Bochner, "Telling and Performing Personal Stories: The Constraints of Choice in Abortion," 79.

4 Ibid., 97.

5 See Celeste Michelle Condit, *Interpreting Abortion Rhetoric: Communicating Social Change*.

6 Alison Norris et al., "Abortion Stigma: A Reconceptualization of Constituents, Causes, and Consequences," 4.

7 On public support for abortion under specific circumstances, see Raymond Tatalovich, *The Politics of Abortion in the United States and Canada: A Comparative Study*, 109–17.

8 Janine Brodie, "Choice and No Choice in the House," 61.

9 For further discussion, see Kate Cockrill and Adina Nack, "'I'm Not That Type of Person': Managing the Stigma of Having an Abortion," 984. See also Dr. Ellen Wiebe's contribution to this volume. As Wiebe has often observed, even women who are seeking an abortion themselves often presume to pass judgment on the motives of others who are doing the same.

10 See, for example, Guttmacher Institute, "States Enact Record Number of Abortion Restrictions," 5 January 2012, http://www.guttmacher.org/media/inthenews/2012/01/05/endofyear.html; and Chuck Raasch, "Abortion Restrictions Gain Steam in the States," *USA Today*, 26 April 2012, http://usatoday30.usatoday.com/news/health/story/2012-04-25/states-anti-abortion-legislation/54538866/1.

11 On Motion 312, see Laura Payton, "Motion to Study When Life Begins Defeated in Parliament," *CBC News*, 26 September 2012, http://www.cbc.ca/news/politics/story/2012/09/26/pol-woodworth-motion-to-study-when-life-begins.html.

12 Websites and blogs such as *I'm Not Sorry* (http://www.imnotsorry.net/) and *Abortion Gang* (http://abortiongang.org/) offered abortion-friendly spaces in which women could share their stories, without the need to reveal their identity. So did *Anti-Choice Is Anti-Awesome* (http://antichoiceantiawesome.blogspot.ca/), a site that is still active. For an analysis of the "coming out" phenomenon, see Steph Herold, "The New Public Face of Abortion: Connecting the Dots Between Abortion Stories," *RH Reality Check*, 8 July 2012, http://rhrealitycheck.org/article/2012/07/08/new-public-face-abortion-connecting-dots-between-abortion-stories/.

13 Kathleen McDonnell, "Claim No Easy Victories: The Fight for Reproductive Rights," 33.

14 Kathleen McDonnell, *Not an Easy Choice: A Feminist Re-examines Abortion*, 71, 77. Perhaps tellingly, when McDonnell's book was reissued in 2003, by Toronto's Second Story Press, the subtitle was changed to *Re-examining Abortion*—which, of course, eliminates the reference to feminism.

15 See Judy Rebick, *Ten Thousand Roses: The Making of a Feminist Revolution*, 35–46, 156–67. On socialist feminism in Canada, see Nancy Adamson, Linda Briskin, and Margaret McPhail, *Feminist Organizing for Change: The Contemporary Women's Movement in Canada*, 97–135; and Meg Luxton, "Feminism as a Class Act: Working-Class Feminism and the Women's Movement in Canada," esp. 66–67.

16 See Stettner, "Women and Abortion in English Canada," 209–16, 249–51, 255–58, 274–76.

17 Writing the opinion in *Roe v. Wade*, Justice Harry Blackmun argued that the right of privacy is "broad enough to encompass a woman's decision whether or not to terminate her pregnancy" and declared: "The detriment that the State would impose upon the pregnant woman by denying this choice altogether is apparent." He then went on to describe the various factors, not only medical but personal and psychological, that play into decisions surrounding abortion, concluding that these factors are something that "the woman and her responsible physician necessarily will consider in consultation." *Roe v. Wade*, 410 U.S. 113 (1973) at 153, available at https://www.law.cornell.edu/supremecourt/text/410/113. In other words, as formulated in *Roe*, a woman's privacy is not absolute: for reasons of

professional responsibility, her doctor also has the right to be involved in her decision.

18 Rosalind Pollack Petchesky, *Abortion and Woman's Choice: The State, Sexuality, and Reproductive Freedom*, 295.

19 Ibid. For an analysis, in the Canadian context, of the constraints on "choice" imposed by legal and medical discourse, including the emphasis on the "rights and responsibilities" associated with reproductive activity (5), see Gail Kellough, *Aborting Law: An Exploration of the Politics of Motherhood and Medicine*. Kellough illustrates her argument by examining OCAC's activist work during the 1980s, at the time of the Morgentaler hearings.

20 Rickie Solinger, *Beggars and Choosers: How the Politics of Choice Shapes Adoption, Abortion, and Welfare in the United States*, 5. As Solinger notes, the shift to "choice" reflected "the determination of abortion rights advocates to develop as respectable, nonconfrontational movement after *Roe*" (5).

21 Ibid., 199–200. For a discussion, in the US context, of the illusory nature of choice for low-income women, many of whom are either black or Hispanic, see Lisa Brown, William Parker, and Jill Morrison, "When a Woman's Choice Is Not a Choice," esp. 25–27.

22 Andrea Smith, "Beyond Pro-Choice Versus Pro-Life: Women of Color and Reproductive Justice," 120, 123, 125.

23 SisterSong, "The Herstory of Reproductive Justice," n.d., http://sistersong. net/reproductive-justice/.

24 Loretta Ross, "Understanding Reproductive Justice: Transforming the Pro-Choice Movement," 14.

25 Miriam Pérez, "The Meaning of Reproductive Justice: Simplifying a Complex Concept," *RH Reality Check*, 8 February 2013, http://rhrealitycheck.org/article/2013/02/08/ communicating-complexity-reproductive-justice/#sthash.vr26Zhd5.dpuf.

26 On the shift to a reproductive justice framework in the United States, see Zaikya T. Luna, "Marching Toward Reproductive Justice: Coalitional (Re) Framing of the March for Women's Lives."

27 As URGE explains on its "About Our Name Change" web page (http://urge.org/about/about-our-name-change/), the organization recognized that "working for choice is not possible without widening our scope to include all of the issues that impact any person's ability to choose." On the rationale for Planned Parenthood's decision, see Anna North, "Planned Parenthood Moving Away from 'Choice,'" *BuzzFeed*, 9 January 2013, http://www.buzzfeed.com/annanorth/

planned-parenthood-moving-away-from-choice#.je06eRqXO. Mainstream organizations, including Planned Parenthood, have been criticized for presenting the shift to a reproductive justice framework as if they had arrived at the idea themselves, without adequately acknowledging the work done by women of colour to develop the concept. For example, see Monica Simpson, "Reproductive Justice and 'Choice': An Open Letter to Planned Parenthood," *RH Reality Check*, 5 August 2014, http://rhrealitycheck.org/ article/2014/08/05/reproductive-justice-choice-open-letter-planned-parenthood/. See also Tracy Weitz, "Planned Parenthood Gives Up the 'Pro-Choice' Label: What Does It Mean for the Movement?" 13 January 2013, *RH Reality Check*, http://rhrealitycheck.org/article/2013/01/13/ planned-parenthood-gives-up-prochoice-label-what-does-it-mean-movement/; Katie Roiphe, "Good Riddance, 'Pro-Choice,'" *Slate*, 16 January 2013, http://www.slate.com/articles/double_x/roiphe/2013/01/ planned_parenthood_abandons_the_term_pro_choice_what_about_pro_ freedom_instead.html; and Dawn Laguens, "Planned Parenthood and the Next Generation of Feminist Activists."

28 Marlene Fried and Susan Yanow, "Abortion Rights and Reproductive Justice," Pro-Choice Public Education Project, n.d., http://www. protectchoice.org/article.php?id=130.

29 See Asian Communities for Reproductive Justice, *A New Vision*.

30 See Jessica Yee, "Reproductive Justice—for Real, for Me, for You, for Now," 6 November 2010, http://jolocas.blogspot.ca/2011/11/reproductive-justice. html. See also Jessica Shaw, "Abortion as a Social Justice Issue in Contemporary Canada," and "Full-Spectrum Reproductive Justice: The Affinity of Abortion Rights and Birth Activism."

31 Jessica Yee, Alisha Nicole Apale, and Melissa Deleary, "Sexual and Reproductive Health, Rights, and Realities and Access to Services for First Nations, Inuit, and Métis in Canada," 633.

32 Abortion Rights Coalition of Canada, "Why ARCC Supports Reproductive Justice," 1.

33 Andrea Smith, "Beyond Pro-Choice Versus Pro-Life: Women of Color and Reproductive Justice," 132; Pérez, "Meaning of Reproductive Justice." As Smith points out, when we rely on dichotomies, "we often lose opportunities to work with people with whom we may have sharp disagreements, but who may, with different political framings and organizing strategies, shift their positions" (133).

34 Jennifer Baumgardner, *Abortion and Life*, 54.

35 An important exception Rebick's Ten Thousand Roses, which incorporates such reminiscences.

36 For a compelling critique of academic feminism, see the essays in Jessica Yee, ed., *Feminism for Real: Deconstructing the Academic Industrial Complex of Feminism*. Much has been written about the tendency of feminist theory, as elaborated within the academy, to become detached not only from activist pursuits from the lived experience of women. See, for example, Elizabeth Fox-Genovese, *Feminism Is NOT the Story of My Life: How Today's Feminist Elite Has Lost Touch with the Real Concerns of Women*; and Christina Hoff Sommers, *Who Stole Feminism? How Women Have Betrayed Women*.

37 For further discussion of the relationship between academic research and activism, see Shannon Stettner and Tracy Penny Light, "The Politics of Reproductive Health History: Visible, Audible, and Consequential." For an effective example of the use of narrative in academic work, see Deborah Davidson, "Reflections on Doing Research Grounded in My Experience of Perinatal Loss: From Auto/biography to Autoethnography."

38 Aspen Baker and Carolina De Robertis, "Pro-Voice: A Vision for the Future," 35.

39 Quoted in Baumgardner, *Abortion and Life*, 60.

40 For insights into women's reactions to abortion, see Eve Kushner, *Experiencing Abortion: A Weaving of Women's Words*. Kushner interviewed more than 150 women who had had an abortion, encouraging them to give voice to what proved to be a broad range of emotional responses. In addition, see Katrina Kimport, Kira Foster, and Tracy A. Weitz, "Social Sources of Women's Emotional Difficulty After Abortion: Lessons from Women's Abortion Narratives," for a discussion of strategies that appear to mitigate post-abortion emotional stress.

41 For a critique of this argument (including the research on which it is based), see Tracy A. Weitz et al., "You Say 'Regret' and I Say 'Relief': A Need to Break the Polemic About Abortion." As the authors point out, the counselling that anti-abortion advocates would make legally mandatory focuses on providing women with (potentially biased) information about the risks associated with abortion, including the possibility of long-term psychological damage. The problem for those who support unfettered access to abortion thus becomes "how to meet women's needs for information regarding abortion without ceding ground to those who use these needs to develop regulations that will make abortion illegal and/or less available" (87).

42 Brenda Major et al., "Abortion and Mental Health: Evaluating the Evidence," 885. As they went on to say, "It is important that all women's experiences be recognized as valid and that women feel free to express

their thoughts and feelings about their abortion regardless of whether those thoughts and feelings are positive or negative" (885). See also Shannon Stettner, "Post-abortion Trauma Syndrome."

43 For an analysis of the issue of abortion counselling from the "pro-choice" perspective, see Dana Goldstein, "The Abortion Counseling Conundrum," *American Prospect*, 30 June 2008, http://prospect.org/article/ abortion-counseling-conundrum. Quoting at length from Goldstein's article, a contributor to an abortion rights blog also tackled the issue in "Pro-choice Post-abortion Counselling," *Dammit Janet!* (blog), 16 February 2009, http://scathinglywrongrightwingnutz.blogspot.ca/2009/02/ pro-choice-post-abortion-counselling.html.

44 Canada Silent No More, "Testimonies," n.d., http://www. canadasilentnomore.com/testimonies.html.

45 "PM Defends Abortion Laws," *Globe and Mail*, 16 June 1970.

46 On the anti-abortion movement in Canada, see, for example, Katrina Rose Ackerman, "'Not in the Atlantic Provinces: The Abortion Debate in New Brunswick, 1980–1987,'" and "In Defence of Reason: Religion, Science, and the Prince Edward Island Anti-abortion Movement, 1969–1988." Additional research is needed, however, especially with regard to the role of fundamentalist Christianity in the movement.

47 On single-issue terrorism in Canada, see G. Davidson (Tim) Smith, "Single Issue Terrorism," Canadian Security Intelligence Service, Commentary No. 74, Winter 1998, http://ftp.fas.org/irp/threat/com74e.htm.

48 Paul Saurette and Kelly Gordon, "Arguing Abortion: The New Anti-Abortion Discourse in Canada."

49 For discussion, see Chris Kaposy, "The Public Funding of Abortion in Canada: Going Beyond the Concept of Medical Necessity."

50 Andrea Mrozek, "The Story," *ProWomanProLife* (blog), n.d., http:// www.prowomanprolife.org/the-story/. For critiques on the new, more "moderate," anti-abortion rhetoric, see Saurette and Gordon, "Arguing Abortion"; Kelly Gordon, "Think About the Women! The New Anti-abortion Discourse in English Canada"; and Jane Cawthorne, this volume.

51 Garson Romalis, "Why I Am an Abortion Doctor," *National Post*, 4 February 2008. See also Mullens, "7:10 am, Nov. 8, 1994"; Jessica Shaw, "November 8, 1994," *ActiveHistory.ca*, 23 July 2014, http://activehistory. ca/2014/07/november-8-1994/; and Jack Fainman, *They Shoot Doctors, Don't They? A Memoir*.

52 See Megan Pritchard, "Can There Be Such a Thing as a 'Wrongful Birth'?" 86; and Victoria Seavilleklein, "Challenging the Rhetoric of Choice in Prenatal Screening."

53 Tom Shakespeare, "Choices and Rights: Eugenics, Genetics, and Disability Equality," 665, and see also 671–73. For additional discussion, see Sandra A. Goundry, "The New Reproductive Technologies, Public Policy, and the Equality Rights of Women and Men with Disabilities"; Ruth Hubbard, "Abortion and Disability: Who Should and Should Not Inhabit the World"; Melissa Masden, "Pre-natal Testing and Selective Abortion: The Development of a Feminist Disability Rights Perspective"; Janice McLaughlin, "Screening Networks: Shared Agendas in Feminist and Disability Movement Challenges to Antenatal Screening and Abortion"; Alison Piepmeier, "The Inadequacy of 'Choice': Disability and What's Wrong with Feminist Framings of Reproduction"; Keith Sharp and Sarah Earle, "Feminism, Abortion, and Disability: Irreconcilable Differences?"; and Alison Sheldon, "Personal and Perplexing: Feminist Disability Politics Evaluated."

References

Abortion Rights Coalition of Canada, "Why ARCC Supports Reproductive Justice." Position Paper #100, December 2015. http://www.arcc-cdac.ca/postionpapers/100-reproductive-justice.pdf.

Ackerman, Katrina Rose. "In Defence of Reason: Religion, Science, and the Prince Edward Island Anti-abortion Movement, 1969–1988." *Canadian Bulletin of Medical History* 31, no. 2 (2014): 117–38.

———. "'Not in the Atlantic Provinces': The Abortion Debate in New Brunswick, 1980–1987." *Acadiensis* 41, no. 1 (2012): 75–101.

Adamson, Nancy, Linda Briskin, and Margaret McPhail. *Feminist Organizing for Change: The Contemporary Women's Movement in Canada.* Toronto: Oxford University Press, 1988.

Asian Communities for Reproductive Justice. *A New Vision.* Oakland, CA: Asian Communities for Reproductive Justice, 2005. http://strongfamiliesmovement.org/assets/docs/ACRJ-A-New-Vision.pdf.

Baker, Aspen, and Carolina De Robertis. "Pro-Voice: A Vision for the Future." *Off Our Backs* 36, no. 4 (2006): 33–36.

Baumgardner, Jennifer. *Abortion and Life.* New York: Akashic Books, 2008.

Brodie, Janine. "Choice and No Choice in the House." In *The Politics of Abortion*, edited by Janine Brodie, Shelley A. M. Gavigan, and Jane Jenson, 57–117. Toronto: Oxford University Press, 1992.

Brown, Lisa, William Parker, and Jill Morrison. "When a Woman's Choice Is Not a Choice." *Health Law and Policy Brief* 3, no. 2 (2009): 25–31.

Childbirth by Choice Trust, ed. *No Choice: Canadian Women Tell Their Stories of Illegal Abortion*. Toronto: Childbirth by Choice Trust, 1998.

Cockrill, Kate, and Adina Nack. "'I'm Not That Type of Person': Managing the Stigma of Having an Abortion." *Deviant Behavior* 34, no. 12 (2013): 973–90.

Condit, Celeste Michelle. *Interpreting Abortion Rhetoric: Communicating Social Change*. Urbana: University of Illinois Press, 1990.

Davidson, Deborah. "Reflections on Doing Research Grounded in My Experience of Perinatal Loss: From Auto/biography to Autoethnography." *Sociological Research Online* 16, no. 1 (2011): 6. http://www.socresonline.org.uk/16/1/6.html.

Ellis, Carolyn, and Arthur P. Bochner. "Telling and Performing Personal Stories: The Constraints of Choice in Abortion." In *Investigating Subjectivity: Research on Lived Experiences*, edited by Carolyn Ellis and Michael G. Flaherty, 79–101. New York: Sage, 1992.

Fainman, Jack, with Roland Penner. *They Shoot Doctors, Don't They? A Memoir*. Winnipeg: Great Plains, 2011.

Fox-Genovese, Elizabeth. *Feminism Is NOT the Story of My Life: How Today's Feminist Elite Has Lost Touch with the Real Concerns of Women*. New York: Anchor Books, 1997.

Gordon, Kelly. "Think About the Women! The New Anti-abortion Discourse in English Canada." Master's thesis, University of Ottawa, 2010.

Goundry, Sandra A. "The New Reproductive Technologies, Public Policy, and the Equality Rights of Women and Men with Disabilities." In *Misconceptions: The Social Construction of Choice and the New Reproductive Technologies*, vol. 1, edited by Gwynne Basen, Margrit Eichler, and Abby Lippman, 154–66. Hull, QC: Voyageur, 1993.

Hubbard, Ruth. "Abortion and Disability: Who Should and Should Not Inhabit the World." In *The Disability Studies Reader*, edited by Lennard J. Davis, 187–202. London: Routledge, 1997.

Kaposy, Chris. "The Public Funding of Abortion in Canada: Going Beyond the Concept of Medical Necessity." *Medicine, Health Care, and Philosophy* 12, no. 3 (2009): 301–11.

Kellough, Gail. *Aborting Law: An Exploration of the Politics of Motherhood and Medicine*. Toronto: University of Toronto Press, 1996.

Kimport, Katrina, Kira Foster, and Tracy A. Weitz. "Social Sources of Women's Emotional Difficulty After Abortion: Lessons from Women's Abortion Narratives." *Perspectives on Sexual Reproductive Health* 43, no. 2 (2011): 103–9.

Kushner, Eve. *Experiencing Abortion: A Weaving of Women's Words.* Binghamton, NY: Haworth Press, 1997.

Laguens, Dawn. "Planned Parenthood and the Next Generation of Feminist Activists." *Feminist Studies* 39, no. 1 (2013): 187–91.

Luna, Zakiya T. "Marching Toward Reproductive Justice: Coalitional (Re) Framing of the March for Women's Lives." *Sociological Inquiry* 80, no. 4 (2010): 554–78.

Luxton, Meg. "Feminism as a Class Act: Working-Class Feminism and the Women's Movement in Canada." *Labour/Le Travail* 48 (Fall 2001): 63–88.

Major, Brenda, Mark Appelbaum, Linda Beckman, Mary Ann Dutton, Nancy Felipe Russo, and Carolyn West. "Abortion and Mental Health: Evaluating the Evidence." *American Psychologist* 64, no. 9 (2009): 863–90.

Masden, Melissa. "Pre-natal Testing and Selective Abortion: The Development of a Feminist Disability Rights Perspective." Women with Disabilities Australia, 1992. http://www.wwda.org.au/masden1.htm.

McDonnell, Kathleen. "Claim No Easy Victories: The Fight for Reproductive Rights." In *Still Ain't Satisfied! Canadian Feminism Today*, edited by Maureen Fitzgerald, Connie Guberman, and Margie Wolfe, 32–42. Toronto: Women's Press, 1982.

———. *Not an Easy Choice: A Feminist Re-examines Abortion*. Toronto: Women's Press, 1984.

McLaughlin, Janice. "Screening Networks: Shared Agendas in Feminist and Disability Movement Challenges to Antenatal Screening and Abortion." *Disability and Society* 18, no. 3 (2003): 297–310.

Mullens, Anne. "7:10 am, Nov. 8, 1994." *Canadian Medical Association Journal* 158, no. 4 (1998): 528–31.

Norris, Alison, Danielle Bessett, Julia R. Steinberg, Megan L. Kavanaugh, Silvia De Zordo, and Davida Becker. "Abortion Stigma: A Reconceptualization of Constituents, Causes, and Consequences." Supplement, *Women's Health Issues* 21, no. 3 (2011): S49–54.

Petchesky, Rosalind Pollack. *Abortion and Woman's Choice: The State, Sexuality, and Reproductive Freedom*. Boston: Northeastern University Press, 1984.

Piepmeier, Alison. "The Inadequacy of 'Choice': Disability and What's Wrong with Feminist Framings of Reproduction." *Feminist Studies* 39, no. 1 (2013): 159–86.

Pritchard, Megan. "Can There Be Such a Thing as a 'Wrongful Birth'?" *Disability and Society* 20, no. 1 (2005): 81–93.

Rebick, Judy. *Ten Thousand Roses: The Making of a Feminist Revolution*. Toronto: Penguin, 2005.

Ross, Loretta. "Understanding Reproductive Justice: Transforming the Pro-Choice Movement." *Off Our Backs* 36, no. 4 (2006): 14–19.

Saurette, Paul, and Kelly Gordon. "Arguing Abortion: The New Anti-Abortion Discourse in Canada." *Canadian Journal of Political Science* 46, no. 1 (2013): 157–85.

Seavilleklein, Victoria. "Challenging the Rhetoric of Choice in Prenatal Screening." *Bioethics* 23, no. 1 (2009): 68–77.

Shakespeare, Tom. "Choices and Rights: Eugenics, Genetics, and Disability Equality." *Disability and Society* 13, no. 5 (1998): 665–81.

Sharp, Keith, and Sarah Earle. "Feminism, Abortion, and Disability: Irreconcilable Differences?" *Disability and Society* 17, no. 2 (2002): 137–45.

Shaw, Jessica. "Abortion as a Social Justice Issue in Contemporary Canada." *Critical Social Work* 14, no. 2 (2013): 2–17. http://www1.uwindsor.ca/criticalsocialwork/system/files/Shaw.pdf.

———. "Full-Spectrum Reproductive Justice: The Affinity of Abortion Rights and Birth Activism." *Studies in Social Justice* 7, no. 1 (2012): 143–59.

Sheldon, Alison. "Personal and Perplexing: Feminist Disability Politics Evaluated." *Disability and Society* 14, no. 5 (1999): 643–57.

Smith, Andrea. "Beyond Pro-Choice Versus Pro-Life: Women of Color and Reproductive Justice." *NWSA Journal* 17, no. 1 (2005): 119–40.

Solinger, Rickie. *Beggars and Choosers: How the Politics of Choice Shapes Adoption, Abortion, and Welfare in the United States*. New York: Hill and Wang, 2001.

Solomon, Martha, ed. *One Kind Word: Women Share Their Abortion Stories*. With photographs by Kathryn Palmateer. Toronto: Three O'Clock Press, 2014.

Sommers, Christina Hoff. *Who Stole Feminism? How Women Have Betrayed Women*. New York: Simon and Schuster, 1994.

Stettner, Shannon. "Post-abortion Trauma Syndrome." In *Encyclopedia of Women in Today's World*, edited by Mary Zeiss Stange, Carol K. Oyster, and Jane E. Sloan, 1126–27. Thousand Oaks, CA: Sage, 2011.

———. "Women and Abortion in English Canada: Public Debates and Political Participation, 1959–1970." PhD diss., York University, Toronto, 2011.

Stettner, Shannon, and Tracy Penny Light. "The Politics of Reproductive Health History: Visible, Audible, and Consequential." *Canadian Bulletin of Medical History* 31, no. 2 (2014): 9–24.

Tatalovich, Raymond. *The Politics of Abortion in the United States and Canada: A Comparative Study*. New York: M. E. Sharpe, 1997.

Weitz, Tracy A. "Rethinking the Mantra That Abortion Should be 'Safe, Legal, and Rare.'" *Journal of Women's History* 22, no. 3 (2010): 161–72.

Weitz, Tracy A., Kristen Moore, Rivka Gordon, and Nancy Adler. "You Say 'Regret' and I Say 'Relief': A Need to Break the Polemic About Abortion." *Contraception* 78, no. 2 (2008): 87–89.

Yee, Jessica, ed. *Feminism for Real: Deconstructing the Academic Industrial Complex of Feminism.* Ottawa: Canadian Centre for Policy Alternatives, 2011.

Yee, Jessica, Alisha Nicole Apale, and Melissa Deleary. "Sexual and Reproductive Health, Rights, and Realities and Access to Services for First Nations, Inuit, and Métis in Canada." Society of Obstetricians and Gynaecologists of Canada Policy Statement No. 259. June 2011. *Journal of Obstetrics and Gynaecology Canada* 33, no. 6 (2011): 633–37. http://sogc.org/wp-content/uploads/2012/12/gui259PS1106E.pdf.

Introduction

A Brief History of
Abortion in Canada

SHANNON STETTNER

The history of abortion is central to the writing of women's history. In the words of Angus McLaren and Arlene Tigar McLaren, abortion reveals much about "women's responses to their physical functions, the medical profession's views of women's health, and male and female attitudes toward sexuality."[1] Perspectives on the female body and on the sexual activity of women are at once conditioned by and integral to the broader social construction of gender. Writing in the mid-1980s, sociologist Susan McDaniel noted that attitudes toward abortion are "closely tied to the social roles women are expected to play" and, by extension, to the perpetuation of patriarchy. "To the extent that women are defined essentially as reproducers," she wrote, "they come to be seen as vessels for carrying out other people's wishes, those of their family, husbands and society."[2] Yet only comparatively recently has the history of abortion in Canada begun to be told from the standpoint of women's lived experience and their reactions to the reproductive definitions thrust upon them. More commonly, the emphasis has fallen on the roles played by the medical, political, legal, and religious sectors and their collective influence on legislation and societal norms. Significantly, these histories often transform women into passive objects—bodies on which laws are imposed and procedures carried out. This focus on external forces, rather than on women's active agency, does not, however, mean that women played no part in the evolution of abortion policy. As legal scholar Shelley Gavigan reminds us, "the history of restrictive abortion legislation is also the history of women's resistance to it."[3]

All the same, despite women's ongoing struggles to assert control over their own bodies and despite an emerging historiographical emphasis on women's experience, histories of abortion have generally foregrounded efforts by physicians, clergy, and politicians to criminalize, decriminalize, and recriminalize abortion.[4] As a result, we know a lot about how these actors have shaped the history of abortion in Canada. We also know that their efforts have been variously affected by a number of factors that combined to shift dominant attitudes about abortion over the course of the nineteenth and twentieth centuries and that continue to do so today. Such factors include urbanization and industrialization; the professionalization of medical practice and the rise of scientific medicine; the connection of moral crusades and social reform to the perceived health of the nation; the increased secularization of Canadian society; the emergence of new reproductive technologies; the rise of protest movements in the 1960s; and the growing entrenchment of the pro-life and pro-choice movements. In what follows, I examine how and why the legal status of and social attitudes toward abortion changed over time, as well as the consequences of these changes. While the history offered below is not comprehensive, in part because so much of that history (especially as it pertains to women's experiences) still needs to be written, it is intended to provide some context for the observations and experiences that are the centrepiece of this book.

The Criminalization of Abortion

Efforts to criminalize abortion began at the start of the nineteenth century. These early laws distinguished between abortions performed before and after quickening—the moment when a pregnant woman first feels the fetus move, which usually occurs sometime between the sixteenth and twentieth week. It was generally held that, once quickening occurred, the fetus was "animated," that is, invested with a soul, and therefore represented a life.[5]

Until the early nineteenth century, abortion prior to quickening was not a criminal offence. This changed in 1803, when the British Parliament passed Lord Ellenborough's Act, which not only criminalized abortion both before and after quickening but also imposed the death penalty for abortions performed after quickening. Colonial administrations in Canada followed suit, enacting legislation modelled on this act.

As the nineteenth century progressed, the nature of abortion legislation began to shift. Under the early laws, in order for a person charged with performing an abortion to be prosecuted successfully, proof was needed that the woman in question was indeed "quick with child." In 1837, revisions to Great Britain's Offences Against the Person Act eliminated the death penalty for performing an abortion, in favour of a maximum sentence of three years' imprisonment, in an effort to make convictions easier to obtain. But the revised law also eliminated the distinction between abortions performed before and after quickening. The distinction was subsequently abolished in Upper Canada and in New Brunswick, which passed amended laws in 1841 and 1842, respectively, with both setting the maximum penalty for abortion at life imprisonment (much harsher than in Britain). New Brunswick soon reduced the sentence to a maximum of fourteen years, but in neighbouring Newfoundland, which had chosen in 1837 to adopt British criminal law as its own, the penalty was only three years.[6] In British North America, the net effect of the revised laws was thus to increase the punishment for abortions prior to quickening. While the rationale for removing the quickening distinction remains uncertain, the change in legislation might have represented what Constance Backhouse describes as an attempt "to eliminate the obvious evidentiary difficulties inherent in determining when a woman had quickened."[7]

The fact that this early legislation punished the abortionist, rather than the woman who sought out the abortion suggests, as Wendy Mitchinson observes, that "the morality of abortion as an act was the focus, not so much the morality of the woman."[8] It was not long, however, before women were drawn into the circle of guilt. In 1849, New Brunswick's anti-abortion legislation was amended to allow criminal charges to be brought against pregnant women who sought out such a procedure, and similar legal changes occurred in Nova Scotia in 1851. Although these amendments may have been prompted, most immediately, by legislation passed by the state of New York in 1845, they clearly reflected changing perceptions of women's participation in and responsibility for abortions. Evidently, Canadian legislators "had come to believe that the women involved were equally the source of the problem and that the full force of the criminal law ought to be brought to bear on them."[9] In 1861, revisions to Britain's Offences Against the Person Act likewise included the pregnant woman among those who could be charged. The 1861 law also allowed for the prosecution of the abortionist regardless of whether the woman "be or be not with Child," thereby eliminating the need for proof of pregnancy, and included a new, lesser offence of acting as an accessory to the procurement of an abortion.[10] In Canada, the Constitution Act of 1867 defined the powers of the federal and provincial governments, at which point criminal law was placed under federal jurisdiction. This division of power enabled the Canadian Parliament to unify abortion laws throughout the existing provinces under Canada's own Offences Against the Person Act, passed in 1869. At that time, the punishment for those convicted of procuring or performing an abortion was set at life in prison.[11]

In 1892, the first Criminal Code of Canada incorporated provisions against abortion. Section 271, captioned "Killing unborn child," mandated life imprisonment for a person "who causes the death of any child which has not become a human being, in such a manner that he would have been guilty of murder if such a child had been born." The same section specified that actions taken "for the preservation of the life of the mother of the child" that resulted in the child's death were not considered an offence, indicating that the same value was not accorded to fetal and maternal life. As in the 1861 legislation enacted in Britain, section 272 of the code made it illegal to attempt an abortion regardless of whether the woman had actually been pregnant:

> Every one is guilty of an indictable offence and liable to imprisonment
> for life who, with intent to procure the miscarriage of any woman,
> whether she is or is not with child, unlawfully administers to her or
> causes to be taken *by* her any drug or other noxious thing, or unlaw-
> fully uses any instrument or other measure whatsoever with the like
> intent.

Section 273 went on to extend these provisions to the woman herself ("whether with child or not"), although with a lesser penalty of seven years' imprisonment.[12] In addition, section 179(c) outlawed the sale, distribution, or advertisement not only of abortifacients but of "any medicine, drug or article intended or represented as a means of preventing contraception."

The criminalization of attempts to induce a miscarriage even if, as it turned out, the woman was not pregnant must be understood in the context of nineteenth-century medical knowledge. At the time, evidence of quickening was, for all practical purposes, the only way to be certain that a woman was pregnant. Thus, even after the distinction between pre- and post-quickening abortions was eliminated, the "proof of pregnancy" requirement rendered prosecution all but impossible in the case of abortions performed prior to quickening. Lifting the pregnancy requirement allowed legal sanctions to be imposed even if the woman had been mistaken about her condition, making it "finally possible to enforce the law against women who were in the early stages of pregnancy."[13]

These legal developments, including the ban on contraceptives, speak to the increasing regulation of women's bodies by the state. And yet existing records indicate that fewer than two dozen abortion cases were tried in Canadian courts during the nineteenth century, and in none of them was a woman prosecuted for procuring an abortion. Rather, those charged were most commonly medical practitioners of some sort or, on occasion, the woman's male partner, typically when he had taken an instrumental role in attempting to end the pregnancy. In other words, from the standpoint of enforcement, the emphasis fell on those who actually carried out the proced-ure. This focus on punishing those who provided medical services reflects the degree to which the evolution of abortion over the course of the nineteenth century was driven by efforts on the part of the nascent medical profession to establish its control over the practice of medicine.[14] As Backhouse argues, especially in the latter half of the century, "regular" physicians—that is, those who had undertaken formal medical training and were duly licensed—used the spectre of illegal abortions performed by "irregular" practitioners to erect and solidify professional boundaries.[15] Unsurprisingly, "regular" physicians were, with rare exception, white males, typically of middle-class origins, whereas "irregular" practitioners were more apt to be women, many of them either Indigenous or from immigrant backgrounds. In short, abortion laws disciplined female bodies in the service of male objectives.

Turn-of-the-Century Sensibilities and Illegal Social Acts

Women's bodies and their reproductive abilities increasingly became a site of contestation not only for physicians who sought to police the scope of medical practice but also for those who saw women's bodies as tied to larger

social, cultural, and economic issues in Canadian society. During the closing decades of the nineteenth century, Euro-Canadian nationalists became
concerned with the decline of Canadian—that is, English and Protestant—
fertility, fearing both "la revanche des berceaux" ("the revenge of the cradles")
of Catholic French Canadians as well as the upsurge in non-British immigration.[16] Evidence that white, Protestant women of middle- or upper-class
origins were seeking abortion in growing numbers only heightened fears of
"race suicide."[17] As historian Tracy Penny Light observes, indications are that
abortion legislation "originated with the middle class, specifically with their
desire to regulate morality in the interest of building a strong and morally
pure nation."[18] The regulation of women's bodies, then, reflected dominant
beliefs about who should, and should not, be encouraged to procreate and,
by extension, about which people were valuable citizens.

The Victorian ideal of womanhood was another important aspect of the
social context of abortion during the latter decades of the nineteenth century. Women (that is, white, middle- or upper-class women) were deemed
to possess natural traits of character such as piety, chastity, domesticity, and
submissiveness that made them perfectly suited to be wives and mothers.[19]
This was the ideal that lower-class women were encouraged to emulate. Of
course, there was a disparity between the conduct prescribed for women and
the ways that women actually behaved, and abortion serves as a good example
of this disparity. In her study of abortion in the nineteenth century, Backhouse
argues that even as laws were being passed to prohibit abortion, they were "at
odds with the views of much of the population."[20] There is ample evidence,
found in criminal records and vital statistics, that despite strict abortion laws,
pregnant women continued to procure abortions. As these records reveal,
during the late nineteenth and early twentieth centuries, those most likely
to seek abortion were in fact married women, often already mothers, who
were looking to limit family size. Since the most common form of birth control prior to the mid-twentieth century was coitus interruptus (withdrawal),
unplanned and unwanted pregnancies occurred with some frequency.[21] There
is also evidence that both married women who were sexually active outside
of marriage, as well as single women who found themselves pregnant, relied
on abortion as a means to cope with unwelcome consequences.[22] What these
patterns clearly suggest is that rather than simply conforming to an ideal of
behaviour ascribed to them, women were active (and sexual) agents who
sought to control not only their fertility but also the shape of their lives.

By examining court documents, we also learn much about the techniques used during the nineteenth and early twentieth centuries to induce miscarriage. Angus McLaren's study of illegal abortion in turn-of-the-century British Columbia reveals that "the use of instruments was by all accounts the leading method of abortion. The women would squat and with the help of a mirror insert in the cervix a catheter, speculum, sound, pencil, bougie, needle, crochet or button hook."[23] The second most popular method was the oral ingestion of herbs or drugs. Of the 108 charges of abortion that Penny Light investigated, for example, 56 included the use of an herbal remedy or patent medicine.[24] The challenge was to take enough of the herb or drug to "irritate the body or digestive system," in order to produce the "abortion of the fetus as a side effect," but not enough to kill the pregnant woman.[25] As historian Eliane Leslau Silverman and others have documented, white settlers in the late nineteenth and early twentieth centuries often relied on the medical knowledge and skills of Indigenous midwives and other healers, who were familiar with methods for inducing abortion. A Métis woman who had lived in Alberta at the turn of the century recalled that local women "used a black bag, from the bladder of a bear. They'd dry it, then mix it with some liquid, and then they'd lose the baby. There must be some medicine in that. They figure that's okay. It's from the land and they figure it didn't do any harm."[26]

Angus McLaren found the third and fourth most common methods to be, respectively, "douching by syringe or enema bag with lysol, carbolic acid, turpentine or simple soap and water" and "dilation of the cervix by inserting slippery elm or packing the vagina with cotton batten."[27] None of these methods guaranteed termination of the pregnancy, and all of them came with risks of infection and hemorrhaging, which, especially in those days, could prove fatal or, short of that, leave the woman sterile. These risks, coupled with the uncertainty of success, demonstrate the degree to which these women did not want to be pregnant. The dangers attaching to abortion were not evenly distributed across social classes. In her study of thirty-four abortion-related deaths in British Columbia between 1917 and 1937, Susanne Klausen found that all of the deceased women belonged to the labouring classes and concludes that it was their need to rely on self-abortion techniques or on dubiously qualified "backstreet" abortionists, as well as a reluctance to incur the cost of seeing physicians should complications arise, that contributed to their deaths. Middle- and upper-class women, she contends, had better access both to contraception and to physicians who "performed abortions under safer circumstances."[28]

As Angus McLaren argues, illegal abortions were "social acts," in the sense that, to procure one, a pregnant woman required help. Faced with an unwanted pregnancy, women relied on the assistance of family and friends, who formed a community of support around her.[29] Indeed, in 70 percent of the cases that Penny Light examined, charges were laid against family and friends of the pregnant women.[30] In the case of single women, McLaren found, the most likely accomplice was their male partner, who often had a vested interest keeping the pregnancy a secret, whether to protect the woman's reputation or his own.[31] Criminal records also show that both regular and irregular doctors performed abortions, whether driven by profit or a sincere desire to help a woman in need.[32]

The social networks surrounding the procuring of illegal abortions remind us of Backhouse's contention that the restrictive abortion legislation enacted in the nineteenth century was out of touch with the reality of people's lives. In part, such legislation attempted to regulate sexual activity, in accordance with Victorian notions of propriety, and such attempts have rarely been successful. In the absence of effective and reliable methods of birth control, unwanted pregnancies were inevitable—a problem in need of a solution. The involvement of lovers, friends, and family in finding that solution suggests that abortion did not necessarily carry the same sense of personal shame that later came to be associated with it. At least among the "respectable" classes, social shame attached to becoming pregnant out of wedlock, although only if the pregnancy became public. Quietly seeking an abortion was therefore the sensible course of action, one in which the woman could depend on help from others. Arguably, it was only when reliable methods of birth control became widespread that (except in cases of rape) a woman who needed an abortion began to be blamed for becoming pregnant—and that she began to blame herself.

A Shift in Consciousness: Birth Control and the Bourne Defence

In the opening decades of the twentieth century, both the legal status and the practice of abortion remained relatively unchanged, with women continuing to use abortion as a means to limit family size. The status quo began to change in the 1930s, however, with the onset of the Great Depression, during

Without Apology

which birth control advocates, many of whom were influenced by eugenics, became increasingly visible.

Although the laws on abortion remained unchanged during the Depression, two important developments occurred in the 1930s that affected abortion. First, a number of groups and individuals became public advocates of birth control. Marie Stopes, in Great Britain, and Margaret Sanger, in the United States, rose to prominence as birth control activists in the second decade of the twentieth century, and they had a great deal of influence on the shape and nature of the birth control movement for several more decades. Neither woman supported abortion, but they both espoused eugenic beliefs regarding who should and should not be allowed to procreate. Accordingly, they felt that the more "desirable" people (that is, people who were white and at least middle class) should be encouraged to reproduce, while "less desirable" people should have smaller families.[33] In 1936, Dorothea Palmer—a nurse who worked for the Parents' Information Bureau, founded by Canadian industrialist and birth control advocate A. R. Kaufman—was tried for distributing birth control information in Eastview (now Vanier), a poor Roman Catholic neighbourhood in Ottawa. Like Sanger and Stopes, Kaufman was motivated by theories of eugenics and sought to make birth control available to working-class people.[34] Ultimately, Palmer was acquitted, on the grounds that her actions had been undertaken as a public service, a decision that reflected the growing popular acceptance of birth control in Canada.[35] Such activism contributed to the normalization of public discussions of birth control, as well as forcing the state, doctors, and churches to acknowledge people's desire to control their fertility. During these years, many countries witnessed the growth of family planning movements that advocated the widespread availability of effective contraception as central to improving the quality of family life.[36]

Another event that influenced the evolution of abortion politics in Canada was the 1938 trial of Dr. Aleck Bourne in the United Kingdom. In Britain, the Infant Life (Preservation) Act of 1929, which amended the 1861 Offences Against the Person Act, had established that an abortion performed solely to preserve the mother's life was not a legal offence. Bourne was charged with performing an abortion on a fourteen-year-old girl who had been raped by several off-duty British soldiers. At his trial, he argued that he had performed the abortion to save the girl's mental health, and he was acquitted by the jury. As John Keown points out, although "long before 1938, therapeutic abortion was judicially approved, both tacitly and expressly" in Britain, the Bourne case was the first time that the principle of medical necessity had been used as a defence in court.[37] Not only was the principle formally upheld, but the decision had the effect of extending the scope of medicine to include mental, as well as physical, health, thereby broadening the range of abortions that could be performed legally, for reasons of medical necessity.[38] Bourne's trial was closely watched in Canada, which lacked the equivalent of Britain's 1929 act. Although no legislative changes occurred at the federal level, the case provided an opening for the argument that abortion should be legal when performed as a medical necessity, that is, when a woman's life or health was endangered by a continued pregnancy.[39] It thus contributed to a growing recognition that abortion should be permitted under certain circumstances.

It is impossible to know what the rate of abortion was before contraception became legal, relatively accessible, and reasonably reliable. As long as abortion itself remained illegal, the fact that one had occurred was generally discovered only when something went wrong. In piecing together the history of abortion, we are thus dependent largely on vital statistics compiled by governments and on legal and medical records, supplemented by stray anecdotal information—sources that, together, provide only a partial picture. In an analysis of maternal mortality statistics in Ontario, historian George Emery, who specializes in interpreting vital statistics, points to several factors that complicate efforts to trace the actual number of deaths from abortion. Whether to protect the woman's reputation or their own, physicians filling out a death certificate might deliberately suppress any reference to abortion—or their diagnostic skills might be inadequate to the task of establishing that abortion was the underlying cause of death. The information they provided was also influenced by the design of the death certificate form, while the resulting statistics depended to some degree on the way that government administrators interpreted this information.[40] As a result, historical estimates vary widely and are inevitably imprecise.[41] While additional research may help to provide us with a clearer sense of how pervasive illegal abortions were, we will never be absolutely certain. It is here that turning to the testimonies of women and physicians makes sense. In the end, the experience of abortion—that is, the motivations for seeking one and for aiding a woman who is looking for one—is perhaps more important than the number that were actually performed.

Without Apology

The Journey to Halfway: The 1969 Amendments to the Criminal Code

From the time of its founding, in 1867, the Canadian Medical Association (CMA) exercised a great deal of influence on Canadian abortion law. During the first half of the twentieth century, maternal and child welfare garnered increasing attention from the medical profession.[42] In the 1950s, the Canadian Medical Association (CMA) established the Maternal Welfare Committee to study issues of maternal health and mortality, including their links to abortion. In August 1961, the BC branch of the CMA began to call for abortion law reform. In 1962, the CMA discussed the issue at its General Council meeting, and, in early 1964, the Maternal Welfare Committee openly raised the issue of legal protection for physicians who performed abortions. At least initially, internal strife over the form that abortion regulations should take frustrated efforts to arrive at a consensus. Alongside these debates within the CMA, the Canadian Bar Association (CBA) began to deliberate on the issue at its annual meetings. At the same time, Canadian churches also began to discuss the place of abortion in a modernizing society.[43] By 1966, both the CMA and the CBA had managed to overcome internal divisions and adopted statements calling for the reform of the abortion law to allow for abortion under certain circumstances. By the end of the decade, several churches had followed their lead. As is important to recognize, although reducing maternal mortality was certainly a concern, all these organizations founded their support for abortion law reform primarily on fears about the potential prosecution of doctors who were willing to risk performing therapeutic abortions, rather than on sympathy for the situation of women who sought abortions for reasons other than medical.

At the same time that physicians, lawyers, clergy, and politicians were growing increasingly concerned about the illegality of abortion regardless of the circumstances, public attitudes also began to shift. In 1957, the British government released the Report of the Departmental Committee on Homosexual Offences and Prostitution (the Wolfenden Report), which recommended that both be decriminalized. Historians view this report as a key moment in the movement away from state regulation of sexual behaviour. Public discussions on issues related to a person's private sexual life took place in Canada in various popular print vehicles, including *Chatelaine* magazine, the *United Church Observer*, and newspapers like the *Toronto Star* and the *Globe and Mail*, through letters to the editors.[44]

Women took an active part in these discussions, with many of them voicing support for the reform of the existing abortion law to make it more responsive to women's needs.

In January 1966, in response to growing concerns from the medical community and the perceived need to clarify the abortion law so as to protect doctors from prosecution, four private member's bills were introduced into the House of Commons. These bills sought to amend the Criminal Code in relation to birth control, with one seeking to modify the abortion law as well, and were duly referred for consideration to the House of Commons Standing Committee on Health and Welfare.[45] The Standing Committee, chaired by Liberal member Dr. Harry C. Harley, sat at different times in 1966, 1967, and 1968 to study contraception and abortion-related issues. In addition to hearing from the members who had proposed the bills, the committee reviewed briefs submitted by individuals and organizations representing a broad spectrum of public opinion. Notable presenters included the CMA, the CBA, the Family Planning Federation of Canada, the Canadian Welfare Council, the Canadian Council of Churches, and the Anglican, United, Lutheran, and Roman Catholic churches. Individual doctors, including Henry Morgentaler, also spoke. Among the women's groups that made presentations were the Voice of Women, the National Council of Women, the Young Women's Christian Association, and the Women's Liberation Group. In December 1967, the committee submitted an interim report to the House of Commons, advocating that the law should be amended to "allow therapeutic abortion under appropriate medical safeguards where a pregnancy will seriously endanger the life or health of the mother."[46]

In the meanwhile, in February 1967, Lester Pearson's Liberal government had established the ground-breaking Royal Commission on the Status of Women (RCSW). According to the official Terms of Reference, the commission was appointed to "inquire into and report on the status of women in Canada, and to recommend what steps might be taken to ensure for women equal opportunities with men in all aspects of Canadian society."[47] The RCSW held public hearings across Canada throughout 1968. Women's letters to the commission and their testimony at public hearings include important examples of how women were affected by the illegal status of abortion (and contraception). One woman, who signed her letter "Desperate," wrote: "I asked my doctor for an operation [sterilization] and he treated me like I had asked for an abortion! I did not! . . . I was . . . *terrified* that

I would have another baby. I only wanted to be sterilized. . . . Isn't that a better solution than *the wish for an abortion* and the *pressure* that comes with *too many children?*"[48] Another woman, a mother of five children, supported legalizing abortion on request, stating, "I think the only person that is affected is the woman with the problem. It is *her* problem only, and she is the one who should decide what she is going to do with her body, a simple matter of—the woman's body, her problem, her decision, her life. She should be able to go to any qualified doctor and have an abortion if she desires."[49] Dozens of women told similar stories about their desire to control their own fertility and the difficulty they encountered in attempting to do so, including their experiences with illegal abortions. These testimonies were relayed to the public through print and television coverage of the RCSW hearings, and they undoubtedly contributed to public support for some degree of abortion law reform, however limited.

In October 1967, the British Parliament passed the Abortion Act, which greatly liberalized the circumstances under which an abortion could be legally performed. In December of that same year, shortly after the Standing Committee on Health and Welfare tabled its interim report, Pierre Trudeau, then Canada's minister of Justice, introduced an omnibus bill (C-195) that contained various amendments to the Criminal Code, including the decriminalization of both homosexuality and therapeutic abortion. Trudeau echoed the sentiments expressed in the Wolfenden Report when he famously stated, in defence of this bill, that "the state has no place in the bedrooms of the nation."[50] After he became prime minister in April 1968, Trudeau continued to advocate for reforms to the Criminal Code. In December of that year, Trudeau's minister of Justice, John Turner, introduced Bill C-150, a revised version of Trudeau's earlier bill, which was passed into law by Parliament in May 1969 by a vote of 149 to 55. The Criminal Law Amendment Act, 1968–69, legalized contraception and also revised section 251 of the Criminal Code so as to partially decriminalize abortion. Under the revised law, the procedure became legal, but only when it was performed in an accredited hospital by a licensed physician and only after a Therapeutic Abortion Committee consisting of at least three doctors had determined that the pregnancy endangered either the life or the health of the pregnant woman.[51]

As noted earlier, despite women's active investment in legal changes, much of the impetus behind the 1969 amendments arose from a desire to clarify the circumstances under which physicians could legally perform an abortion.

While the amendments to the Criminal Code did liberalize the existing law, from the standpoint of women access to abortion was still quite restricted. The new law also did nothing to end the public discussion of abortion. If anything, the law was a turning point that initiated the deepening polarization of those for and against the legalization of abortion.

The New Law: Ideological Divides and Practical Difficulties

Although the new law may have satisfied politicians and physicians, Canadians who supported either greater access or no access to abortion were unhappy with the changes. Those who found the new abortion law to be inadequate responded quickly to Bill C-150. The May 1970 Abortion Caravan, the first national pro-choice protest in the country, clearly demonstrated many women's rejection of the 1969 law. Originating in Vancouver under the direction of the Vancouver Women's Caucus, the Abortion Caravan travelled across the country to Ottawa, stopping in eleven cities along the way to connect with other women's groups, engage in public education and outreach, and gather supporters for the Ottawa protests. The Caravan culminated in two protests on 11 May 1970 on Parliament Hill—one outside the House, in which protesters circled the centennial flame, and another inside the House, during which thirty-six women, many of whom had chained themselves to their seats in the galleries, shouted "Free abortion on demand!" and ultimately succeeded in causing a temporary adjournment of House proceedings.[52]

During that weekend of protest, Margo Dunn, a Caravan participant, made a speech about the tools of the illegal abortionist and how each one contributed to the death of Canadian women:

> There are garbage bags on top of that coffin. These are used to pack the uterus to induce labor. Since they are not sterile, they often cause massive infection, resulting in sterilization, permanent disability, or death. . . . There are knitting needles on top of that coffin. These are used to put in the vagina in order to pierce the uterus. Severe bleeding results. . . . There is a bottle which is a container of Lysol, on top of that coffin. When used for cleaning, it is in solution. Women seeking to abort themselves inject it full strength into their vaginas. This results in severe burning of tissues, haemorrhage, and shock. Death comes within a matter of minutes. Intense, agonizing pain is suffered until the time of death. . . . There is part of a vacuum cleaner on top of that

coffin. The hose is placed in the vagina in order to extract the fetus, but results in the whole uterus being sucked from the pelvic cavity.[53]

Dunn's speech highlighted the fact that the liberalization of the abortion laws did not end illegal abortions. Women wishing to abort for non-medical reasons were still left with little recourse. Some women could afford to travel to the United States, where abortion was already legal in many states (and, after 1973, with *Roe v. Wade*, would be so throughout the country), others were left with no choice but to seek an illegal abortion in Canada.[54]

At the same time, many were staunchly opposed to any liberalization of the abortion law. In the years leading up to and following the 1969 changes, several anti-abortion organizations came into existence. Many of these groups, which divide their focus between political and educational goals, are still operating: Alliance for Life Canada (ALC), founded in 1968; Toronto Right to Life (TRL), founded in 1971; Campaign Life Coalition (CLC), formed in 1978; and REAL (Realistic, Equal, Active, for Life) Women of Canada, founded in 1983, among others. Although REAL Women has a broader mandate than abortion, the "right to life" position is fundamental to the organization: one of its founders, Gwen Landolt, also founded the TRL and was involved in the creation of the Coalition for Life as well. In 1973 and 1975, national anti-abortion groups petitioned the Canadian Parliament, having collected more than one million signatures opposing the 1969 liberalization of the abortion law. The political silence with which the 1975 anti-abortion petition was received was, in the words of Michael Cuneo, "a watershed in the movement's history, setting the stage for disillusionment, the growth of extremism, and heightened organizational panic."[55] By the early 1980s, Canada's anti-abortion movement had become a part of a larger "pro-family" movement, which offered deeply conservative critiques of issues such as sex education, feminism, pornography, gay rights, and, especially, abortion.[56]

Opposition notwithstanding, in the period following the 1969 amendments, it rapidly became evident that "gross inequities existed in the availability of therapeutic abortion to the women of Canada."[57] In 1975, following widespread complaints, the federal government established the Committee on the Operation of the Abortion Law, with the goal of determining whether the abortion law was being equitably applied throughout the country. The three-member committee, chaired by University of Toronto professor Robin F. Badgley, tabled its report in January 1977. It found that many hospitals, especially those with religious affiliations, had not established Therapeutic

Abortion Committees at all, and, when such committees did exist, they varied widely in their procedures and overall approach. In particular, in deciding whether continuing a pregnancy posed a threat to a woman's health, committees were left to decide for themselves how to interpret the term *health*. In short, Canadian women were not guaranteed equal access to abortion, with women living in rural parts of the country especially likely to encounter obstacles because they did not have local access to accredited hospitals.[58] In addition, significant numbers of women were still leaving Canada to obtain an abortion. Despite the fact that 49,300 abortions were performed in Canadian hospitals in 1975, another 9,700 women travelled to the United States for the procedure.[59] To make matters worse, the waiting period in Canada for a legal abortion was averaging eight weeks.[60] Clearly, in both its scope and its application, the new law was failing to address women's needs.

The same year that the Badgley Committee submitted its report, another development occurred that would have a lasting effect on abortion politics in the country. In 1977, the Established Programs Financing Act (EPF) altered the arrangement whereby the federal government transferred funds to provinces to help cover the cost of both health care and post-secondary education (the "established programs" referred to in the act), responsibility for which lay with individual provinces. Formerly, funding had been provided on a cost-sharing basis, with certain conditions attached to the award of federal funds. The EPF instead introduced a set formula, which operated on a per capita basis: provinces would receive a standard amount of funding (in the form of a percentage of federal tax revenues, supplemented by cash grants) for each resident of the province. This funding was, moreover, unconditional: no mechanism existed whereby the government could withhold funds should a province fail to provide specific services. In other words, the EPF represented a move toward decentralization, in which the provinces were allowed considerable latitude in the delivery of health services. Thus, while the new funding model guaranteed provinces a steady supply of federal funds, it also aggravated the problem of procedural inconsistencies and inequities in access.

The Canada Health Act (CHA), passed in 1984, was intended, in part, to address this problem, by imposing some degree of uniformity on the health care plans offered by individual provinces. According to section 3 of the CHA, Canadian health care policy has as its primary goal "to protect, promote and restore the physical and mental well-being of residents of Canada and to facilitate reasonable access to health services without financial or other barriers." To this end, the act specified five criteria that provincial health plans must meet in order to be eligible for federal funding.[61] In the words of a subsequent parliamentary report, the CHA sought to ensure that "every Canadian has *timely* access to all medically necessary health services *regardless* of his or her ability to pay for those services."[62] The act does not, however, explicitly define what constitutes a "medically necessary" health service; rather, provinces are left to decide precisely which health services will be insured.[63] Given that, in 1984, abortions could legally be performed only in a hospital, after a Therapeutic Abortion Committee had certified that the procedure was necessary to preserve the life or health of the mother, any legal abortion would, by definition, be medically necessary. This situation would change, however, only four years later.

"Fighting for Fundamental Justice": Dr. Henry Morgentaler

One of the voices advocating for reform of the abortion law during the 1960s was that of Dr. Henry Morgentaler. Like many others, Morgentaler was dissatisfied with the restrictions imposed by the 1969 amendments to section 251 of the Criminal Code. In response, he began publicly defying that law in order to underscore the need for further liberalization. Morgentaler was by no means the only physician who was willing to perform abortions during the time that they were illegal. What separated Morgentaler from other physicians, at least during the 1960s and 1970s, was his openness about his illegal activities.

Morgentaler began his career in medicine in Montréal in 1953 as a general practitioner, but he focused increasingly on the reproductive health needs of his patients. He was a member of the Humanist Association of Canada, and it was as a representative of that organization that he first spoke out publicly about abortion, before the Standing Committee on Health and Welfare on 19 October 1967. Born in Poland in 1923, Morgentaler survived imprisonment in Auschwitz and Dachau, an experience, he said, that led to his later advocacy for women's right to an abortion: "I was sensitized to injustice and when I was in a position to do something about it, I felt it was a duty to do so, at whatever risk there was. I had a feeling I was fighting for fundamental justice."[64] After his speech in front of the Standing Committee, he was increasingly contacted by women across Canada in search of a safe abortion.

In 1968, Morgentaler abandoned his general practice and instead focused on abortion provision at his private clinic in Montréal. The police arrested him for the first time on 1 June 1970. In December 1973, in an article published in the *Canadian Medical Association Journal*, Morgentaler reported on the more than five thousand abortions he had performed using vacuum suction curettage—a technique, he argued, that could replace the traditional method of dilation and curettage used in most hospitals. Whereas dilation and curettage required general anesthesia, vacuum suction curettage could be performed under local anesthesia, which meant that abortions could be performed in clinics or doctors' offices, thereby freeing up hospital beds.[65]

In the period from 1973 to 1976, Morgentaler was tried on three separate occasions; each time he was acquitted by a jury. Following his first acquittal, the Province of Québec appealed the decision, and, in 1974, the Québec Court of Appeal went so far as to overturn a decision made by a jury and substitute a guilty verdict. After an unsuccessful appeal to the Supreme Court of Canada, Morgentaler began serving an eighteen-month prison term. However, in response to the unprecedented action taken by the Québec Court of Appeal, in 1975, the Government of Canada passed the so-called Morgentaler Amendment, which states that a court of appeal cannot substitute a conviction for a jury acquittal; rather, if the appeal court overturns a jury acquittal, the case must be returned to trial court. At two subsequent trials, the first in 1975 (while he was still in jail) and the second in 1976, Morgentaler was again acquitted by juries.[66]

This series of acquittals strongly suggests the degree to which the abortion law was out of touch with social attitudes in Québec, which had been transformed by the Quiet Revolution of the 1960s—a decade that, among other things, saw the founding of family planning associations in the province. In the early 1970s, however, despite the recent amendments to the federal law, access to abortion remained scarce in Québec, with the vast majority of legal abortions performed in anglophone hospitals, and a full four out of five taking place at Montreal General.[67] Almost immediately after the federal law was amended, numerous groups throughout the province began agitating for improved access to abortion. These included the Fédération du Québec pour le planning des naissances, founded in 1972, which joined in the protests against Morgentaler's 1974 conviction. In November 1976 (roughly two months after Morgentaler's third acquittal), the Parti Québécois came to power. In defiance of federal law, the new government quickly granted

Without Apology

immunity from prosecution to all doctors qualified to perform abortions, regardless of the circumstances under which the procedure was carried out. Although abortions continued to be performed in hospitals in accordance with federal law, legal action could no longer be brought against physicians, such as Morgentaler, who provided abortions in clinics or private offices and without the prior approval of a Therapeutic Abortion Committee.[68]

Despite the newly supportive environment in Québec, Morgentaler was not finished challenging Canada's abortion law. In 1983, along with two colleagues, Dr. Robert Scott and Dr. Leslie Frank Smoling, Morgentaler opened an abortion clinic in Toronto with the intention of challenging the abortion law in Ontario. That same year, the Toronto police raided the clinic and charged the doctors with illegally providing abortions. When, in 1984, a jury acquitted the doctors, the Ontario government appealed the decision. The Ontario Court of Appeals ordered a retrial, and Morgentaler appealed that decision to the Supreme Court of Canada. In 1982, however, just a few years before this case began its journey through the court system, the Canadian Charter of Rights and Freedoms had been adopted, providing crucial support for Morgentaler's fight and, more importantly, for Canadian women generally. According to section 7 of the Charter, "Everyone has the right to life, liberty and security of the person and the right not to be deprived thereof except in accordance with the principles of fundamental justice." In January 1988, the Supreme Court of Canada declared, in *R. v. Morgentaler* ([1988] 1 S.C.R. 30), that section 251 of the Criminal Code violated section 7 of the Charter, arguing that the law infringed upon a woman's right to security of the person and that the procedures whereby women were deprived of this right did not accord with fundamental justice. The Court further argued that the infringement of this right could not be justified under section 1 of the Charter, which guarantees that the rights it lays out will be "subject only to such reasonable limits prescribed by law as can be demonstrably justified in a free and democratic society." By striking down the 1969 law, the Supreme Court created an opening for new abortion legislation.[69]

Although Morgentaler's name stands out in history, it is important to remember that he was far from alone in his struggles. During the 1970s and early 1980s, a number of abortion rights groups fought, often alongside Morgentaler, to have abortion fully legalized. The Canadian Association for Repeal of the Abortion Law (CARAL), founded in 1974 to protest Dr. Morgentaler's incarceration for performing abortions, focused its efforts on overturning the abortion law, providing both political and fundraising support to Morgentaler's own efforts. In 1980, the organization adopted a new name, the Canadian Abortion Rights Action League, and, two years later, narrowed its mission to political activism, moving its educational and research activities into a separate organization, the Childbirth by Choice Trust. Provincial and local chapters of CARAL quickly spread across the country. Similarly, the Ontario Coalition for Abortion Clinics (OCAC) was established, in 1982, with the specific goal of helping Morgentaler fight for legal abortion in the province. In addition to raising funds to aid Morgentaler's legal challenges to the abortion law, both CARAL and OCAC worked to shift public opinion so as to broaden support for the unconditional decriminalization of abortion. For example, OCAC organized a number of "abortion tribunals" throughout the 1970s and 1980s to highlight the ways in which the law was unresponsive to women's needs.[70] Through petitions, protests, and public education campaigns, the women in these organizations—women like Judy Rebick, Carolyn Egan, and Norma Scarborough—contributed to a greater awareness of the issues at stake in the struggle for access to abortion. While, until 1988, legal and political challenges to the law remained the primary focus of activism, these same women, and others, would go on to speak out against efforts to recriminalize abortion and to defend women's right to control their reproductive lives.

Retrenchment: The Reaction from the Right

Canada has been without an abortion law since the Supreme Court's 1988 decision, yet women continue to struggle for accessible, affordable, and safe abortions. Although a province cannot outlaw abortion, it can, under the Canada Health Act, refuse to fund it by arguing that it is not a medically necessary service unless certain conditions are met. Thus, in response to the Supreme Court's ruling, a number of provinces quickly moved to limit access to abortion. While the legal backlash was by no means limited to the Maritimes, it was especially evident there. In 1989, the Nova Scotia government passed a regulation that prohibited abortions unless they were performed in a hospital, although the regulation was subsequently struck down on the grounds that the province was attempting to legislate in the area of criminal law (a federal domain).[71] That same year, New Brunswick amended its Medical Services Payment Act so as to exclude abortion from coverage except when the procedure was performed by a specialist in obstetrics and gynecology, at an approved hospital, and only after two physicians had certified, in writing, that the abortion was medically necessary.[72] At the time, Newfoundland was home to only a single doctor willing to perform abortions (who later retired), and although a Morgentaler clinic opened in St. John's in 1990, abortion was not covered by provincial health insurance until 1998.[73] Abortion services had not been available in Prince Edward Island since 1982, and this situation remained in place, with the provincial government signing a resolution, in the wake of the Supreme Court's ruling, urging the federal government to enact a new abortion law.[74]

Quite apart from the response of individual provinces, attempts have repeatedly been made at the federal level to introduce new legislation limiting access to abortion. In November 1989, less than two years after the Supreme Court's ruling, Brian Mulroney's Conservative government introduced Bill C-43, which would have recriminalized abortion except when performed by or under the direction of a physician in whose opinion the woman's health or life might otherwise be endangered. By substituting the opinion of a single doctor for the earlier review by a Therapeutic Abortion Committee, the bill attempted to circumvent the legal grounds on which the Supreme Court had struck down the 1969 law. Although, in May 1990, the bill managed to pass in the House of Commons, it was ultimately defeated in the Senate, albeit only by a tie vote.[75] In addition, the years since 1988 have witnessed a steady stream of private member's bills and motions introduced into Parliament, all seeking in some way to curtail access to abortion—the first of them a motion, in June 1987, to amend section 7 of the Canadian Charter of Rights and Freedoms itself.[76]

In addition to legislative challenges, the anti-abortion movement has exerted a significant influence on the political and social landscape surrounding access to and discussions about abortion. One early and continuing manifestation of anti-abortion organizing is the development of crisis pregnancy centres (CPCs), which purport to offer women professional counselling about how to cope with an unplanned pregnancy. Their overriding goal, however, is to deter women from having an abortion. Such centres were first established in Canada in the 1960s as a response by opponents of abortion to the growing public conversation about the need to liberalize abortion laws. One of the first CPCs in Canada was Birthright, founded in Toronto in 1968 by Louise Summerhill. As the mother of seven children herself, Summerhill believed that women needed support with unplanned pregnancies as an alternative to abortion.[77] Although Birthright, which is now an international organization, seeks to adopt "a non-moralistic, non-judgmental approach toward helping women through their pregnancy dilemmas," and although the organization has no formal religious affiliations and always avoided political engagement with the abortion issue, its "pro-life" orientation is clear from its very name.[78]

In contrast to Birthright, many (and possibly most) CPCs are funded by religious groups that are directly involved with anti-abortion activism. Many CPCs are affiliated with the Canadian Association for Pregnancy Support Services, which describes itself as a "Christ-centered national ministry dedicated to providing support for life and sexual health by partnering with Pregnancy Centres across Canada."[79] Nor do most CPCs adopt an approach that could reasonably be described as nonjudgmental. For the most part, those who volunteer at CPCs have no formal medical or mental health training, and investigations into such centres reveal that they offer disturbingly inaccurate information about abortion in an effort to steer women away from the idea of terminating an unwanted pregnancy. Such misinformation includes claims for which no scientific support exists, such as the notion that abortion is linked to breast cancer, to a higher risk of miscarriage in future pregnancies, and even to infertility.[80]

The turn toward radicalism of the anti-abortion movement in the United States also had an impact in Canada, especially during the 1990s. Following the Supreme Court's 1988 decision, the tactics of Operation Rescue, a pro-life organization founded in the United States in 1986, began to be employed in Canada. These tactics included aggressive picketing campaigns outside abortion clinics and an escalation in violence against abortion providers. In May 1992, Morgentaler's Toronto clinic was fire-bombed, and the 1990s brought several further attacks on abortion providers. On 8 November 1994, Dr. Garson Romalis was shot through a window in his Vancouver home and seriously wounded. A year later, on 10 November 1995, Dr. Hugh Short, of Ancaster, Ontario, was likewise shot and wounded in his home, and, two years after that, on 11 November 1997, a similar attack was made on Dr. Jack Fainman, in Winnipeg. In July 2000, Dr. Romalis was attacked again, this time stabbed and wounded in the lobby of his Vancouver clinic. An American, James Kopp, was convicted in 2003 of the October 1998 murder of Dr. Barnett Slepian—who was also shot through a window in his home, in a suburb of Buffalo, New York—is strongly suspected in the shootings of Romalis, Short, and Fainman as well.[81] Although violence has subsided in recent years, abortion opponents persist in their efforts to recriminalize abortion through such events as the annual national pro-life march in Ottawa, media and poster campaigns, and the continued picketing of clinics.

A Precarious Victory: Abortion Rights Today

What does abortion in Canada look like today? Statistics provide some idea of the frequency of abortion and also hint at certain patterns surrounding access to abortion services. Even though about 80 percent of Canadian women use contraception of some sort, a significant proportion (perhaps somewhere around 40 percent) of all pregnancies in Canada are unplanned, with the annual abortion rate estimated to range between 12 and 16 abortions per 1,000 women of reproductive age.[82] According to data compiled by the Canadian Institute for Health Information, 81,897 abortions were performed in Canada in 2014, although this number includes only those performed at hospitals and clinics (and thus omits abortions carried out in a doctor's office). Of these 81,897 women, three in five were under the age of thirty: 11.1 percent were 19 years old or younger; 27.9 percent were aged 20 to 24 years; and 22.5 percent were 25 to 29 years. Of the remainder, 17.0 percent were 30 to 34 years, and 15.3 percent were 35 or older, with the age of the other 6.2 percent unknown.[83] Abortion is not only a commonplace medical procedure but a remarkably safe one, with 97.7 percent of women reporting no complications.[84] In Canada, roughly three-quarters of all abortions are performed during the first trimester; only a very small percentage occur after twenty-one weeks and always in response to significant genetic or health concerns.[85] Statistics like these are illuminating, but they tell us little about the women who are choosing abortion or about how they arrive at the decision to terminate a pregnancy. This gap in our knowledge is one of the reasons why it is so important for women to share their abortion stories. And yet, while we may not know the individual stories, we do know that, in 2014, there were at least 81,897 reasons not to recriminalize abortion.

At the same time, access to abortion services continues to vary widely across the country and is especially poor in rural areas, in the Atlantic provinces, and in Northern communities.[86] And, of course, the anti-abortion movement remains a source of concern. In recent years, the movement has developed new strategies, which have included an unapologetic effort to appropriate the history of the abortion rights movement for their own purposes. The 2012 "New Abortion Caravan," orchestrated by the Canadian Centre for Bio-ethical Reform (CCBR), sought to mimic the 1970 Abortion Caravan that challenged the restrictions imposed by the 1969 amendments to the abortion law. The CCBR expressed the goals of the New Abortion Caravan in this way: "The New Abortion Caravan will signal the beginning of the end of Canada's greatest human rights violation: the wholesale, state-funded slaughter of the youngest members of our society." Retracing the steps of the original Caravan, the group sought to make "the victims of Canada's abortion holocaust visible to the entire country" by displaying graphic images of the alleged victims of abortion at stops throughout its cross-county tour.[87] Unsurprisingly, the New Abortion Caravan garnered much attention from the media—and, as many observers have noted, anti-abortion extremists, despite reflecting the views of a minority, arguably receive a disproportionate share of media coverage. They also appear to be well funded, and not only by religious organizations within Canada. According to one report, "Research on tax filings and joint ventures of charitable organizations show support for Canada's pro-life movement from Catholic groups in the United States, as well as increasing support for the cause among MPs aligned with religious organizations."[88]

From 2006 until 2015, anti-abortion advocates hoped to find legislative support from the Conservative government of Stephen Harper. The election of the Conservative Party in February 2006, after more than a dozen years of Liberal rule, was a cause for great concern among abortion rights supporters. Although Harper had vowed not to reopen the abortion debate, it was not long before new private member bills were put forward in Parliament. Among the more notable of these were Bill C-338, first introduced in June 2006, which would have criminalized abortion after twenty weeks of gestation, and Bill C-484, the "Unborn Victims of Crime Act," introduced in November 2007, which sought to criminalize any attempt to "injure, cause the death of or attempt to cause the death of a child before or during its birth while committing or attempting to commit an offence against the mother."[89]

Harper reiterated his promise not to reopen the abortion debate in April 2011, not long before the federal election, when his party was still a minority government. That situation changed the following month, when the Conservatives won a majority in the House of Commons. On 6 February 2012, the Conservative MP for Kitchener, Ontario, Stephen Woodworth, introduced Motion 312, which called for the creation of a House committee "to review the declaration in Subsection 223(1) of the Criminal Code which states that a child becomes a human being only at the moment of complete birth."[90] Pro-choice Canadians were quick to respond to the bill with a coordinated campaign, spearheaded by the Abortion Rights Coalition of Canada; the campaign included petitions, postcards, and protests against reopening any discussions on abortion. On 26 September 2012, Motion 312 was defeated by a vote of 202 to 91.

Although that bill died, Conservative MP Mark Warawa introduced a new anti-abortion bill, Motion 408, the very next day. Motion 408, which sought to outlaw sex-selective abortion, illustrates another recent tactic of those who would recriminalize abortion: the attempt to portray themselves as champions of women—and, more generally, to temper their language and style of argument in order to appear more moderate.[91] Supporters of Motion 408 thus claimed that their main interest lay in preventing discrimination against females—meaning, of course, female fetuses. In fact, such legislation would have the effect of targeting women in certain ethnic groups, thereby promoting discrimination, an issue that H. Bindy K. Kang explores later in this collection. In short, despite their consistent lack of legislative success, those in the anti-abortion movement are not likely to abandon their efforts to sway public opinion, in hopes of tipping the balance.

The face of pro-choice organizing has also changed significantly since the turn of the twenty-first century. In 2004, CARAL disbanded, and a new organization, Canadians for Choice, was launched, with a focus not on political activism but on education and research. The following year saw the founding of a new national activist organization, the Abortion Rights Coalition of Canada / Coalition pour le droit à l'avortement au Canada, which has taken over where CARAL left off. In 2014, Canadians for Choice joined forces with two other reproductive rights groups to form Action Canada for Sexual Health and Rights / Action Canada pour la santé et les droits sexuels, an organization that combines advocacy with education in all areas of reproductive health.[92]

Canadian abortion rights organizations currently face several significant challenges, however. One is complacency. Canadians who favour abortion rights are, for the most part, not active in pro-choice organizing. Despite surveys suggesting that support for unrestricted access to abortion is not quite as overwhelming as we might like to believe, the assumption seems to be that the issue is resolved, perhaps because opponents of abortion have (so far) failed in their efforts to recriminalize abortion.[93] The activist base is therefore relatively small and tends to be reactive rather than proactive on the issue of abortion access, mobilizing more on an ad hoc basis, in response to threats. Another challenge is chronic underfunding, which may reflect the same assumption that the victory has already been won. In 2014, for example, lack of funding forced the Canadian Women's Health Network to suspend its operations.[94] In contrast, as noted above, the anti-abortion movement in Canada receives funding from various faith-based organizations, as well as from individual donors sympathetic to the cause and, at least to some extent, from groups in the United States. In addition, the abortion rights movement in Canada is in the process of shifting toward a reproductive justice framework, the meaning of which is very much a work in progress.

The movement has also had to contend with the death of Dr. Henry Morgentaler, on 29 May 2013. Although the role of Morgentaler as the face of the "pro-choice" movement has been overstated in the media, his death did have its impact, at least temporarily. In July 2014, the Morgentaler Clinic in Fredericton, New Brunswick, was forced to close because the province provided no funding for abortions performed at clinics, and, without contributions from Morgentaler himself, the clinic could not afford to stay open. Before it closed, the clinic was performing some 60 percent of the province's abortions, approximately six hundred per year.[95] Following a fundraising campaign by reproductive justice activists in the province, the clinic reopened as Clinic 554 in 2015, restoring clinic abortions to the province.[96] These same reproductive justice activists made the issue of abortion access a central focus of the September 2014 provincial election. As noted earlier, New Brunswick had, in 1989, altered its health plan so as to place draconian restrictions on abortions eligible for provincial funding. Liberal leader Brian Gallant was elected on a promise that he would review that policy, with a view to removing barriers to access. As of January 2015, New Brunswick eliminated two of the three restrictions: the province no longer requires that two doctors provide prior certification that an abortion is medically necessary, and abortions can now be performed by doctors who are not specialists in obstetrics and gynecology. However, to qualify for provincial funding, an abortion must still be performed in a hospital, not in a clinic.[97]

Two further developments should soon improve abortion access not only in PEI but across the nation as a whole. In July 2015, Health Canada finally approved the use of the abortion drug RU-486 to terminate pregnancies, although only up to the end of the seventh week of gestation. The drug, to be sold in Canada under the name Mifegymiso, will be available by prescription only, at an estimated cost of $270, and will be administered under medical supervision.[98] Despite these restrictions, the availability of the drug should improve access to abortion for those who live at some distance from a hospital or clinic that provides abortions. In addition, women using the drug will be spared the experience of having to cross anti-abortion pickets in order to enter a clinic. Additionally, in March 2016, in response to a legal challenge launched by an abortion rights group on the island, the PEI government announced that abortion services would be available on the island by the end of the year. The province was responding to a legal challenge launched by Abortion Access Now, which, two months earlier, had notified provincial authorities of its intention to file a lawsuit charging the PEI government with violating the Charter of Rights and Freedoms. Liberal Premier Wade MacLauchlan acknowledged that the PEI government would almost certainly have been unable to defend its prohibitive provincial legislation against such a charge. Abortion Access Now credits the work of abortion rights activists in helping to create an environment that made change a necessity, observing that "this outcome would not have been possible without the tremendous efforts of the activists in P.E.I. who have tirelessly advocated for abortion access in the province over the last three decades."[99]

The October 2015 federal election saw a majority win for Justin Trudeau's Liberal Party. After assuming party leadership in 2013, Trudeau made it clear, in June 2014, that "every single Liberal MP will be expected to stand up for women's rights to choose" and that those who had previously opposed abortion and were returned to office in the upcoming election would be obliged to vote pro-choice on any subsequent legislation concerning abortion.[100] He has, since becoming prime minister, repeatedly referred to himself as a feminist.[101] It remains to be seen, however, whether his political stance and self-identification will translate into ensuring that women not only have unfettered access to abortion but also the resources they need to make meaningful choices. Certainly, for those of us who advocate for reproductive rights and, indeed, for reproductive justice, the defeat of the Harper Conservatives was a welcome outcome—but a more sympathetic governing party does not automatically guarantee greater rights or improved conditions. It is not merely a matter of safeguarding the rights that we have: we must work to improve access to abortion all across the country and to ameliorate the structural conditions that make genuine choice impossible.

Notes

1 Angus McLaren and Arlene Tigar McLaren, *The Bedroom and the State: The Changing Practices and Politics of Contraception and Abortion in Canada, 1880–1997*, 32.

2 Susan A. McDaniel, "Implementation of Abortion Policy in Canada as a Women's Issue," 80.

3 Shelley A. M. Gavigan, "On 'Bringing on the Menses': The Criminal Liability of Women and the Therapeutic Exception in Canadian Abortion Law," 284.

4 For further discussion, see Shannon Stettner, "Women and Abortion in English Canada: Public Debates and Political Participation, 1959–1970," 4–22.

5 On quickening, see John Keown, *Abortion, Doctors, and the Law: Some Aspects of the Legal Regulation of Abortion in England from 1803 to 1982*, 3–4; and Shelley A. M. Gavigan, "The Criminal Sanction as It Relates to Human Reproduction: The Genesis of the Statutory Prohibition of Abortion," 20–21. See also Constance Backhouse, *Petticoats and Prejudice: Women and Law in Nineteenth-Century Canada*, 146; and Gavigan, "On 'Bringing on the Menses,'" 299.

6 On these legal developments, see Constance Backhouse, "Involuntary Motherhood: Abortion, Birth Control and the Law in Nineteenth-Century Canada," 67–71. Prince Edward Island, however, retained its original law, which included both the quickening distinction and capital punishment, until 1877, when federal criminal law was extended to the island.

7 Backhouse, "Involuntary Motherhood," 70. Courts were reluctant to trust a woman's own testimony in this matter (assuming that she had survived the abortion), especially when the punishment for post-quickening abortions was death. Instead, early-nineteenth-century courts tended to rely on a "jury of matrons" consisting of twelve married women of good character to determine whether a woman had quickened, supplemented, as need be, by the opinion of a physician. See Gavigan, "Criminal Sanction," 34–35; and Backhouse, "Involuntary Motherhood," 67, 75.

8 Wendy Mitchinson, *Body Failure: Medical Views of Women, 1900–1950*, 176. See also McLaren and McLaren, *Bedroom and the State*, 38–39.

9 Backhouse, "Involuntary Motherhood," 74.

10 *An Act to Consolidate and Amend the Statute Law of England and Ireland Relating to Offences Against the Person*, 6 August 1861, http://www.legislation.gov.uk/ukpga/1861/100/pdfs/ukpga_18610100_en.pdf, secs. 58 and 59. See also Keown, *Abortion, Doctors, and the Law*, 33.

11 A. Anne McLellan, "Abortion Law in Canada," 334; Gavigan, "On 'Bringing on the Menses,'" 295.

12 See Canada, *Criminal Code, 1892*. Only in 1954 was section 273 amended such that charges could be laid against a woman only if the she had, in fact, been pregnant. McLellan, "Abortion Law in Canada," 333–34.

13 Backhouse, "Involuntary Motherhood," 75.

14 See Backhouse, "Involuntary Motherhood," 82–85. As Backhouse explains, "If the abortion laws were primarily considered to be a method of regulating the practice of medicine, it should not be surprising that they were predominantly enforced against the individuals who were providing the medical services, rather than against the patient, who was merely the recipient of the treatment" (85).

15 See Backhouse, "Involuntary Motherhood," 76–82, and *Petticoats and Prejudice*, 142–43. On professionalization, see also Michael McCulloch, "'Doctor Tumblety, the Indian Herb Doctor': Politics, Professionalism, and Abortion in Mid-Nineteenth-Century Montreal."

16 On the decline in fertility rates, see McLaren and McLaren, *Bedroom and the State*, 17–22.

17 Backhouse, "Involuntary Motherhood," 76, 80. Although physicians spoke out vehemently against abortion, Backhouse found no evidence that they expressed similar outrage about a considerably more common occurrence, namely, infanticide. Unlike abortion, however, infanticide was practiced chiefly by lower-class women and thus "would not have fueled the doctors' fears about the declining fertility rate of the 'better classes.'" Moreover, given that women did not require medical assistance in order to kill an infant, doctors did not have to worry about competition from "irregular" practitioners. As considerations such as these illustrate, objections to abortion did not arise from concerns for the welfare of the fetus. See Backhouse, "Involuntary Motherhood," 79.

18 Tracy Penny [Light], "'Getting Rid of My Trouble: A Social History of Abortion in Ontario, 1880–1929,'" 47, 68–69.

19 See Wendy Mitchinson, *The Nature of Their Bodies: Women and Their Doctors in Victorian Canada*, 14–15.

20 Backhouse, *Petticoats and Prejudice*, 147. Backhouse argues that a woman would not so much have perceived herself as pregnant but would have noticed that her period was "irregular" and undertaken

various actions (pills, vigorous exercise, hot baths) to restore her period (146–47). For other historical accounts of abortion during its period of illegality, see Backhouse, "Physicians, Abortions, and the Law in Early Twentieth-Century Ontario," and "The Celebrated Abortion Trial of Dr. Emily Stowe, Toronto, 1879."

21 Angus McLaren, "Illegal Operations: Women, Doctors and Abortion, 1886–1939," 797.

22 Susanne Klausen, "Doctors and Dying Declarations: The Role of the State in Abortion Regulation in British Columbia, 1917–37," 60–61; Penny, "'Getting Rid of My Trouble,'" 25–33.

23 McLaren, "Illegal Operations," 800.

24 Penny, "'Getting Rid of My Trouble,'" 82. Herbs and drugs used included tansy, pennyroyal, cotton root, oil of cedar, and ergot of rye. See also McLaren and McLaren, *Bedroom and the State*, 34–35.

25 Penny, "'Getting Rid of My Trouble,'" 83.

26 Quoted in Eliane Leslau Silverman, *Last Best West Women on the Alberta Frontier, 1880–1930*, 62. On the interface between Indigenous healing practices and colonial medicine, see also Kristin Burnett, *Taking Medicine: Women's Healing Work and Colonial Contact in Southern Alberta, 1880–1930*.

27 McLaren, "Illegal Operations," 800–801.

28 Klausen, "Doctors and Dying Declarations," 60.

29 McLaren, "Illegal Operations," 797. Klausen's study similarly revealed the role of friends, family, and especially lovers in women's pursuit of abortion. See Klausen, "Doctors and Dying Declarations," 71–73.

30 Penny, "'Getting Rid of My Trouble,'" 62.

31 McLaren, "Illegal Operations," 800.

32 Penny, "'Getting Rid of My Trouble,'" 53–62. Examples of physicians performing abortions despite restrictive abortion laws can be found throughout the nineteenth and twentieth centuries. See, for example, Carole Joffe, *Doctors of Conscience: The Struggle to Provide Abortion Before and After Roe v. Wade*; and Childbirth by Choice Trust, *No Choice: Canadian Women Tell Their Stories of Illegal Abortions*.

33 Regarding the influence of Sanger and Stopes in Canada, see McLaren and McLaren, Bedroom and the State, 54–91. On eugenics, see Erika Dyck, Facing Eugenics: Reproduction, Sterilization, and the Politics of Choice.

34 On Kaufman, see Linda Revie, "More Than Just Boots! The Eugenic and Commercial Concerns Behind A. R. Kaufman's Birth Controlling Activities"; and McLaren and McLaren, Bedroom and the State, 92–123.

Without Apology

35 For an account of the Palmer trial, see Gerald Stortz and Murray E. Eaton, "'Pro Bono Publico': The Eastview Birth Control Trial."

36 Jane Jenson, "Getting to Morgentaler: From One Representation to Another," 21–22.

37 Keown, Abortion, Doctors, and the Law, 53. As Keown goes on to argue, "That the defence was not raised until R. v. Bourne is due less to doubts as to its validity than to the reluctance of prosecutors to question medical discretion" (53).

38 Barbara Brookes and Paul Roth, "*Rex v. Bourne* and the Medicalization of Abortion," 315.

39 On the Bourne precedent, see Jenson, Getting to *Morgentaler*, 24–25; and Gavigan, "On 'Bringing on the Menses,'" 307. As Gavigan notes, Bourne charged no fee for performing the abortion, and he performed it openly, so as not to evade prosecution. As a result, he could not be accused of felonious intent. But prevailing social attitudes, influenced by notions grounded in eugenics, also played a part. Bourne believed the girl to be ordinary and decent: "Had she been 'feebleminded' or 'of a prostitute mind,'" Gavigan argues, "her mental health, in Aleck Bourne's judgment, would not have been adversely affected and she would not have been entitled to the abortion" (308). In other words, it was important that the young girl be the "right" kind of patient.

40 See George Emery, *Facts of Life: The Social Construction of Vital Statistics, Ontario, 1869–1952*, esp. chap. 6. Emery has also critiqued research presented by Angus McLaren and Arlene Tigar McLaren in "Discoveries and Dissimulations: The Impact of Abortion Deaths on Maternal Mortality in British Columbia," *BC Studies* 64 (1985–86): 3–26. He argues that not only did the McLarens exaggerate the proportion of maternal deaths that resulted from criminal abortions but probably also overestimated the total number of illegal abortions, from which he concludes that "illegal abortion quite possibly was *less traditional* than they suggest and *much riskier* than they realize." George Emery, "British Columbia's Criminal Abortion History, 1922–1949: A Critique of the Evidence and Methods in the Work of Angus and Arlene Tigar McLaren," 56.

41 In 1970, the Royal Commission on the Status of Women in Canada reported that estimates of the number of illegal abortions in Canada ranged from 30,000 to 300,000 a year. Citing a Québec study, which put the figure at 10,000 to 25,000 annually in that province, the commissioners indicated that, for Canada overall, the figure would be 40,000 to 100,000 illegal abortions annually. If the latter figure were correct, this would mean that one in five pregnancies was ending in an illegal abortion. As

they noted, however, the number of illegal abortions "cannot be accurately known." *Report of the Royal Commission on the Status of Women in Canada*, 284, citing Serge Mongeau and Reneé Cloutier, *L'avortement* (Montréal: Les Éditions du Jour, 1968).

42 For an analysis of these developments, see Cynthia R. Comacchio, *Nations Are Built of Babies: Saving Ontario's Mothers and Children, 1900–1940*. As Comacchio argues, seeking to address problems such as infant mortality and the risks associated with childbirth, the medical profession, with the backing of the state, promoted a "scientific" approach to motherhood that, among other things, effectively elevated (mostly male) doctors into the position of experts on mothering. On the evolution of physicians' attitudes toward abortion in particular, see Tracy Penny Light, "Shifting Interests: The Medical Discourse on Abortion in English Canada, 1850–1969."

43 See Brenda Margaret Appleby, *Responsible Parenthood: Decriminalizing Contraception in Canada*.

44 For further discussion, see Stettner, "Women and Abortion in English Canada," 62–137.

45 See Appleby, *Responsible Parenthood*, 19–36, 201–21. The four bills were C-22 and C-64, which pertained to exemptions from prosecution for social workers and health care personnel who distributed contraceptives, and C-40 and C-71, which aimed to remove the words "preventing conception" from the relevant section of the Criminal Code. Bill C-40, introduced by Liberal Ian Wahn, additionally sought to liberalize the abortion laws.

46 Quoted in Melissa Haussman, "'What Does Gender Have to Do with Abortion Law?' Canadian Women's Movement–Parliamentary Interactions on Reform Attempts, 1969–91," 131.

47 *Report of the Royal Commission on the Status of Women in Canada*, vii.

48 Library and Archives Canada (hereafter LAC), Royal Commission on the Status of Women in Canada fonds, RG 33/89, vol. 8, file: Letters of Opinion—Alberta. See also Shannon Stettner, "'He Is Still Unwanted': Women's Assertions of Authority over Abortion in Letters to the Royal Commission on the Status of Women in Canada."

49 LAC, RG 33/89, Royal Commission on the Status of Women in Canada fonds, RG 33/89, vol. 7, file: Letters of Opinion—British Columbia.

50 Quoted in McLaren and McLaren, *Bedroom and the State*, 135.

51 These changes were contained in sec. 16 of the Criminal Law Amendment Act, 1968–69 (S.C. 1968–69, c. 38), which amended section 237 of the 1953–54 version of the Criminal Code (which became section 251 in the 1970 version). On these amendments, see Appleby, *Responsible Parenthood*, 87–197.

52 For more on the Caravan, see Frances Wasserlein, "'An Arrow Aimed at the Heart': The Vancouver Women's Caucus and the Abortion Campaign, 1969–1971"; Christabelle Sethna and Steve Hewitt, "Clandestine Operations: The Vancouver Women's Caucus, the Abortion Caravan, and the RCMP"; Barbara M. Freeman, *Beyond Bylines: Media Workers and Women's Rights in Canada*, 123–56; Stettner, "Women and Abortion in English Canada," 231–97; Ann Thomson, *Winning Choice on Abortion: How British Columbian and Canadian Feminists Won the Battles of the 1970s and 1980s*; and Judy Rebick, *Ten Thousand Roses: The Making of a Feminist Revolution*.

53 Quoted in Kathryn Keate, "'Out from Under, Women Unite!': Personal Notes of an Activist in the Women's Liberation Movement," 17.

54 For more on these travels, see Christabelle Sethna, "All Aboard? Canadian Women's Abortion Tourism, 1960–1980"; Christabelle Sethna and Marion Doull, "Accidental Tourists: Canadian Women, Abortion Tourism, and Travel"; and Beth Palmer, "'Lonely, Tragic, but Legally Necessary Pilgrimages': Transnational Abortion Travel in the 1970s." See also Christabelle Sethna and Marion Doull, "Far from Home? A Pilot Study Tracking Women's Journeys to a Canadian Abortion Clinic."

55 Michael W. Cuneo, *Catholics Against the Church: Anti-abortion Protest in Toronto, 1969–1985*, 12.

56 For more on the pro-family movement in Canada, see Margrit Eichler, *The Pro-family Movement: Are They For or Against Families?*; Lorna Erwin, "What Feminists Should Know About the Pro-family Movement in Canada: A Report on a Recent Survey of Rank-and-File Members"; and Donna Gill, "REAL Women and the Press: An Ideological Alliance of Convenience."

57 William D. S. Thomas, "The Badgley Report on the Abortion Law."

58 Palmer, "'Lonely, Tragic, but Legally Necessary Pilgrimages,'" 643. For the complete report, see Robin F. Badgley, *Report of the Committee on the Operation of the Abortion Law*.

59 McLaren and McLaren, *Bedroom and the State*, 137, citing Roderic P. Beaujot, "Canada's Population: Growth and Dualism," *Population Bulletin* 33, no. 2 (1978): 1–48.

60 Thomas, "Badgley Report on the Abortion Law."

61 See Canada Health Act (R.S.C. 1985, c. C-6), http://laws-lois.justice.gc.ca/PDF/C-6.pdf. The five criteria—public administration, comprehensiveness, universality, portability, and accessibility—are described in sections 7 to 12 of the act. According to section 12 (1) (a), in order to satisfy the criterion of accessibility, provinces "must provide for insured health services on

uniform terms and conditions and on a basis that does not impede or preclude, either directly or indirectly whether by charges made to insured persons or otherwise, reasonable access to those services by insured persons." The act offers no definition of "reasonable" access, however.

62 Parliament of Canada, Standing Senate Committee on Social Affairs, Science and Technology, "The Canada Health Act," para. 4.

63 As defined in the act, neither "universality" nor "comprehensiveness" refers to the range of services offered by a given province. The former demands that provincial health plans cover everyone who lives in the province (section 10). The latter stipulates only that provincial health insurance plans "must insure all insured health services provided by hospitals, medical practitioners or dentists, and where the law of the province so permits, similar or additional services rendered by other health care practitioners" (section 9). In section 2, "insured health services" are defined simply as "hospital services, physician services and surgical-dental services provided to insured persons," with these three sets of services then defined in terms of medical necessity. "Physician services" are, for example, "any medically required services rendered by medical practitioners."

64 Henry Morgentaler, Sam Solomon, and Gillian Woodford, "The Interview: The Morgentaler Decision Turns Twenty." Morgentaler's father was killed by the Gestapo during the German occupation of Poland; his mother died in Auschwitz, and his sister at Treblinka.

65 Henry Morgentaler, "Report on 5,641 Outpatient Abortions by Vacuum Suction Curettage." As Morgentaler noted, complication rates were extremely low, with only twenty-seven patients (0.48%) requiring hospitalization.

66 For a useful discussion of these cases, see McLellan, "Abortion Law in Canada," 335–37.

67 Monica Dunn et al., *Focus on Abortion Services in Quebec*, 12, 14; Nora Milne, "Creating Change to Maintaining Change: The Fédération du Québec pour le planning des naissances and the Pro-choice Movement," 11–12. On shifting attitudes in Québec toward birth control and abortion, see Rachel Johnstone, "The Politics of Abortion in Canada After Morgentaler: Women's Rights as Citizenship Rights," 155–59.

68 Dunn et al., *Focus on Abortion Services*, 15.

69 For a discussion of the three majority opinions and one dissenting opinion in *Morgentaler*, see Karine Richer, "Abortion in Canada: Twenty Years After *R. v. Morgentaler*," 2–4.

70 See Beth Palmer, "Choices and Compromises: The Abortion Rights Movement in Canada, 1969–1988," 218–29. For a comprehensive

examination of the campaigns surrounding Morgentaler's own activism, see Catherine Dunphy's 1996 biography, *Morgentaler: A Difficult Hero*.

71 See Johnstone, "Politics of Abortion in Canada After Morgentaler," 129–30. Morgentaler reacted to the Nova Scotia regulation by opening an abortion clinic in Halifax. He was duly charged by the province but acquitted, first by a provincial judge (in 1991) and, following a provincial appeal, ultimately by the Supreme Court (in 1993).

72 Ibid., 86 (and see 83–87 for the legal situation in New Brunswick at the time). The regulation remained in force until the start of 2015. A similar situation developed in British Columbia when, immediately following the Supreme Court's ruling, Premier Bill Vander Zalm—a staunch "pro-lifer"—attempted to cut off funding for abortions. The reaction in BC was rather different, however, and Vander Zalm was obliged to back down. See Shelley A. M. Gavigan, "*Morgentaler* and Beyond: Abortion, Reproduction, and the Courts," 141.

73 Gavigan, "*Morgentaler* and Beyond," 140–45.

74 Katrina Rose Ackerman, "In Defence of Reason: Religion, Science, and the Prince Edward Island Anti-abortion Movement, 1969–1988."

75 See Janine Brodie, "Choice and No Choice in the House," 66–70. The bill passed in the House of Commons by fairly slim majority: 140 to 131. The Senate vote was 43 to 43.

76 See Abortion Rights Coalition of Canada, "Anti-Choice Private Member Bills and Motions Introduced in Canada Since 1987," 2 October 2012, http://www.arcc-cdac.ca/presentations/anti-bills.html, which lists forty-five attempts in the period from June 1987 to September 2012. The June 1987 motion, introduced roughly six months prior to the Supreme Court ruling, sought to add a reference to "unborn persons" to section 7 of the Charter.

77 Cuneo, *Catholics Against the Church*, 9–10.

78 Birthright International, "Discover Birthright," 2013, http://birthright. org/en/discover-birthright. Birthright describes itself as "independent, interdenominational, and not affiliated with any religious or political group or public agency." See Birthright International, "Our Philosophy," 2013, http://birthright.org/en/our-philosophy.

79 Canadian Association for Pregnancy Support Services, "Our Mission," 2016, http://www.capss.com/about-us/our-mission.

80 Jessica Shaw, "Abortion as a Social Justice Issue in Contemporary Canada," 11. Shaw reports having been told, for example, that if she had an abortion, she would be drawn to abusive men in the future, as she would subconsciously know that she deserves punishment, and would be likely to

turn to drugs or alcohol. See also Joyce Arthur, *Exposing Crisis Pregnancy Centres in British Columbia*, esp. 3–4; Joyce Arthur et al., *Review of "Crisis Pregnancy Centre" Websites in Canada*; and Shannon Stettner, "Crisis Pregnancy Centers."

81 Abortion Rights Coalition of Canada, "Anti-choice Violence and Harassment," 2. See also Canadian Press, "Anti-abortion Sniper Won't Face Justice in Canada," *CTV News*, 8 August 2010, http://www.ctvnews.ca/anti-abortion-sniper-won-t-face-justice-in-canada-1.540326.

82 "Facts and Figures on Abortion in Canada," Society, the Individual, and Medicine, University of Ottawa, 24 July 2015, http://www.med.uottawa.ca/sim/data/Abortion_e.htm. According to comparative statistics compiled by the United Nations Population Division, the abortion rate in Canada was 13.7 in 2009, slightly lower than the rate in most northern European countries and considerably below the rate in the United States, which stood at 19.6 in 2008. See United Nations, Department of Economic and Social Affairs, Population Division, *World Abortion Policies 2013*, http://www.un.org/en/development/desa/population/publications/pdf/policy/WorldAbortionPolicies2013/WorldAbortionPolicies2013_WallChart.pdf.

83 Canadian Institute for Health Information, *Induced Abortions Reported in Canada in 2014*, Table 1: Number of Induced Abortions Reported in Canada in 2014, by Province/Territory of Hospital or Clinic and Age Group. Percentages are calculated from the hard numbers.

84 Ibid., Table 8: Number and Percentage Distribution of Induced Abortions Reported by Canadian Hospitals (Excluding Quebec) in 2014, by Complication Within 28 Days of Initial Induced Abortion.

85 Ibid., Table 4: Number and Percentage Distribution of Induced Abortions Reported by Canadian Hospitals (Excluding Quebec) in 2014, by Gestational Age. According to these figures, 75.1% of abortions took place within the first sixteen weeks of pregnancy (29.2% under 8 weeks; 39.0% from 9 to 12 weeks; and 6.9% from 13 to 16 weeks). Only 3.4 percent occurred in the range of 17 to 20 weeks, and 2.4 percent at 21 weeks or beyond. (For the remaining 19.0 percent, the gestational age was unknown.) See also "Facts and Figures on Abortion in Canada."

86 For an analysis of these inequities and the multiple burdens they place on women seeking abortions, see Christabelle Sethna and Marion Doull, "Spatial Disparities and Travel to Freestanding Abortion Clinics in Canada." See also Howard A. Palley, "Canadian Abortion Policy: National Policy and the Impact of Federalism and Political Implementation on Access to Services."

87 Canadian Centre for Bio-Ethical Reform, "The New Abortion Caravan," 2015, http://www.unmaskingchoice.ca/caravan. On the CCBR's deliberate manipulation of the original Abortion Caravan, see Karissa Patton, "The New Abortion Caravan," *ActiveHistory.ca*, 26 May 2015, http://activehistory.ca/2015/05/the-new-abortion-caravan/.

88 Sasha Lakic, "U.S. Funding Helped to Re-open the Canadian Abortion Debate," *Vancouver Observer*, 23 October 2012, http://www.vancouverobserver.com/politics/investigations/canadian-pro-life-fueled-us-lobbyists.

89 Bill C-338, *An Act to Amend the Criminal Code (Procuring a Miscarriage After Twenty Weeks of Gestation)*, 1st sess., 39th Parliament, 21 June 2006 (first reading), http://www.parl.gc.ca/HousePublications/Publication.aspx?DocId=2494993&Language=E&Mode=1; Bill C-484, *An Act to Amend the Criminal Code (Injuring or Causing the Death of an Unborn Child While Committing an Offence)*, 2nd sess., 39th Parliament, 21 November 2007 (first reading), http://www.parl.gc.ca/HousePublications/Publication.aspx?Docid=3127600&file=4.

90 For the text of Woodworth's motion, see "Vote No. 466," 1st sess., 41st Parliament, 26 September 2012, http://www.parl.gc.ca/HouseChamberBusiness/ChamberVoteDetail.aspx?Language=E&Mode=1&Parl=41&Ses=1&Vote=466.

91 On the shift in discursive strategies evident in both Motion 408 and Motion 312, see Paul Saurette and Kelly Gordon, "Anti-abortion Movement Rebrands Itself," *Toronto Star*, 12 January 2013. See also Jane Cawthorne's chapter in this volume, for an examination of "third way" tactics in relation to the New Abortion Caravan.

92 The other two groups are the Canadian Federation for Sexual Health (formerly Planned Parenthood Canada) and Action Canada for Population and Development. See Laura Payton, "Pro-choice Groups Merge Amid Abortion Access Concerns," *CBC News*, 14 November 2014, http://www.cbc.ca/news/politics/pro-choice-groups-merge-amid-abortion-access-concerns-1.2833982.

93 An Ipsos poll, taken between 22 January and 5 February 2016, found that roughly six in ten Canadians (57%) feel that abortion should be permitted whenever a woman decides she wants one, while very few (3%) are opposed to abortion under any circumstances whatsoever. At the same time, 21 percent believe that abortion should be permitted only in certain situations (such as pregnancies resulting from rape), and another 8 percent believe abortion should not be permitted except to save the life of the mother. Although the poll rightly identified Canada as one of the "most

progressive" of the twenty-three countries surveyed, we ranked seventh on the list, behind France (69%) and the United Kingdom (62%), as well as Sweden (84%). See Andrew Russell, "6 in 10 Canadians Support Abortion Under Any Circumstances: Ipsos Poll," *Global News*, 23 February 2016, http://globalnews.ca/news/2535846/6-in-10-canadians-support-abortion-under-any-circumstances-ipsos-poll/.

94 Canadian Women's Health Network, "WHN Announces Suspension of Activities Due to Lack of Funds," news release, 21 November 2014, http://www.cwhn.ca/en/node/46597.

95 "Morgentaler Clinic in Fredericton Performs Last Abortions Before Closure," *CBC News*, 18 July 2014, http://www.cbc.ca/news/canada/new-brunswick/morgentaler-clinic-in-fredericton-performs-last-abortions-before-closure-1.2710909. On the clinic's financial situation, see "Morgentaler Abortion Clinic in Fredericton to Close," *CBC News*, 10 April 2014, http://www.cbc.ca/news/canada/new-brunswick/morgentaler-abortion-clinic-in-fredericton-to-close-1.2604535.

96 Tracy Glynn, "Service Restored: New Abortion Clinic Opens in Fredericton," *Rabble*, 20 January 2015, http://rabble.ca/news/2015/01/service-restored-new-abortion-clinic-opens-fredericton.

97 See "New Brunswick Abortion Restriction Lifted by Premier Brian Gallant," *CBC News*, 26 November 2014, http://www.cbc.ca/news/canada/new-brunswick/new-brunswick-abortion-restriction-lifted-by-premier-brian-gallant-1.2850474; Tracy Glynn, "Abortion Restriction in New Brunswick Lifted but Access Still a Problem," *Rabble*, 28 November 2014, http://rabble.ca/news/2014/11/abortion-restriction-new-brunswick-lifted-access-still-problem.

98 "RU-486 Abortion Pill Approved by Health Canada," *CBC News*, 30 July 2015, http://www.cbc.ca/news/health/ru-486-abortion-pill-approved-by-health-canada-1.3173515. For a critical look at some of the implications of Health Canada's decision, see Grace Lisa Scott, "A New Abortion Pill Will Be Available in Canada Soon, but It's Not a Simple Solution to Access," *VICE*, 21 January 2016, http://www.vice.com/en_ca/read/new-abortion-pill-not-a-simple-solution-to-abortion-access-in-canada.

99 Canadian Press, "PEI to Provide Access to Abortions by End of 2016," *Toronto Star*, 31 March 2016, http://www.thestar.com/news/canada/2016/03/31/pei-agrees-to-provide-abortions-by-end-of-2016.html; Alison Auld, "P.E.I. Abortion Rights Group to Sue Province for Not Providing Access to Procedure," *Toronto Star*, 5 January 2016, http://www.thestar.com/news/canada/2016/01/05/pei-abortion-rights-group-to-sue-province-over-not-providing-procedure.html.

100 Quoted in Laura Payton, "Justin Trudeau Clarifies Abortion Stance for Liberal MPs," *CBC News*, 18 June 2014, http://www.cbc.ca/news/politics/justin-trudeau-clarifies-abortion-stance-for-liberal-mps-1.2679783.

101 See, for example, Alexander Panetta, "'I Am a Feminist,' Trudeau Tells UN Crowd," *Toronto Star*, 16 March 2016, http://www.thestar.com/news/canada/2016/03/16/i-am-a-feminist-trudeau-tells-un-crowd.html.

References

Abortion Rights Coalition of Canada. "Anti-choice Violence and Harassment." Position Paper #73, September 2006. http://www.arcc-cdac.ca/postionpapers/73-Anti-choice-Violence-Harassment.pdf.

Ackerman, Katrina Rose. "In Defence of Reason: Religion, Science, and the Prince Edward Island Anti-abortion Movement, 1969–1988." *Canadian Bulletin of Medical History* 31, no. 2 (2014): 117–38.

Appleby, Brenda Margaret. *Responsible Parenthood: Decriminalizing Contraception in Canada*. Toronto: University of Toronto Press, 1999.

Arthur, Joyce. *Exposing Crisis Pregnancy Centres in British Columbia*. Vancouver: Pro-Choice Action Network, 2009. http://www.prochoiceactionnetwork-canada.org/Exposing-CPCs-in-BC.pdf.

Arthur, Joyce, Rebecca Bailin, Kathy Dawson, Megan Glenwright, Autumn Reinhardt-Simpson, Meg Sykes, and Alison Zimmer. *Review of "Crisis Pregnancy Centre" Websites in Canada*. Vancouver: Abortion Rights Coalition of Canada, 2016. http://www.arcc-cdac.ca/CPC-study/CPC-Website-Study-ARCC-2016.pdf.

Backhouse, Constance. "The Celebrated Abortion Trial of Dr. Emily Stowe, Toronto, 1879." *Canadian Bulletin of Medical History* 8, no. 2 (1991): 159–87.

———. "Involuntary Motherhood: Abortion, Birth Control and the Law in Nineteenth-Century Canada." *Windsor Yearbook of Access to Justice* 3 (1983): 61–130.

———. *Petticoats and Prejudice: Women and Law in Nineteenth-Century Canada*. Toronto: Women's Press for the Osgood Society, 1991.

———. "Physicians, Abortions, and the Law in Early Twentieth-Century Ontario." *Canadian Bulletin of Medical History* 10, no. 2 (1993): 229–49.

Badgley, Robin F. *Report of the Committee on the Operation of the Abortion Law*. Ottawa: Supply and Services Canada, 1977.

Brodie, Janine. "Choice and No Choice in the House." In Brodie, Gavigan, and Jenson, *Politics of Abortion*, 57–117.

Brodie, Janine, Shelley A. M. Gavigan, and Jane Jenson. *The Politics of Abortion*. Toronto: Oxford University Press, 1992.

Brookes, Barbara, and Paul Roth. *"Rex v. Bourne* and the Medicalization of Abortion." In *Legal Medicine in History*, edited by Michael Clark and Catherine Crawford, 314–43. Cambridge: Cambridge University Press, 1994.

Burnett, Kristin. *Taking Medicine: Women's Healing Work and Colonial Contact in Southern Alberta, 1880–1930*. Vancouver: University of British Columbia Press, 2010.

Canada. *Criminal Code, 1892*. 55–56 Victoria, c. 29. Ottawa: Queen's Printer, 1892. https://archive.org/details/criminalcodevic00canagoog.

Canadian Institute for Health Information. *Induced Abortions Reported in Canada in 2014*. Ottawa: CIHI, 2014. https://www.cihi.ca/sites/default/files/document/induced_abortion_can_2014_en_web.xlsx.

Childbirth by Choice Trust. *No Choice: Canadian Women Tell Their Stories of Illegal Abortions*. Toronto: Childbirth by Choice Trust, 1998.

Comacchio, Cynthia R. *Nations Are Built of Babies: Saving Ontario's Mothers and Children, 1900–1940*. Montreal and Kingston: McGill-Queen's University Press, 1993.

Cuneo, Michael W. *Catholics Against the Church: Anti-abortion Protest in Toronto, 1969–1985*. Toronto: University of Toronto Press, 1989.

Dunn, Monica, Marie-Eve Quirion, Nathalie Parent, Patricia LaRue, Sabina Grabowiecka, and Julie Charbonneau. *Focus on Abortion Services in Quebec*. Ottawa: Canadians for Choice and Fédération du Québec pour le planning des naissances, 2010.

Dunphy, Catherine. *Morgentaler: A Difficult Hero*. Toronto: Random House, 1996.

Dyck, Erika. *Facing Eugenics: Reproduction, Sterilization, and the Politics of Choice*. Toronto: University of Toronto Press, 2013.

Eichler, Margrit. *The Pro-family Movement: Are They For or Against Families?* Ottawa: Canadian Research Institute for the Advancement of Women, 1986.

Emery, George. "British Columbia's Criminal Abortion History, 1922–1949: A Critique of the Evidence and Methods in the Work of Angus and Arlene Tigar McLaren." *BC Studies* 82 (1989): 39–60.

———. *Facts of Life: The Social Construction of Vital Statistics, Ontario, 1869–1952*. Montréal and Kingston: McGill-Queen's University Press, 1993.

Erwin, Lorna. "What Feminists Should Know About the Pro-family Movement in Canada: A Report on a Recent Survey of Rank-and-File Members." In *Feminist Research: Prospect and Retrospect*, edited by Peta Tancred-Sheriff, 266–78. Ottawa: Canadian Research Institute for the Advancement of Women, 1998.

Freeman, Barbara M. *Beyond Bylines: Media Workers and Women's Rights in Canada*. Waterloo, ON: Wilfrid Laurier University Press, 2011.

Gavigan, Shelley A. M. "The Criminal Sanction as It Relates to Human Reproduction: The Genesis of the Statutory Prohibition of Abortion." *Journal of Legal History* 5 (1984): 20–43.

———. "On 'Bringing on the Menses': The Criminal Liability of Women and the Therapeutic Exception in Canadian Abortion Law." *Canadian Journal of Women and the Law* 1, no. 2 (1986): 279–312.

———. "*Morgentaler* and Beyond: Abortion, Reproduction, and the Courts." In Brodie, Gavigan, and Jenson, *Politics of Abortion*, 117–46.

Gill, Donna. "REAL Women and the Press: An Ideological Alliance of Convenience." *Canadian Journal of Communication* 14, no. 3 (1989): 1–16.

Haussman, Melissa. "'What Does Gender Have to Do with Abortion Law?' Canadian Women's Movement–Parliamentary Interactions on Reform Attempts, 1969–91." *International Journal of Canadian Studies* 21 (Spring 2000): 127–51.

Jenson, Jane. "Getting to *Morgentaler*: From One Representation to Another." In Brodie, Gavigan, and Jenson, *Politics of Abortion*, 15–55.

Joffe, Carole. *Doctors of Conscience: The Struggle to Provide Abortion Before and After Roe v. Wade.* Boston: Beacon Press, 1995.

Johnstone, Rachel. "The Politics of Abortion in Canada After Morgentaler: Women's Rights as Citizenship Rights." PhD diss., Department of Political Studies, Queen's University, 2012.

Keate, Kathryn. "'Out from Under, Women Unite!': Personal Notes of an Activist in the Women's Liberation Movement." *Saturday Night*, July 1970.

Keown, John. *Abortion, Doctors, and the Law: Some Aspects of the Legal Regulation of Abortion in England from 1803 to 1982.* Cambridge: Cambridge University Press, 1988.

Klausen, Susanne. "Doctors and Dying Declarations: The Role of the State in Abortion Regulation in British Columbia, 1917–37." *Canadian Bulletin of Medical History* 13, no. 1 (1996): 53–81.

McCulloch, Michael. "'Doctor Tumblety, the Indian Herb Doctor': Politics, Professionalism, and Abortion in Mid-Nineteenth-Century Montreal." *Canadian Bulletin of Medical History* 10, no. 1 (1993): 49–66.

McDaniel, Susan A. "Implementation of Abortion Policy in Canada as a Women's Issue." *Atlantis* 10, no. 2 (1985): 75–91.

McLaren, Angus. "Illegal Operations: Women, Doctors and Abortion, 1886–1939." *Journal of Social History* 26, no. 4 (1993): 797–816.

McLaren, Angus, and Arlene Tigar McLaren. *The Bedroom and the State: The Changing Practices and Politics of Contraception and Abortion in Canada, 1880–1997.* 2nd ed. Toronto: Oxford University Press, 1997.

McLellan, A. Anne. "Abortion Law in Canada." In *Abortion, Medicine, and the Law*, edited by J. Douglas Butler and David F. Walbert, 333–67. New York: Facts on File, 1992.

Milne, Nora. "Creating Change to Maintaining Change: The Fédération du Québec pour le planning des naissances and the Pro-choice Movement." Master's thesis, Deaprtment of History and Classical Studies, McGill University, Montréal, 2011.

Mitchinson, Wendy. *Body Failure: Medical Views of Women, 1900–1950*. Toronto: University of Toronto Press, 2013.

———. *The Nature of Their Bodies: Women and Their Doctors in Victorian Canada*. Toronto: University of Toronto Press, 1994.

Morgentaler, Henry. "Report on 5,641 Outpatient Abortions by Vacuum Suction Curettage." *Canadian Medical Association Journal* 109, no. 12 (1973): 1202–5.

Morgentaler, Henry, Sam Solomon, and Gillian Woodford. "The Interview: The Morgentaler Decision Turns Twenty." *National Review of Medicine* 5, no. 1 (2008). http://www.nationalreviewofmedicine.com/issue/interview/2008/5_interview_01.html.

Palley, Howard A. "Canadian Abortion Policy: National Policy and the Impact of Federalism and Political Implementation on Access to Services." *Publius* 36, no. 4 (2006): 565–86.

Palmer, Beth. "Choices and Compromises: The Abortion Rights Movement in Canada, 1969–1988." PhD diss., Department of History, York University, 2012.

———. "'Lonely, Tragic, but Legally Necessary Pilgrimages': Transnational Abortion Travel in the 1970s." *Canadian Historical Review* 92, no. 4 (2011): 637–64.

Parliament of Canada. Standing Senate Committee on Social Affairs, Science and Technology. "The Canada Health Act." Chap. 17 in *The Health of Canadians: The Federal Role—Final Report*, vol. 6, *Recommendations for Reform*. Ottawa: Parliament of Canada, 2002. http://www.parl.gc.ca/Content/SEN/Committee/372/soci/rep/repoct02vol6part7-e.htm.

Penny [Light], Tracy. "'Getting Rid of My Trouble': A Social History of Abortion in Ontario, 1880–1929." Master's thesis, Department of History, Laurentian University, 1995.

Penny Light, Tracy. "Shifting Interests: The Medical Discourse on Abortion in English Canada, 1850–1969." PhD diss., Department of History, University of Waterloo, 2003.

Rebick, Judy. *Ten Thousand Roses: The Making of a Feminist Revolution*. Toronto: Penguin, 2005.

Report of the Royal Commission on the Status of Women in Canada. Ottawa: Information Canada, 1970.

Revie, Linda. "More Than Just Boots! The Eugenic and Commercial Concerns Behind A. R. Kaufman's Birth Controlling Activities." *Canadian Bulletin of Medical History* 23, no. 1 (2006): 119–43.

Richer, Karine. "Abortion in Canada: Twenty Years After *R. v. Morgentaler.*" Ottawa: Library of Parliament, Parliamentary Information and Research Service, 2008. http://www.lop.parl.gc.ca/content/lop/researchpublications/prb0822-e.pdf.

Sethna, Christabelle. "All Aboard? Canadian Women's Abortion Tourism, 1960–1980." In *Gender, Health, and Popular Culture: Historical Perspectives*, edited by Cheryl Krasnich Warsh, 89–108. Waterloo, ON: Wilfrid Laurier University Press, 2011.

Sethna, Christabelle, and Marion Doull. "Accidental Tourists: Canadian Women, Abortion Tourism, and Travel." *Women's Studies: An Interdisciplinary Journal* 41, no. 4 (2012): 457–75.

———. "Far from Home? A Pilot Study Tracking Women's Journeys to a Canadian Abortion Clinic." *Journal of Obstetrics and Gynaecologists of Canada* 27, no. 8 (2007): 640–47.

———. "Spatial Disparities and Travel to Freestanding Abortion Clinics in Canada." *Women's Studies International Forum* 38 (2013): 52–62.

Sethna, Christabelle, and Steve Hewitt. "Clandestine Operations: The Vancouver Women's Caucus, the Abortion Caravan, and the RCMP." *Canadian Historical Review* 90, no. 3 (2009): 463–95.

Shaw, Jessica. "Abortion as a Social Justice Issue in Contemporary Canada." *Critical Social Work* 14, no. 2 (2013): 2–17. http://www1.uwindsor.ca/criticalsocialwork/system/files/Shaw.pdf.

Silverman, Eliane Leslau. *The Last Best West Women on the Alberta Frontier, 1880–1930*. Montréal: Eden Press, 1984.

Stettner, Shannon. "Crisis Pregnancy Centers." In *Encyclopedia of Women in Today's World*, edited by Mary Zeiss Stange and Carol K. Oyster, and Jane E. Sloan, 363–64. Thousand Oaks, CA: Sage, 2011.

———. "'He Is Still Unwanted': Women's Assertions of Authority over Abortion in Letters to the Royal Commission on the Status of Women in Canada." *Canadian Bulletin of Medical History* 29, no. 1 (2012): 151–71.

———. "Women and Abortion in English Canada: Public Debates and Political Participation, 1959–1970." PhD diss., Department of History, York University, 2011.

Stortz, Gerald, and Murray E. Eaton. "'Pro Bono Publico': The Eastview Birth Control Trial." *Atlantis* 8, no. 2 (1983): 51–60.

Thomas, William D. S. "The Badgley Report on the Abortion Law." *Canadian Medical Association Journal* 116, no. 9 (1977): 966.

Thomson, Ann. *Winning Choice on Abortion: How British Columbian and Canadian Feminists Won the Battles of the 1970s and 1980s*. Victoria, BC: Trafford, 2004.

Wasserlein, Frances. "'An Arrow Aimed at the Heart': The Vancouver Women's Caucus and the Abortion Campaign, 1969–1971." Master's thesis, Department of History, Simon Fraser University, 1990.

part one

Speaking from Experience

An Abortion Palimpsest

Writing the Hidden Stories of Our Bodies

JUDITH MINTZ

> *Women's autobiography is distinguished by its uneasy relationship to the body and maternity.*
>
> Kristi Siegel

> *Woman must write her self: must write about women and bring women to writing, from which they have been driven away as violently as from their own bodies—for the same reasons, by the same law, with the same fatal goal. Woman must put herself into the text—as into the world and into history—by her own movement.*
>
> Hélène Cixous

Time measures our experiences and gives perspective. When we read texts that we ourselves have written about our experiences, we often can regard these pasts with a clarity that we only wish we had had when we recorded them. Feminist life-writing theorist Helen Buss points out that autobiographical writing also allows for a discursive construction of the self, the meanings of which are encoded within the writing itself.[1] In other words, women have often constructed their lives through writing in order to simultaneously reveal and conceal particular issues related to experiences such as pregnancy, miscarriage, and childbirth. In earlier writings, Buss explains the importance of decoding such writing: the decoding "allows the researcher to mitigate the silence that male-centred language imposed on women's real lives."[2]

The following personal narrative traces my own coded experience of abortion in Ontario, Canada, at the turn of the twenty-first century. This narrative attempts to unwind some of the tangled social stigma associated with abortion by revealing the psychosocial considerations of such a decision. The diary entries illustrate the tension between maintaining a normal appearance and negotiating the embodied changes associated with the first trimester of pregnancy. By analyzing my own diary and comparing what I wrote with my memory, I will decode missing information in an effort to give voice to the stories that remain hidden in my body. As Cixous says, it is imperative that women put themselves back into texts, which is my intention in this narrative. My text becomes the source for my analysis of the discourse that filtered my emotional experience of abortion. Despite abortion being legal in Ontario, it still is a site of constrained expression.

I take the liberty here to suggest that the discourse that I deconstruct is not unlike that of other women whose careers and relationships were in their infancy. I liked the idea of becoming a mother and anticipated the potential joys that I imagined children could bring into my life, but only on terms that could accommodate my life's path and personal timeline. Sometimes, I felt this craving in my body, but it persisted in issuing monthly bloody reminders to my mind that, at the age of twenty-nine, I hadn't yet established a solid career or relationship.

22 February 2001
I took the morning-after pill yesterday. We needed to make a quick
decision about our mistake. This big dose of estrogen and progesterone
is making me nauseous so I take Gravol. I feel stoned and go to sleep.
My stomach is giving me mixed signals between nausea and hunger

and pain. I'll get over this. I am trying to get through this on my own because I want to be my own strong container for myself.

Contemplating my situation, I also struggled with what I thought I should be as a woman versus what I thought my partner wanted me to be.

22 February 2001
Stopping the potential conception of a child was almost difficult to do. But now is definitely not the time for us to get pregnant.

23 February
Fatigue today, feet hurt during yoga practice and mild headache. Took a sauna and felt better, but fatigue lingers. I taught a private yoga class and came home wanting to nap when I usually feel energized from teaching. I had planned to help S with his business, but when he came to pick me up tonight, I told him I had to stay home and rest.[3] He left, but I wish I could have seen him for longer, touched him and talked to him. But life is not like that, not right now.

My diary entries sound like a cry for help as I rationalized why it was okay that I did not receive more support as I moved through the discomfort of taking the emergency contraceptive pill (ECP). But the entries also read like a shopping list of things I had promised to do for S to help him with his business. On the same page where I made business notes, I also jotted down the date, 28 February, for an appointment at the Hassle Free Clinic in Toronto. I did not yet know I was pregnant, not having anticipated that the ECP would not work. I can barely decipher which notes are for S's business and which ones relate to the situation in which I had found myself. What is clear now is that I had no plans on making changes to my lifestyle that I felt a mother should make when planning for a child to come into being.

"Open her heart and let healing start," I wrote somewhere around 10 March. The bottom half of the page is torn out, but I don't know why anymore. Perhaps I ripped it out because I needed to protect myself from painful truths. This filtering of my experience enabled me to compartmentalize my inner and outer lives and to perpetuate dualizing frameworks that alienate body from mind.

13 March 2001
Pouring rain. Swelling breasts, sore. No period after thirty-three days. If I don't bleed by the dark of the moon, which is ten days from now,

I will worry. But that morning-after pill has really screwed up my system. S's mother is in hospital again.

I dreamed last night of building a garden. I bought a ten-kilo bag each of geranium seeds, clove seeds, and lettuce. I had peaches, which I planted individually, whole, with the help of a young child. The garden was somewhat prepared already, I just had to turn the soil to wake up the ground. I had no help and I was puzzled as to how I would get around the huge puddles.

I realized a few weeks later why I continued to feel so exhausted: as in my dream, I actually was growing something. At the time of the dream, I was unable to hear its prophetic message. Interestingly, my diary never actually reveals when, exactly, I went to the doctor and got a blood test for pregnancy. I never wrote anything about that moment, and yet I recall it viscerally—hearing the results of that blood test on the phone while standing in the personal trainer office at the gym where I taught yoga and did shiatsu treatments. I did not need to record it, because I will always remember the surge of queasiness and heat in my belly when the doctor told me that I was pregnant despite having taken the ECP.

My notes in the diary describe a yoga workshop I led for high school students who were learning to become leaders in their community. I now recall how tired and nauseated I felt that evening, and how I could not consider cancelling the workshop for fear of seeming unprofessional. On 26 March, I wrote more notes from a phone call I made to Motherisk: we talked about the risk of birth defects from the ECP to the fetus. A sharp line divides the page and a note underneath declares, "ECP didn't work!" More notes detail information about a possible abortion procedure, but nowhere on the page did I write the word *abortion*. Nowhere did I write how I felt. That part, I had to shut out.

In 2001, abortion was legal in Ontario, but it was, as it is now, a contested issue. Clinics that provided abortion services in Toronto in 2001 still had to protect themselves and their clients from protesters and other threats. I knew, however, that abortion services were available to me and were covered by OHIP, the Ontario Health Insurance Program. Even though a simmering stew of anti-abortion sentiment lurked near clinics, I felt secure that I could indeed have my abortion "hassle free." I never questioned, as my mother's generation had, whether I could have an abortion should I have an unplanned pregnancy. The historical tension from so-called pro-lifers still coloured abortion clinic protocol. My notes about the Choices in Health Clinic say that I could bring one support person with me to the procedure and that this person would be required to provide photo identification. A note in my diary suggests that I was concerned that S would not prioritize me and the procedure, which I had by now reluctantly agreed to undergo. I was deeply conflicted about my own choice. The idea that I was the "right" age for having a baby and settling down was not congruent with the truth of my actual life: I had a budding career as a yoga instructor and shiatsu therapist, and my relationship with the father of this child was not stable.

> 2 April 2001
> Jennifer gave me a little foot massage and made me tea at her studio today. Nurturing is what I need and she gives. My mother told me, "there are so many people who want to take care of you," meaning herself and my sister. I am fully aware that S may want to but is unable to take care of me. I have to let this being inside myself go. I couldn't/ don't want to do it [have the baby and raise it] by myself, so this "accident" we've created must not be brought to term.

> 3 April
> While making lunch today, the voice inside said, "I'm going against myself." For years I have wondered, what would I do if I accidentally conceived now? I never wanted to have to go through this.

> 5 April
> Abort baby or abort my career. And then he reminds me: "We tried to kill it."

> 9 April
> I called him to see if he was okay with all the plans for everything tomorrow, and he actually asked me if I could meet him there! I was so astounded I forgot to tell him that he must come in with me, otherwise they won't let him in.

As much research and oral history has demonstrated, my mother's generation and others before hers did not have as easy access to abortion as I did.[4] Indeed, many women in my own generation cannot access abortion services because of their location, race, or class. The fact that my partner had to show identification and come in with me rather than his preference to either drop me off or meet me at the clinic after the procedure clearly shows that abortion service providers advocate for women's health, safety, and agency by insisting that women receive support from someone throughout the entire process. My diaries from spring 2001 show that I had no awareness of women's uneven access to abortion services in Canada. It was so simple for me to procure a timely abortion appointment in Toronto that I did not need to worry about my safety; the abortion service providers did that for me. The relative ease of having the procedure allowed me to focus instead on grieving the loss of the baby and healing my own body.

Despite the fact that abortion is legal in Ontario, many barriers remain that prevent women from receiving this medically and socially necessary service. The continuing controversy and outright condemnation of abortion by some groups means that many women are unable to find support when facing an unplanned pregnancy. My identity as a white, educated urban dweller made obtaining abortion services a trouble-free privilege. It is my hope that writing about my personal abortion experience may open doors for the expression of other people's narratives. This narrative also demonstrates the ways in which I was, like many women, wrestling with my authentic truth, but through decoding the writing, I have revealed it.

Notes

1   Helen Buss, "Katie.com: My Story: Memoir Writing, the Internet, and Embodied Discursive Agency," in *Tracing the Autobiographical*, ed. Marlene Kadar, Linda Warley, Jeanne Perrault, and Susanna Egan, 9–24 (Waterloo, ON: Wilfrid Laurier University Press, 2005), 9. The opening epigraphs are from Kristi Siegel, *Women, Autobiographies, Culture, Feminism* (New York: Peter Lang, 2001), 12; and Hélène Cixous, "Laugh of the Medusa," trans. Keith Cohen and Paula Cohen, *Signs* 1, no. 4 (1976): 875.

2   Helen Buss, "Anna Jameson's Winter Studies and Summer Rambles in Canada as Epistolary Dijournal," in *Essays on Life Writing: From Genre to Critical Practice*, ed. Marlene Kadar, 42–60 (Toronto: University of Toronto, 1992), 24.

3   I have used random letters of the alphabet as pseudonyms in order to protect the identities of individuals who are part of the narrative.

4   See, for example, Childbirth by Choice Trust, *No Choice: Canadian Women Tell Their Stories of Illegal Abortions* (Toronto: Childbirth by Choice Trust, 1998).

T.A.

Clarissa Hurley

There's small choice in rotten apples.

The Taming of the Shrew, I, i.

Time: St. Patrick's Day, 1988
Place: Dr. Everett Chalmers Hospital, Fredericton, New Brunswick
Appointment: T.A. Check-in: 6 a.m. Procedure: 11 a.m.

There were presurgery complications: I lived at home with my parents and had not risen at 5:00 a.m. since early childhood Christmases. I concocted a dubious story about making breakfast for my boyfriend before his long hiking trip in Maine. My parents found this hilarious and offered advice. Father: "Remember to cook sausages! No man can climb a mountain sans sausages!" Mother: "It's a bad precedent, darling! They are all but stomachs and we all but food!" Laughter.

In the silent Lenten darkness, I pulled the front door shut. Wet, early spring snowflakes slapped the dark pavement and vanished as

I waited for the taxi at the end of the street, well away from my house. The friendly, flirtatious driver complimented my outfit, was curious why I was going to the hospital so early, looking so nice. Was someone in my family sick? I said I was a volunteer. I said it was my choice.

In an odd conjuncture of events to which I was oblivious at the time, the judgment of the Supreme Court, two years in the making, had been announced a few weeks earlier, on 28 January. In a split decision, a majority of five judges declared section 251 of the Criminal Code of Canada unconstitutional, in conflict with section 7 of the Charter of Rights and Freedoms, which guarantees the right to "security of the person." My ill-starred pregnancy may have been conceived at the very hour the red-suited sages, like seven sombre Santas, delivered their judgments. About six weeks later, I would act upon a judgment of my own.

My grad school boyfriend and I had agreed there was no point in his coming with me, nothing he could do to help. Actually, he had suggested that, and I had acquiesced. "I'd just be sitting around waiting, wouldn't I?" Perhaps it sounded reasonable in his British accent. I was twenty-two; he was twenty-five. The discussion had been brief. He was on a student visa and not ready to father a child. I was on my own if I wanted to mother one. For the first time in our seven-month relationship, he said he loved me. He said it right after I agreed to the abortion.

Momentous in principle, *R. v. Morgentaler* removed abortion from the criminal code—and it did remarkably little else. Provinces grappled skittishly with the implications of the judgment and delivery of the service was largely unaffected. Then, as now, access depended on location. I was one of the fortunate ones. My doctor was sympathetic, directing my performance in her office as she explained the process by which a committee of physicians would adjudicate my situation and approve, hopefully, my termination.

"I need to see tears," she prompted.

"I don't feel like crying," I protested.

"I know, but the committee likes tears."

I obliged, summoning tears of frustration at the humiliating insult added to the bewildering injury of contraception-evading fertility. But her letter convinced the jury of my nonpeers. I received notice of my appointment, sent to a postal box I had rented for the purpose. I was determined, then, that no one should know. Fredericton is a small town and talk is the oxygen that sustains it. Abortion invites outrage and condemnation; unwed mothers receive disdain and pity. Abortion is slatternly and immoral; single motherhood is pathetic and expensive to the community that enforces it. A committee would know my identity, but not I theirs. I was assured the anonymous jurors who vetted my appeal would be discreet, but I knew they were likely to be friends of my parents.

The doctor who would perform the procedure was professional and remote. His tousled, healthy children and toothsome, fecund wife beamed from the picture frame behind his left shoulder.

"Are you sure this is what you want to do?"

"I don't feel I have any choice."

He briefly described the procedure, to be performed under a superfluous general anesthetic. No doubt intending to be reassuring, carefully smiling, he said chances were low that he would perforate my uterus and perform an emergency hysterectomy. All surgery carries risk, but more women die in childbirth. He must have felt some compulsion to perform the surgery, so I appreciated him as one condemned might appreciate a benevolent prison guard. Years later, I would meet him at a lavish gala fundraiser for the regional theatre company he generously supported. He thanked me profusely, with genuine emotion, for the tax receipt I issued. If he recognized me, he made no sign.

An elegant young woman, alarmingly well-coiffed for 6:00 a.m., registered me at the outpatients' desk. She perused the details of my appointment, pausing to stare at me as a languid disdainful cat watches rain from the shelter of a doorframe. In my world, "T.A." meant teaching assistant. I owed my department twelve hours a week, marking undergrad essays or looking up books for my supervising professor. Now the letters assumed a sinister euphemism and vague inanity. What was therapeutic in the prurient, prying eyes of strangers, absurd appointment times, the scowling anesthetist clumsily skewering the back of my hand, his punitive rage belied by my transparent skin, the lavender veins lying plump and present, mapping his way to my unconscious. My mother's shocked gasp days later: "How *did* you get that ghastly bruise?"

St. Patrick's Day was big in my family. My father was third-generation Miramichi and spoke in a brogue-tinged dialect. My mother had spent her early years in Cloyne, before poverty sent her family to England and marriage brought her to Canada, where she finally had the two children she craved but had such trouble conceiving. When I arrived home in late afternoon from the hospital, drinks with friends were well underway. Bright red vinyl played Fenian rebel music on the scratchy old turntable. "We *are* the boys of Wexford . . ." Dad poured me a Bushmills.

"I shouldn't drink . . . Seminar tomorrow."

"It's St. Patrick's Day."

It was instruction, not information. I drank it and went to bed, lamely protesting my early morning, my limbs leaden from anesthetic and alcohol. I went to my Middle English poetry seminar the next morning. I finished my MA a few months later. I broke up with the nonfather. We remain friendly, if not friends. We were young, by middle-class Western standards.

———◆———

Time: Late summer, 1998
Place: Morgentaler Clinic, Fredericton, New Brunswick
Appointment: T.A. Check-in: 11:00 a.m. Procedure: 12:00 p.m.

The new Morgantaler clinic had opened in Fredericton in 1994 on a quiet street on the north side of the river in a building that had been a private home and later a posh restaurant. Protesters regularly picketed, heads bowed, reverently clutching placards displaying vaguely cartoonish representations of bloodstained full-term infants. They were generally quiet and not importunate. My beloved elderly aunt would sometimes come by bus from her convent in Saint John to pray with them. I often offered to drive her so I could listen to her animated stories of wartime, her years of nursing in postwar Japan, the welcome hysterectomy she had had in the 1950s at an American military hospital. I discreetly checked with her about her plans before I made my appointment.

In many ways, the experience was strikingly different. No panel of elders would "yay or nay" my actions; no general anesthetic would augment the risks inherent in surgery. I was older and had my own apartment—no subterfuge was necessary. In other ways, it was remarkably similar. My then-partner, a professional in his forties, possessed an Olympian intellect and the emotional stability of a hormonal adolescent. He left for a research trip in Britain a few days after I told him of my pregnancy. He wanted children, ideally, in principle, but on his terms, his schedule. My timing was bad, he informed me. I also wanted children, ideally, but children are not ideals, abstractions, principles, acquisitions for a CV, or items to be checked on a to-do list. I felt they were a privilege, not a right. Again, I was on my own. Florynce Kennedy famously quipped that if men could conceive, abortion would be a sacrament. For the women who do conceive, abortion is frequently a sacrifice—a giving up of, not a getting rid of.

The appointment was in midday. Clinic staff members were supportive, respectful, and efficient. A sensible nurse held my hand and talked to me through the uncomfortable but brief procedure. The price, of course, was the price. As in many provinces, clinic abortions are a private matter, and the cost of privacy is high.[1]

———————◆———————

Time: Recent
Place: Fredericton Medical Clinic
Appointment: Introduction to new physician

Having moved back to Fredericton from Toronto three years ago, I am relieved and elated to be matched finally with a family physician, following a three-year wait with over four thousand others on an official registry. I am fortunate to be in good health and have not had to rely often on the physician lottery of after-hours clinics or the hospital ER. The administrative assistant hands me a clipboard and requests that I read carefully and sign the "Office Policies" form. I browse through the list of "please do not wear scent" and "please arrive ten minutes early," etc. The final point makes me draw a sharp breath and I read it repeatedly, as if translating from a language I had not used in years: "This office will not aid or facilitate in the termination of pregnancies."

I briefly consider throwing the clipboard through the sliding glass partition but decide against the risk of criminal charges—and yet another protracted wait on the family doctor registry. Across the waiting room a nervous young woman texts discreetly on her smart phone as she waits for her appointment. I wonder why she is here, whether she is facing a "choice" that may well be as fraught as mine were in previous decades; whether she will have to scramble to find another doctor in time for a time-sensitive procedure, or raise a month's rent to pay for a clinic abortion. Reluctantly, I sign the bottom of the form, breaking the pencil lead twice in my furiously clenched fingers.

My enquiry to the NB College of Physicians and Surgeons the following day results in vague responses about "grey areas" and glib optimism that such situations "usually work themselves out."

———◆———

The reproductive rights movement in Canada reveres the principle of freedom of choice. It is attractive, compelling rhetoric with which I am loath to quibble. The idea draws on principles held dear in post-Enlightenment Western thought; that we are free to choose seems mulishly axiomatic. Yet I cannot help but feel discomfort, for reasons both psychological and material, with the implications of this emphasis on choice. "Choice" implies that desire trumps circumstance, while I believe the opposite is frequently true. At least since Aristotle's *De Caelo*, Western philosophy has problematized the notion of a purely free will. Late medieval philosopher Jean Buridan's doctrine of moral determinism was satirized in the paradox of Buridan's Ass, in which a donkey, hungry and thirsty, is set midway between a pail of water and a bale of hay. Paralyzed by the equally compelling choices, the animal dies of hunger and thirst. Options may also be similarly repellent or terrifying. I have several friends who have had abortions: most have had more than one; some have had more than three. In no case have I spoken to a woman who came to the decision based on abstractions of what was most desirable.

The administrative and jurisdictional inequality of abortion access in Canada is well documented. The $450 I paid fifteen years ago at the Fredericton Morgentaler Clinic, a fee that would render the service a fantasy for most teens and disadvantaged women, has risen to over $700 and the provincial Medical Services Payment Act remains unchanged.

In New Brunswick, three hospitals in two cities at opposite poles of the province currently provide abortions, in addition to Fredericton's Clinic 554, which opened following the closure of the Morgentaler Clinic. More encouraging has been Premier Brian Gallant's long-overdue removal of the anomalous two-doctor rule in New Brunswick, as well as the decisive majority government election of the Liberal party and its leader Justin Trudeau, an openly pro-choice prime minister.

Given that only seventeen percent of hospitals nationwide offer terminations and nearly all abortion access in the country is restricted to urban centres, the focus of discussion, particularly among young people, has shifted away from abstract moral debate to the pertinent and pressing issue of access.[2] Abortion remains most elusive to the women—and communities—who most need it.

Less quantifiable barriers are equally powerful. Gender roles are more confusingly scripted than ever, and young people are steeped in the hyper-sexualized worlds of social media. To be sexual—and sexy—is virtually mandatory for young women; to be pregnant outside of a conventional partnership remains problematic in all but the most privileged contexts. Birth control, even when easily available, is never fully reliable.

Unfettered choice cannot exist in a world that remains judgmental, unaccommodating, and punitive to unpartnered pregnant women and mothers. While I still support the possibly utopian quest for women's full reproductive control, the slogan of "choice," I fear, has not significantly advanced this cause.

Notes

1 This situation has evolved in many provinces. Currently, every province except New Brunswick funds most abortions performed in approved clinics. PEI has no clinic but funds at least some terminations for their residents who must travel to Moncton. Almost every clinic in the country is located in an urban centre. See Abortion Rights Coalition of Canada, "List of Abortion Clinics in Canada," 16 June 2016, http://www.arcc-cdac. ca/list-abortion-clinics-canada.pdf.

2 This statistic comes provided by the Abortion Rights Coalition of Canada in an email communication and is current as of February 2016.

But I Kept All These Things, and Pondered Them in My Heart

JESS WOOLFORD

I took my third pregnancy test at a clinic. While Jon and I waited for the results, I visualized the word PLEASE. When it looked as bold as I could make it, my mind gave it a shove and the entreaty drifted out into the ether. I hoped it would catch the eye of a merciful deity, one who had perhaps been off-duty before but who would now take hold of the situation and reduce it to a false alarm.

Jon sat with his arms crossed and his eyes closed, his head tilted back against the wall. We did not speak, but the jittering of his boot on the dull floor tiles told me exactly how he felt.

After a time, the clinician came in, closed the door behind her, and sat down at the desk. Laying out a file, she quickly scanned its contents before looking up at us. Then she said, "The results are positive."

Her words lacked the power to surprise me. Instead, they shook the last scrap of hope I'd been clutching and sent it wafting away like a leaf in the wind. Glancing at Jon, I saw dismay flood his face.

"We want an abortion," I said.

"That's a big decision, one you need to think about carefully. Have you considered other options? Adoption is a possibility or . . ."

Surprised and irritated by the clinician's response, I didn't let her finish.

"We've already thought about it," I said, "and we want an abortion."

"Well, I'm afraid we can't get you in for at least another week. Look, why don't you think about it over the weekend and give us a call on Monday? Here, take these pamphlets."

———————◆———————

Jon thumped the dashboard with his fist. "Now we have to wait? Just in case we haven't *thought* about it enough? I can *not* fuckin' believe this."

I thought I knew what he meant. For days, it seemed like I'd been thinking about our dilemma and little else. *What am I going to do?* Either the question shouted and swelled so that it threatened to burst my cranium or it stood off to one side and whispered a relentless interrogation.

"You might as well get rid of those pamphlets," Jon said. "Why'd you even bother to take 'em?"

"I don't know."

"Come on."

"I guess it just seemed rude not to."

"Well, all I can say is, you'd better not be backing out on me, Jess. You *said* you'd have an abortion. When we talked about it before, that's what you said. Remember?"

"Of course I remember. In case you didn't notice, Jon, *I'm* the one who told her we want one."

"Okay, okay. You don't hafta bitch at me. Just don't go getting any crazy ideas about keeping it."

I knew Jon was right. After all, I hadn't set out to become pregnant. When it came to sex, I wasn't a reckless person. Far from it: I had consistently used birth control, but *it* had failed *me*. I didn't see why I should be punished for that and so part of me resented the creature unfurling in my womb. Abortion was the logical choice.

Still, logic couldn't appease another part of me. Since the moment I'd realized I was pregnant, it seemed that babies waited for me around every corner, and each time I saw one, the life I carried felt more compelling than everything else put together. It was disconcerting. In the days when the idea of a surprise pregnancy was only an abstraction, I had never suspected that I could feel fierce love for an embryo.

I wanted to discuss my mixed-up feelings with Jon, but I didn't know how, especially since it was clear that his mind was already made up. I needed to talk to someone who would understand. My mother? Maybe. She had chosen to have four children, but she had also taught me that a woman has options beyond motherhood. Even though we weren't as close as we had once been, she might still be able to help me untangle this knot.

Back at Jon's house, I stopped long enough to shove a few things into my pack before telling him I was going to stay at my parents' for a while. He didn't try to stop me. "Okay," he said, and that was all.

———◆———

Driving alone down the highway, I felt as though Jon was still beside me. I kept hearing his demand: *Remember?* How could I forget? In my mind's eye, I saw us the summer before. Conjuring my old Kent Street apartment, I lifted the roof and peeked in like a child cracking open a dollhouse. There we were, Jon and I, supine on carpet as bland as porridge, our heads pressed so close together that strands of our hair touched. From the tape deck, Taj Mahal's voice crackled and crooned . . . *How can you sleep when your baby is gone?* . . . and a hot breeze carried the spicy-sweet scent of wild roses through the open window. We had not yet had sex, but we were dancing toward it, and, as though we were the stars of a film about sexual responsibility, we had already begun to strategize about birth control. Jon had told me that he and his last girlfriend had tried everything except intercourse, so he was technically still a virgin. That made me the font of experience, and I thought that in order for his first time to be perfect, he should be able to feel everything, so I vetoed condoms. He didn't object—why should he have? We were free of disease. I wanted to take the pill, but Jon worried that its chemicals might harm me. His concern for my health, for *me*, was something new in my experience of men, and it left me giddy with gratitude and tenderness. When Jon suggested the diaphragm, I agreed. A few days later, I would go for a fitting.

Lounging on the floor next to Jon, I felt pleased that we were taking such an open, practical, mature approach to sex, and I was thinking that that was just one of many reasons Jon outshone every other guy I had dated. It wasn't long, though, before something began to disturb my glistening bubble of competence. It was the Worst Case Scenario, an entity that I seem unable to hold at bay for long, no matter what the situation. The problem was that I didn't know what Jon thought about abortion. I had a choice: I could keep quiet and just go along hoping I never got pregnant or I could ask him. I was tempted to keep my worry to myself. Jon and I shared similar views on most things, but what if it turned out that we were at odds on this one issue? It would rend my heart to have to let him go, but I also knew that I couldn't leave this detail to chance. I had to say something.

I turned on my side so that I could see Jon's face. His eyes were closed and he was smiling. I rested my head on his chest and closed my eyes too. The sound of his heart plodding beneath my ear lulled me and I wanted to follow it into sleep, but I forced myself to take a steadying breath instead.

"Can I ask you something?"

"Sure," Jon said, his long fingers in my hair.

"I was just wondering what would happen if . . ." I shifted so that my chin was propped on his chest. He opened his eyes and lifted his head. "I mean, if I accidentally got pregnant, what would you want to do?" There. I had said it.

Jon let his head fall back to the floor. He was quiet long enough for me to regret speaking. *I should have kept my mouth shut!* At last, he turned on his elbow and looked at me again. "Well . . . I'm not ready to be a father. I mean, I have to finish school and then I want to do a bunch of other things . . . you know, drive across the country, play my guitar. Besides, we're too young to have a kid."

I felt my face warming. Did he think I meant that I *wanted* to have a baby?

"Oh, I agree," I said. "That's what I was hoping you'd say. I mean, I'm sure I won't get pregnant, but what if I did and I didn't want to have it, but you wanted me to? God, what a mess that would be!"

"So, you'd have an abortion?"

"Yeah, of course. I wanna finish school too and even if I wasn't doing that, I'm pretty sure I couldn't handle having a kid. I mean, I can hardly care for myself. And anyway, I'm probably too crazy to be a good mother."

"You're not crazy." Jon pulled my head down to his chest and resumed stroking my hair. I wasn't sure I agreed with his assessment of my mental health, but I kept quiet and snuggled closer to him.

———◆———

Without Apology

When I reached my parents' house, it was nearly dinnertime and I found my mother standing at the stove. On the iron skillet, fat hamburgers spat gobs of grease and the stench of searing flesh filled the kitchen and made my stomach wobble.

"Hi, Mom."

She glanced over her shoulder at me. "I wasn't expecting you," she said.

"Well, here I am." I hoped she would hug me, but she stayed where she was.

"No Jon?"

"No. He's working late."

She gave her attention back to the skillet. "You should have called first. I would have made an extra burger."

"That's okay. I'm really not hungry."

"You have to eat."

"I know. It's just the smell."

"The smell?"

"Yeah. Of the meat. It's kind of getting to me."

My mother turned to face me then, a hand on her hip, her mouth barbed. "What's the matter? Preggers, Jess?"

Beneath her gaze, my body seemed a clear pool, but if my mother truly glimpsed what stirred there, she was unmoved. Jostled by her scorn, I placed a hand on the counter to steady myself. I was too rattled to look her in the eye and say, "Well, as a matter of fact, I *am* pregnant, mother dear." Instead all I could manage was, "No. I just don't like the smell of meat anymore. I *do* work in a vegetarian restaurant, you know." A bowl of salad sat nearby. I grabbed it and hurried out to the picnic table.

———◆———

At dinner, my parents hardly looked at each other and when one of them spoke, the other pretended not to understand. Though long accustomed to this routine, it still rankled. In the past, I had often acted as interpreter, but that night I sat still and silent and wished for them both to be struck dumb.

When the meal finally ended, I shouldered my pack and walked through the shadows lengthening in the sugar bush. At the top of the hill, I clambered over the mossy stone wall and into a neighbour's field. Purple vetch tangled the high grass and I stretched myself out in it. Closing my eyes, I slid a hand over my stomach. Now I knew better than to expect any help from my mother, but little else was clear. My emotions were still jumbled. It seemed incomprehensible that I could feel both love and hate for the thing inside me, and I turned the riddle of my responses this way and that. I couldn't make much sense of them, though, so I decided to draw up a list. I rolled onto my stomach, pulled my journal out of my pack, turned to a blank page, and drew a line down the middle of it. At the top of one half I wrote PRO, and on the other CON. What could be simpler? Then I noted every reason I could think of to support or oppose having an abortion. This is what I ended up with:

ABORTION

PRO	CON
too young / still learning to care for self	*feel attached to it, somehow*
have few $$ / skills	*damnation?*
still in school	
history of depression!	

It was four to two with PRO in the lead. I had hoped that seeing my reasons inscribed in black and white would free me from uncertainty, but I remained troubled.

Everything I'd written in the left-hand column was undeniable. I had turned twenty-one two months earlier and I felt like I was only just beginning to be able to look after myself. Furthermore, I didn't know how to do much besides clean and cook—hardly the sort of skills that would bring in enough money to support a child. Besides, I needed to finish school. While it was true that I had no idea what, exactly, I wanted to do, the spark of the past semester still shone within me. Didn't I have a right to figure out my own life before bringing another one into it? How could I be a good student and a good mother at the same time? And even if I could manage to tend to both books and baby, what if it turned out that my depressive tendencies were genetic? The year before, I'd been hospitalized because I couldn't seem to haul myself out of despair. What if my potential child were to fall into the same hole? I imagined a small black spot of a mouth screaming *How could you do this to me? I never asked to be born!* Besides, it wasn't just the illness that concerned me, it was also the cure. As my psychiatrist had written out a prescription for Prozac, he'd remarked that the drug was so new he considered it somewhat experimental. Though at first the absinthe-and-cream-coloured capsules had guided me back into the world, ten months later, they'd boomeranged and shot me right back to melancholia. I had recently shaken the pills into the trash, but I assumed their trace still lurked inside me. Might it affect the developing embryo?

Surely, caring about this tiny thing meant protecting it. I knew that for some people, that's where adoption came in. They preferred to allow their embryo to grow into a fetus and then a baby so they could give it away. Maybe that was noble. My brother Nate was adopted, and loving him made me think I appreciated something of the sacrifice his biological parents had made. Yet when I remembered Nate's habit of calling himself "ugly" every time he looked in the mirror or was asked to pose for a picture, I couldn't help wondering if that initial rejection had scarred his psyche. What's more, I also knew that red tape had bound my brother for two years when he could have been with us. Anyway, how could I ensure that my potential child would be adopted by good people? Or even adopted at all? Given the way it was already demanding my allegiance, I suspected that if it spent nine months snug inside me, I would love it too much to be able to give it up. And then where would we be? I could see us wailing together in a peeling apartment behind Dunkin' Donuts, me adding Green Stamps to my welfare check in an endless attempt to create something that resembled security. We would have no one but each other. Grandparents, probably. But no partner for me and no father for the child. Jon had made that clear.

To the PRO side of my list I added:

Jon doesn't want it

That one obstacle trumped all my other concerns. I imagined myself pleading with Jon to demonstrate even the slightest interest in his child: *If you can't bother to visit, you could at least call!* At the same time, I heard myself trying to reassure our little one: *Daddy's very busy, but I know he thinks about you all the time.* Whatever else I might be able to do for our child, I knew I could never force Jon to love it. Of all the pains that await us in this world, I most desired to protect it from feeling unwanted. I knew something about that and I was damned if I'd subject anyone else to it.

As for God, well, I'd just have to take my chances. If He really existed, rumour had it that He was either a well of infinite compassion or a control freak gone galactic. I thought I'd rather take responsibility for my own soul and risk hell than accept being moved about like a tyrant's chess piece. Besides, wasn't it sinful to give birth to a child you didn't really want and couldn't properly care for? The truth of that conjecture hummed through me, but it didn't make me feel better.

I stood and looked about but it had become too dark to see much. Clouds sailing across the indigo sky caused the stars to blink and stutter like flames in a draft. As I followed an old wagon track through the field to the road below, I sometimes caught an incandescent glimpse of Queen Anne's lace stirring the night like a ghost's frilled skirt.

Keep It Small

E.K. HORNBECK

When the elevator doors slide open, we step into an empty corridor. The nurse leads; the other patient and I follow. After our walk through the early morning bustle of the hospital, the quiet rings in my ears. My rubber boots thud on the shiny floors. The other patient wears black sweatpants and slouchy boots, blonde hair up with a stretchy band. I'm wearing jeans and a green fall jacket. Neither Blonde nor I are wearing makeup.

A sign on the metal doors ahead warns RESTRICTED ACCESS NO THOROUGHFARE. Blonde chuckles once and says, "That's welcoming." I smile politely at her as the nurse picks up a phone by the doors. They buzz open and we step forward into the locked ward.

I was told that I could expect to wait three to six hours. That there is a TV but I should bring my own reading material. As directed, I haven't eaten since the night before. My heart is racing.

First, a nurse hands me a clipboard with the usual outpatient surgery check-in list (no allergies, nonsmoker, etc.). The waiting room has pastel walls and padded chairs that face each other along the long walls. There's a door off the side to the nurses' station. There is indeed a small TV, but it's turned off. Blonde and I are the only ones in the room, but soon I'll discover there are other women in the ward, already part of the complicated dance of the day—first meeting, second meeting, change room, procedure room . . .

I fill out the form quickly and wait. Soon a well-dressed girl—let's call her Fashion Girl—sits down across from me. She barely speaks and looks out of place in her fur-trimmed wool coat, silk scarf, and fashionable boots. As she reads the form, I see her stop at the same question that tripped me. Fashion Girl calls over the nurse, who quickly says, "Oh yes. We know." Two-thirds of the way down the list, question 23 asks if there is any chance we may be pregnant.

But this is the Termination of Pregnancy Unit. Confirmed pregnancy is the reason we have come here.

In another room across the hospital, my friend is waiting. This is part of the strangeness of the day: in order to guard our privacy, the only ones allowed to enter the ward are the women seeking abortions. Though almost 100,000 abortions are performed each year in Canada, utter secrecy muffles the sisterhood. I begrudge no one her privacy, but I wish there was more openness, that I could have some support here with me. In abortion clinics, where a larger proportion of Canadian abortions take place each year, women wait with their hands held and shoulders to lean on. But in Nova Scotia, there are no abortion clinics. The unit I've walked into, at the Victoria General Hospital in Halifax, performs 95 percent of the abortions in the province, with other hospitals performing them irregularly. This is what abortion looks like in Nova Scotia.

The mothers and partners and friends of the women in the ward leave us in the elevator between outpatient check-in and the ward. After the rushed goodbyes before the metal doors slide closed, we disappear into the mysterious world of the TPU, to spend the day with women we have never met but with whom we share one significant biological process. After days, weeks of hiding my truth, I have arrived in a place that defines me.

———◆———

Two weeks earlier, my friend, my roommate, and I were caucusing in my room. I sat on the bed, feeling numb and resigned. My roommate sat on the floor, which she always did. When I had told her the news, minutes earlier, just out of earshot of the boys we live with, she began laughing uncontrollably. My friend, who had run over from her house across the street, perched on a box.

"Of course this would happen to me. Everything happens to me first, doesn't it?" I'd addressed this to my friend, and we both laughed bitterly. Through eighteen years of friendship, of important and insignificant changes, I've always been the first. First period, first kiss, first boyfriend, first to lose my virginity . . . First. Again.

"Oh my God, I know," she said. "I actually thought that when you texted me. Of course. So do you know . . . who . . . ?" my friend asked.

"Charlie. Yeah. It is. It must be."

My voice was calm and even, but my mind was racing. I still could not believe the truth that sat in a drawer in the bathroom.

Seconds after awkwardly peeing on the pink and white stick, I was staring reality in the face. As my urine travelled up the testing stick, two little lines appeared in the white window.

Maybe sometimes one of them disappears, I silently suggested to the empty bathroom.

I had waited the prescribed three minutes. But I already knew.

I realized I'd known since I grumbled idly about being two days late, and then ignored it until I discovered—oh shit—it's now two weeks. I'd known since I wondered why the hell the cold made my tits hurt so much this winter. I'd known since I started waking in the darkness each morning to relieve new pressure on my bladder. My body knew, but my brain fell behind.

"And what . . . will you do?" My friend did most of the talking.

What I had done, first, was place the test face down in the drawer across from the toilet and pull up my pants. I sent one text message to two people: "I took a test. It says I'm pregnant." I chose the wording carefully, guarding against what I was not yet ready to admit.

"I don't want a baby. And if *Teen Mom* has taught me anything, it's that adoption is hard." It felt good to joke about this. Dark humour bends pain into manageable shapes. "Who says you don't learn anything from MTV?"

As a pro-choice feminist who had just turned twenty-one and was about to graduate from university and start my own life, I wasn't ready to start someone else's. I knew what would come next.

Later, my roommate told me she had felt very awkward in that room. "I just thought, oh my God, what if she wants to keep it and we're participating in this awful peer pressure?" I remember that she was pretty quiet.

"Will you tell him?" my friend asked.

I found it impossibly hard to keep answering questions. I'd only known about this for twenty minutes.

"I don't know. I mean, I want to," I said.

My roommate piped up. "Maybe after you have your first appointment?" I'd said I would call the sexual health centre in the morning, to get a referral. "Maybe when you have more information?"

"Yeah . . . maybe."

There was something extremely unfair going on. For weeks, my body had been quietly changing, rearranging its depths to prepare the way for what was growing inside of me. Now the burden of this change rested on my shoulders. But my uterus wasn't acting alone. And he deserved to feel this stress; I deserved help bearing the load. But I wasn't sure I had the strength to tell him. Or maybe I feared he wouldn't have the strength to help me.

"It doesn't feel fair! That the girl has to deal with this and he doesn't. The guy should have to suffer through it."

"Yeah."

"Yeah."

Together, we lined up tasks. I would make appointments. I would tell my other roommates. I would carefully guard the truth. I would keep it small. It would not grow.

There were hugs. Laughs. I wondered if they felt in over their heads. Were they watching me to see what I would do? If I was okay? Had I proven I was? Was I?

———◆———

After waiting a while, I'm led by a nurse to a small room to talk. We go over the form I've filled out and she asks a few questions. Would I like to take narcotics against the pain? Though this means staying an extra twenty minutes after the procedure, I say yes. I am concerned about the pain. I remember how much my IUD insertion hurt.

Would I like the anti-anxiety medication? I dither for a bit but decide I don't need it.

"Now," she asks, "have you decided what kind of contraception you'll use after the procedure?"

That's the thing about pre-abortion counselling. It's a lot like health class, only no one pretends you aren't having sex.

I'd been using the copper intrauterine device, until it migrated down to a corner of my uterus and "failed." They'd found it during my ultrasound ("Oh yeah, it's quite low down there") and would remove it today, along with the "products of conception." All the same, I decide to stay with a copper IUD—I've had poor experiences with hormonal contraception—and the nurse notes it on her chart.

"Does your partner know? About the pregnancy?" she asks.

"I . . . I don't have . . ." I stop. "The guy involved does know. Yeah. And he's been great."

"Good, that's good," she says encouragingly. She tells me I'm number six in line, that the doctor will meet with me soon, and sends me back to wait.

◆

By this time, the room has filled somewhat. Blonde is still there, reading her paperback. A girl in green sweats sniffling quietly, a girl in a black tracksuit, a Southeast Asian girl in a huge hoodie. A wiry woman with a long pony-tail. A girl with olive skin and embellished jeans picks up a copy of a teen tabloid. I would have guessed they would all be my age, but that's not true. Our vulnerability makes us all look younger.

The mood of the room has changed while I was gone. The sleepy silence with which I had been happily insulating myself has dissolved. I've been back a few minutes when the Southeast Asian girl speaks.

"Do you have kids?" she asks Ponytail.

"Yeah," says Ponytail. She has five kids. She explains a complicated mess of fathers and breakups. She has two at home right now. "You?"

"I have two," the Southeast Asian girl responds, and then she begins to sob. Now she's Sobbing Girl.

I am mortified. The unspoken rules of waiting rooms are three: stay quiet, act deaf, and never make eye contact. In a strange place, treading unfamiliar paths, I'd had no idea what to expect, least of all the loss of these social mores.

I look around the room without lifting my head from my magazine. Fashion Girl is staring straight ahead. Green Sweats is looking out the window, tears still quietly rolling down her face. Later, she mentions that someone named Corey is waiting for her downstairs. I text this to my friend, and she guesses that Corey is the rural Nova Scotian boy trying not to cry in her waiting room.

Ponytail is leaning forward toward Sobbing Girl. She lets her speak.

"I have two, and . . . I just don't know. It's hard. I mean, they showed me the ultrasound."

My mind reels. Certainly, such an experience would test my resolve, my sanity. My ultrasound was short, the screen turned away from me, and the sound was off, though the gel made that squirting sound it does in all the movies about pregnancy.

While I try to prevent my mind from contemplating too carefully the inside of my womb, I lose the conversation. When I come back, Blonde has set aside her paperback and joined in.

"I have a ten-month-old at home," she says. "It took me a long time to decide. I'm at fifteen weeks."

There is a murmur in response. The cut-off for abortion in Nova Scotia is fifteen weeks and six days pregnant.

"Nah, I knew right away," says Ponytail. She tells us she's eight weeks.

"Eight," says Black Tracksuit.

"Eight," I say.

"I can't wait 'til it's over," Ponytail goes on. She'd been having acne problems and terrible morning sickness.

"Oh, I know!" Blonde pipes up.

I'm next in line. I shrug and offer, "I haven't been sick at all. My skin's actually been kind of great."

Blonde and Ponytail laugh jealously.

A woman comes in and takes Sobbing Girl away, to "go talk." I realize this must be the counsellor we've been told is on call for us.

Once she leaves, the mood lifts. But the talking stresses me.

"It hurts so much, you know, oh yeah," Ponytail says to the room, unprompted. She's had two abortions before. "It's the worst thing I've ever felt. You're gonna yell for sure. Oh boy." She never takes the narcotics, she says, because she doesn't like staying longer to let them wear off.

My stomach clenches. The idea of pain sinks into my limbs and a wave of nausea hits me.

Blonde asks Ponytail to compare it to birthing pains, and then they're off. Black Tracksuit jumps in, and they're soon comparing birth stories. But by now I'm so scared of the pain, my head is spinning. To distract myself, I pick up my phone.

I've been texting my friend all along, but since we arrived so early in the morning, I've been out of touch with anyone outside the hospital. It's now 9:00 a.m., so I scroll to the guy's name and write, "This waiting room could be a sitcom."

He tells me he's already picked up the car from his mom's, so he can drive me home later.

"The talking is weird," I write. "I don't like talking about the pain."

I try to keep the conversation light, but I'm scared and he knows it. "I wish I could bear hug you right now," he writes, and I smile, with tears behind my eyes.

———◆———

Neither the guy nor I were looking for anything serious, which added another whole level of complexity to the situation. We'd been "casually" spending a lot of time together, but we'd begun drifting apart by the time I found out I was pregnant.

I had pulled the "need to talk about something serious" card, so I knew he must be pretty worked up by the time we sat down on his bed. I took some deep breaths and just blurted it out.

"It's fine. I'm fine. Everything is fine but . . . I'm pregnant." Before he could say anything, I slumped into the fetal position, my head in his lap.

It's quite something to bring this news to a man. For all of the physical pain and responsibility that ultimately falls to the woman in these situations, there is a painful powerlessness for him. The biological process is outside his control, and, ultimately, so is the final say. He struggled to find words as I trembled.

"What . . . do you want to . . . do?" he asked me.

"I figured I should nip it in the bud. You know, before it gets worse." I was quoting a line I'd heard somewhere.

This seemed to be the right answer. He relaxed slightly.

"Oh E–," he said, "you're so strong."

We were both in shock, so we crawled under the covers. We lay there for a long time, holding each other and periodically saying "Holy shit!" and "Is this really happening?" I didn't cry. I hadn't yet.

By the time I left, we'd decided he would tell his roommates. We both realized we wouldn't be able to focus on anything else, so we spent the next few days in a bubble we created, surrounded by those who knew. We watched movies and he cooked for me. Our roommates made jokes; we shook our heads in disbelief. Once, the hormones made me faint in the shower, and we both worried. But with him there, the anxiety in my stomach calmed down, for a few days. He carried me through beautifully.

By the time it is my turn to meet with the doctor, I'm worked up from listening to the others go on. I don't know if Ponytail is looking to be the queen bee or what, but she's certainly been holding court, offering painful tidbits to the rest of us.

The doctor is neat and gruff, and—isn't life funny—I recognize her as the doctor who inserted my IUD at the Halifax Sexual Health Centre two years before. She goes over my form, again, and asks if I have any questions. I've glanced over the "Abortion Procedure" explanation form I received at the centre a few days ago—the friendly nurse with the short hair and skinny scarf had gone over it with me. Her face earnest and concerned, she'd given me the pre-abortion counselling, discussing options and medical jargon.

I shake my head, but one last thing nags me.

"Sorry, I changed my mind . . . Could I have the anxiety medication?"

The doctor notes it on her form, and after another brief contraception chat, our meeting is over.

Without Apology

The ward is laid out in two sections. One side has the main waiting room, the nurses' station, the meeting rooms, and a bathroom. This is the side I've been on. The other side, behind heavy metal doors, has the procedure room and recovery area. You can also get there by walking through the bathroom, into a sitting and changing room that adjoins it, and out another door.

After my meeting with the doctor, one of the nurses leads me into the changing room and explains to me what will happen next. I'm to take a locker, put on the robe and jacket inside it, and put my clothes inside. There's a menstrual pad in there too, and I must apply it before my turn. Since the lockers don't lock, the nurse advises me to keep my bag with me. She looks down at the rubber boots I'm wearing and says, "Well, I guess you'll have to wear those."

"After you're done," she adds, "you can wait wherever you'd like."

Once I've changed, the quiet of the sitting room seems a vast improvement over the frightening chatter. Fashion Girl sits curled up in a chair, staring into space; now wearing a gown like mine, she looks diminished. I take the couch and breathe in the silence.

People come and go from the room. Sobbing Girl follows a nurse in and stands by the lockers. She opens one but closes it again, leaves and doesn't come back.

The girl with embellished jeans comes in from the recovery side of the ward and changes out of her hospital gear. I study her closely as she moves in and out of the bathroom, watching for signs of pain or trauma, but notice nothing.

Waiting is the hard part. My stomach growls and I'm tired from waking before dawn. The silent seconds stretch out. Though I've taken the anxiety drug, half a pill of Ativan melted under my tongue, waves of anxiety wash over me. I take deep breaths. I try to relax every part of me to let the knots of fear come undone.

First, the form from the health centre told me, the speculum. Then the freezing. "The next step is the dilation or opening of the cervix; and this is done by putting small rods into the cervix starting with a very small one, taking it out, putting in a slightly larger one, and so on, until the cervix is open one centimeter . . . then doctor puts a sterile tube in the cervix . . . attached to the aspirator or suction machine . . . Your level of pain is often affected by feeling frightened or anxious."

Open. Aspirate. My poor, poor body. I know this will be a deep trauma, tearing and forcing open the closed places inside me. The violence of it scares me. I tremble, saying silent prayers to my body, asking for forgiveness. I spread a protective hand over my abdomen, but it's not love stirring, it's self-preservation. When it seems too much, when the guilt and blame move over me, I remember the words that a wise friend gave me the day before. "It's such a tender, vulnerable place in your life and body," she wrote to me. "Be gentle with yourself . . . self-care is not selfish, is never a violence."

I care, I tell my body. *I'm so, so sorry. Please let's get through this.*

◆

The physicality of the trauma had come to me only the afternoon before. I'd just finished my requisite day of tests, the blood work, the ultrasound. After he nagged me, I allowed the guy to come, and I was glad to have him. We retreated back to his home, under the blankets. My phone rang, and I knew in my belly what would come next.

"Tomorrow? Oh, that's fast. Yes."

I made the calls I needed to make, I cancelled work and excused myself from class for the week. The guy made arrangements to borrow his mom's car. I put my friend on alert. I returned to the couch, and the guy went to make dinner.

Once I was alone, once the actions were done, it caught me. Until that moment, my pregnancy had been a piece of information. I'd managed it carefully, deciding who would know, who wouldn't know, who I had to tell and when. All of a sudden, I realized I needed to come to terms with my pregnant body and let it go, all in twenty-four hours.

For the first time, the tears came easily. My silence was conspicuous, and soon the guy found me. He knew it would happen eventually, he told me.

"Oh, E–," he said, and took me into his arms. That's when I fell apart.

"I don't regret my decision," I told him, "but this is really hard . . . I was really hoping that my body would end this before I had to do anything." Between sobs, I finally let my fears come out of my mouth.

"I know this is something I'll have to forgive myself for."

He kissed me on the head and held me close until my breathing evened.

The pain isn't in the choice. It's in finding the peace in it.

A nurse fetches me to insert an IV for the narcotic they'll use to numb me during the procedure. She takes me to the recovery room, and I see Ponytail and Blonde sitting in recliner chairs, chatting and laughing. I avoid eye contact and hurry back to the quiet room. Now is the final wait. I've been in the ward for three hours, but this wait feels the longest. Every time I hear footsteps, my heart jumps, wondering if a nurse will enter and call me in. They come first for Fashionable Girl.

I'm so, so sorry.

I abandon my magazine and let the waves of fear run through me. I feel a strange calm in letting them come. I don't cry again. I sit as if in the eye of the storm, accepting some calm.

Ponytail comes in to get dressed. Instead of leaving straight away, she sits down next to me. They've asked her to wait to talk to the counsellor before she leaves, but it's plain that Sobbing Girl is keeping the counsellor busy.

"Have you ever had one before?" she asks me.

I tell her I haven't and look quickly back to my magazine, staring intently and hoping she'll realize I don't want to talk.

"Oh boy. Yeah, it'll hurt. You'll yell for sure. Did you take the pain stuff?"

"Yeah."

"I don't. I don't like to wait longer. I want to be done and get out of here."

I don't answer. She wonders aloud where the counsellor is.

"That girl was pretty freaked out," I say. "I can't believe they showed her the ultrasound."

"Yeah, but she's had kids, you know? She should know. She knows what it looks like then. She's seen it."

Her jeans are old, she's too thin, and there are lines forming on her still-young face. And she's just had her third abortion. I wonder what comfort she gets from scaring someone like me.

"I just want to leave. Gotta go," she repeats. Her kids will be done at daycare before long, and now she won't have time for a nap.

Finally, the nurse fetches her, and she goes out. She wishes me luck as she leaves.

Minutes later, at 11:30, the door opens, but I don't turn until the nurse addresses me.

"E–?"

"Yes?"

"It's your turn, hon."

I stuff my magazine haphazardly into my bag, and send a few hasty texts. *It's my turn*, to my friend and to the guy. Wearing rainboots and my robe, I follow the nurse out of the room, into the other half of the ward.

We enter a room with a cushioned table in the middle and a rolling cart with a tray on it holding instruments I decide not to think about. Despite the half pill of Ativan, I begin to shake. The room is cool, and I feel as though my blood has stopped circulating.

In a dance I've become used to, the nurse tells me to lie down, scoot down to the edge, and cover myself with the waxy paper sheet she hands me. I've gone through this process over and over in the past few days, so many times that I wondered whose body this was anyway. But soon it would be all mine again. Very soon.

I put my bag down next to the table and hop up, pulling my feet out of my boots. I feel so small, so young, coming in from recess, exchanging boots for indoor shoes. I leave my socks on for warmth. I lie back and shake.

The nurse goes about hooking up the medication to my IV. She tells me to lie with my heels up under my buttocks. I take deep breaths and try to will my body not to shake, first by tensing my muscles then releasing them. "It's cold in here," I say, teeth nearly chattering.

She finds a thick sheet, folded several times, and drapes it across me. The weight of it calms me a bit, settles the shaking. I thank her and breathe slowly.

The table has two stirrups at the end, but they are not the gynecological stirrups for heels. They are wider, and curved. They are for knees.

The nurse tells me that once she has injected the narcotic painkiller, I'll feel loopy, but I'll still be conscious. There is no escaping this moment. As she lowers the plunger and the cool neurological balm moves up my arm, I feel drunk. I wish I felt more drunk, blackout drunk. I already feel scared enough to throw up. She tells me the doctor won't be long. She takes out what looks like a blue paper shower cap and wraps it around my left foot.

"What's that for?" I ask.

She explains to me that it's a precaution, that my left foot would hang close to "the tray."

I curl my toes.

"So," I ask, trying to distract myself, "do you work here often? Or is this like a rotation?"

"No," she says, her tone serious. "You have to apply here specially. You wouldn't want the wrong kind of person to work in here."

I consider these words as she fixes a heart rate monitor to my finger. These women, the ones who'd been poking and prodding, guarding and holding us all day, these women chose this. Day after day, they see women shaking, crying; they watch women struggling against themselves. They are our guardian angels, stand-ins for mothers and partners and girlfriends.

Once the doctor arrives, things happen fast. She greets me and then begins preparing efficiently: gown, gloves, I can't see what else. I stare straight up, willing my consciousness into my body to slow my heart and my breath. Strong hands move my legs into the stirrups, arrange the sheet to obscure my view. As the doctor inserts the speculum, my nurse is back at my side. She starts to explain what's happening—the speculum, the cervix freezing. When the doctor starts the dilation, I gasp in pain.

Before I can react any more, the nurse reaches under the blanket and grabs my hand, tight. She speaks in soft, soothing tones. It's all right. It won't be long.

Please let's get through this, I pray to my body. *I'm so sorry.*

It's very strange to feel a part of your body you've never felt before. It must shock pregnant women at the quickening. It's like having the circulation return to a limb, only unpleasant. It doesn't hurt exactly. It's intense discomfort. It's deep cramping and a dull ache. It feels utterly wrong. I feel the suction reach inside of me and my breathing comes hard. The nurse lets go of my hand to help the doctor, but she returns quickly and takes it again. She has never asked if I want this; she knows. For those brief moments, we bond.

And then the doctor turns off the machine and leaves the room, the tray in hand. She must check to ensure that the abortion is "complete." She returns in a moment and interrupts my relief to go in again to get my IUD, which is stuck. I must have whimpered or moaned, because the nurse squeezes my hand. Moments later, the doctor is done. I thank her, and she leaves.

It's over. It's done. We made it.

◆

The nurse brings my knees down and helps me sit up and put on my underwear.

"How are you feeling?" she asks. She offers to go get a wheelchair.

I'm achy and woozy, but I don't want to hold up the room, so I let her help me to my feet. She carries my backpack, and we walk carefully out and down the hall. I have to lean on her heavily and take deeps breaths to avoid fainting. She settles me into a chair in the recovery room and leaves.

The clock tells me it's been only minutes since I left the sitting room. I watch them continue to tick by while I wait to regain full consciousness. The nurses offer me water and ibuprofen, and then saltine crackers, a stick of cheddar cheese, and jam cookies. Behind a curtain to my left, a girl moans with pain. I feel deep cramps, but I'm told this is good: my emptied uterus is contracting. The pregnancy is over. I suck on my water and wait.

After two trips to a small bathroom to check my bleeding, the nurses decide I can leave. I put on my own clothes carefully, and they lead me to doors at the opposite end of the ward. On the other side, my friend is waiting for me.

A Bad Law and
a Bold Woman

BERNADETTE WAGNER

1985. I've always called it the worst year of my life. A series of unfortunate events tripped me up the summer I turned twenty-three. In no
particular order: sex, a really bad boss, unemployment, and a 1968
Buick.

The sex: great! One of my first orgasms.

The job: itself, not bad. Great pay for typing and answering phones.
But when I lost my only pair of glasses, I couldn't work. The boss I had
considered nice convinced me to quit. She suggested that missing a
week of work while I waited for new specs to arrive would "let down
the team." Fine, I thought. I didn't really love the job. I'd had great
student placements there in the past; this one wasn't one of them.
Earlier that year, another boss, a.k.a. The Dragon Lady, had hauled
me into her office and tried to guilt-trip me into taking full-time
hours during the summer months. I told her I couldn't. She shouted.
I cried and insisted I was taking summer classes. Had I known then
what I now know about collective agreements and workers' rights,
that meeting would have gone differently!

So when the nice boss started in on me, I quit. Unemployment meant spare time. On my way to my dad's for coffee one summery day, a teenager failed to yield as posted. His hot red car smashed into the rear driver's side door of my blue Buick. My car spun counterclockwise through the intersection, up onto the sidewalk, and stopped abruptly when the passenger side door hit the solid steel light post. Police eventually arrived to take my shaky statement. An ambulance hauled me to the hospital, where my dad met me. I was diagnosed with sprains and whiplash and sent on my way with a back brace and painkillers. Flexoril, a painkiller, became my friend.

In Canada in 1985, Madame Justice Bertha Wilson had not yet played her role in striking down Canada's abortion law, the law that created regulations so strict that it was nigh impossible for women to access the procedure. It required a woman to secure the approval of a doctor and the local hospital's Therapeutic Abortion Committee (TAC) if she wanted to terminate a pregnancy. In Saskatchewan, only two hospitals performed abortions, Regina General and Saskatoon City. Few women received the necessary approval in Regina. Some sought services elsewhere. My friend travelled nine hours to a private clinic in North Dakota and experienced severe complications afterward. Wealthy women, and those who could find the money to do so, flew to Toronto, where the Morgentaler Clinic operated. Still others tried to induce their own abortions by various means. Knitting needles, coat hangers, and onions were a few of the methods I'd read about.

My injury had me back and forth to the doctor's office. I'd been thinking that having unprotected sex with a friend was probably not wise. So on one of those trips, I told my doctor I wanted to try the pill. During his process of figuring out which one would work, I learned I was pregnant. I immediately knew I'd have the pregnancy terminated. I did not want, and was not ready for, parenthood. Adoption was out of the question, along with travelling to Toronto or anywhere out of province, for that matter.

The friend who'd had post-abortion complications told me about an underground network she had learned about. This led to my first visit to the Regina Women's Community Centre, an organization to which I would give volunteer time in the future. The woman who offered counsel, Abby, had counselled many women like me over the years. She shared the options available to me. I took a chance on the one doctor in Regina who occasionally supported a woman in jumping through the TAC's hoops.

His office was an ordinary one for older buildings in the downtown core.

The lobby, lined with rows of black vinyl and chrome chairs, had white walls and dark-stained wood trim. Three of us, in various stages of pregnancy, waited. A faint quiver ran through my body. My face felt flushed. He made me nervous. After the physical exam, he confirmed my pregnancy. I then explained why I needed an abortion. I told him it had been the first time this man and I had had intercourse, that I was studying to be a teacher and wanted to finish my degree, that I couldn't afford parenthood. Before I could finish, the doctor turned and walked away from me, shouting, "I will not be a welfare doctor!" What the hell that meant, I did not know. I can suppose, now, that he meant he wouldn't terminate a pregnancy in order to keep a young woman off of welfare. I'll never know for sure. I didn't stick around to quiz him; I left, in tears, more determined than ever to put an end to the pregnancy.

The TACs operated under a residency restriction regarding which hospital could treat which woman. The town of Davidson divided the province. Women living to the north were to use Saskatoon; women in the south, Regina. I lived in Regina, and a woman with the underground network informed me that Dr. John Bury, a Saskatoon doctor sympathetic to women's rights, would perform abortions on women who could provide a Saskatoon address. This option didn't sit too well with me—I didn't want to lie. But I knew beyond a doubt that this road would be the only one available to me. It meant I'd have to tell more people about my pregnancy. I could live with that. But could I live with lying to officials to secure the procedure?

I pulled Lesley, my former roommate and friend living in Saskatoon, in on my plan, made an appointment, and travelled to Saskatoon. My official identification had me living at my dad's house in Regina, but I offered Lesley's Saskatoon address as my own to the intake worker at Dr. Bury's clinic. She did not ask about the address discrepancy. Per the advice I'd received, I added that my studies at the University of Saskatchewan brought me to live here in Saskatoon. Until then, I'd believed my capacity as a liar lacked a certain strength of conviction, but in that moment, I surely could have convinced anyone of the veracity of my statement. I held my quivering nerves in check from the time I arrived until I left. My resolve was firm.

I thought she'd bought my story, along with my very real concerns about the consumption of pain medication during my early pregnancy. She informed me that the doctor's office would call the first week in September. I had a long, sweaty month ahead of me. What if they discovered I'd lied? What if the TAC denied my request?

A Lonely Ride

KRISTEN

If I had known then what I know now—the isolation and fear, the lack of support, both before and after the procedure—I might have a nine-year-old running around. But the abortion I had in 2006 left me with an irreplaceable experience and with knowledge about my rights as a woman and as a person.

My parents were the models for my initial decision. They had decided to have children together. But my partner and I disagreed. He stood his ground and said he'd leave me if I went through with the pregnancy, even if it ended in adoption. I was seventeen years old, suffering from chronic depression, and the thought of being alone was horrible, even life-ending. We had only been together for three months, but I loved him. I relented and made an appointment at a clinic in Toronto, which had been recommended to me by a local youth clinic.

I skipped school two weeks later, with the gracious help of my vice principal, to go to my appointment. It was a forty-five-minute drive to downtown Toronto. I knew the clinic was close when I saw two people standing on the sidewalk with pro-life signs. One showed a picture of a small, bloody fetus. I turned my head away, swearing at them in my mind for being so inconsiderate. I wasn't having this abortion because I wanted to! This wasn't exactly a date night! I didn't want to have a baby on my own, I didn't want to have to tell my parents I was pregnant, and I was only seventeen. Couldn't these pro-life people understand that? Didn't they know that I had agonized over this decision? They knew nothing about me!

We arrived at the clinic and I sat nervously on a couch and waited. My boyfriend whispered to me, "If they ask you if you're sure you want to have an abortion, lie and say yes." I nodded, pained that he would say such a thing to me. A nurse explained to me what would happen during the abortion procedure and handed me a form with a list of general health questions. I found myself asking her for the answers. "Why are you having an abortion?" the questionnaire asked. I asked the nurse if I could say "Because I'm too young to have a baby." If that was my reason, she said, write it down. She proceeded to tell me that the youngest girl served by the clinic was twelve years old. That's so young, I thought. If she can do this, then so can I. I was filled with a courage that wasn't there before. I would be okay.

After speaking with the nurse, I met with Dr. X, the clinic's founder. With a female nurse nearby, he performed my first ultrasound. I should have asked why I needed one; I assumed that it was just for visual confirmation of size or something medical like that. I didn't see the picture. I wasn't asked if I wanted to, and I didn't ask to. We then had a great talk with some laughs about how I came to be at the clinic, and I felt even more courage. Dr. X was a good man.

While I had gone through the intake procedure, the waiting room had filled with more women and their male counterparts. I sat beside mine once again and, while waiting for my name to be called, discreetly checked out the newcomers. They were not all young like me. One woman was probably in her mid-twenties and another in her forties. It was becoming clear that an abortion wasn't something that only "stupid teenagers" needed. It was a service that was required by a variety of women for a variety of reasons. None of us talked to each other. The atmosphere was sombre.

When it was my turn, I was given a local anaesthetic, and any remaining fear dissipated as the drug kicked in. There were two women in the procedure room along with Dr. X. One was the nurse I had spoken to earlier and the other was Dr. X's medical assistant. The drug left me worry free, and we began talking about my pets, my Mormon upbringing, and the musical I had been in recently. The abortion was over in about ten minutes, and I was sent to a reclining chair to recover.

After approximately three hours, I was able to go home under strict instructions: do not use a tampon to collect the blood that would flow out, do not have vaginal sex, and take this pill to prevent infection from occurring in your wide open cervix. It would take two weeks for things down there to go back to normal. I was also sent home with a prescription for birth control pills. The whole ride home, I was quiet and listened to my boyfriend talk about how proud he was—not of me, but of his ability to navigate the city streets.

I didn't do well after the abortion. I wouldn't blame the actual abortion, not now. For a while, my depression and self-harming became worse, but I emphasize that I was subject to both of these prior to the abortion. I couldn't handle the gravity of the decision I had made. My seventeen-year-old mind had to grapple with what an abortion meant. Before my pregnancy, I had said I would never have an abortion. Am I a murderer? Did I do the right thing? Will anyone be able to understand why I had an abortion? I felt tremendous guilt, and I felt it alone.

I've had nine years to think about it, and I now believe that it was the lack of support, not the abortion itself, that made this experience horrible. The religious beliefs of my parents created a fear in me that prevented me from telling them that I was pregnant or that I was having/had had an abortion. They could have been great supporters. To my knowledge, my parents still do not know about this event. If they do, they haven't said anything to me about it.

My friends and partner presented me with no options. It was assumed that I would have an abortion. One friend told me that the abortion procedure was painful and that I would be out of school for a week. But she was wrong. I felt pain for a split second when my cervix was frozen open, and I was back at school the next day.

My partner would not let me grieve. Whenever I became upset, he would begin to cry, which would make me push aside what I was feeling to make sure he was okay. My inability to grieve had some painful results. I ignored my youngest cousin, born a few months after the abortion, for the first six months of his life; I spent a lot of my time blaming myself, and I still experience extreme jealousy and emotional pain when I find out that people I know are going to have children. It's been a lonely ride.

Because of my experience, I feel we need aftercare for women who experience abortions, as well as for the men involved. The clinic knew about my mental health issues, yet there appeared to be no concern about how I might be affected by the abortion. There was no offer of post-abortion support. I have tried to find such support in Toronto, but it seems to be nonexistent. This can be an emotional journey, and the isolation can be a large contributing factor to the negative thoughts and emotions experienced by women and men after abortions.

Fear keeps me from starting my own support group, which friends have suggested I do. Fear keeps me from attending pro-choice events because of the pro-life individuals who may be in attendance. Fear keeps me from talking openly or in depth about the abortion.

I'm tired of the fear and I'm tired of doing this alone. I want to be able to openly share with people my experience. I want to support other women and men who have experienced abortion. I want to be a part of the pro-choice movement openly. I want to eradicate the stigma that surrounds abortion and that keeps some of us silent. But I will still write this without using my real name.

Do I regret the abortion? No. I regret putting myself in the situation, at such a young age, where the decision had to be made. I am lucky that abortion was even an option. I am lucky that the procedure was covered under my provincial health insurance. I am lucky that I lived close to an amazing clinic. Many Canadian women are not this lucky.

What does my abortion mean to me nine years later? It means that even if I didn't know my rights, I had the choice. I didn't have to think twice about where I would go or whether I could afford it. It means that I had an experience that gave me great personal knowledge on a complex moral and medical issue, which is more than a lot of people involved in the pro-life/anti-abortion movement can say. My abortion means that I learned how to be angry about injustice and how to stand up for myself, which is something I had previously found impossible to do. It means that I have given myself the chance to be the mother I want to be—a mother with a loving partner, a stable job, and an emotionally healthy self. It means that I can be a rare support to young women and couples who wish to pursue an abortion. I want to give what I never had.

Without Apology

My abortion was a pivotal experience in my life, but it was difficult. I have never been more aware of the hatred some people feel toward women who undergo the procedure than I have been over the past few years. Fortunately, they don't get to choose what I do, and I firmly believe that I would not be where I am today if I had a child. I am happy with my life and excited to be a mother when I decide the time is right.

[untitled]

Mackenzie

My motivation for sharing my experience of abortion is twofold. First, this is an opportunity to expose Canadians to another unique narrative, to expand our understanding of this complex issue, and to break through some of the stereotypes surrounding who gets abortions and why. Second, this is an excellent outlet for me to unpack and process my own experience. Despite having an amazing partner at the time of my abortion with whom to share my story, for many years I chose not to share it with many important people in my life. This was extremely isolating and difficult. Writing this piece assisted me in further working through my experience.

My previous partner and I found out that I was pregnant in the fall of 2011 a few weeks before my twenty-third birthday. We happen to live about five units down from our city's Planned Parenthood office, and we walked there immediately after getting positive results from several at-home pregnancy tests. We were able to schedule an appointment for the next day.

We knew that we wanted to get an abortion and did not even consider any other options. We had been dating for nine months and had recently moved in together. We were very much in love but were not ready to have a child, the primary reason being that we both wanted to pursue graduate school in our field of study. We were planning to apply the following spring, with a start date of September if we were successful candidates. We also had dreams of travelling and seeing the world together, which would become much more difficult with a child on the way. With jobs in the field of social services, our combined income was not very high. Having a child would certainly strain our financial resources and would inevitably either delay or cancel the possibility of further education, training that would enable us to get better jobs. Finally, I had made many choices that would have negatively impacted the fetus, including smoking cigarettes, drinking alcohol, and using recreational drugs while on vacation.

Our appointment at Planned Parenthood was very difficult for me. The staff members were great and very supportive. They did not try force me to talk about options in which I had no interest. They offered to share as little or as much information about the procedure as I wanted. I chose to hear all of it. I do not deal well with medical interventions; my biggest fear is syringes. However, I knew that this was a decision I was accountable for and therefore I needed to know exactly what I was getting into. As a staff member explained the details of the abortion procedure, I felt extremely sick. I started to cry and became pale and dizzy. I needed to take a break. I was very grateful that my partner was able to be present at this meeting. The staff member left the room for some time so he could comfort me, returning when I was ready to finish the meeting. We then booked my procedure at the local hospital, which was scheduled within two weeks.

The waiting period was also difficult, in two ways. While I was afraid of and dreading the procedure, it was also very difficult to be pregnant and know that I was not planning on keeping the baby. Having to book time off of work was also anxiety provoking. At the time, my partner and I worked at the same agency and we both had to arrange for time off. I was afraid that my employer would find out why we needed time off and would not give it to us. Fortunately, this did not happen.

My procedure took place on 15 September 2011. It was a long day. I had to work the night shift just before that day. It was difficult not to eat or drink all night and not to have the chance to sleep. I had had to arrange to get the end

Without Apology

of my shift covered that morning. My partner met me at the bus terminal, and we left together for the hospital. Upon checking in, the process started fairly quickly. In the waiting room, I completed the necessary paperwork. Next, I was told I would be separated from my partner until the procedure, which wouldn't be for several hours. I was given the choice of having him present at the procedure, which I opted for.

I was taken to have my blood work done, at which time I had an IV inserted into my arm. This was the second worst part of the day. The IV disgusted me and I did my best to ignore it. Then I had to meet with a nurse, who asked me medical questions and explained the procedure. Some of her questions were asked to ensure that I was not being pressured into the procedure. She also encouraged me to go on birth control and referred me to the necessary follow-up appointments through public health. Although I had been on birth control from the age of fifteen to twenty-one, I had used none since then. Admittedly, my partner and I did not make use of other adequate contraceptive methods. We knew better, and we now had to face the consequences of our irresponsibility.

The nurse led me to a locker room, where I was directed to strip down to all but a hospital gown and socks. Next came another waiting room, where all the women waited alone, without their support person, until it was their turn for the procedure. The exception was one woman who, it seemed, did not know English and so was allowed a companion. I remember being extremely angry and jealous about this in the moment, but now, looking at the situation rationally, I completely understand. I waited in this room for about three hours. I was surprised by the variety of women in that room. I expected to see mostly young teenagers; instead, I saw women of many ages and cultures. I was also surprised by the sheer number of women in the room.

The only time I left that second waiting room was for my ultrasound. The technician informed me that the fetus was approximately five weeks old. She did not offer to show me the picture, even on the screen. I'm still not sure if I wanted to see it or not. I'm certainly glad it was not forced on me, but it would have been nice to have been offered the choice. I'm sure if I had asked, she would have shown me.

Immediately after being called in for my procedure, two medications were administered through my IV. One was to soften and dilate my cervix and the other was an anaesthetic, which I opted to take. I was so relieved to be reunited with my partner for the procedure. I was not nearly as enthused to be informed that a student would be performing the procedure, under the direct supervision of a doctor. This really scared me, and I wish I had been told this ahead of time, so I could process it before being drugged up. After hours of waiting, I just wanted to get this over with, and I didn't want to make others wait longer. At this point, I was told that they would be doing a D&C. I was happy to know I would not have to hear the suction machine, which I expected to be traumatizing. My cervix was further dilated with a tenaculum, and the procedure was done very quickly. Although it was painful, the drugs eased the discomfort and clouded my mind. My partner was holding my hand and was very comforting, keeping eye contact with me the whole time. All I felt was the pain and the tears dripping down my cheeks, but I knew he was there with me.

After the procedure, a big pad was placed against my vulva and mesh underwear pulled over me. I was then escorted, without my partner, to the recovery room, where I spent the next half hour and was given antibiotics, crackers, and ginger ale. We took a cab home and spent the day on the couch watching *Gilmore Girls*. Later, my partner cycled over to pick up my favourite Chinese takeout.

I did bleed and spot for quite a while after the procedure, but it was nothing abnormal. My six-week check-up also came back normal. At this appointment, I was again pressured to go on birth control. This irritated me. I knew that I had made poor decisions, and I felt that the public health nurse was rubbing it in my face. As a woman who had consistently taken care of my sexual health since the age of fifteen, in addition to having a university degree in sexuality, I did not feel this was necessary. Please, make me aware of my options, but do not tell me what to do with my body.

The worst part of this whole experience was the shame and isolation. I was so lucky to have the support of my partner and a few close friends with whom I had shared the situation. We did not tell any family members, although this changed over the years. I remember one particular conversation, about a month after my abortion, when I was visiting my father. He was talking about abortions—in particular, how irresponsible the women who have them are—and he said that he was so relieved that *his* daughters would never need any such service or make that choice. I, of course, argued against his position, but not on the basis of personal experience. I felt horrible hearing my father say that. But I felt even more horrible for not having stood up for women's choice by sharing my experience—for not having revealed that even his own daughter would choose to have an abortion. I felt guilty for not disclosing this, believing that I was contributing to the perpetuation of the stereotypes and discrimination that women from all walks of life face when making this difficult decision.

At the time, I didn't know if I wanted to tell my family. I did know that I didn't want to feel shame about a decision that I needed to make in order to make my life and future better. I feel like my silence may have contributed to these negative feelings. Every time I disclose my story, I do feel slightly more empowered. Abortion is a huge taboo. But fuck it. Don't expect to bring up abortion and not have people challenge your beliefs when they do not come from a place of personal experience. I am not trying to say that people do not have a right to their own opinions—they do. But I also think that lived experience is a huge part of understanding this very complex issue.

When I originally wrote this, seven months after my abortion, my partner and I were still together and stronger than ever. However, this time was not without its difficulties. Being around friends who were pregnant was challenging. We both ended up being accepted into grad school and went on to complete our programs and get jobs in our field. We also got married in the summer of 2013 and spent our honeymoon backpacking across Europe. All of our dreams were right before our eyes. These were dreams that probably would not have been possible, or at least not until the far future, if we had gone through with our pregnancy. We were also using contraception *every* time!

One of the hardest parts of processing the abortion was knowing that, despite the hardships we would have experienced, we could have done it. We could have raised our child, whom we would have loved dearly. We did want children in the future. I think it would have been a challenge to have these children and know of the child who never had the chance to be part of our family. But this was part of our story together: it made us who we were as a couple. We knew that if we decided to have children, it would be on our own schedule—when we were ready and prepared to fully embrace and appreciate such a blessing.

part two

**Abortion
Rights
Activism**

Reproductive Freedom

The Ontario Coalition for Abortion Clinics and the Campaign to Overturn the Federal Abortion Law

CAROLYN EGAN & LINDA GARDNER

A historic battle took place in this country in the late twentieth century between the women's movement and the Canadian state. Advocates for women's rights won a major victory when the Supreme Court of Canada overturned the federal abortion law in January 1988. At the time, the campaign for full access to free abortion was situated in the broader context of reproductive freedom. Abortion rights was seen as only one of a number of demands of the women's movement in the fight for reproductive rights for all.[1]

Before the law was struck down, women had access to abortion, but it was a very privileged access. In 1969, legislation was passed that allowed abortions to be performed if they took place in an approved or accredited hospital with the consent of a Therapeutic Abortion Committee. The committee had to comprise three doctors whose role was to determine whether the continuation of a pregnancy would impact on the physical or mental health of the woman. If they decided that it would, the woman would be allowed an abortion.

There was uneven interpretation of the law across the country, and many hospitals did not establish committees. The law was unjust in that it denied women the right to make decisions over their reproductive health.

In practice, the 1969 law resulted in very inequitable access. Women with economic resources who could afford a private gynecologist or travel to the United States or Montréal could get an abortion. Many racialized, Indigenous, working-class, rural, and young women did not have access. In spite of the claims that Canada had universal health care, there was a two-tiered system.

In Toronto, workers from the Immigrant Women's Health Centre, the Birth Control and VD Information Centre, and the Hassle Free Clinic decided that they had to challenge a system that was denying abortions to many of those using their services. They spoke every day with women who were being treated in a humiliating and degrading manner and were made to leap through hoops to access abortion. They felt strongly that the federal law was fundamentally flawed: not only did it take the decision out of the hands of women but it was racist and class biased in its application. They and others (ourselves included) formed the Ontario Coalition for Abortion Clinics (OCAC) in 1982.

The group thought long and hard about how best to change an increasingly desperate situation for so many women. We looked at the province of Québec, where CLSCs (Centres locaux de services communautaires, or local community services centres) and Centres de santé des femmes (women's health centres) were providing abortions to women in their own communities. We modelled our campaign on that of our sisters in Québec. The strategy involved a combination of a doctor willing to challenge the law and a broad and representative movement willing to fight for the necessary changes.

OCAC was a grassroots, activist organization. The immediate objectives were to overturn the federal law and to legalize free-standing clinics providing medically insured abortions. The membership set out to win full access to free abortion for all women. OCAC made clear in its organizing that it should be a fundamental right for women to make the decision to terminate a pregnancy and that the facilities must be in place to allow them to do so. Members also felt that the movement needed an analysis that went much further. OCAC believed that women must also have the right to bear the children they choose to bear. This was a perspective that activists from the

Immigrant Women's Health Centre had put forward in earlier campaigns to remove barriers to abortion and sexual health services.

We were aware of the limits of the notion of "choice." Full access to free abortion, as significant an advance as that would be, does not guarantee that all women have choices in directing their lives or in having or raising children. The definition of "choice" was broadened in our organizing. OCAC stated that for all women to have real choices in our society, they require safe and effective birth control services in their own languages and their own communities, decent jobs, paid parental leave, child care, the right to live freely and openly regardless of their sexuality, an end to forced or coerced sterilization, employment equity, and, of course, full access to free abortion. All were required if women were to have reproductive freedom.[2]

OCAC tried to ensure that the demand for abortion access was never seen in isolation but as one of a number of interdependent struggles. We tried to make this concrete by challenging the coerced sterilization that Indigenous women, women with disabilities, and black women were facing. We held joint forums on the issues, at which women spoke about the injustices that they were experiencing. Health care workers told us that Therapeutic Abortion Committees sometimes refused abortions unless a woman agreed to be sterilized. We fought for child care as a woman's right and campaigned against extra billing by doctors. AIDS activists spoke at our rallies, describing the pressures exerted on HIV-positive women to have abortions and tubal ligations. We worked very closely with the Midwives Collective.

We believed that the choice to have a child can never be free in a society where many women earn much less than men, where quality child care and affordable housing are not available, where inequity and discrimination are systemic. We found this reproductive rights perspective (today often referred to as reproductive justice) to be vital to the success of our organizing, because it reflected the reality of women's lives, broadened the base of the movement, and explicitly dealt with issues of class and race. A long campaign against two levels of government and an organized anti-choice movement began.

OCAC worked with Dr. Henry Morgentaler, who, in 1983, opened a clinic challenging the federal Criminal Code. He agreed to establish the clinic if we mobilized broad support and built a movement to defend it. The clinic became a symbol of women's resistance to an unjust law. Women made appointments for abortions at the clinic knowing full well that the government viewed it to be illegal. They faced police surveillance and anti-choice harassment, standing up to both and demanding their right to abortion by defying the law. They were a varied group, including women without health cards, Indigenous women from northern reserves, and women who could not speak English. They were the true heroines of the movement, risking exposure and arrest, and they continued to come. Safe houses were established in the neighbourhood, and volunteer escorts accompanied them to the clinic.

It did not take long before the facility was raided by the police: Drs. Morgentaler, Scott, and Smoling were arrested and the medical equipment seized. This was not unexpected, and OCAC had been building broad support. We knew we were going to be in a long, drawn-out campaign. We had to change the balance of power in the country; while the issue had to be in the courts because of the arrests, the critical task was mobilizing the strong support that we knew was there for women's reproductive rights. Judges do not sit in isolation, and we had to show that the law was unenforceable and ensure that a jury would not convict the doctors.

OCAC took a mass action approach. We did not leave the campaign to the lawyers or to the lobbying of politicians. We believed that tens of thousands of women and men would come into the streets across the country to fight for women's reproductive freedom. Groups took up the cause in every province, and the Canadian Abortion Rights Action League fought side by side with us. Members and allies spoke at labour conventions, to community organizations, on campuses, and to faith communities. At the very start, we won a resolution at the Ontario Federation of Labour convention, and individual unions followed suit. Women Working with Immigrant Women in Toronto was a strong supporter, helping to organizing meetings in diverse communities. We began building step by step, and the popular support grew.

In linking its various struggles together, OCAC was able to build a wide campaign through demonstrations, marches, and rallies in which thousands participated. Speakers from many communities spoke about the situation they were facing and about the importance of working together to address the inequities that so many women were up against. We always tried to involve ourselves in movement building. Through our organizing, we were able to broaden participation in the campaign to trade unionists, students, AIDS activists, people of colour, and immigrant women's organizations. We understood that without active participation and the support of thousands, no change would occur.

After the raid of the Morgentaler Clinic, we were caught in the courts for almost a year on a constitutional challenge, through which the state tried to demobilize the movement. An Ontario Supreme Court Justice ruled that the federal abortion law was constitutional. He stated that the Canadian Charter of Rights and Freedoms protects only those rights that are spelled out in law or "rooted deeply in our traditions." Well, abortion is certainly rooted in women's traditions. In the actual trial, the jury unanimously rejected this interpretation by finding the doctors innocent. The government appealed the acquittal, but the clinic reopened and the movement gained tremendous momentum.

Our goal was to build a visible, mass movement that fought as one for women's reproductive freedom. The full message was often lost in the media presentations, where most of the attention was given to the single issue of overturning the federal abortion law. We undoubtedly could have done it better. Achieving the best balance between short- and long-term goals, between the polemical value of the "choice" slogan and the constraints of such arguments was difficult sometimes. We didn't always make the right decisions and were under tremendous pressure with so much at stake. There were many debates about the best way forward. Strategic complexities and dilemmas were not made easier in a movement that was constantly under direct attack from the state and the conservative right.[3]

OCAC was a voluntary organization raising money though donations, garage sales, and benefits, with only one staff person at the height of the struggle. We openly debated questions, scheduling general membership meetings every two weeks, and always tried to choose the course of action that would involve the largest number of people. At strategic junctures, we advertised open public strategy meetings to involve everyone interested in determining our next steps. Many people who could not commit themselves to the organization in an ongoing way could attend such meetings.

When the Supreme Court finally overturned the existing abortion law in 1988, it was through the strength of a broad and representative movement. It was a collective victory in which tens of thousands played an active role. The fact that OCAC understood that the state was not neutral and was not acting in the interests of women was critical to the success of our campaign. We believed that only a mass movement could change the balance of forces in the interest of all women.

There was a spontaneous demonstration of thousands of supporters outside the Morgentaler Clinic when the decision of the Supreme Court was announced. Women and men were dancing in the street! Similar rallies erupted across the country. Freestanding clinics were legalized in Ontario, fully covered by the health care system, and clinics began to open in other parts of the country as well. A number of facilities in Ontario were able to provide abortions to women without health cards as a result of our organizing.

It did not take long before the Conservative government in Ottawa began the process of introducing new legislation recriminalizing abortion, with Bill C-43 in 1990. Because of the strong roots that had been developed, a major campaign against a new law was launched. There was wide support from groups such as the National Organization of Immigrant and Visible Minority Women, the Canadian Labour Congress, the National Council of Jewish Women, the Federation des femmes du Québec, the United Church of Canada, the Canadian Medical Association, AIDS Action Now! and a large range of provincial and local organizations across the country. On national days of action, thousands poured into the streets. Tragically, during this period, a young woman in Toronto died from a self-induced abortion because she believed a legal procedure was not available.

During the campaign against the new law and for increased access, anti-choice forces continued another assault. Operation Rescue, as they called it, had started in Toronto in the fall of 1988 and attempted to blockade the entrance to the Morgentaler Clinic. They physically and verbally harassed women seeking abortions. OCAC organized defence of clinics in Toronto, a number of which had opened after the law was struck down, rejecting the argument that it should be left to the police to protect these facilities. Supporters would sometimes spend the night when we were given advance warning and would be outside waiting for Operation Rescue members to arrive in the early morning. We would link arms and chant: "Racist, sexist, anti-gay, born again bigots, go away" and "Campaign Life, your name's a lie. You don't care if women die"—chants that reflected the politics of the campaign.

It was not unusual for members of the United Steelworkers, the Black Women's Coalition, Women Working with Immigrant Women, EcoMedia, AIDS Action Now! and the Canadian Auto Workers, along with Indigenous activists, to stand shoulder to shoulder to defend the clinics. Because of this strong mobilization and community support, Operation Rescue was stopped. This speaks to the strength of the movement-building strategy and the active alliance building. Those who defended the services believed that the clinics were legal and accessible as a result of their collective struggle, and they were committed to defending them. This broad support created the political pressure to defeat Bill C-43 in the Senate in January 1991, after it narrowly passed in the House of Commons.

As Women Working with Immigrant Women (WWIW) said in a statement when the law was defeated,

> Today, we applaud the death of Bill C43 acknowledging that collective visible actions by many different constituencies led to its defeat. We strongly support OCAC's position that the legal right to choose, as important as it is, is meaningless unless fully funded services exist to give every woman the opportunity to make that choice in her own language and her own community. WWIW will continue to work with OCAC to pressure the federal government to implement the Canada Health Act to ensure that every province provides full access to free abortion and to insist that the provinces provide this critical service with all the other demands that will ensure real choices in our lives.[4]

There are now more than thirty free-standing clinics providing funded abortions across the country. Access is much wider than when the OCAC campaign began in the early 1980s, and sexual health services are more widely available. A major victory was finally won when, in response to a legal challenge by Abortion Access Now PEI, the province announced its intention to make abortion services available by the end of 2016, at which point women living in Prince Edward Island will no longer be forced to go to the mainland to access abortions. But the fight for reproductive justice is far from over. New Brunswick still refuses to fund clinic procedures. Hospital amalgamations and health care cuts are reducing reproductive services in many areas. Women are still being harassed as they enter clinics. The Harper government initially refused to fund International Planned Parenthood Federation and then decided to give money on the condition that it be allocated only in countries where abortion is illegal. The Liberal government elected in 2015 has reversed this decision. In Canada, there is no national child care program, equal pay for work of equal value is still a dream for many, employment equity has not been implemented, systemic discrimination still exists, and many of the other services necessary for women to have real choices in their lives are not in place. Private members' bills are regularly being introduced in the House of Commons to create barriers for women to access abortion. To date, all have been defeated.

Support for reproductive justice is still very strong across the country. While the overall strategic situation has changed and will continue to change, the lessons of the campaign waged in the 1980s still remain relevant. The principles and tactics that were used created a broad-based movement that overturned the federal abortion law and created a network of clinics, making abortion much more accessible for women who were previously denied that service. We must continue to put pressure on the federal and provincial governments today so that all women have what is required to live their lives with the dignity and respect they deserve. What we won are initial and partial victories, to be sure, but still major gains for women's reproductive justice.

Notes

1 Carolyn Egan, "The Right to Choose," *Our Times*, June 1985, 30.
2 Ibid.
3 Ontario Coalition for Abortion Clinics, "Feminist Struggles and State Regulation: Controlling Women's Reproductive Rights," *Resources for Feminist Research / Documentation sur la recherche féministe* 17, no. 3 (1998): 111.
4 Women Working with Immigrant Women, statement on the defeat of Bill C-43 (news release), 31 January 1991. The statement was written by Judy Vashti Persad and Salome Loucas.

Handmaids on the Hill

Defending Our Rights One Womb at a Time

AALYA AHMAD & THE RADICAL HANDMAIDS

On 25 April 2012, a small grassroots group of (mostly) young women donned outfits inspired by Margaret Atwood's 1985 novel, *The Handmaid's Tale*, and went to Parliament Hill for a little "cosplay" to protest Motion 312—Conservative MP Stephen Woodworth's attempt to reopen the abortion debate by proposing that a Parliamentary committee be established to revisit the question of fetal personhood. We called ourselves the Radical Handmaids.

In addition to our red dresses and white "flying nun" hats or gauzy red veils, à la Volker Schlöndorff's 1990 film adaptation of Atwood's book, we carried a fabric-covered plywood "wall" to which we pinned many colourful knitted wombs and vulvas. These had been knitted by groups of people united under a Facebook page titled "Womb Swarm Parliament: Textile Artists United Against Motion M-312" and sent to the Handmaids (care of the Canadian Union of Postal Workers) from all over the country. The reasoning behind these multicoloured

Figure 1. The Radical Handmaids arrive on Parliament Hill to protest Motion 312.
Photograph: Garth Gullekson, Darlington Mediaworks.

woolly parts was that if politicians wanted to control uteruses so badly, they should have "a womb of their own" to lord it over so that they could leave ours alone. The group's stated goal was to collect enough uteruses and vulvas to send one to each MP in Parliament. Had we kept going with our call beyond the protest, we would certainly have succeeded.

It was a moving experience to see these knitted works of activism come in. Some arrived with accompanying cards and little notes to the Handmaids. One, from "The Rhizome Kids" in Vancouver, read:

> To the Radical Handmaids,
> Thank you so much for representing us in Ottawa and taking our crafts to the streets!! You all rock! Enjoy the protest and the wombs and vulvas.

Another read:

> Hello,
> Here are the 2 wombs I managed to complete. I haven't stuffed them so they fit in an envelope. I'm sorry there isn't more, it's a little difficult with my 4-month-old. If we plan on sending more past the beginning of the debate, please let me know and I'll try to send more.

Our protest took place the day before the opening debate on Woodworth's Motion 312, on 26 April 2012. The motion was supposed to return to the House of Commons in June but was postponed until 21 September, with the vote taking place on 26 September. As expected, the motion did not pass, but ninety-one MPs—four Liberals and the rest Conservatives—voted in favour of reopening the abortion debate, including the minister responsible for the Status of Women, Rona Ambrose (who, after the election of the Trudeau-led Liberals in October 2015, became the interim leader of the Conservative Party). Woodworth's initiative has not been, nor will it be, the only attempt to recriminalize abortion in Canada. In May 2012, another Conservative MP, Maurice Vellacott, tried to appropriate the International Day Against Homophobia and Transphobia to suggest, bizarrely, that abortion bullies the fetus in the womb.[1]

It's tempting to regard these anti-choice proposals as little more than quaint flare-ups of an outmoded and marginal ideology. Eyebrows may be raised at the suggestion that campaigns against bullying should extend to fetuses, but no matter what's happening south of the border, in Canada, a perception endures that the War on Women is only a silly skirmish—

Figure 2. Wombs of their own for members of Parliament.

Photograph: Garth Gullekson, Darlington Mediaworks.

Figure 3. Knitted works of activism from all across the country.
Photograph: Radical Handmaids.

interesting to observe or debate but unlikely to have any real consequences for women's lives, even with a Conservative federal government in power. Therefore, the Radical Handmaids were met with shrugs and why-bothers from some quarters. Even Margaret Atwood herself said in 2011, prior to the Conservatives' return as a majority, that a debate on abortion ought to be had, albeit located within its proper context:

> Harper says he will not allow a debate on abortion. But he should allow it. All aspects of this troublesome question—and it has been trouble-some throughout history, as there are no lovely answers—should be thoroughly discussed. There should be clarity on Harper's attitude to women and children and their well-being. Let them die of mal-nutrition? Supply adequate diet, public support if there's no income, protection from rape and enforced prostitution, improved adoption procedures, education, better hospitals and access to drugs, new orphanages, enforced chastity, unwillingly pregnant women locked up in mega-jails, payment per baby if baby-making is service provided to the state, pace Napoleon? What's it to be? Spit it out. Let us know what may be coming soon to a neighbourhood near us.[2]

Of course—and Atwood's intention was undoubtedly to highlight this dismal reality—those whose bodies and lives are particularly vulnerable to such debates, fertile women, are condemned to watch from the sidelines.

As Atwood makes clear, the problem with the view that such a debate is harmless is its dislocation from the context in which it needs to be firmly situated—the Harper Conservatives' relentless erosion of hard-won feminist gains since their first rise to power as a minority in 2006. Looked at in this way, the attacks on reproductive rights, however silly, become not marginal but central to the steady pattern of an anti-feminist backlash. Too often, abortion rights are isolated from their intrinsic connection with the other rights that feminists have fought for. And yet those rights—including access to education, affordable child care, freedom from stifling poverty, and the ability to leave abusive partners, to name only a few—are integral to women's ability to choose whether, when, and with whom they will have children.

We know that something is wrong with debating fetal personhood, as M-312 would have had us do, as if the woman carrying the fetus has no personhood of her own. Since 2006, feminist organizations have been incessantly battered by policies that treat women as "baby-makers," as the irrepressible feminist journalist Antonia Zerbisias puts it, without even the traditional respect for that role that is supposed to be its partial reward.[3]

Figure 4. Saying no to the recriminalization of abortion.
Photograph: Garth Gullekson, Darlington Mediaworks.

Take, for example, child care—or the lack of it. We live in a society that richly rewards financial "experts" who swindle and bankrupt its citizens but that deems it perfectly acceptable to pay its child care workers peanuts. The lack of concern for children and the women who do most of the caregiving work is blatant. One of the first acts of the newly elected Conservative government in 2006 was to kill provincial child care agreements that would have led to the creation of a universal child care program, implementing instead a monthly taxable $100 handout that does nothing to address the lack of child care spaces so desperately needed by working parents.[4] In Canada, the percentage of women aged fifteen and over who participate in the workforce increased from 45.7 percent in 1976 to 61.8 percent in 2005. In 2001, 69.8 percent of women with children at home (regardless of age) and 65.8 percent of women with children under two years of age participated in the labour force.[5] Feminists have been struggling for decades to get this through to people, which is why it was so painful to see the

Conservatives—at the time of M-312 still a minority—block our baby steps toward a national child care program that would have been Canada's first universal social program since the achievement of health care.

Anti-choicers have very little to say on the subject of child care. At the March 4 Life on 9 May 2012, for which tax-subsidized Catholic school boards sent busloads of kids to Parliament Hill, one sign held by a high school student suggested that forced pregnancies were rightful punishments for women who were supposed to have "kept your legs shut," conveying a demeaning stereotype of promiscuous young women and ignoring the fact that many married women with children also get abortions.

One might suppose that those professing concern for the fetus would support good-quality, accessible, universal child care, but the reverse seems to hold true—the idea that a child is punishment for the mother forces her to drop out of the workforce altogether or, more commonly, in these days of struggling working parents, accept precarious or inferior working conditions and scramble for whatever child care she can find. Such conditions are hardly the best for children to grow up in, but for those who are anti-choice, concern for children appears to evaporate once they are no longer in utero. In a press release issued just prior to our day of protest, we tried to make this connection to affordable child care very clear in our closing comment: "Affordable daycare for working parents isn't on the agenda," we wrote. "Apparently you have to be a fetus to matter to a Conservative."[6] To nobody's surprise, none of the many mainstream media covering our protest made such a connection.

One goal of our event was to have a protest that was not the officious and boring type of rally so often seen in Ottawa. We wanted a funky, cheeky third-wave feminist protest that would respect the grassroots nature of our group and its roots in cultural production, as well as the DIY spirit of the Womb Swarm. Many of us in the group were veterans of social justice and reproductive rights activism and did not want to simply reproduce the same old hierarchies of tub-thumping speakers and yelling crowds. At the same time, a certain degree of scripting was necessary for us to have an organized event. Representatives of the Canadian Labour Congress and political parties, particularly the NDP, showed up to support us, which we appreciated, and they all wanted to speak at our rally.

One of the ways in which we accommodated our allies while countering the tendency to fall into the familiar patterns of speaker hierarchies was to

Figure 5. Anti-bullying? March 4 Lifers engage in verbal assaults on women.
Photograph: Jordan Reid.

Figure 6. Fighting not only for women's reproductive rights but for social justice.
Photograph: Garth Gullekson, Darlington Mediaworks.

form circles wherever possible. We held hands around the Centennial Flame, and we closed the event by fanning out on the lawns of the Hill in a large circle and then coming together while chanting slogans. In this way, we literally put our bodies "out there" to dramatize our solidarity and unity. With the help of some protesters from Montréal who regaled us with funny parodies of pop song medleys—"You Can't Touch This" being one favourite—we ended our protest in a positive and upbeat spirit, vowing to continue our fight.

Figure 7. Circling the Centennial Flame in solidarity.
Photograph: Garth Gullekson, Darlington Mediaworks.

Since then, the Radical Handmaids have shown up at anti-abortion events such as the annual March 4 Life and the New Abortion Caravan, which appropriated feminist herstory for a drive across Canada in trucks bearing graphic oversized photos of dismembered fetuses. In Ottawa, Handmaids participated in the protest against the Caravan organized by the Canadian Auto Workers and held a public education awareness day in Byward Market. Radical Handmaids in Vancouver and other parts of the country are also getting active. Despite the election of a new, pro-choice government in 2015, we know the struggle is not over.

Acknowledgements

Many thanks to photographers Garth Gullekson, Jordan Reid, and Jenn Farr for documenting our activism in images. The Radical Handmaids also wish to thank the Canadian Union of Postal Workers for its support. For more information about the Radical Handmaids, please visit our Facebook page and website.

Notes

1   Jennifer Ditchburn, "For Tory Backbencher, Abortion Is 'Bullying in the Worst Degree," *Globe and Mail*, 17 May 2012.

2   Margaret Atwood, "My Paper Napkin Guide to the Election," *Toronto Star*, 25 April 2011.

3   Antonia Zerbisias, "Harper's Plan Helps Women Only as Baby-makers," *Toronto Star*, 29 January 2010.

4   Moma Ballantyne, "Harper and Child Care," in *The Harper Record*, ed. Teresa Healey (Ottawa: Canadian Centre for Policy Alternatives, 2008), 339–44.

5   Statistics Canada, *Canada's Workforce: Paid Work, 2001 Census*, catalogue no. 95F0378XIE2001004. See "Indicators of Well-Being in Canada—Canadians in Context: Households and Families," Employment and Social Development Canada, http://well-being.esdc.gc.ca/misme-iowb/.3ndic.1t.4r@-eng.jsp?iid=37.

6   "Handmaids on the Hill Protest Conservatives' Anti-abortion Bill," news release, 25 April 2012, http://www.newswire.ca/news-releases/handmaids-on-the-hill-protest-conservatives-anti-abortion-bill-510088251.html.

Breaking the Silence Through Portrait and Story

Arts4Choice

MARTHA SOLOMON

When I was about six or seven years old, I came across a box of tampons in our bathroom cupboard. I knew I had seen it before and had probably looked inside, but until that point, I had just classified the box and its contents as "adult stuff" that wasn't particularly interesting or noteworthy. But for some reason, on this day, I asked my mother what these things were.

"Tampons," she replied.

"What are they for?" I asked.

"Women use them when they menstruate."

"When they what?"

My mother has always been great at explaining things—she is straightforward, almost clinical. I appreciate this. But her explanation on that day shocked me. I was rattled. Women bleed every month? This seemed so improbable to me, but I knew my mother would not lie to me about this. I remember feeling the room spin slightly. How could I not have known? I remember asking my mother about each and every woman I knew—aunts, teachers, and friends of the family. Did they all menstruate? Yes, she assured me, they all did.

I was so disturbed by the fact that I had not known about this deeply important—even sacred—bodily function and that all the women I knew not only experienced this but hid it, kept it secret, did their best never to discuss it. Questions raced through my mind: How did I not know? Why did they keep this a secret? And most importantly—what else were they keeping secret?

Noticing that women kept their reproductive lives secret stayed with me as I grew older. In my teen years and early twenties, I noticed that this secrecy also applied to sexuality, birth control, abortion, pregnancy, birth, and menopause.

When a close friend of mine became pregnant in her early twenties, she stayed with my mother and I while she had her abortion. It was a difficult time, and once again, I noticed this secrecy creeping up. My friend was feeling very alone and isolated; she did not want her family to know that she was pregnant. At one point, my mother had a friend over for dinner, and the four of us were sitting around the table chatting. In a very nonchalant way, my mom's friend asked my friend why she was staying with us, and there was an uncomfortable silence. While my mind was racing, trying to figure out a way to "fix" the situation, my friend replied that she was staying with us while she had an abortion. My mother's friend very quickly responded that she too had had an abortion and shared her story. For me, this experience was the antithesis of that first experience with the secrecy surrounding women's reproductive lives. This was a warm, compassionate, open, and caring response. The urge to share, to comfort and reassure, was palpable and keenly felt. It was a remarkable moment that stayed with me as a touchstone for the importance of sharing our stories with each other, of breaking down the habit of secrecy.

This idea of keeping secrets, of not sharing our stories, has been an integral part of my own feminist research over the years and was the major impetus for the founding of Arts4Choice (www.arts4choice.com). In 2007, the *Ottawa Citizen* published an article about the lengthy wait times faced by many women seeking abortions in the National Capital Region. The author claimed that women were not interested in the abortion issue, were not even thinking about abortion, and until they were, nothing would change. Angered by the article, my friend and colleague, Kathryn Palmateer, and I founded Arts4Choice. The goal of Arts4Choice was to kick-start discussion about women's real experiences of abortion in Canada, to break the silence and replace secrecy with open and compassionate sharing. We firmly believe that every woman should have the right to a timely abortion on demand, no questions asked. We also believe that no woman should be made to feel fearful or ashamed for having exercised her right to reproductive freedom. We want to show Canadians that women are indeed interested in the abortion issue and that women who have had abortions are their neighbours, sisters, mothers, and friends.

It seemed to us that photographic portraits and personal stories would be the boldest and potentially the most transformative means to achieving the goals of Arts4Choice. Breaking the taboo about discussing women's abortion experiences in a genuine and accessible way meant that readers must be able to "meet" each woman, almost as though they were sitting around the table together. The portraits and stories, working together, do just this. The result is a deeply personal and political experience for both the readers/viewers and the participants. For many participants, this is the first time they have gone public with their experience, the first time they have taken pen to paper (or fingers to keyboard) to write about the events surrounding their abortion(s), the first time they have put their faces forward. For many readers/viewers, this is the first time they have read about women's abortion experiences, seen the faces of women just like them or their partners. One of our main hopes was that the process and the result would be empowering for both the readers/viewers and the participants.

The response to the project has been overwhelming. The Arts4Choice photos and stories have been part of two Toronto exhibits, have been featured in the *Globe and Mail*, and were awarded a Multi-Arts Grant in 2008 from the Ontario Arts Council. In 2014, we celebrated the publication of an Arts4Choice book, *One Kind Word: Women Share Their Abortion Stories* (released by Toronto's Three O'Clock Press).

But breaking the silence is hard work. It involves courage and compassion, for others and for ourselves. It involves undoing years and years of habitually silencing ourselves about our reproductive lives. The good news is that when one woman shares her abortion experience, she inspires many more to do so as well. Apparently, sharing stories is infectious!

Many women who have taken part in Arts4Choice have mentioned that they would have felt so much less isolated during their abortion experiences if they had known of other women's experiences. Again and again, the story-tellers mention that one of their motivations for participating is that they do not want other women to feel this same sense of isolation. We care about each other and want to help each other, but, to do this, we must stop keeping parts of our lives secret.

Keeping secrets is not the same as respecting privacy. For many women, having an abortion is a deeply private event in their lives, one that they do not wish to share publicly. But the line between privacy and secrecy can be a thin one. Secrets are invariably tinged with a fear of discovery. Secrets can leave people feeling muzzled, fearful, and ashamed. Privacy, however, involves the ability to determine where and with whom we share information without fear of shame or retribution.

During my years at Arts4Choice, my understanding of the importance of sharing abortion experiences has become more nuanced, and despite the recent change in federal government to a party that identifies itself as pro-choice, I believe that such sharing of stories is becoming even more imperative. It is essential that together we create a safe and accessible space for women to come together to learn from one another and support one another. We must share our abortion stories for many reasons:

- To ensure that women's lived experiences are front and centre in any abortion debate in this country and to expose the lies of anti-choicers.

- To create, together, safe and accessible spaces for women to come together to learn from one another and support one another. Telling our stories inspires other women to do the same and creates a community of support and activism.

- To provide support for women who are currently making their decision about abortion or who have had an abortion and feel isolated or alone.

- To counter the anti-choice rhetoric that seeks to create a monolithic and negative stereotype about women who have abortions. Women who have abortions are our friends, neighbours, teachers, aunts, nieces, daughters, and political leaders.

- To place abortion and abortion care squarely within the continuum of women's reproductive lives as a normal and common event.

- To help illuminate the very real problem of access to abortion in Canada today. We need to hear women's real experiences of barriers to reproductive freedom, especially those that are geographical and financial.

- To ensure that women receive excellent medical care and support in hospitals and clinics across the country. Without women stepping forward to report instances of anti-choice pressure or subpar services, problems of quality and accessibility will not be resolved.

The primary lesson underlying my drive to share women's abortion experiences is that we cannot leave the abortion issue in someone else's hands. These are our rights, our bodies, our choices. Our reproductive freedom is our own: we cannot allow others to make decisions for us. Wendy M's story of her pre-Morgentaler abortion in 1986 reminds us of this:

> Though it is now quite a long time ago and some of my memories are gone, I remember feeling very daunted by the screening of the Therapeutic Abortion Committee at the hospital. It was clear to me, at every step, that the process could be denied to me. Such a momentous decision about my life was in the hands of others—people who did not know me, people who went home at the end of the day after having done their jobs. I remember being quite frightened. I don't remember talking with anyone about these feelings.

"We Can Get There Faster If We All Move Together"

The Birth and Evolution of a Reproductive Justice Activist

COLLEEN MACQUARRIE

By the time I am five, sexual assault has branded me with shame, fragmented my heart, and bit my tongue with silence. At twelve, a daytime assault in my home coagulates the message that my body is not my own. I hear every demeaning sexual slur and know that, but for the direction of the wind, it could be directed at me. Perhaps this is every woman's story and I don't know it. Twelve becomes sixteen—I want to keep my boyfriend, so even though I say no, and mean it, he pushes, and cajoles, and I give in. The social scripts are tedious in their predictability here as elsewhere. At sixteen, date rape isn't yet a concept in my mind, but pregnancy is. I recoil from the scrutiny: death might be better than public shaming, and my community knows how to shame a "knocked-up slut" to death. I know nothing about safe abortion. My period returns. I have a birth control prescription but feel too ashamed to have it filled at the pharmacy. Besides, I am without a job to pay for it. So I return home and disclose that I am sexually active to my mother, who helps me. Thank you, Mom. You are loving and kind and supportive, and I need that.

Protections from sexually transmitted infections are unheard of in my teen heterosexual world. I am unaware, uninformed, unprotected, all the while smugly encircled by the preventable pregnancy myth. There is no information, no health class in which to talk about positive relationships, let alone sexual ones, and the role models are caricatures. My girlfriends and I trade information; cautiously, we build our sisterhood. Despite precautions, at least three become unexpectedly pregnant and end up being parents before their time. "Choice" is not a word on any of our lips. Abortion is not even considered, given the public furor over it, led intensely by the Catholic Church, with which our school and community is closely affiliated. Abortion is just not an option for a teen in Prince Edward Island in the early 1980s, nor is it an option for anyone in the province, really.

The PEI Right to Life Association, heavily funded by faith-based organizations, has been aiming to eradicate from the province what few reproductive options we have. Submissions to the Therapeutic Abortion Committees (TACs)—which often result in humiliating, unfair, and debasing trials before a panel of physicians—usually end with denials. In a series of nasty public battles, anti-choice forces target the hospital boards and systematically buy enough membership votes to disband the TACs in the province. The last safe abortion is performed in the Prince County Hospital in 1982, and the last TAC is dissolved in 1986. Women in PEI are left to our own devices. Those who can manage it leave the province and travel long distances to terminate their pregnancies.

When I am twenty-four, I am galvanized to seek out analysis and understanding by the Montréal Massacre of 6 December 1989, when fourteen young engineering students were murdered because they were women. In the aftermath, the women's movement makes connections among the different types of violence against women: sexual assault, intimate partner violence, external control over our reproductive lives. The confusion and fragmentation of ideas I had felt about the violence are resolved and new understandings emerge through the illumination of feminist perspectives; analysis replaces the silence, and unleashed tongues speak truths. Feminists know how women struggle in all areas of our lives. We are adamant that women must know that our bodies are our own. The concept of reproductive justice emerges: we should get to decide if and when we will have children and how many we will have. Without access to affordable, safe abortions, we are not yet equal.

In 1988, when the Supreme Court's *Morgentaler* decision increases access to abortion for women in the rest of Canada, the PEI legislature responds with Resolution 17, which decrees that ours is an anti-choice province. Women in PEI are to remain without access. Anti-choice lobby groups exercise incredible power, and the PEI government sanctions a Campaign for Life, which involves every Grade 7 student being bussed to the provincial capital for a pro-life rally at the University of PEI's Student Union Building. The junior high students are subjected to an emotionally charged graphic presentation. To show that they are against abortions, they are all instructed to wear their "little feet" pins, which purport to show the size of a fetus's feet. I wonder how the Department of Education can get away with such an act, but then, the department's minister wears his own "little feet" pin on his lapel.

Somehow, feminists persevere in the belief that PEI women will get access to this basic medical procedure, and I join in their optimism, protests, and lobbying, feeling to the depths of my being that genuine equality means access to safe abortion. Without unfettered access as part of a reproductive justice policy, women are second-class citizens. I vow that this will change someday. For a brief time in my early thirties, I work inside government to better understand the PEI health policy environment.

Finally, at forty-four, by then a tenured professor at UPEI, I decide that the moment has arrived to return to reproductive justice, and I begin working on the abortion issue in earnest. I gather a broad research advisory group and create with them the conditions for a participatory action research project. Our goal is to address the unfair situation through an analysis of the impacts of the abortion policies in the province over the last twenty years. Our proposal is turned back by the UPEI ethics review board. Some members, unaccustomed to qualitative approaches and unschooled in participatory action research, block the project, citing it as activism rather than research. This is unprecedented. In previous projects on the impact of tobacco on teen mothers, women leaving violent relationships, and palliative care, I was never told that my research was suspect because I didn't want to encourage teen smoking, or women staying in violent relationships, or unnecessary suffering while dying. Clearly, this challenge stems from the issue being abortion and my use of activist research methods. Thankfully, the chair of the committee facilitates an external review.

The external review is a stunning fifteen-page endorsement of the project, including an admonishment to the ethics committee for attempting to stop important, ground-breaking research. Citing the need for action research that challenges the status quo, this review is an invigorating turning point in my research journey. I feel the full weight of what our participatory action project is attempting to achieve. While before this enthusiastic endorsement I felt exclusion and derision, I now feel validation from the academy. We want to challenge injustice with academic activism. It becomes clear that the ethics review committee has some members whose own world view blinds them to the value of the research and from whom I will never earn either respect or academic freedom.

Community members embrace the participatory action project with deep and abiding enthusiasm. Ethics approval in hand, we post advertisements on 13 July 2011. Within two days, the online posting receives more than five hundred hits. I easily book interviews for research conversations with PEI women and their family, friends, and physicians who have all been deeply affected by the lack of access to abortion services. Our conversations are rich with details and ideas on how to improve the situation. The participants voice painful realities that clearly express the urgency of changing the status quo. The project is a magnet for volunteers both within and outside the academy: a highly skilled feminist therapist donates many hours to the project, and honours students invest their scholarship in the topic.

The spectre of the anti-choice movement is often larger than its actual effect. Yes, I receive anti-choice harassment emails, but they are few and far between, as are the handful of oppositional phone calls. I think through more contingency plans than I ever need. In early September 2011, I receive a supportive phone call from the vice-president of Research. Both she and the president have met with a sophomore in my department who was protesting my "biased abortion" research and wanted the university administration to intervene. The VP of Research took time out of her day to go over the ethics review process with the student to explain why the project was ethical and to educate her on participatory action research. Later, I discover that she is the student leader for the anti-choice group on campus.

The academy continues to be a paradoxical site of intense support and equally fierce opposition. At a peer-reviewed conference in 2012, I am part of a feminist reproductive justice panel with two other women. Just five minutes into my talk, I am interrupted by an older male audience member challenging my right to be there—an unprecedented interruption within the collegial environment of a conference where questions are withheld until the speaker finishes. He is successful in halting my presentation for about three minutes while I deal with his protestations. When I finish, several people affirm the value of the work, posing excellent questions. After the presentation, some audience members commiserate with me about the harasser's misconduct; I see him speaking with several people at the back of the room and wonder if more will come of the exchange. He makes his way to me after the room clears to have a more private conversation. He apologizes for having inter-rupted me. I ask why he chose to behave so "unprofessionally." He felt that my presentation violated his sense of "his" discipline, he says, and that I am outside the bounds of acceptable scholarship with my activist standpoint: he expects a more objective perspective. "I couldn't help myself, I just had to say something, it raised my ire so much!" he says to justify his outburst. Socrat-ically, I ask if he is familiar with qualitative methodologies? With paradigms that question objectivity? With participatory action research or scholarship in action? He is not, but he is certain I do not belong in the academy.

Many academics are becoming tuned into the paradigm shift toward scholarship in action. Together, we are starting a revolution. The revolution may not be funded, but parts of it will be highly subsidized! The University Research Committee grants the project a full internal research grant to help defray costs. This modest amount is awarded without any question, although I did attach the external ethics review to the application, which may have assisted in the committee's deliberations. Perhaps the colleagues on the ethics committee who were anti-choice and anti-action research actually ended up doing me a favour by having the proposal reviewed so rigorously.

Granted, I could have faced insurmountable obstacles if I hadn't had a feminist community from which to draw, both in terms of the research and the community outreach. If I hadn't had an external reviewer who under-stood the significance of the issue and the validity and appropriateness of the participatory action research design, the project would have stalled. If I hadn't had a broad community of reproductive justice advocates to bolster the project, it would have failed. Academic activism is done with the com-munity, for the community, and that is making all the difference.

My colleagues and I are still working on changing the status quo. The plan is to take the research findings on the road, back to the community, to have discussions about what participants shared so movingly. A fortuitous reorganization within the province's health system resulted in an eradication of the hospital boards, thereby removing their strictures against abortions and, as we discover through our research, opening the system wide for a pro-choice physician to step up. But we need the social conditions for a physician to provide that service. Aside from the direct community discussions about the research, it seems that just giving people the opportunity to express openly how women have been affected by the lack of abortion access has created momentum for community change. For example, our project has provided the necessary spark to inspire a whole new group into action. One young activist publicly credited a research conversation with me for her incipient activism: she discovered new information that made her so angry she decided something had to be done. Within weeks, six young women had organized the PEI Reproductive Rights Organization. They sponsored the first PEI pro-choice rally in more than twenty years on 19 November 2011, created a pro-choice social media campaign, pressured the provincial government, succeeded in having the Province post access-to-abortion information on its website, presented to high school students, garnered national and international coverage about the lack of abortion access in PEI, and engaged in a host of other community actions. That is the value of collective organizing: together, we are making a difference.

As I write this, women still do not have access to abortion in PEI, but my colleagues and I have made changes in that direction. Ours is a story of making connections in an environment that seeks to dissociate, of speaking truths out of shame, of articulating ongoing violence that began with child sexual abuse in a world claiming that our bodies were not our own. It is a story of resistance born out of the everyday challenges to our spirits, minds, and bodies. Our path may be long, but, in the lyrics of Ndidi Onukwulu's "Move Together," "We can get there faster if we all move together."

Waves of Change in Prince Edward Island

Opening the Dialogue on Abortion Access

Sadie Roberts

When I finished my undergraduate degree from the University of Prince Edward Island, I had the good fortune to embark on a master's thesis in which I examined the barriers faced by women from Prince Edward Island (PEI) in their attempts to obtain a safe and legal abortion from the perspective of allies and advocates. This project was part of a larger study called "Trials and Trails of Accessing Abortion in PEI: Reporting on the Impact of PEI's Abortion Policies on Women." I had the honour of listening to women who have been helping women and girls navigate an inhumane health care system and fighting to change that policy. This research also helped me extend my own advocacy efforts and gave me more clarity on my own abortion experience.

A different set of emotions and circumstances frames each experience of abortion. My problem pregnancy occurred from an incident that resulted in a loss of trust in my partner at the time, who preferred not to use condoms, wanted to have a baby, and would sometimes joke about getting me pregnant. I believe that my partner impregnated me against my wishes. Aware that I was ovulating, I warned him to take precautions and pull out very early. In this regard, he failed me, as did the morning-after pill. My abortion was not difficult, but my pregnancy was. For seven weeks, I endured coercion, guilt, and my partner's anger with my desire to terminate. My difficulties did not include finding car rides, money, time off work, or privacy; they arose mainly from struggles with my partner, who wanted to "keep the baby." The procedure itself was actually a very redemptive experience—through it, I was finally able to regain control over my own body, which I felt had been hijacked for many weeks. Dr. Morgentaler, who performed my abortion, became one of my heroes, and reproductive justice one of my passions. Because of my own abortion experience, this project has become very important to me.

Years after my abortion, when I moved to PEI to do my undergraduate degree, I was shocked to learn that islanders finding themselves regrettably pregnant must contend with many more barriers than I faced to get the care they need. I was disturbed by stories of women waiting weeks for an ultrasound, having to travel far out of province, and losing their privacy. I was appalled that although Canada mandates abortion access in every province and territory, islanders have been denied this basic medical procedure. When I brought up this lack of abortion access in PEI within a university setting, I was shamed by my professor. I also noticed that students generally spoke about the subject very quietly.

With the help and encouragement of another trusted professor, I decided to break this silence with a class project. I asked my classmates to participate by reading aloud, to the class, stories of circumstances surrounding problem pregnancies (poverty, substance abuse, incest, youth, etc.) and then to select a fortune cookie in order to find out whether their story-character would be able to access a legal and safe abortion, depending on her government's policy. All of my classmates agreed to read the stories aloud, and the overall response was encouraging and supportive, with personal reactions ranging from silence to tears. The project was successful in showing PEI's current policies as unjust and out of step with the more progressive stances on reproductive health in much of the world. Most satisfying, however, was the uninhibited and exploratory class discussion that followed. My professor responded by offering me the opportunity to collaborate in a large study with her and many others with a long history of fighting for access in PEI, and I was very happy to accept. "Trials and Trails" is now completed, and the findings expose injustices far beyond those I had originally expected.[1]

Interviews from this study have shown that the policies in place in PEI act, in various ways, as barriers to accessing a basic procedure covered by public health care, creating a web of obstacles that is particularly opaque for those who are less privileged. For example, obtaining a referral for an ultrasound may take over fifteen weeks—which is also the cut-off gestation period for an abortion in both of the nearest clinics on the mainland. If you are an islander attempting to access an abortion covered by health care, your first task is to find a pro-choice doctor to provide a referral, as many doctors will, in fact, deny you this service. It is also not uncommon to be shamed by other staff such as nurses or receptionists. Knowledge of which doctor to ask depends, to a large extent, on familiarity with the island community. Minors are less likely to have access to such information, and since they are also less likely to be employed and to have a driver's licence or a car, they will have more difficulty in accessing a public, out-of-province clinic.

The prohibitive costs associated with a private clinic are often exacerbated by the costs of travel arrangements, time off from work, or hiring a babysitter. For people in controlling or abusive relationships, getting off the island may simply be unachievable. Indeed, data from "Trials and Trails" have shown that some islanders have been blocked entirely from getting the care they need, with outcomes ranging from self-imposed bodily harm resulting from attempting a self-induced abortion to problem pregnancies being brought to term. In short, PEI's abortion restrictions have the largest impact on those who need the support the most. Unequal distribution in abortion access thus sharpens the divide in the province between rich and poor, adults and youth, educated and uneducated.

Responding to inquiries from curious islanders about my thesis topic has been difficult at times, since abortion is still very much contested terrain in PEI. More recently, however, I have found it increasingly rewarding. With the launch of this major research project, the cloak of silence that has, for many years, prevented open discussion of abortion on the Island has been lifted. Several abortion rights advocacy groups have formed that continually and publicly take issue with the Island's unjust policies. Letters to the editor can now often be found in the local paper, brave leaders are coming forward, protests are gaining momentum, and local campaigns have garnered international attention. Increasing numbers of islanders are speaking up, calling for control over our reproductive choices and demanding that our constitutional rights be upheld—and these voices are gaining ground. I have added my voice to this chorus because my studies and research have confirmed what I learned from personal experience: access to care is vital to a community's health and equality. Anything less is an injustice.

Note

1   The final report, *Trials and Trails of Accessing Abortion in PEI: Reporting on the Impact of PEI's Abortion Policies on Women,* was released in January 2014 and is available at http://projects.upei.ca/cmacquarrie/files/2014/01/trials_and_trails_final.pdf.

part three

Challenging Opposing Positions

Blinded by the Right

My Past as an Anti-abortion Activist

NATALIE LOCHWIN

To start, I didn't want to write this. So I searched, hoping to find someone who had a similar experience to share so that I could read their own take on their progression from a "pro-life/anti-choice/anti-abortion" position to believing in and advocating for abortion rights. I'm sharing this story of my past anti-choice activism because it is a past I have been ashamed of. Yet it also shaped me and is part of what, ironically, made me who I am today.

This, in the end, is a story about how destructive the anti-abortion movement can be not only to society but to individuals as well.

In the late 1980s, when I was sixteen, my mother decided to move our family away from the "rough" inner city of Toronto and tuck us away in safe, clean, boring suburbia.

This essay originally appeared as a guest blog on Michael Laxer's Blog, 17 October 2012. http://mlaxer.blogspot.ca/2012/10/guest-blog-blinded-by-right-my-past-as_17.html. It is reprinted here with minor revisions.

The day Canada's abortion law was struck down, I recall my mother watching the news and listening to the reaction from the public. She was motivated to do something, to get involved. She was determined to take a stand. I didn't really know or care about this issue. I was still just a kid, really, in high school, sort of geeky, blessed with an awkward nature and a teenager's skin.

My mother, however, decided that we (that is, my mom, my sisters, and I) would go picket the hospital circuit with our homemade anti-choice signs and hand out pamphlets spouting anti-abortion propaganda. Regularly, after school, we would travel downtown with her from Etobicoke, grabbing some veggie pitas en route, and protest the "killing" of the unborn in front of the hospitals. I'd beg to do something else after school, to go out with friends, but the answer was always no. There was no other option. Picketing and homework were my lot.

We had become born-again Christians. My mother had faith that this would save her crumbling marriage and stop her kids from turning into wayward anarchist heathens. For my mother, Christianity and pro-life activism changed everything. It delivered us from skull earrings, multicoloured hair, and "satanic" black nail polish. We were saved!

We began to "fellowship" with other like-minded folks, as is done in movements like this. We were constantly going to church and to youth events.

As our involvement in anti-choice activism developed, I grew to like the attention, negative or positive. We became known and even somewhat famous in the movement as an "activist family." At one point, *Toronto Life* magazine even featured us in a piece.

A sick and paranoid mythology was part of the anti-choice ideology. We'd hear about the evil "pro-aborts," how they hated children, how they'd get pregnant intentionally and then have abortions. The anti-choicers really believed that "feminazis," as they called feminists, were evil, that they sacrificed fetuses in some sort of satanic ceremony. Clinics were rumoured to sell fetal parts to research facilities for medical experiments and to meat processing plants and fancy cosmetics companies for the collagen. They claimed that experiments were performed on "living" fetuses, decapitated fetuses, and so forth.

We'd hang out at Aid to Women, an anti-choice "counselling" organization that was littered with Christian propaganda and expressed a truly extremist anti-abortion ideology. The atmosphere in the movement was extremely oppressive and very controlling. According to the anti-choicers, the mainstream, secular media were all liars, and any statistics or information that seemed to contradict their views were lies or government conspiracies. Followers were strongly encouraged to rely only on Christian or Catholic sources and to avoid mainstream media. The world presented through their eyes was a very ugly place.

Virtually everyone in the movement was religious—Catholic, born-again evangelicals, or members of some other Christian faction. Their stated goal was to save babies. But their broader agenda was to "save the world" from the secular, non-Christian agenda, and they were armed with an over-the-top anti-gay and anti-woman manifesto. Homosexuals were seen as "AIDS carriers" who were out to "get the family." Abortion was ultimately just a stepping stone, a point of entry into their paranoid, homophobic, hate-filled world.

Accosting female patients on their way to abortion clinics was like a game for them, some sort of competition. One day, my mother, who had begun to regularly do sidewalk "counselling," cornered a nineteen-year-old woman from Grenada in an alleyway and convinced her not to have an abortion. My mother dragged her into the fake "pregnancy counselling centre," the one beside the Morgentaler Clinic on Harbord Street, shoved a bunch of pamphlets and a plastic fetus in her face, and asked her why she wanted to "kill her baby." The young woman began to weep. This was a "victory" for my mother and made her the envy of other, more experienced sidewalk "counsellors." "Why do you get to save a baby?" they lamented. "I've been doing this longer than you."

Eventually, we joined Campaign Life Coalition (CLC). My mother was rather generously supporting them—this was back in the days when they had charitable status—with donations to the tune of tens of thousands of dollars. We became involved with many truly extreme characters. There was Vlad, a Soviet defector, who actually lived at CLC's Dundas Street headquarters. He was an eccentric who worked in the office, and he was devoutly religious. He would accompany us on regular trips across the border to Buffalo to participate in Operation Rescue efforts. He hated abortion providers. I asked him once why he never took part in traditional protests. His answer was that he would kill the doctors if he saw them. I don't think I brought it up with him again.

We also came to know Ken Campbell, a prominent anti-choice evangelical Christian who spewed his own special brand of reactionary hatred via a Christian radio show in the early 1990s. He would pontificate on air at great length, supported by the blessings and dollars of his faithful listeners, who included my mother and also my father. Sadly, they must have donated tens of thousands of dollars to him as well. Campbell would rant about the "pro-aborts" and how anti-family they were. He was also extremely fixated on homosexuality, even relating stories of how he was tormented by gay men in his dreams! This seemed rather odd for someone who despised gays: every broadcast was a call to action against the supposed anti-family, anti-traditional marriage, homosexual agenda. Then, of course, he would beg for money. Eventually, my mother had a falling out with him when he kept pushing for more and more money. The last straw was when he showed up at our home with prearranged loan papers all ready for my parents to sign. Fortunately, they declined.

Meanwhile, lots of exciting things were happening in the anti-choice movement in the United States, led by the Christian hard-line fanatic pastor Randall Terry, whose Operation Rescue movement appropriated civil rights activist tactics and then dared to compare itself with the civil rights movement, even going so far as to sing their songs and twist their slogans. "They ended slavery, we're ending slavery in the womb!" his followers would shout. Randall Terry embraced the role of "prophet" that his devotees cast him in. In the early 1990s, he, along with a bunch of others, worked the faithful up into a frenzy in Washington, DC, with calls to take action against the murderous doctors who performed abortions. Unfortunately, some of his followers did just that.

In 1994, the Morgentaler Clinic in Toronto was bombed. Within the anti-choice movement, the anonymous cowards who had done this were seen as heroes and extolled as noble. They had obeyed a higher law. Morgentaler had "deserved" it, they said. They would make comments about how ironic it was that he had survived the Holocaust only to go on and kill North American babies.

Emulating the United States activists, we started to block clinics too. The movement's male leaders, preferring to lead by words rather than by example, never put their necks on the line. Often, the front-line activists at the Toronto clinics—Morgentaler's, the Scott, the one in Cabbagetown— were children and teens. My ten- and fourteen-year-old sisters were arrested

Without Apology

while protesting, as were many other children. Time after time, kids and teens were encouraged to engage in activism by the anti-abortion adults, who liked the media attention we got.

Sometimes, we'd use Kryptonite locks to attach our necks to gates or to each other, imitating the Lambs of Christ, an extremist American anti-abortion group. A good family friend of ours was a "Lamb." He was a single forty-year-old who wanted nothing more, as he put it, than "to die in service to the Lord." He also had ties to the Army of God, a group of Christian anti-choice terrorists, and was proud of his Army of God manual, an underground "how-to" guide full of explicit instructions for vandalism and violence against abortion clinics and providers. He was such a fanatic that his father had taken out a million-dollar life insurance policy on him. He would accompany my mother and younger sisters on their strange and confusing "missions" to many US cities, where they would campaign against Christians using birth control. Sometimes, my mother would suggest that I marry him. Given that I was seventeen at the time, I have always hoped she was joking!

A big part of being a pro-life youth involved socializing with others in the movement and attending various conferences across Ontario and the United States. This was all part of our socialization into extremism and the ideology of control. At a Human Life International conference, one of my sisters and I were "shamed" for being vegetarians, since this meant we were going against the Bible and against our parents' wishes. Our vegetarianism was deemed anti-Christian.

At our evangelical church, there were people who spoke in tongues—people who had been "chosen" to convey a special message from "the Lord." It was, of course, always the same two people who "received" and interpreted. One of the tongue speakers looked me over one time and proclaimed to my mother that she detected witchcraft. This started a whole mess of trouble for me, and my mother got rid of my palm-reading books, along with many other suspect possessions.

No matter what, I felt as though I could do nothing right. Thoughts, especially sexual thoughts, which were normal for a girl my age to have, were considered sinful. We were taught that we could not trust a single natural thought. Everything about being a teenage girl was evil and unclean. I was convinced, after constant reminders at church and at home, that God would judge us and that His vengeance would be visited upon us.

My mother would inquire about our sexuality and remind us that mastur-
bation was wrong and sinful. We were to practice chastity until marriage.
Their answers to teenage hormones were lame. "I'm worth waiting for" but-
tons were thrust into our palms. Those in the anti-abortion movement and
the Christian churches associated with it had a fundamental mistrust of
youth and felt that all of us were in grave danger of becoming sex-crazed
animals and drug addicts. It was as though they had simply forgotten, or
perhaps never knew, what it means to be human, to be a young adult, and
were unwilling to accept that this is an awkward age meant for discovering
and learning about who you are and what you believe.

Why did I go along with all this? I think that, for me as a young person,
it was about the attention and the thrills—the excitement of the lead-up to
an Operation Rescue action, the camaraderie, the police, the media interest, and all the people watching. Then to get arrested, to go to jail for a few
weeks (even if you were starting to have doubts about the tactics that got
you there), and to get even more attention from those within the cult, all the
greater because of your youth and "dedication." I'd been involved for a few
years now, and the magic number, 18, wasn't too far off, which would mean
the end of my young offender charges and sentences. Soon I would be in
adult court. Just how dedicated was I?

If I could speak to my now long-dead mother, I might ask her why she let
this happen. It destroyed our already fractured family. All we did was obsess
over "the cause," and it ate up every weekend and all our free time. It was as
though a stranger had moved into our lives.

What did the pro-life movement teach us as kids and young adults? It
taught us that God's "law" overrides any other laws or rights. These were the
anti-social "values" that anti-choice advocates instilled. Their family values
involved showing graphic and misleading images to kids and repeatedly
violating the rights of women. Upholding their values involved invading
privacy, stealing clinic garbage to scrounge for fetal parts, picketing escorts'
homes, committing vandalism, and condoning and even encouraging violence against abortion providers and their property. They taught us to have
no concern for anyone's rights or property because we were obeying a higher
law and we answered only to "God."

When I read about current anti-choice activists, or when I see them at
demonstrations or in their propaganda videos, they seem so sincere. Yet
many are full of hatred and are sickened by the sight of women standing up

for their reproductive rights. They see us as the enemy and as bloodthirsty "baby killers." I see familiar faces in the news—the McCashes, Jim Hughes, Linda Gibbons. I see other people I once stood alongside now involve their own offspring in the movement, creating future generations of activists in the cause of quashing women's reproductive autonomy and carrying out a reactionary agenda.

Painting a false portrait of abortion rights activists is key to the anti-choice movement. To convince the flock, this portrayal must be as ugly and paranoid as possible. Just have a look at the website of the Canadian Centre for Bio-ethical Reform (CCBR) or at *LifeSite News*. Anti-choicers choose to perpetuate lies, and the tactics they use are fundamentally unethical. They are manipulative, anti-woman, and anti-family.

Their agenda reaches far beyond abortion. The beliefs they hold dear are part of an unholy trinity of hate that is anti-abortion, anti-homosexual, and anti-feminist. They work tirelessly at scheming new ways to complete or promote their agenda, using abortion as an issue to draw people in. This broader agenda is why Campaign Life was so prominent in opposing Ontario's Bill 13 (an anti-bullying amendment to the Education Act), as well as the Gay-Straight Alliance in general, even though homosexuality has nothing at all to do with abortion.

The anti-choice vision is of a world where women are happy breeders, at home making dinner and raising their children, fulfilled by their duties as baby makers with no selfish thoughts of education, career, or personal achievement. Pregnancy is viewed as a duty, a must, a necessary rite of passage. As anti-choice activists see it, making babies is for everyone. Whether you're a fifteen-year-old girl who had sex only once and got pregnant, or a rape victim, or a single "slut," or a woman who's been diagnosed with cancer: it doesn't matter. To them, the circumstances are irrelevant.

It would make sense that such a movement, if it were actually about the love of "unborn babies," would be concerned with the well-being of both pregnant women and the potential life they carry. You might think that these activists would support a government that would fund daycare, prenatal programs, affordable housing, and programs to assist single-parent families and that would fight to end hunger and poverty in our country so that more women would be in a position to bring a new life into the world, when the time is right for them, without fear of the future. But this is not so. Anti-abortionists are encouraged to vote according to one issue:

abortion and abortion alone. They are fixated, paranoid, and poisoned with an anti-female ideology. This is why their heroes are the Mitt Romneys, Rush Limbaughs, and Michael Corens of the world. Anti-choicers are not at all concerned with children or women—only with fetuses.

The anti-abortion movement is truly cult-like. Cutting ties with it, if one wants to, is not simple, since so many of your friends are anti-choice and are either evangelical Christians or devout Catholics. Leaders of the movement make sure of that. I remember how weekend retreats and pro-chastity, anti-abortion conferences were always held in out-of-town locations, far from most attendees' homes. This made them a great opportunity for bonding and brainwashing. We really believed that when we blocked clinics, we were doing something good, that we were doing the right thing. We believed we were involved in the noble cause of saving women and babies from being dragged to a horrible fate.

———◆———

I can't exactly say what opened my eyes. It wasn't one specific incident but several. The shootings and other anti-abortion violence helped to wake me up, of course.

Then there was the anti-choice hysteria surrounding the Nancy Cruzan case in Missouri. In 1983, she was in a terrible car accident, which left her in a coma, a vegetative state from which she would never recover. Four years after the accident, her family requested that she be removed from life support. They believed that they were following what would have been her wishes. The right-to-life movement in the United States and Canada went berserk, hatching plans to go and "rescue" Nancy. They claimed that she showed signs of brain activity and that her doctors and family were out to kill her. There were protests and legal challenges. The court ruled in favour of her family, and, on 26 December 1990, Nancy was finally allowed to die. The movement's heartless actions against Nancy and her family were pivotal in changing my mind.

In 1992, I happened to watch an incredible *Frontline* documentary titled "The Death of Nancy Cruzan." The tenderness and love that her father showed for Nancy really moved me. I wondered why those involved in the right-to-life movement didn't talk about this. Surely, they could see how much her family loved her and how painful it was for them to watch this once vibrant young woman brought back by "roadside heroics" to be an empty shell. The real Nancy was never coming back. Her body, now pale and bloated, would be unrecognizable to her former self. This was not living with dignity.

I was in art school by then and was being exposed to liberal thinking. I flourished. My best friend was a wonderful gay man; we were kindred spirits. I read authors like Toni Morrison and experienced the arts education I'd only dreamed of before. And yet I avoided intimate relationships, drinking, and most types of socializing. Feeling uncomfortable in my own skin, I was unable and unwilling to connect in a healthy, nonparanoid way because I was so used to having a movement and a religion looking over my shoulder.

Fortunately, the next twenty years would take me on a new personal and political journey. Having become a feminist and socialist, as well as the proud mother of a daughter who I hope will embrace the freedoms her foremothers fought for, I now see things very differently. I understand that anti-choice extremists view the world through hate-tinted glasses. They are the proverbial wolves in sheep's clothing. Their ugly construct of women and the world bears no resemblance to reality.

One Life Change
Leads to Another

My Evolving View of Abortion

Tracey L. Anderson

During my early teenage and young adult years, I firmly believed in the right-to-life side of the endless abortion debate. My view slowly began to change during my early twenties. Now, in my forties, I see that, as my life has evolved, so, too, has my view of abortion.

I was raised in a Catholic household. Premarital sex was a sin, but abortion was a bigger sin. To me, abortion was unequivocally immoral; it was tantamount to murder.

At seventeen, when I fell in love with my first real boyfriend, I chose to save sex until after marriage. Early in our relationship, I made my feelings clear to my boyfriend, who accepted how I felt. As our relationship developed over several years, my desire to show my love physically grew. I knew it would go against Catholic teaching, but I thought it would be acceptable because, although we weren't married, we loved each other. Besides, at the time, I truly believed he was the man I would one day marry. In that frame of heart, I overrode the church's teachings on premarital sex—and on birth control.

Like all young women, I had goals and dreams. I didn't want to lose any opportunities by getting pregnant, so I got a prescription for birth control pills. Every time you have sex, of course, the risk of pregnancy exists. I thought often in those years about what I'd do if I ever got pregnant despite my precautions. I knew that I'd be devastated and that my parents' disappointment would be hard for me to bear. I knew that, technically, I'd have three choices: seek an abortion, choose adoption, or accept motherhood. Realistically and idealistically, though, I knew I had only two choices: I could never accept abortion as a valid option.

I believed that abortion was morally wrong, but I'm adopted, so I also wondered: *What if your birth mother had believed in abortion? You wouldn't be here now.* My strong, idealistic views made me argue—loudly and often—that abortion should only be allowed in exceptional circumstances. I could understand how a woman could—and should be able to—abort if she had suffered the horrors of rape, or if she or the child might die or suffer severe genetic or medical problems; I could not accept any other justification for abortion. The thought of the procedure made my stomach heave.

Anyone who advocated for the right to choose abortion was immediately immoral in my eyes. Even my best friend was the recipient of my swift reaction. I couldn't believe that she thought killing an unborn child was acceptable: I became incensed whenever the topic came up between us. It was always the same endless circle.

"How can you justify killing an unborn baby?"

"Why should a woman be forced to deliver a baby she doesn't want? It's her body. She should have the right to choose what happens to it."

Around and around we'd go, spinning like an angry tornado. To save our friendship, we finally agreed to disagree on the subject and to stop discussing it.

Because abortion was out of the question for me, I knew that I'd carry any unplanned baby to term, whether I kept it or gave it up for adoption. I wondered, though, whether I'd have the courage to give up a baby, so I considered my future life plans: *Now wouldn't be a good time for it, but you want a child someday. Why not keep the baby if you get pregnant?* I also thought about the future consequences of choosing adoption for me and for the child: *How could you give away a child never knowing if that might be your only chance to have one? And what if the child grew up as angry and resentful toward you as you've been toward your birth mother? Or feels rejected and unloved like you did for so long? How would you feel if you spent the rest of your life not knowing how your child felt about being given away?*

The longer I thought about the potential of an unwanted pregnancy, the more I suspected that I wouldn't be able to live with myself if I chose adoption. I knew I'd probably keep the baby and try to forget that it had come at the wrong time in my life.

My view of abortion remained deep and unbending for almost a decade, until some point in my early twenties. Suddenly I was living a surprising life—one I hadn't expected, one I couldn't even have conceived of a year or two earlier. In an instant, the six-year relationship with my first boyfriend had ended badly, and I was alone. A year later, I lost my dream teaching job because of harsh government cutbacks and then spent a year un- and under-employed. To add insult to injury, I was rear-ended at a stoplight—on Christmas Eve—and was left with chronic neck and back pain. My life was a muddled mess, and I felt shattered.

Out of the grey mist that my life had become, an unanticipated offer to teach English as a Second Language at a private school in China arrived. To escape the chaos in my personal and professional worlds, I accepted the job. Perhaps it was because this new life abroad was so unexpected and because most of my previous mental photographs of my life had remained undeveloped—no marriage to the love of my life, no permanent teaching job in my hometown, no financial security—that I suddenly began to see that I could live a different life than the one I'd envisioned when I was growing up. I also realized that many of those images had not been my own; they'd been drawn in my mind by society and by my parents. Getting married and raising a family was what I'd thought I was supposed to do.

But I'd broken the mold. I'd left the comfortable circle of family and friends and moved to the other side of the globe. And I was having a great time, testing my limits and trying new things. Suddenly, those old expectations lost their hold on me. I saw that I could finish my contract in China, move home, find a partner, get married, and raise a family. But those were choices, not requirements. I could also take a thousand other paths.

So I chose one of those alternate paths. I stayed in China for another year. I eventually lived in Macedonia, Morocco, and the United Arab Emirates. I travelled and took photos and met new people. I married the best man I have ever met. And somewhere along that meandering road—I don't recall noticing precisely when or where—I realized a startling thing: I don't want children. I also realized that choosing to be childless was perfectly acceptable.

Once I understood those two things, an interesting change happened: my views on abortion began to shift. When my desire to have children dissolved, the picture of what would happen if I accidentally got pregnant became very different. When I wanted kids, choosing abortion didn't make sense. A child might come into my life too soon, but I planned to have one eventually, so I'd probably keep it. After I realized that I didn't want kids, having one would have been devastating. It would have meant life-style changes I didn't want to make, obligations I didn't want to meet, and worries I didn't want to endure. I could suddenly see how a woman could choose an abortion in an unplanned-pregnancy scenario. I could suddenly see how *I* could choose an abortion; in fact, I began to believe that might be the choice I would make.

Acknowledging that was quite a shock at first, but I've accepted that change in my point of view. I understand that we gain new perspectives as we evolve. I see, too, that the abortion equation comes down to a basic question: Should women have the right to make choices about all matters that deeply affect their lives? The answer, of course, is a resounding yes.

In the same way that women should be able to choose such parts of their lives as their life partners and their jobs, they should also be able to choose whether to have a family. No woman should be forced by law or by religion or by societal pressure to give birth if she is unready or unwilling. If we believe in women's rights such as the right to vote and the right to work, we must also believe in women's right to choose their reproductive futures. Although I never thought I'd say it, every woman should be free to choose an abortion if she believes it's the right thing to do. Nobody else should be allowed to make that choice for her.

Without Apology

Pro-Choice for God's Sake

Shannon West

When I was in Grade 7, I had a friend named Nina (as I will call her here), a lovely Métis girl. She "passed" for white, which is why she had no problems in my very, very, very white school. One day, after Nina and I had been friends for a while, she took me home after school, where I was greeted by her Cree mother. They didn't warn me. They thought it would be funny. And it apparently was, because they both howled with laughter at my obvious shock. Once I got over it, and I'm not sure it was even the same day, I said something stupid about Nina obviously having a white father, and her mother, who pulled no punches, said, "Yeah, they were white." I must have looked confused, because she then told me that two young white guys had raped her, and the result was Nina. I was horrified and on the verge of tears. That's when she got really gentle and said, "It's okay honey. I made peace with it. And I chose to have her. I figured some good should come of it all. I didn't have to do that. It'd be different if they made me." Then she looked a bit haunted and said, "Like my sister."

And there's the heart of the issue: choice. Women get pregnant in all sorts of ways: expected, unexpected, carefully planned, in vitro fertilization, and rape. I don't think rape is on the top of anyone's list of fun ways to get pregnant. It's a crime; it's a trauma that people live with for the rest of their lives. And sometimes it results in pregnancy. At that point, like every pregnant woman, the woman has a choice to make: Do I want to carry this to term? Do I want a baby now? Do I want to abort? Do I want to give it up for adoption?

I'd hazard a guess that most women who get pregnant by a rapist don't want to carry the pregnancy to term. They don't want a physical reminder of the violation. They don't want to worry that they'll look into their baby's eyes and see their rapist. They don't want to worry that nature will outsmart nurture and that their baby will grow up to be a rapist. And so they choose to stop it.

And some women choose to go on with it. Perhaps, like my friend's mom, they view a new life as something wonderful coming from a trauma (I might have named that girl Phoenix!), or perhaps they don't have access to a safe abortion and won't risk a back alley job or perhaps they are anti-choice themselves. Or maybe they decide to give it up for adoption. I can't fathom this one myself—carrying a pregnancy from rape to term and then giving up the baby? It boggles my mind. But that's the point. I don't have to be the one to understand it. Only the woman making the decision does.

But they're all valid choices. And they should all be supported. Can we please stop mocking the idea that some women might actually want a pregnancy that we couldn't conceive of? I understand the impulse to mock. We tend to mock those whose beliefs are so different from ours that we can't even imagine how the thought process works. This is especially true when there is fear involved. When I was pregnant with my second child, a woman in my pregnancy group was carrying a baby who was conceived by rape. She had decided to keep the baby, but she actually had to fight with her family (read: parents), who tried to get her to abort, because they had all the fears listed above. And they were afraid that she wouldn't be able to love her baby. They were probably afraid that *they* wouldn't love the baby. They wanted to protect her. But she said the same thing my old girlfriend's mom said: "I wanted something good to come of it. And what could be better than a new baby?" (My thoughts were wine, chocolate, a hot bath, and some bubblewrap therapy, but to each her own.) And so she decided to carry on.

In 2012, an American politician, Richard Mourdock, found himself in the media spotlight when he tried to defend his objection to a rape exclusion to an abortion ban. His argument, if you can call it that, was that a pregnancy from rape is "something that God intended to happen."[1] I understand his logic, actually. He believes that God creates all life and that life begins at conception. So he says it's God's will. Not the rape, but the pregnancy that came from it. I'm not sure how one can separate them, but maybe he thinks God is micromanaging the sperm. Or that God is some sort of weird doorman at the egg barrier. I have no clue, and Mourdoch isn't saying, probably because he doesn't know either. In "Pregnancy from Rape Is Not 'God's Will,'" an article that appeared in the *Washington Post* on 24 October 2012, Susan Brooks Thistlethwaite, a former professor at the Chicago Theological Seminary, disagrees with him on all of it. She says that making God the author of conception after rape makes God the author of the crime as well. Where I disagree with her is in her statement that "conception following rape is a tragedy, not part of 'God's will.'" I say that tragedy is defined by the victim of the crime. It is a tragedy if the woman perceives it as one. Like rain is a tragedy in a flood but a blessing in a drought, a conception from a rape is what the woman perceives it to be in her particular circumstances.

Actually, that's where the religious anti-choice people make the least sense. They claim that all conceptions are gifts and blessings, and we just need to shut up and see it that way. Oh, I suppose that's possible. Any belief is changeable. It's like saying that rain is always a blessing, a gift from God. Just get in a boat and enjoy it. Swept away in a flood? Intended by God. Crops failing? God's will. Can't eat this winter? God must be teaching you a lesson. Conception is just something that happens. We define its value. But that's the problem too. Anti-choice Christians have made their beliefs into dogma, incontrovertible truth, and are attempting to enforce it as law on all of us. They want to be the ones defining the belief for everyone.

And where do the Christian anti-choice people get the idea that a fetus is a blessing, each and every time? Where do they get the idea that the life growing inside a pregnant woman is a full person? I'm Christian, with thirteen years of Catholic school, so I know my Bible pretty well, but I had to go looking for explicit references. I could not find a single reference to "abortion," "caused herself to miscarry," or any variation of those. Even "unborn" got me only a single reference, and it was to "a people yet unborn." But there are plenty of references to babies in wombs and pregnant women—here are some of them.

Psalm 139:13
For you created my inmost being; you knit me together in my mother's womb.

Lovely image, that. Of course, we know that's not quite right, but it is a lovely image. The Bible is full of lovely imagery. And some not-so-lovely imagery . . . see below.

Isaiah 44:2
This is what the LORD says—he who made you, who formed you in the womb, and who will help you: Do not be afraid, Jacob, my servant, Jeshurun, whom I have chosen.

Same idea, God actively forming the fetus.

Jeremiah 1:5
Before I formed you in the womb I knew you, before you were born I set you apart; I appointed you as a prophet to the nations.

Jeremiah 20:17
For he did not kill me in the womb, with my mother as my grave, her womb enlarged forever.

Okay, Jeremiah definitely feels like he was an individual in the womb, and that in the womb, he could be killed. And God said he knew him in the womb. Okay, I am definitely on board with the idea that this is an argument for the fetus being a separate entity from its mother. But so what? Does that mean that his mother, or any mother, is morally obliged (never mind legally obliged) to allow it to continue to develop? At that time in history, certainly. Because the fetus belonged to her husband. (Many a woman, though, found a way to abort; it seems that if that had been a big deal, they'd have mentioned it.) But today? No. Not for a woman who isn't Christian, certainly. And for Christians? I think that's between them and God, because there's nothing in here that is completely clear.

Luke 1:44
As soon as the sound of your greeting reached my ears, the baby in my womb leaped for joy.

Oh boy. A fetus with emotions. Or maybe he just decided to kick. Mine liked to do that when I ate spicy food. Joy? A pretty image again, but I see no evidence of anything other than wishful thinking. Interestingly, this is the only reference in the Greek scriptures bestowing any sort of awareness upon a fetus.

Amos 1:13–14

This is what the Lord says: "For three sins of Ammon, even for four, I will not relent. Because he ripped open the pregnant women of Gilead in order to extend his borders, I will set fire to the walls of Rabbah that will consume her fortresses amid war cries on the day of battle, amid violent winds on a stormy day."

There's a fair bit about the crime of ripping open pregnant women in the Hebrew scriptures (a.k.a. the Old Testament)—in Hosea and 2 Kings, especially. Looks like this was a worse offence than just killing the women or the children because pregnant women were property carrying other property. Children, in utero or not, were property of their fathers, and women, property of their husbands. So pregnant women were especially valuable. And I'm sure there was plenty of emotional value involved, too. These people, like people everywhere, had hopes and dreams for the future. To have them so cruelly taken away could drive almost anyone to revenge.

Genesis 38:24

About three months later Judah was told, "Your daughter-in-law Tamar is guilty of prostitution, and as a result she is now pregnant." Judah said, "Bring her out and have her burned to death!"

Well then. Nice guy. I guess that fetus was worthless. It certainly didn't seem to have any value to Judah at all. And when a fetus does have value in the Bible, well, we're back to property value. Since the fetus's owner could not be determined, it had no value at all.

Exodus 21:22–23

If people are fighting and hit a pregnant woman and she gives birth prematurely but there is no serious injury, the offender must be fined whatever the woman's husband demands and the court allows. But if there is serious injury, you are to take life for life.

"Gives birth prematurely" means miscarriage, since in those times, preemies didn't have a chance. (The King James Version reads "and her fruit depart from her"; the Good News Bible says "and loses the child.") There are lots of laws set out in Exodus about what could be done to slaves, children, people who curse their parents. And this one is right smack in the middle of them. It is absolutely clear in this passage that fetuses were not to be considered of equal value to women. Killing a woman (accidentally, that is—go ahead and beat her to death if she cheated on you) was punishable by death. Killing a fetus, but not the woman, was punishable by fine. This is a clear reference to the value of a fetus being less than that of a wife.

It might appear that this is another example of the Bible contradicting itself, but assuming you take everything in the Bible to be golden and completely relevant today, what all of this says is that God forms life in women's wombs, little lives, capable of experiencing joy. And that these lives are just not as valuable as fully formed ones. They're valuable, certainly, as the property of men. God never really says anything about their inherent value as souls— oh sure, God had plans for some of those fetuses, and God's plans can't be thwarted by mere women with inconvenient pregnancies. Maybe that's why God bothered to send angels to Mary and some of the other women who found themselves inconveniently pregnant. So they wouldn't find a good herbalist.

But perhaps, like me and many other Progressive Christians, you view the Bible as a holy, sacred book of stories of our ancestors in faith and how they understood God, a divine set of moral stories, history, and mythology to learn from, not as a revelation of God's Law, enshrined on paper, divinely translated and transcribed perfectly for all eternity. So no, I don't think that Exodus's law about killing a fetus really proves what God thinks (because I'm pretty positive God doesn't want us keeping slaves and beating them— same book, same chapter), but it does show clearly that the people of the day didn't value fetuses like the anti-choice crowd now does, and claim that God does (using scripture as backup). They're the first to jump on the likes of me for cherry-picking quotes, but they're leaving out a pretty damning one themselves.

We pray "Thy will be done, on earth as it is in heaven," so I'm pretty sure God would really like our world to be such that no woman ever felt the need to abort, and that we are fucking it up royally. *My God values human life: fetal life, child life, adult life, elderly life.* But my God is not an idiot. God knows that women will choose abortion, for all sorts of reasons, some good, some terrible (for God to judge though, not me!). And God will want them to be safe about it, because God loves them and would rather lose one precious life than two. And so I am vehemently pro-choice, because abortion restrictions do not prevent abortions. They push them underground, and instead of one life lost, there are sometimes two.

And that's what the anti-choicers miss. They're so concerned about the "right" of the fetus to live (I disagree with that too, but on different grounds) that they forget to care about the mother. They say horrible things like "If a woman doesn't want to die of an illegal abortion, she shouldn't have one," which can be translated as "You get what you deserve, slut." They don't care that there are situations where the choice to abort is better than to carry to term—an abusive marriage, the precarious mental or physical health of the mother, the needs of existing children, just for starters. They live in a world of black and white, right and wrong. And that's just simply not reality. We live in a world where there's wrong and more wrong. Right and more right. Where children starve if Mom can't work, and Mom can't work if she's on bed rest. Where husbands beat women for being pregnant, even when they're the ones who got them that way. Where fragile minds would break down if the body had to carry a fetus to term. Where crappy Dads beat the shit out of kids, so maybe it's a bad idea to give them more victims. Where nine-year-olds, whose bodies aren't ready to have babies, are impregnated by their stepfathers.

And NONE of that shit is God's plan. That's us fucking up God's plan. So we can make it worse by limiting women's options, driving them into situations in which they're willing to risk death to end a pregnancy, and blaming them for their predicament, or we can create a world where every pregnancy is a wanted pregnancy. Where every child is cherished. You tell me, just how could God not want that?

I'm still not sure how I feel about the idea that God creates all life. What I think might be true is that God created life and that we propagate it—similar to how I planted the mint in my backyard, and it's spreading. Not by my will, but not against it either. Not that I'm God—it's not a perfect analogy, but something along those lines. We have free will, so we can choose to reproduce or not. I don't believe in predestination or in God as the ultimate puppeteer. I believe that God is with us—nudging us through various means, including conscience, to do the right thing—and we do what we'll do. Sometimes that's what God wants, sometimes it's not. So when a man rapes a woman and God is there, begging him not to, and he does it anyway, it's not God's will that she is impregnated. It just happens. And whether that pregnancy is a tragedy or not is up to her. There will be no judgments from me, because I don't have her experience. I don't have her life. I don't have her beliefs. I don't have her conscience. I don't have her knowledge. We need to trust women to do what is right for them (us) and shut our mouths about it.

The very last bit of Thistlethwaite's *Washington Post* article really struck me, so I'll end with it, too:

> There is, however, no failure of compassion so glaring as the way rape survivors are being made into political and religious scapegoats today.
> Stop that. In God's name, stop it.

Note

1   Richard Mourdock, "On Abortion: Pregnancy from Rape Is 'Something God Intended,'" *Huffington Post*, 23 October 2012, http://www.huffingtonpost.com/2012/10/23/richard-mourdock-abortion_n_2007482.html.

Pro-Choice with No "Buts"

Three Commentaries

LAURA WERSHLER

Between 2004 and 2010, while I was executive director of Planned Parenthood Alberta, which became Sexual Health Access Alberta in 2006, I wrote several commentaries on abortion for the *Calgary Herald*. Some I initiated; others were invited. Two of the commentaries republished here are as pertinent today as they were at the time I wrote them. The first speaks to the stigma of abortion, a stigma that effectively silences the voices of the majority of women who've had abortions and robs the abortion discourse of its most valuable asset: first-hand personal experience. The second addresses a recurring theme in Canadian abortion politics—the idea that it just isn't right that Canada has no laws restricting abortion. The third commentary written for this collection, attempts to convey what it means to me to be "truly pro-choice," to believe in a woman's right to choose to have an abortion without feeling the need to justify or seek approval of her reasons for doing so.

In the summer of 2004, the Planned Parenthood Federation of America raised controversy throughout North America for selling "I had an abortion" T-shirts. Unsurprisingly, the public assumed that all organizations with Planned Parenthood in their name were selling the shirts. I received several angry phone calls and emails from Albertans appalled at the idea of women wearing the message "I had an abortion." While I explained that Planned Parenthood Alberta was not selling the shirts, I also defended the right of women to wear the T-shirts and felt compelled to make a case for their value.

The column was published in the *Calgary Herald* on 30 July 2004. By the time I got to work that morning, I had a phone message from a woman who worked in the same building as I did, the executive director of another non-profit organization. Her message stated that she thought the T-shirts were a bad idea until she read the column. "I hadn't thought about it like that," she said. "You changed my mind."

The Effort to Understand Can Begin with an Unemotional Statement of Fact

"I had an abortion." Why has this statement of fact elicited such fear and loathing from so many?

The furor was sparked by the news that the Planned Parenthood Federation of America is selling T-shirts with the simple statement "I had an abortion."

Neither the Planned Parenthood Federation of Canada nor Planned Parenthood Alberta is involved with this campaign. Canadians have chosen a gentler approach to the abortion debate that rages on in the United States. Yet the very thought of millions of American women calmly announcing "I had an abortion" to friends, neighbours, and strangers has the Canadian public squirming.

If the power of an idea can be measured by the virulence of the response it receives, then the idea of women refusing to be silenced or shamed for choosing a safe, legal, and common procedure to manage their own reproductive lives is a very powerful one.

The words "I had an abortion" do not overtly express sorrow or shame, joy or sadness, fear or relief. It is the lack of emotion in the statement that seems to offend so many, including the gentleman who

Without Apology

called me to express his objection to the T-shirt caption. As I told him, this does not mean these or other emotions were not felt by the women who chose abortion. It's just that the emotional content of each woman's story belongs to her.

The critics' response to these T-shirts superimposes their own vitriolic emotions onto the prospective wearers. They seem to think it is fine and dandy for others to walk around in "Abortion is Homicide" T-shirts, expressing an opinion not shared by the courts or the majority of citizens in either the United States or Canada and one that could be construed as libellous to those who provide or choose abortions, while those who have the courage or gall to reveal a personal truth should be ashamed of themselves.

What do the critics know about each and every woman's abortion experience? Absolutely nothing. And therein lies the power of the T-shirt idea.

It is one thing to heap scorn on abortion as a concept, a choice, or a medical procedure. It is quite another to heap scorn on a real woman with a face, a family, and an abortion story who refuses to be silenced, shamed, or ignored because she made a choice that millions of women have made since the beginning of time.

Perhaps the knee-jerk negative reaction to the T-shirts reflects the shame and helplessness many of us feel, consciously or not, about our failure as a culture to diminish the need for girls and women to choose abortion.

Despite all our reproductive technology and our public education efforts, many women daily still face the tough decision about whether or not to continue a pregnancy they did not plan or intend. What failure of responsibility do we all, individually and collectively, have to account for?

According to the Planned Parenthood Federation of America, one in three women in the United States will have had an abortion before the age of forty-five. Because of universal health care and better sexuality education, Canadian figures may be less, but the point is made.

Abortion is part of many women's experience. Blame these women if you dare, but one day they may decide to stand up en masse and ask you to hear their stories and compel you to start asking questions that lead to understanding, compassion, and action.

If, by some chance, every single woman in North America who has had an abortion chose to acknowledge this tomorrow by wearing the T-shirt, we would all be shocked by how many of these women we know. And truly humbled by the depth and breadth of the abortion experience.

The anti-choice movement would be over and the effort to understand would begin.

———◆———

This second commentary appeared in the *Calgary Herald* on 28 January 2008, a day that marked the twentieth anniversary of the *Morgentaler* decision. I was asked by the *Calgary Herald* to write a column from the pro-choice perspective. The papers had been full of commentaries in the week leading up to the anniversary, so I was able to push back against some of the arguments calling for the decision to be revisited. The arguments I made then are the same I'd make today against those who insist that Canadians reopen the debate on abortion. As I write, this commentary is still posted on the websites of the International Medical Abortion Consortium and the Safe and Legal in Ireland Abortion Rights Campaign.

A Canadian Controversy—a Wise and Just Decision, Worthy of Canadians

As Canadians celebrate, agitate, or ruminate on the twentieth anniversary of the Supreme Court decision to strike down Canada's abortion laws, it is time to consider the general impact of this judgment.

Twenty years without any abortion law is considered scandalous by some. Yet, when compared to other countries with laws governing abortion, Canada is an intriguing example of how unnecessary such laws actually may be.

Writing in a *National Post* commentary on 22 January 2008, David Frum called the Canadian situation "the Western world's most radical abortion regime." In this case, "radical" is best defined as going to the root or foundation of something. Radical as in fundamental.

The fundamental truth of having no abortion laws (and having universal health care) is that positive outcomes have ensued. When comparing the US situation to ours, a reasonable, thinking person would admit that having no law has been more effective at managing outcomes than has the morass of restrictions legislated south of the border.

Canadian women have about one-quarter fewer abortions per 1,000 women than American women.[1] In Canada, a greater percentage of abortions are done before twelve weeks than in the United States. Canada also has one of the lowest maternal mortality and complication rates for abortion in the world. In addition, Canada's abortion rates are similar to or lower than those in European countries that do have laws restricting abortion and have generally been in decline since 1997.

What the *Morgentaler* decision has meant for Canada is that abortion has settled into the domain in which it rightly belongs—the health care system. It is a medical procedure that, as two decades have proved, can be appropriately regulated by provincial Colleges of Physicians and Surgeons.

Canada's abortion statistics bear this out, including those related to the most controversial aspect of our no law status—that there are no legal restrictions on late-term abortions.

Procedures occurring after twenty weeks gestation make up less than 0.6 percent of abortions.[2] Late-term abortion is rare, difficult to access, and provided only in cases of serious maternal or fetal health problems.

It is inflammatory to suggest, as does a recent national billboard campaign by LifeCanada, that women do or can access abortion on demand when they are nine months pregnant.

To further demonstrate how abortion laws have no real power to impact actual abortion rates, consider a study by the Guttmacher Institute and the World Health Organization published in October 2007 by the medical journal *The Lancet*.[3] It found that abortion rates in countries worldwide are similar regardless of whether the procedure is legal or not. "The legal status of abortion has never dissuaded women and couples, who, for whatever reason, seek to end pregnancy," said Beth Fredrick of the International Women's Health Coalition, commenting on the study.

Herein lies another fundamental truth about abortion: that whether legal or not, safe or not, abortion is a choice often made by normal women all around the world. We cannot deny this. We could do worse as a society than to normalize abortion as a fact of human experience. Not normal as in blasé, but normal as in standard, natural, common.

Canada, it could be argued, has been doing just this for the past twenty years. We have, to a lesser or greater degree, depending on where you live in this expansive country, normalized abortion as a medically necessary, reasonably accessible, and compassionately delivered health care procedure.

Canada also continues striving, through sexual health education and services, to reduce the need for abortion.

Perhaps this normalization is what most aggravates those who want to keep the abortion controversy simmering—or boiling over onto the political stovetop.

Barbara Kay, also writing in the *National Post* last week, argued that Canadians who believe abortion should be restricted in some cases have been silenced. She noted astutely that "the 20-year anniversary of any transformative social decision is a good moment for a dispassionate review of the decision's consequences."

Could it be the consequences of the *Morgentaler* decision that have kept our politicians from responding to calls for discussion on legal restrictions to abortion?

After all, a dispassionate review reveals that abortion in Canada is being appropriately regulated by the medical profession with reasonable outcomes equal to or better than countries that do have laws restricting abortion.

All things considered, it appears the decision made twenty years ago today by the Supreme Court of Canada was wise, just, and worthy of Canadians.

———◆———

To these commentaries I now add a third that challenges what it really means to support a woman's right to abortion and explores what appears to be the habitual need to qualify the morality of women's decision-making.

So You Think You Want an Abortion

In my evolution as a sexual, reproductive, and abortion rights advocate, I can almost remember the day when the penny dropped and I understood what it meant to be truly pro-choice. *Pro-choice with no provisos.*

Not: *"I support abortion, but not when it's used as birth control."*

Not: *"I believe in a woman's right to choose, but not her right to have multiple abortions."*

Not: *"I support abortion rights, but no one should be able to have an abortion after twelve weeks."*

Not: *"I am a pro-choice feminist, but I can't condone the selective abortion of female fetuses."*

Just: *"I support a woman's right to choose to have an abortion."*

Proviso thinking stems from the belief that, surely, to be moral and upstanding as both individuals and a nation, we must impose *some* restrictions on abortion. This opinion continues to ignore the fact that since 1988, abortion in Canada has been effectively regulated by the Canadian Medical Association and provincial medical governing bodies. Having no law does not mean that there are no restrictions on abortion: no woman who is thirty-nine weeks pregnant can walk into an abortion clinic in Canada and demand an abortion.

The proviso game is really about judging women's reasons. Many people who consider themselves pro-choice find it hard *not* to judge women's reasons for choosing abortion, yet they fail to realize that it's a no-win pursuit. It ends in a tangle of circular argument:

> *She didn't use birth control so she can't have an abortion. . . . Her birth control failed, but she can't have an abortion because she's already had one. . . . Another abortion? Oh, she was sexually assaulted. . . . She's eighteen weeks pregnant? Well, she can't have an abortion, it's too late! . . . Why did she wait so long? Oh, her pro-life doctor lied and told her she wasn't pregnant. . . . If she can't figure out how to get an abortion before twelve weeks she shouldn't be able to have one. Oh, she was living in rural PEI, and it took her a month to plan a trip to the abortion clinic in New Brunswick. . . . Oh my, this does get complicated.*

Beyond the issues of contraceptive failure and timely access to abortion services, it gets even more complicated. Disability rights activists are concerned that the selective abortion of fetuses with disabilities devalues the lives of people with disabilities and that genetic testing revealing fetal anomalies may result in undue pressure on women to abort. Undue pressure on women to abort for any reason is unacceptable, but the idea of restricting access to abortion to protect fetuses with disabilities is illogical. Why should it be legal to abort a fetus without a genetic disorder but not a fetus with a genetic disorder?

Opponents to abortion in the United States have recently begun to push for laws that would ban abortion on the basis of a Down syndrome diagnosis. Rachel Adams, the mother of a Down syndrome child, believes these laws are not about fighting prejudice but about limiting women's reproductive rights. In a column for the *Washington Post* she writes that "we won't end discrimination by limiting access to abortion, which will have the unwanted consequence of driving some women to risk their health by seeking illegal alternatives and other women to bear children they are not prepared to raise."[4]

Sex-selective abortion has also attracted controversy, along with calls for restrictions such as denying parents information about the sex of their baby until after the second trimester of pregnancy or making sex-selective abortion illegal altogether. The abortion of female fetuses is problematic for many feminists, but are legal restrictions an effective way to change deeply engrained cultural attitudes that value boys over girls?

This issue provides an example of how, in Canada, the medical profession can address such concerns in a way that precludes the need to enact laws restricting abortion. In February 2014, the Society of Obstetricians and Gynaecologists of Canada (SOGC) and the Canadian Association of Radiologists (CAR) issued a joint policy statement on the nonmedical use of fetal ultrasound. The statement specifically addresses what the authors refer to as "entertainment" ultrasounds performed for nonmedical reasons without guarantee of technical safeguards and operator qualifications. The policy states that ultrasound technology "should *not* be used for the sole purpose of determining fetal gender without a medical indication for that scan." Without calling for restrictions to abortion, the SOGC and CAR "encourage governments to join with our organizations to find appropriate means to deal with this public health issue."[5]

The bottom line for this abortion rights advocate is that the reason a woman chooses to end a pregnancy in any situation is none of my business. I don't know her story or her situation. How can I presume to judge or condone or reject her reason? I may not agree with her reason, I may not like her reason, but it is her reason to have and to act on. To believe otherwise is to believe that I'm more qualified to make this decision for her than she is.

Politicians and pundits who keep insisting that it's time to talk about imposing a set of restrictions on abortion in Canada should ask themselves why they believe that they, or any of us, qualify to be the arbiters of women's reasons for choosing abortion.

The no-proviso pro-choice position acknowledges that there are as many reasons for choosing to have an abortion as there are women who choose to have one. I can't understand them all, nor do I have to agree with them all, but I will not support any effort to deny any woman the right to act upon her self-determined reason for having an abortion.

◆

Will there come a time when these kinds of commentaries in support of a woman's right to have an abortion are no longer needed? We might hope so, but I think the reality is that reproductive health advocates will continue to face challenges that demand reaction, response, and action, such as the sustained pressure that abortion activists on Prince Edward Island put on the provincial government in order to make abortion services at long last accessible in that province.

Maintaining abortion rights requires vigilance, as our American colleagues know all too well. But, in Canada, the legacy of the 1988 *Morgentaler* decision that struck down this country's abortion laws continues to inform public sentiment. Ipsos poll results released on 24 February 2016 show that the percentage of "Canadians who believe abortion should be permitted whenever a woman decides she wants one" has steadily increased, from 36 percent in 1998, a decade after *Morgentaler*, to 57 percent at present.[6] And we can be assured that the pro-choice, majority Liberal government elected in October 2015 will not challenge the position of the majority of Canadians.

Notes

1   The statistics here and below were accurate at the time the article was written; I have appended a few notes for the present publication. According to the United Nations, in 2007, the abortion rate in Canada stood at 15.2 per 1,000 women of childbearing age and at 20.8 in the United States. By 2013, the numbers had fallen slightly, to 13.7 in Canada and 19.6 in the US. See United Nations, Department of Social and Economic Affairs, Population Division, *World Abortion Policies 2007* and *World Abortion Policies 2013*. In Canada, statistics about abortion are now compiled annually by the Canadian Institute for Health Information (CIHI). In the US, similar statistics are periodically released by the Centers for Disease Control and Prevention. See, for example, "Abortion

Surveillance—United States, 2011," Center for Disease Control and Prevention, *Morbidity and Mortality Weekly Report*, 28 November 2014, http://www.cdc.gov/mmwr/preview/mmwrhtml/ss6311a1.htm.

2   Although these statistics would not yet have been available at the time this article was written, according to the CIHI, 98,762 abortions were performed in Canada in 2007, of which only 549 (0.56%) were reported to have occurred at a gestational age of 21 or more weeks.

3   See Gilda Sedgh, Stanley Henshaw, Susheela Singh, Elisabeth Åhman, and Iqbal H. Shah, "Induced Abortion: Estimated Rates and Trends Worldwide," *The Lancet* 370, no. 9595 (13 October 2007): 1338–45.

4   Rachel E. Adams, "My Son with Down Syndrome Is Not a Mascot for Abortion Restrictions," *Washington Post*, 19 February 2016.

5   Shia Salem, Kenneth Lim, and Michiel Van den Hof, "Joint SOGC/CAR Policy Statement on Mon-medical Use of Fetal Ultrasound," SOGC Policy Statement no. 304, Society of Obstetricians and Gynaecologists of Canada, February 2014, http://sogc.org/wp-content/uploads/2014/02/gui304PS1402Erev.pdf.

6   For the results of the poll, see Andrew Russell, "6 in 10 Canadians Support Abortion Under Any Circumstances: Ipsos Poll," *Global News*, 23 February 2016, http://globalnews.ca/news/2535846/6-in-10-canadians-support-abor tion-under-any-circumstances-ipsos-poll/.

Expanding the Reproductive Justice Lexicon

A Case for the Label *Pro-abortion*

LAURA GILLESPIE

"Pro-choice is not pro-abortion; no one is pro-abortion." As an avid Internet peruser and social media enthusiast, this is a sentiment I frequently, and unfortunately, see bandied about by pro-choice activists online.[1] It's unfortunate because while it is true that these terms are not equivalent, it's also true that they are not incompatible. Yet when this notion is expressed by those in the pro-choice community, it usually carries with it the implication that *pro-choice* is a noble label and worthy cause—a sentiment with which I heartily agree—while *pro-abortion* is an insulting attack on a person's moral fibre. This does not have to be the case. *Pro-abortion* need not be an inherently disparaging term; rather, it has abundant potential to be utilized within a positive and empowering framework. In this context; the term is worth exploring: What exactly does it mean to be pro-abortion? How can we, as a movement, shift the discourse to elicit more positive associations? And, perhaps more importantly, why should we do so?

First, it is imperative to recognize that *pro-abortion*, like most labels, carries with it no uncomplicated, cut-and-dried definition. When used by those who are anti-choice, it tends to carry the implication that they are exposing the term *pro-choice* as a euphemism used to gain support for a cause based solely around providing abortions; thus, in their opinion, *pro-abortion* is a more transparent, direct, and accurate label. For instance, in 2013, when Planned Parenthood announced its decision to move on from the pro-choice label, Jill Stanek, writing for the anti-abortion LifeSite News, rallied behind this shift, claiming that *pro-choice* was initially developed as a way "to counter 'pro-life' with an 'anything-but-abortion' phrase."[2] She goes on to assert that Planned Parenthood's linguistic shift should be viewed as a victory for the anti-choice movement, since they had successfully "made the term 'pro-choice' synonymous with 'pro-abortion.'"

While this anti-choice misunderstanding is worrisome and a worthy topic of discussion in and of itself, what predominantly elicits my concern is the way in which *pro-abortion* is comprehended by those who identify as pro-choice. Common, though not ubiquitous, within the pro-choice discussion of this term is the understanding that *pro-abortion* necessarily entails the pursuit of coerced termination and a belief in abortion as the preferred choice for all pregnant persons. For instance, in her article "What Pro-choice Really Means," Joyce Arthur, founder and executive director of the Abortion Rights Coalition of Canada, asserts that "pro-choice does not mean pro-abortion. We do not advocate for abortion over birth."[3] Likewise, Stacey Jacobs, a Canadian Planned Parenthood sexual health educator, explicitly argues that "no one is pro-abortion."[4] She explains this position by stating her hope that "no one would want a woman to be in a position where she has to make the decision to terminate her pregnancy," thus implying that such a belief would be intrinsic to a pro-abortion stance. In essence, although statements such as these do reject the problematic anti-choice notion that *pro-choice* and *pro-abortion* are synonymous, in doing so, they concede the point that pro-abortion is a derogatory term and therefore seek to distance themselves—and, by extension, the pro-choice movement—from it.

These interpretations, both anti- and pro-choice alike, seem to stem from a variety of sources, including fear of abortion and the fact that abortion is entrenched in social stigma. But particularly significant for my defence of the term here is the fact that its rejection by pro-choice activists seems to be a defensive reaction to its misappropriation by abortion opponents, who hurl it derisively at the pro-choice cause. Of course, if we are to accept the pejorative definitions of *pro-abortion* ascribed by abortion opponents, then intelligent and thoughtful pro-choice advocates, such as Arthur and Jacobs, are correct to argue that no one is pro-abortion. It hardly needs saying that there are few people—if any—who advocate for coercive abortion practices or the termination of all pregnancies, or who take pleasure in a person's experience with an unwanted pregnancy. Moreover, such sentiments are certainly not within the purview of a pro-choice stance. However, while I agree that the aforementioned formulations of *pro-abortion* are abhorrent, it is also possible to consciously and actively reject these negative characterizations in favour of a positive, empowering definition of the term. When I state that I'm pro-abortion, what I hope to convey is that I unequivocally and unconditionally support the existence of safe, legal, accessible abortion services; I recognize that abortion is a common, necessary medical procedure that is undeserving of the shame and stigma it currently receives; I acknowledge that any reason for choosing abortion is a valid one; and I understand that it's not up to me, nor anyone else, to police individuals' motivations for exercising control over their own reproductive lives. I do not, however, advocate for the termination of all pregnancies, nor do I condone coercing individuals into accessing abortion.

Plainly stated, I do not believe that every pregnant person should have an abortion—only those who require one. And to be clear, by "those who require," I mean anyone who is pregnant and either does not want to be or wants to be but is unable to continue on with the pregnancy for whatever reason. With this in mind, it is pertinent to reinforce the point that *pro-choice* and *pro-abortion*, though correlated, are not interchangeable, despite the anti-choice assertion to the contrary. My identity as pro-abortion is only a part of my identity as pro-choice, which, in turn, is only one component of being a reproductive rights advocate. Along this vein, I consider myself the bearer of many simultaneous and intersecting labels including pro-choice, pro–birth rights, pro–pregnant person, pro-family, pro-child, pro-adoption, and pro-abortion. None of these labels is equivalent or contradictory to any of the others, though I do consider them each to fall under the rubric of reproductive justice.[5] Effectively, what I hope this far-from-exhaustive list is able to convey is that although *pro-abortion* and *pro-choice* may not be interchangeable, they need not exist in conflict; in fact, they have great capacity to complement each other.

I understand that even with a positive definition available, there will be those who identify as pro-choice who will still not feel comfortable calling themselves pro-abortion, and that's okay; it's not up to me, or anyone else, to tell others how they should self-identify. There is still an overwhelming amount of societally imposed stigma surrounding abortion, and even people who recognize the need for it to be an available choice may still not look too kindly upon the procedure itself. This can be clearly seen, for example, in the oft-quoted and pervasive motto—initiated by Bill Clinton and adopted by many in the pro-choice community—that abortion ought to be "safe, legal, and rare." This seemingly enviable goal of ensuring the rarity of abortion is itself a value judgement, however, as it implies there is something invalid and shameful about abortion as a procedure. In her 2010 research article, which seeks to re-examine the "safe, legal, rare" mantra, Tracy Weitz, director for Advancing New Standards in Reproductive Health, argues that "'rare' suggests that abortion is happening more than it should, and that there are some conditions for which abortion should and should not occur. It separates good abortions from bad abortions."[6] Jessica Valenti, author and co-founder of Feministing.com, agrees, stating that "the 'rare' framework adds to the stigmatisation of the procedure."[7] That is, rather than focusing on reducing the number of unwanted pregnancies, increasing knowledge of and access to contraception, or expanding support for new parents, this viewpoint problematizes abortion as something we should strive to diminish, even while recognizing its necessity. Overall, it is unlikely that those who subscribe to the perspective that abortion is a morally fraught, though necessary, procedure will be apt to call themselves pro-abortion, despite identifying as pro-choice.

This may lead one to question my ultimate goal of appropriating the term if I do not hold the expectation that all who identify as pro-choice will also adopt the *pro-abortion* label for themselves. While I strive for a more common and normalized inclusion of the label into the pro-choice discourse, what I would most like to see is for fellow reproductive rights advocates to simply have a more genial view of the term. More specifically, I would urge allies not to dismiss the label entirely or, at the very least, not to disparage it alongside abortion opponents. I realize this is no easy feat, as the term *pro-abortion* often gets thrust upon those who are pro-choice by the anti-choice crowd with the intent of making our movement seem reductive and cold. Of course, this only works if we accept the pejorative connotations with which it has been imbued; moreover, it only works if we accept that abortion is a shameful word, capable of breeding insult.

Words carry incredible power, and it's a clever rhetorical trick to take something a group supports, make it sound disgraceful, and then proceed to throw it back in their faces. Not only is it clever; it's apparently also effective, since many who are pro-choice seem not to think twice about deriding the term *pro-abortion* in tandem with those who are anti-choice. However, when pro-choice advocates spew forth this internalized invective, they are perpetuating the idea that abortion is a shameful procedure worthy of derision, which only furthers anti-choice sentiments regarding the morality of abortion and those who access it. It's a divisive practice that leads to pro-choice infighting and derails the movement from its ultimate goal of reproductive justice for all. That is, focus shifts from concerns such as expanding access to and knowledge about reproductive services to a defensive rejection of *pro-abortion*, a label that has potential to be used productively as a way to express acceptance of a procedure that is integral to achieving comprehensive reproductive health care.

It's important to remember that language is malleable, and we have the power to resist shame-inducing and restrictive definitions of *pro-abortion*. Whether by not reacting defensively when we are labelled *pro-abortion* by those who are anti-choice, or by not capitulating to the notion that it's an inherently vicious label, or by explicitly and unapologetically identifying ourselves as pro-abortion, we can challenge how this term is currently defined. In doing so, we can shift the discourse so that *pro-abortion* connotes nothing less than support for abortion as a valid medical procedure and support for those who require access to abortion services. This does not mean, however, that we should leave unchallenged any assertion that *pro-abortion* is synonymous with *pro-choice*. We can and should dispute this equivalency. As previously stated, pro-choice is indicative of much more than abortion access; moreover, there are numerous issues unrelated to abortion that are central to the reproductive rights movement. It is a dynamic and complex movement that cannot be reduced to a single cause. Thus, regardless of whether individuals incorporate the pro-abortion label into their personal repertoires, we, as a movement, should ensure that we're not denigrating the term or making those who do choose to adopt it feel ashamed, or as if they're somehow faulty reproductive rights advocates, for doing so.

What is central to this discussion is the understanding that abortion is neither a shameful word nor a shameful concept, so why would we treat it as if it were? By incorporating *pro-abortion* into the reproductive justice discourse within a positive capacity, we can actively work to reduce the shame and stigma that are needlessly and undeservedly associated with this common, legal medical procedure. As a wise, albeit fictional, professor once said, "Fear of a name increases fear of the thing itself."[8] Abortion and those who access abortion services do not deserve fear or shame; they deserve support and compassion, as well as the knowledge that their choice is a valid one. Therefore, let's not sit complacently by and accept the hostile and insulting implications associated with current usage; instead, let's actively reject attempts to imbue *pro-abortion*, and thus abortion itself, with negative connotations. I, for one, am proud to be pro-abortion.

Notes

1   In addition to hostile interpretations by those who are anti-choice, a quick Internet search using the phrase "pro-choice is not pro-abortion" will reveal that pro-choice advocates also have many antagonistic understandings of *pro-abortion*. For a few examples, see Corey Purdy-Smith, "Pro-choice Is Not Pro-abortion," Abortion Rights Coalition of Canada, September 2008, http://www.arcc-cdac.ca/presentations/smith. html; Kimberly Johnson, "I'm Pro-choice Not Pro-abortion," *Liberals Unite*, 8 August 2014, http://samuel-warde.com/2014/08/im-pro-choice-pro-abortion/; and responses to the question "Is Pro-choice a Code Name for Pro-abortion?" at *Debate.org*, n.d., http://www.debate.org/opinions/is-pro-choice-a-code-name-for-pro-abortion.

2   Jill Stanek, "Planned Parenthood Quietly Abandons Term 'Pro-choice,'" *LifeSite* USA, 11 January 2013, http://www.lifesitenews.com/opinion/planned-parenthood-abandons-term-pro-choice.

3   Joyce Arthur, "What Pro-choice Really Means," Pro-choice Action Network, 2000, http://www.prochoiceactionnetwork-canada.org/articles/realchoice.shtml.

4   Stacey Jacobs, "Sexplanations with Stacey: Defining Pro-choice," *The Cord: The Community Edition*, 3 July 2014, http://community.thecord.ca/blog/2014/07/03/defining-pro-choice/.

5   I say this with the acknowledgement that *reproductive justice* is a historically rich term that was developed by women of colour to account for disparities between their experiences with reproductive health care and

those of middle-class white women. See Jennifer Nelson, *Women of Color and the Reproductive Rights Movement* (New York: New York University Press, 2003).

6   Tracy A. Weitz, "Rethinking the Mantra That Abortion Should Be 'Safe, Legal, and Rare,'" *Journal of Women's History* 22, no. 3 (2010): 164.

7   Jessica Valenti, "Hillary Clinton Must Reject the Stigma That Abortion Should Be Legal but 'Rare,'" *The Guardian*, 9 July 2014.

8   J. K. Rowling, *Harry Potter and the Philosopher's Stone* (London: Bloomsbury, 1997), 216.

Same as It Ever Was

Anti-choice Extremism and the "Third Way"

JANE CAWTHORNE

For many years, right-wing anti-abortion proponents have adopted the language and tactics of the Left in order to implement an agenda that rescinds the accomplishments of the latter. Like citizens of a democracy using their freedom to elect a dictator, these activists use the freedom gained through the successes of anti-oppression movements to rebuild oppression. Some have abandoned the religious rhetoric of the past and are now using the language of science and human rights to make their case. They seek a renewed debate on abortion in Canada. They propose changes to legislation that would incrementally chip away at access to abortion by prioritizing the rights of the fetus over the rights of women. But otherwise, the movement is the same as it ever was. The absolute prohibition of abortion remains its goal, and violence underwrites its tactics. Those of us who consider ourselves truly moderate, pro-choice, and progressive Canadians must understand how our best practices, including our respect for free speech and human rights, are being used by anti-choice groups to undermine the gains we have made in promoting respect for women's rights.

In a June 2009 article in the *National Post* about an anti-abortion group called Signal Hill, commentator Charles Lewis refers to the new methods of the anti-choice movement as a "third-way approach." He quotes Yvonne Douma, the organization's executive director, as saying that Signal Hill has given up seeking legislation to criminalize abortion and instead wants to "create a Canada where demand for abortions dwindles and decreases until there's none left—not because it was forced upon anyone, but because that is what women choose." As Lewis goes on to remark, "For an anti-abortion group, it is a radical approach—relying on soft options of winning hearts and minds rather than hard-hitting campaigns and protests."[1] In other words, it is radical for an anti-choice group to be moderate. Stephen Harper, our former prime minister, seems to be a proponent of this "third way." In a January 2011 interview with CBC's Peter Mansbridge, he declared, "What I say to people, if you want to diminish the number of abortions, you've got to change hearts and not laws. And I'm not interested in having a debate over abortion law."[2] Harper's lack of interest may be because Canadians generally feel that the issue has been decided and because efforts to enact a law restricting access to abortion have not met with success.[3]

Opening hearts and minds, though, requires ongoing discussion. That is why anti-choice groups in Canada have made reopening the debate on abortion a priority. Calling for debate is a seemingly reasonable request: debate is a tool of democracy, a fair and balanced means of swaying opinion. It is difficult for a moderate person to refuse such a modest request. On the one hand, rejecting debate is seen as intransigent and possibly petulant, as a sign that the side that is refusing discussion is doomed and cannot defend itself. On the other hand, only those interested in upending the status quo on abortion push for a renewed debate. No one else has anything to gain. As the Abortion Rights Coalition of Canada has made clear, all requests to reopen the debate are thinly disguised attempts to recriminalize abortion.[4]

Knowing this, pro-choice groups have consistently refused to debate abortion. A typical response, one I have given myself, is, "I don't debate abortion because abortion is a human right and human rights are not up for debate." Yet even I have been sucked into debate. While Stephen Harper grandstanded his Maternal Health Initiative in front of the 2010 G8 and G20 summits, an initiative that failed to include abortion care, I agreed to be part of the Munk Debates to highlight this critical failure. My reasoning was that the debate was not about abortion itself but about the inclusion of funding for abortion care in international aid. But this is exactly the kind of hair-splitting that opens the door for a debate on abortion itself. I should have known better. In fact, the Maternal Health Initiative was a critical wedge used to reopen the debate in Canada, something Harper still denies having done.

The "third way" position is an effort to put a foot in the door and generate talk around the issue. According to Lewis, groups like Signal Hill "want to radically shift the conversation from the polarized rut it has been stuck in for years to something more productive."[5] What Lewis doesn't say is that Signal Hill and other proponents of the "third way" want to reshape the debate so that it is more productive *for them*. The tactic has caught on throughout the anti-choice movement, and all parts of it have adopted the language. For example, anti-choice blogger Andrea Mrozek, my opponent in the Munk Debates, represents a "third way" position. According to her blog, *ProWomanProLife*, she "desires to bring an end to abortion, not by coercion, but by choice."[6] There is recognition by Signal Hill that even with laws, abortion continues. In the Lewis article, Mrozek concurs with Signal Hill: "My approach was to go after cultural change and pull it out of the legislative arena and not even talk about it or discuss it. Politicians will not take this on anytime soon."[7]

But when the topic turns to rights, there is no middle ground for Mrozek. In her blog, she states, "It's not a woman's right to have an abortion. . . . There's no such thing as a right to an abortion, not for women, not for men. It doesn't contribute to women's rights and freedoms at all, because having an abortion is, put simply, not a right."[8] Here, Mrozek disagrees with the Supreme Court of Canada, which upheld women's right to abortion in the 1988 *Morgentaler* decision. This decision asserts that women must have access to abortion to ensure their right to security of the person and to freedom of conscience, thought, and belief. It says, among other things, that

> the right to "liberty" contained in s. 7 guarantees to every individual
> a degree of personal autonomy over important decisions intimately
> affecting his or her private life. Liberty in a free and democratic society
> does not require the state to approve such decisions but it does require
> the state to respect them. A woman's decision to terminate her preg-
> nancy falls within this class of protected decisions.[9]

While Mrozek is correct in that the word "abortion" isn't found in the Canadian Charter of Rights and Freedoms, the words that *are* there have been interpreted to include that right.

Although Signal Hill no longer works toward the change they seek through legal means, other abortion opponents do. For example, in 2014, Conservative MP Jim Hillyer sent out a flyer to his constituents asking, "Do you agree with Jim Hillyer that abortion is NOT a human right?"[10] The question lays the groundwork for a future appeal to the objectivity of law in the form of legislation concerning human rights. Another way in which anti-choice groups attempt to unravel the status quo is by taking issue with the use of the word "everyone" in the Charter. The Charter uses the word to describe who is entitled to the rights and freedoms it outlines.[11] Anti-choice advocates want to include the fetus in "everyone," giving the fetus the same protections as women. As a result, anti-choice MPs have attempted, on numerous occasions, to introduce legislation through private members' bills that would give the fetus the same status as women. For example, a 2008 private member's bill called the Unborn Victims of Crime Act (C-484) attempted to amend the Criminal Code to allow separate criminal charges to be laid in the case of injury or death of a fetus that results from a pregnant woman being the victim of an offence. Had it passed, this bill would have been a step toward giving "personhood" to the fetus. It did not pass, in part because it would have been an unconstitutional infringement on women's rights and would probably have resulted in criminalizing pregnant women for behaviours perceived to harm their fetuses.

These efforts obscure an irreconcilable difference between the pro-choice and anti-choice positions. The woman and the fetus are not two separate entities but exist within one body. How can two entities have rights within the same body, and what is to be done if these rights conflict? The Wisdom of Solomon cannot resolve the conflict. Anti-choice advocates privilege the rights of the fetus, while pro-choice advocates privilege the rights of the woman who carries it. If anti-choice advocates such as Mrozek were to state unequivocally that they prioritize the rights of the fetus over those of the woman, they could surely not claim to be pro-woman at the same time, at least not beyond supporting a woman in her very narrowly defined role in reproduction. To Mrozek and her allies, there is only one important right at stake—the right of the fetus to be born.

Without Apology

At the same time as this irreconcilable difference is ignored, anti-choice proponents promote a philosophical paradigm in which the woman and her fetus are in conflict. In doing so, they assert that such conflict needs to be resolved by someone other than the woman, because she may choose an abortion. She cannot be trusted to make a choice that favours the fetus. The organization We Need a Law, another group working toward recriminalization, focuses on enacting new laws to protect the fetus. In its mission statement, We Need a Law claims that as "the only nation in the Western world without abortion legislation," Canada needs to "fall into step" with other nations and "enact a law that protects pre-born humans." The group further asserts that Canada's lack of an abortion law "is a sad reflection on a country that prides itself on a high standard of human rights" and that this "egregious violation of rights against pre-born children needs to be addressed."[12] Again, the rights of the "pre-born" are privileged over the rights of the "post-born." The rights of the "post-born" are not in the organization's bailiwick.

But as former prime minister Stephen Harper and others have admitted, getting a law, getting "the" law, is unlikely. Like the 2008 effort to include the fetus as a possible victim of crime, another backbench initiative, introduced in 2012 as Motion 312, asked Parliament to study medical evidence about when life begins. Instead of going straight to a demand for new legislation to recriminalize abortion or prohibit it, the author of the motion, Stephen Woodworth, then a Conservative MP, took a step backwards in the process. All he wanted was a committee to determine when a fetus becomes human. It is likely that, had the motion passed, such a committee would have asserted that zygotes, embryos, and fetuses are human beings from conception since they possess human DNA. (But the reasoning is nonsensical because an eyelash or a malignant tumour also includes human DNA.) One imagines that at that point, Woodworth and his allies would have asked Parliament to change the Criminal Code to reflect the new definition and scientific evidence. But the motion conflates the legal issue of personhood with a medical understanding of what it means to be human. In doing so, the motion is intended to be a first step to giving the fetus legal personhood, at which point it would be entitled to human rights, a cause that would then be taken up with gusto by those on the Right. Again, the fact that such rights would subordinate the rights of pregnant women is not their concern. As Gordon O'Connor, then the Conservative Party whip, said while speaking against the motion in the House, "The ultimate intention of this motion is to restrict abortions in Canada at some fetal development stage."[13]

The call for a seemingly unbiased committee to define "human" is appealing, then, but only until one remembers that it obscures the real dilemma of potentially having two entities with (possibly conflicting) rights existing in one body. It might also seem reasonable because it is an improvement on the violence that characterizes the so-called pro-life movement. For years we have seen women harangued and harassed for exercising their legal rights; clinics targeted and bombed; and doctors threatened, injured, and murdered by anti-choice activists who claim to speak for the "pre-born." Although anti-choice groups are generally quick to denounce the violence within their movement and distance themselves from perpetrators, they benefit from the culture of fear that the violence creates.[14] A bully needs only to throw an occasional punch to maintain dominance, whether in the schoolyard or in wider society. One of the results of this violence is that pro-choice advocates are sometimes reluctant to engage with those who are anti-choice, knowing that others who have done so have been targeted with hate mail, harassment, and physical violence. It is tempting to let an unknown "committee" settle the question instead of risking one's personal safety. As Sam Harris writes in *Letter to a Christian Nation*, "Our fear of provoking religious hatred has rendered us unwilling to criticize ideas that are increasingly maladaptive and patently ridiculous."[15]

All of the "third way" strategies considered thus far are blatantly evident in one of the least moderate anti-choice groups in Canada, the Canadian Centre for Bio-ethical Reform (CCBR). It too uses "third way" language. The group's name infers its assertion that the "bio-ethics" of Canadians are in need of reform. Such reform would privilege the rights of the fetus. "Bio-ethical" is an interesting choice of words. Again, it has secular appeal. The "bio" makes it appear scientific and a matter for academics rather than theologians.

The CCBR's tagline is "See it. Believe it. End it." Like its American cousin, the Center for Bio-ethical Reform, the CCBR considers abortion the greatest evil of our time and is dedicated to "making abortion unthinkable," a phrase that is ubiquitous on the group's website. Although a disclaimer runs across the bottom of its home page saying it denounces violence, the CCBR seems to have a limited understanding of what constitutes violence. In more socially progressive contexts, we understand that violence doesn't always leave a physical mark. Violence can be emotional, psychological, and verbal. In this wider context, some CCBR tactics can be considered violent. For example, in its Genocide Awareness Project (GAP), the CCBR uses graphic imagery to equate legal abortion with genocide. GAP activists sets up graphic side-walk displays of allegedly aborted fetuses next to images of victims of the Holocaust, lynchings in the American south, and other genocides. They place these displays in high traffic areas, near abortion clinics, in front of pro-choice sexual health centres, in schools, and at the entrances to events that are likely to draw a crowd, including family events such as the Calgary Stampede. Passersby come upon the images without warning. No attempts are made to prevent children from seeing the images, and they do—these are public spaces.

The graphic nature of the displays is designed to provoke and trigger distress, which it does. Carol Williams and Don Gill explain that the tactics of the Genocide Awareness Project should make us wary. Wrenching images from their specific historical context and attaching them to an unrelated cause is a tactic of propaganda. Williams and Gill explain that GAP proponents "exploit unsuspecting younger or naïve viewers who may have little familiarity with the history or motivations of lynchings or the Holocaust. Targeted are those who may be visually unsophisticated in the sense they possess only a nascent capability to interrogate the immersive excess" of the images.[16]

The CCBR recycles the GAP display in mailings and often meets resistance. For example, in Charlottetown, Prince Edward Island, a petition was started to ban the distribution of the images. The mayor, who called them "repulsive and disrespectful to the community," said he could not enact a bylaw prohibiting the distribution of the images because his lawyers advised that it would not withstand a Charter challenge.[17] The CCBR also hangs banners on highway overpasses and has been allowed to do so despite the existence of laws against "stunting" (any act along a highway that can distract a driver) that exist in every provincial highway traffic act. Complaints from drivers about the distraction—and at least one accident—prompted the city of Hamilton, Ontario, to pass a bylaw against the practice.[18]

The use of graphic imagery is hardly new or original. The government uses graphic imagery to deter people from smoking when it puts images of cancer on cigarette packages. Mothers Against Drunk Driving (MADD) uses graphic imagery of victims at accident scenes to deter driving while under the influence of alcohol. In these cases, the images are also meant to change "hearts and minds" rather than laws. However, unlike those images, the graphic images of the CCBR are often thought to defy "community standards" as defined by the Canadian Code of Advertising Standards.[19] They target women for discrimination and potentially incite hatred by equating women with the perpetrators of genocide. To date, the CCBR's right to free speech has been upheld. But even Bishop Frederick Henry, the current bishop of the Roman Catholic Diocese of Calgary, Alberta, has denounced the tactics of this group, calling them a "violation of human dignity" and saying, "In no way may these pictures be construed as healing, nor can the project be described as 'tough love,' and I am not in favour of this kind of pedagogy. In my opinion it does more harm than good to the pro-life cause.[20]

A favourite place for the CCBR to set up the displays is on university campuses. A student at the University of British Columbia was inspired to strip naked in front of the display to make a statement about her right to control her own body. The student captures the essence of why the display is so deeply offensive in a blog post about the incident:

> They are saying that a woman who chooses to terminate her pregnancy is akin to Nazis, terrorists, Klu [sic] Klux Klan members and the Santebal—all groups which set out to systematically destroy or enslave entire groups of people out of a sense of God-given superiority. And it is not just a woman who actually has an abortion who is labelled as—at the very least—a cog in a genocide machine. The implication is that anyone who supports a woman's right to choose is also participating in mass, organized murder, and that the very act of supporting the right to choose is violent and inherently evil.[21]

At some universities, attempts have been made to ban the display and these have resulted in expensive and protracted legal battles over free speech. Jane Kirby, in an article for *Briarpatch* titled "Freedom of (Hate) Speech," describes the dangers of the GAP approach:

> These presentations and displays have provoked a pro-choice response in a way the activities of other anti-choice groups have not. Pro-choice activists find the activities of the CCBR particularly inflammatory and dangerous because of the extent to which they demonize women who have had, or who support the right to have, abortions. When abortion is equated not only with murder but with genocide, women who have had an abortion are cast as perpetrators of vicious and systematic violence. For women who have had abortions, confronting this portrayal

can be an emotionally distressing experience, as it's intended to be. More importantly, some pro-choice activists fear that the comparison invites, or could fuel, extremist violence against pro-choice organizations and advocates.[22]

Williams and Gill note that the CCBR "conceives the university as a 'marketplaces of ideas'" and uses the GAP display "to market extremism."[23] Universities, however, need to be concerned with the ethical production of knowledge, and they violate their mandate when they promote pernicious historical misrepresentations as "just another idea." Unlike a municipality, a university has ample and varied resources to counter misinformation.

The New Abortion Caravan is yet another project of the CCBR, and it, too, misrepresents history, although in a much less egregious way. It explicitly co-opts and perverts the historic Abortion Caravan, a successful feminist project of the Vancouver Women's Caucus in 1970. The Abortion Caravan is often credited with galvanizing the emerging women's movement in Canada and with ultimately bringing an end to the criminalization of abortion. It is therefore a target for CCBR wrath. In the summer of 2012, the CCBR literally took their show on the road and drove panel vans bearing the usual graphic images along the route of the original Abortion Caravan to Ottawa. They stopped in the same towns along the way. The organization's embrace of third-way tactics in is evident in the strategy outlined on their website, as well as in the deceptively moderate language used to describe it:

> In each city, the media will inevitably be compelled to cover the abortion issue once again as the New Abortion Caravan passes through. The presence of the dismembered pre-born victims will force Canadians and the media to recognize their plight. The historical resonance of the New Abortion Caravan confronting the injustices brought about by the original Abortion Caravan will force people to re-examine their conceptions about abortion.[24]

The CCBR justifies its use of graphic imagery in various ways but, oddly, not by aligning itself with a tradition of similar advocacy from groups like MADD. With the New Abortion Caravan, they applied "tit for tat" reasoning, arguing that the women who took part in the original Abortion Caravan, women they refer to as "abortion advocates," also "used vivid imagery— coffins and coat hangers—to draw attention away from the pre-born and force politicians and the public to focus on the women in front of them."[25]

The implication is that they are doing the same thing that the Vancouver Women's Caucus did. But the comparison of the gory imagery used by the CCBR and imagery used by the original Abortion Caravan is hardly that of apples to apples. The Abortion Caravan vehicles were decorated, and one carried a black coffin representing all of the women who had died in botched abortions. There were banners, one of which read, "We Are Furious Women." In Ottawa, after rallying on Parliament Hill, some of the Caravan's members went to the home of then prime minister Pierre Trudeau and delivered the tools of a home abortion kit they had carried with them on their journey. The Caravaners also left their coffin behind on the lawn of 24 Sussex Drive. The following Monday, they disrupted Parliament for over a half an hour, chaining themselves to seats in the gallery and reciting speeches. It was the first time that Parliament in Canada had ever been forced to stop.

In a CBC *Daybreak* interview with Margo Dunn, one of the original Abortion Caravaners, host Chris Walker, voiced the perspective of the CCBR: "Along the way, you used some of what, at the time especially, were shocking tactics." He mentioned the illegal abortion kit and said that the new Caravan is different but the tactics are similar. Dunn disagreed: "What we didn't do, I mean, I see these images, as a kind of pornography. . . . But we didn't use scare tactics in that particular kind of way. We always attempted to, as the suffragists did, act with dignity." Walker did not give up on this line of questioning: "Abortion is such a personal and deeply divisive topic where, it seems to me, people of honest conscience can come to different conclusions. Why is it wrong for this group to use methods to argue what they believe?"[26] The implication again is that the imagery used by the two Caravans are equivalent and that the CCBR is doing nothing that the original Caravan did not do.

If the original Caravan had used images of dead women, exposed and crumpled on bathroom floors in pools of blood as a result of botched abortions or bleeding out on kitchen tables with their legs splayed apart, the comparison would be valid. The "vivid imagery" of the Abortion Caravan was symbolic and did not exploit or objectify anybody, pre-born or otherwise.

The "vivid imagery" of the Abortion Caravan included the performance of skits:

> The mimed performance illustrated the unequal and cruel treatment
> meted out to women who applied for legal abortions under the new
> law. Three "doctors," representing a hospital Therapeutic Abortion

Committee, stood with their hands thrust through a large piece of cardboard that was hung by a cord around their necks. Another "sympathetic doctor" presented this "board" with anxious women, wearing identifying signs. The shabbily dressed "Mother of Six" was summarily turned down for an abortion, as the TAC doctors wound her in red tape and thrust forth signs saying "NO." An applicant with "German Measles" and one who had been raped met the same fate. A user of the Catholic method of birth control wore a sign saying, "I Got Rhythm"; she was also turned down. But when a woman appeared in a fur coat, with a "Silver Spoon" in her mouth and handfuls of money, the TAC doctors signaled "Yes."[27]

The imagery seems somewhat quaint today.

In contrast, the images and tactics used by the CCBR are violent. According to Stephanie Gray, then CCBR's executive director, the images are absolutely necessary. Canadians must see them, no matter how upsetting they are. "Abortion is tolerated by the Canadian public because it is invisible to them," she says. "We use our graphic projects to make the victims of abortion visible, showing abortion as an act of violence that kills a baby, so that abortion becomes an unthinkable option."[28] Gray described an incident at one of their Caravan's stops that eerily echoes domestic abuse, citing it as part of a "positive response" to the display, in which they "helped connect a woman with a support group to help her cope with a previous abortion, after she burst into tears upon seeing the placards."[29] This can be spun another way. A woman who had an abortion came across the images, and after calling her a genocidal murderer, her abusers, like any textbook abuser, told her that they cared and set her up for potentially more indoctrination and abuse.

In any case, it is hard to imagine that abortion is invisible to Canadians. Thirty-one percent of Canadian women who turned forty-five in 2005 have had an abortion at some point in their life.[30] Abortion is a topic to which we often return, as is capital punishment, gun control, and prayer in school. It is one of the issues that voters use to help them distinguish and define the beliefs of political candidates. It is widely understood as an issue that tells us something critical about a constellation of related beliefs. If I want to get a sense of who someone is, asking them how they feel about abortion can be a quick, if not necessarily accurate, shortcut.

The images used by the CCBR are not the only images of abortion in existence. The Abortion Rights Coalition of Canada has posted other stock images available for media use that are quite different and have a different impact.[31] They include a photo of a blastocyst—an early embryo—at five weeks next to a ruler indicating that it is about two to three centimeters across. Such images are downright boring compared to the highly manipulated images of the GAP display. Some might argue that the former, too, are propaganda. Perhaps so. Various media have a habit of placing an image of obviously pregnant women, often women almost at term, with articles about abortion. Since most women have the procedure very early in their pregnancy, such images are entirely inappropriate and even misleading. If we can admit that everything is political, we can also admit that some things are more political than others.

Whether or not pro-choice advocates wish to fight a battle of images is beside the point, and challenging the veracity of the CCBR's images is only likely to result in more protracted legal battles. Whether we are looking at a minute blob of tissue or a gory image of an allegedly aborted fetus, the fact that we don't generally look at images of the procedure or the products of conception is not a surprise. We tend not to look at images of heart transplants or knee replacements either. As a patient, I don't need to watch a video of a procedure before I have it, and generally, I would prefer not to. My preference to avoid such images does not make the procedure any less necessary. Nor does a preference not to look at images of an abortion procedure mean that women who support or choose abortion are in any kind of denial about what abortion means to us, our individual consciences, our families, and our lives. As Charlotte Taft has said, "Women who have abortions do so because they value life and because they take very seriously the myriad responsibilities that come not just with birth, but with nurturing a human being."[32]

It would be hard to overstate or exaggerate the hyperbolic rhetoric of the New Abortion Caravan Web page. It speaks for itself. It calls the participants "a team of young people who are survivors—all born at a time when their peers were being killed."[33] The word "survivor" tends to be associated with tragedies such as the Holocaust, and is also typically associated with living through illness (particularly cancer) or abuse. To be a survivor is also to be a victim, and that is why many progressive people are moving away from using the word to describe people. The appropriation of the term by the

CCBR is part of the explicit comparison between legal abortion and genocide. According to the site,

> Over 3 million Canadian children have been brutally dismembered, decapitated, and disembowelled through abortion. Our taxes pay for this grotesque human rights violation. . . .
>
> In 1970, the Abortion Caravan heralded the arrival of a great injustice. But in 2012, the New Abortion Caravan will make the victims of Canada's abortion holocaust visible to the entire country. The New Abortion Caravan will signal the beginning of the end of Canada's . . . wholesale, state-funded slaughter of the youngest members of our society.[34]

The language indicates that CCBR members and supporters consider every birth a victory—evidence that somehow all the young people alive today survived despite the fact that abortion exists. In their fantasy world, every woman contemplates abortion with every pregnancy, and every birth is an event that somehow "slipped by" the abortionists.

The organization also draws attention to any opposition, positioning its supporters again as victims of wrongdoing. Referring to an "assault" in which CCBR protesters were doused with chocolate milk by a passerby who was incensed that his three-year-old had seen the images, Gray said, "We will continue with our tour regardless of violence or threats of opposition because someone has to speak for the pre-born children who cannot speak for themselves."[35] The passerby spent a night in jail, and the CCBR has highlighted this incident on its website, characterizing itself as the victim. Anti-choice groups appear to be very concerned with their safety. It is common for participants in the GAP displays to film passersby and take photos. Perhaps they want to be able to identify future chocolate milk assailants. In the United States, anti-choice groups train their members to track licence plates and take descriptions of people approaching clinics so that they can differentiate between clients and staff and determine whether a woman has come back and had an abortion or has not come back and possibly decided against it.[36] They would consider the latter a victory. The other possible uses to which this information could be put are cause for concern. Although there is never a justification for violence, being doused with chocolate milk is hardly the same as being murdered in your own church in front of friends and family while taking up the collection, the fate of Dr. George Tiller, one of the few providers of late-term abortions in the United States, nor does it compare with the shootings of Canadian doctors Garson Romalis, Hugh Short, or Jack Fainman or the 1992 firebombing of the Morgentaler Clinic in Toronto. But in describing the chocolate milk incident, the site, referring to the passerby's young child, claims,

> This little girl is the perfect illustration of what pro-life activists have found to be true time and time again: Children have functioning consciences. When they see a dismembered baby, they want to know what happened, and who allowed it to happen. They do not get disturbed by the pictures so much as the obscene language and temper tantrums of their parents.[37]

Releasing themselves from any responsibility for traumatizing the child, the CCBR and its supporters displace the blame for any trauma onto the angry parent. They appropriate his role as parent, taking away his ability to introduce to his child complex issues surrounding life, death, and sexuality at a time he deems appropriate. The group has consistently refused to position its display in a way that would give passersby a choice about whether to view it. Even the CCBR's American counterpart has a seven-second warning on their main page prior to the start of their graphic video. The Canadian group does not offer even this opportunity to look away. This could speak to their desperation.

In 2012, Andrea Mrozek embedded a New Abortion Caravan video (which has since been "removed as a violation of YouTube's policy on shocking and disgusting content") into her own *ProWomanProLife* blog and wrote,

> Be forewarned that this YouTube clip about the start of this new campaign has graphic content. I know our readers are split on whether to use graphic content like this. However, in overturning the old status quo the "angry women" who wanted abortion certainly used graphics—what do you call dumping a coffin in front of the Prime Minister's residence? Killing is bloody and messy. Therefore, abortion is bloody and messy. While I don't use those posters myself, I do support those who do, because I believe it reminds the complacent and the apathetic that abortion is the killing of a human being, something our country chooses not to notice or care about.[38]

Again, an anti-choice proponent equates one type of imagery with the other. And although Mrozek says she does not use these images herself, she does exactly that by embedding them in her blog. Furthermore, she admits that

Without Apology

she supports the tactics of the CCBR. She tries to have it both ways here, indicating that her "moderate" stance is merely a way to wedge the door open for the typical radicalism of the anti-choice movement.

The CCBR also highlights the use of the word "everyone" in the Charter (a tactic discussed above). Stephanie Gray and the CCBR feel that it applies to the "pre-born" as much as it does to a toddler.[39] In Winnipeg, as the Canadian Museum for Human Rights was being built in that city, Gray said that "abortion is Canada's greatest human-rights violation."[40] She repeated this in an interview on CBC's *Daybreak*. In a telling moment, Gray was asked what the punishment should be for a woman who has an abortion. She replied, "Once abortion becomes illegal, I would say the consequences for a woman who has an abortion at that point, breaking the law, would be no different from the consequences for a woman who kills her born children." When the interviewer asked if this would mean life in prison, Grey added that it depends, and said that some women who have abortions might instead be considered "clinically insane," like women who "drown their kids in a bathtub."[41]

On her *ProWomanProLife* blog, Mrozek explains her position against seeking legislation: "I don't know a single person who thinks about what should be a legal punishment for an abortion doctor and I don't know a single pro-lifer who thinks the woman should be put in jail for going to have an abortion."[42] I guess she has never met Stephanie Gray.

For secular and pro-choice Canadians, it is difficult to resist the call for debate, especially when the terms of the debate have left God behind and focus instead on human rights and Charter rights. Calls for a "rational" debate are coming from many quarters now. In an article for *This Magazine* about the New Abortion Caravan, writer Kyle Dupont expresses surprise that this New Abortion Caravan is "pro-life" and worries about the tactics. "If we are to have a debate," he writes, "we should strive to make both sides of the debate respectful. There needs to be some kind of line drawn; without it there is no telling how far shock value may go."[43] His call for moderation implies that there is moderation to be found in the CCBR. There is not. The very act of debating implies that minds can be changed. Changing minds appears unlikely in this case. To attempt to change a mind on abortion is, according to Walter Benn Michaels, akin to an attempt at religious conversion.[44] There is little hope for success. Lines are sharply drawn.

Encouraging people to be respectful, as Dupont does, is laudable, but it can do nothing to alter the fact that our differences are irreconcilable. Sometimes, there is no middle ground to be found. In this case, the fetus is a person, or it is not. The woman is entitled to rights, or she is not. The best we can do is "agree to disagree." But anti-choice activists will not settle for that. Anti-choice perspectives will continue to perpetuate the inferiority of women. They will continue to sacrifice women's rights for those of the fetus. While some may accuse pro-choice activists of being just as rigid as their opponents, this is not the case, for there is moderation to be found in the pro-choice stance. The very nature of the pro-choice position asserts both a woman's right to an abortion and her right not to have one. It asserts a woman's right to give birth, or not to give birth, as she sees fit. As Gordon O'Connor said in Parliament, speaking against Motion 312:

> Whether one accepts it or not, abortion is and always will be part of society. There will always be dire situations in which some women may have to choose the option of abortion. No matter how many laws some people may want government to institute against abortion, abortion cannot be eliminated. It is part of the human condition.
>
> I cannot understand why those who are adamantly opposed to abortion want to impose their beliefs on others by way of the Criminal Code. There is no law that says that a woman must have an abortion. No one is forcing those who oppose abortion to have one.
>
> Within the free and democratic society of Canada, if one has a world view based on a personal moral code that is somewhat different from others, then live according to those views as long as they are within the current laws. On the other hand, citizens who are also living within the reasonable limits of our culture and who may not agree with another's particular moral principles should not be compelled to follow them by the force of a new law.[45]

Or, in the pithy words of the pro-choice movement, "If you're against abortion, don't have one."

Being pro-choice is the most moderate position we can take in a civil and democratic society on this issue. The alternative results in what activists and others have deemed a war on women. Such a war is already evident in the United States. According to the Guttmacher Institute, two hundred and eighty-two restrictive laws on abortion have been enacted in the United States since 2010.[46] These laws have made it extremely difficult and sometimes impossible for many American women to access abortion services. Molly Redden, writing for *Mother Jones*, found that despite *Roe v. Wade*, conservatives in the US have been able to fundamentally rewrite abortion laws and "the onslaught of new abortion restrictions has been so successful, so strategically designed, and so well coordinated that the war in many places has essentially been lost."[47] In Canada, those involved in the anti-choice movement seek the same outcome. They are determined to end abortion and will welcome incursions on women's rights to achieve that goal. The "third way" is nothing more than new packaging on old goals; goals which pose the same threat to women's life, liberty, and security as they ever did and expose women, abortion providers, clinic workers, and pro-choice advocates to abuse. Truly moderate, pro-choice, and progressive Canadians must continue to support the gains we have made in assuring women's rights and push for access to abortion services throughout Canada, particularly in places where women are underserved. Most importantly, we must continue to challenge the agenda, be it "bio-ethical" or otherwise, of those who would have us deny women their rights.

Notes

1   Charles Lewis, "BC Anti-Abortion Group Takes Radical Stance," *National Post*, 12 June 2009.
2   David Anderson, "Transcript: Stephen Harper—The Mansbridge Interview (Part Two)," *CBC News*, 18 January 2011, http://www.cbc.ca/newsblogs/politics/inside-politics-blog/2011/01/transcript-stephen-harper-the-mansbridge-interview-part-two.html.
3   According to a July 2014 poll taken shortly after New Brunswick's one and only private abortion clinic, Fredericton's Morgentaler Clinic, announced its plans to close because it could not afford to continue operating without funding from the province, 59 percent of those polled indicated that they were "fine" with Canada's lack of a law restricting access to abortions. Angus Reid Global, "Canadians Express Little Desire to Re-introduce Abortion Laws in Their Country," 21 July 2014, http://angusreidglobal.com/wp-content/uploads/2014/07/ARG-Abortion-2014.pdf.
4   Abortion Rights Coalition of Canada, "Abortion: There's Nothing to Debate," news release, 3 November 2011, http://www.arcc-cdac.ca/press/ARCC-CDAC-release-nov3-11-english.pdf.
5   Lewis, "BC Anti-Abortion Group Takes Radical Stance."

6   Andrea Mrozek, "The Story," *ProWomanProLife* (blog), 2015, http://www.prowomanprolife.org/the-story/.

7   Quoted in Lewis, "BC Anti-Abortion Group Takes Radical Stance."

8   Mrozek, "Story."

9   R. v. Morgentaler, [1988] 1 SCR 30, http://scc-csc.lexum.com/scc-csc/scc-csc/en/item/288/index.do.

10 Charlie Smith, "Conservative MP Declares That Abortion Is Not a Human Right," *Georgia Straight* (Vancouver), 25 July 2014, http://www.straight.com/blogra/694856/conservative-mp-declares-abortion-not-human-right.

11 Indeed, the Charter of Rights and Freedoms does not grant a specific right to abortion in that the specific word is never used. But to make such an argument as Mrozek does is to misunderstand the purpose of the Charter. The Charter offers Canadians a framework within which more specific decisions can be made consistent with principles it upholds. According to section 2,"Everyone has the following fundamental freedoms: (*a*) freedom of conscience and religion; (*b*) freedom of thought, belief, opinion and expression, including freedom of the press and other media of communication; (*c*) freedom of peaceful assembly; and (*d*) freedom of association." Section 7 goes on to state, "Everyone has the right to life, liberty and security of the person and the right not to be deprived thereof except in accordance with the principles of fundamental justice." See "Constitution Act, 1982: Part 1, Canadian Charter of Rights and Freedoms," Justice Laws Website, 2015, http://laws-lois.justice.gc.ca/eng/const/page-15.html.

12 We Need a Law, "Mission," n.d., http://www.weneedalaw.ca/about/mission.

13 Gordon O'Connor, "Private Members' Business: Special Committee on Subsection 223(1) of the Criminal Code," *Hansard*, 26 April 2012, http://www.parl.gc.ca/HousePublications/Publication.aspx?Language=E&Mode=1&Parl=41&Ses=1&DocId=5524696.

14 One often hears such denouncements of violence from the anti-choice groups that the media turn to for comments on abortion-related issues that arise from time to time. Journalists justify quoting the opinions of such groups on the grounds that doing so provides balance to a story. What balance is there, however, when views espoused by, say 20 percent of the population (at best) are given 50 percent of the column space?

15 Sam Harris, *Letter to a Christian Nation* (New York: Vintage Books, 2006), 80.

16 Carol Williams and Don Gill, "Visual Spectacle as Propaganda," *The Meliorist*, 7 November 2013, http://themeliorist.ca/2013/11/visual-spectacle-as-propaganda/.

17 "Abortion Protest Prompts Graphic Images Ban Petition," *CBC News*, 13 August 2014, http://www.cbc.ca/news/canada/prince-edward-island/abortion-protest-prompts-graphic-images-ban-petition-1.2735048.

18 Kevin Werner, "Hamilton Prohibits Overpass Banners," *Hamilton Community News*, 22 May 2014, http://www.hamiltonnews.com/news/hamilton-prohibits-overpass-banners/.

19 See Advertising Standards Canada, "The Canadian Code of Advertising Standards," 2015, particularly section 14, "Unacceptable Depictions and Portrayals," http://www.adstandards.com/en/standards/canCodeOfAdStandards.aspx.

20 Jennifer Wiley, "Little Truck of Horrors," *FFWD* (Calgary), 9 August 2007.

21 Justine Davidson, "Why the Hell Did That Woman Take Her Clothes Off on Campus?!" *Naked at UBC* (blog), 22 March 2012, http://www.nakedubc.blogspot.ca/2012/03/why-hell-did-that-woman-take-her.html.

22 Jane Kirby, "Freedom of (Hate) Speech: The Rise of Anti-choice Activities on Canadian Campuses," *Briarpatch Magazine*, 9 September 2010, http://briarpatchmagazine.com/articles/view/freedom-of-hate-speech.

23 Williams and Gill, "Visual Spectacle as Propaganda."

24 "The New Abortion Caravan," Canadian Centre for Bio-ethical Reform, 2015, www.unmaskingchoice.ca/caravan.

25 Ibid.

26 "Original Abortion Caravan Activist Horrified at Pro-life Tour," interview with Margo Dunn by Chris Walker on *Daybreak*, CBC Radio, 6 June 2012, http://www.cbc.ca/daybreaksouth/2012/06/06/original-abortion-caravan-activist-horrified-at-pro-life-tour/.

27 Ann Thomson, *Winning Choice on Abortion: How British Columbian and Canadian Feminists Won the Battles of the 1970s and 1980s* (Victoria, BC: Trafford, 2004), 32–33. Thomson quotes from Jeannine Mitchell's "Abortion March a Success," *Georgia Straight*, 18 February 1970, 2.

28 Canadian Centre for Bio-ethical Reform, "'New Abortion Caravan' Brings Bloody Anti-abortion Trucks and Signs to Sault Ste. Marie as They Head to the GTA," news release, 19 June 2012, http://www.unmaskingchoice.ca/blog/2012/06/18/new-abortion-caravan-brings-bloody-anti-abortion-trucks-and-signs-sault-ste-marie-th.

29 Joyanne Pursaga, "Graphic Anti-abortion Bus Sparks Anger," *Canoe.com*, 15 June 2012, http://cnews.canoe.com/CNEWS/Canada/2012/06/15/19883751.html.

30 Wendy V. Norman, "Induced Abortion in Canada, 1974–2005: Trends over the First Generation with Legal Access," *Contraception* 85, no. 2 (2012): 188–89.

31 Abortion Rights Coalition of Canada, "Abortion Stock Photos for Media Use," n.d., http://www.arcc-cdac.ca/backrounders/media-photos.html.

32 Charlotte Taft, "Reproductive Rights: Sinking or Swimming?" *On the Issues*, 3 April 2012, http://www.ontheissuesmagazine.com/cafe2/article/206.

33 Canadian Centre for Bio-ethical Reform, "The New Abortion Caravan," n.d., http://www.unmaskingchoice.ca/caravan.

34 Ibid.

35 Quoted in Canadian Centre for Bio-ethical Reform, "'New Abortion Caravan' Brings Bloody Anti-abortion Trucks." On the chocolate milk incident, see Patrick Craine, "Pro-lifers Doused with Chocolate Milk While Protesting Abortion in Thunder Bay," *LifeSite USA*, 18 June 2012, https://www.lifesitenews.com/news/what-if-christians-dumped-chocolate-milk-on-feminists.

36 Progress Texas, "Undercover Audio Reveals Intimidation Tactics of Anti-Abortion Groups," 12 August 2014, http://progresstexas.org/blog/undercover-audio-reveals-intimidation-tactics-texas-anti-abortion-groups?utm_content=bufferf3cbb&utm_medium=social&utm_source=facebook.com&utm_campaign=buffer.

37 Jonathon Van Maren, "The Thunder Bay Assault: A Child's Conscience Versus A Man's Anger," Canadian Centre for Bio-ethical Reform, 18 June 2012, http://www.unmaskingchoice.ca/blog/2012/06/18/thunder-bay-assault-childs-conscience-versus-mans-anger.

38 Andrea Mrozek, "The New Abortion Caravan Gets Started Today in Vancouver," *ProWomanProLife* (blog), 29 May 2012, http://www.prowomanprolife.org/2012/05/29/the-new-abortion-caravan-gets-started-today-in-vancouver/.

39 Stephanie Gray, "The Canadian Charter of Rights and Freedoms Is Anti-abortion," Canadian Centre for Bio-ethical Reform, 14 June 2012, http://www.unmaskingchoice.ca/blog/2012/06/14/canadian-charter-rights-and-freedoms-anti-abortion.

40 Quoted in "Anti-abortion Activists Go Door-to-Door in Winnipeg," *CBC News*, 14 June 2012, http://www.cbc.ca/news/canada/manitoba/story/2012/06/13/mb-anti-abortion-protest-winnipeg.html.

41 "Anti-abortion Caravan Rolls Through Kelowna," radio interview, *CBC News*, 4 June 2012, http://www.cbc.ca/daybreaksouth/coming-up/2012/06/04/anti-abortion-caravan-in-kelowna-on-monday/.

42 Lewis, "BC Anti-abortion Group Takes Radical Stance."

43 Kyle Dupont, "WTF Wednesday: The New Abortion Caravan Is Pro-Life," *This Magazine*, 13 June 2012, http://this.org/2012/06/13/wtf-wednesday-the-new-abortion-caravan-is-pro-life/.

44 Walter Benn Michaels, *The Trouble with Diversity* (New York: Metropolitan Books, 2006), 182.

45 O'Connor, "Private Members' Business."

46 Guttmacher Institute, "Laws Affecting Reproductive Health and Rights: State Trends at Midyear, 2015," 1 July 2015, http://www.guttmacher.org/media/inthenews/2015/07/01/.

47 Molly Redden, "The War on Women Is Over—and Women Lost," *Mother Jones*, September–October 2015, http://www.motherjones.com/politics/2015/07/planned-parenthood-abortion-the-war-is-over.

Women over Ideology

Nick Van der Graaf

The pro-choice struggle for reproductive justice is a noble one. For decades, in Canada and around the world, feminist activists have taken to the streets and the courts to decriminalize abortion and to make it safe and legal. By doing so, we have saved countless women's lives and helped families grow in health and prosperity.

But what of the future of the pro-choice movement? While around the world the fight continues for decriminalization of abortion and even for access to basic birth control, in Canada our focus is shifting toward ensuring access to abortion services across a large and thinly populated country, where access can be fraught for those living in remote and northern communities.

We also continue to oppose the anti-choice movement. It remains an active threat even though, at present, roughly six out of ten Canadians apparently have no interest in recriminalizing abortion.[1] Anti-choice advocates continue to lobby Parliament for legal restrictions and to engage in street-level activism, many of them protesting outside abortion clinics and high schools. Pro- and anti-choice activists often counter-demonstrate at each other's events, which all too often leads to ugly and juvenile confrontations in the streets. Will this fight with the anti-choice movement continue in this mode forever? Or can two adversaries—both of whom have genuine concerns about profound issues such as the meaning of life, the nature of personhood, and the ethics of personal autonomy—move toward a more mature, respectful dialogue? Such a shift will be a challenge for both sides, but I believe the benefits to women and to society at large make this a legitimate goal.

No doubt you're thinking, *Dialogue with the anti-choice? Why would I talk to people trying to take my rights away?* I can hardly blame you. The anti-choice movement's attacks on women's autonomy, the shocking dishonesty manifested by so-called crisis pregnancy centres, and, of course, occasional acts of violence against abortion clinic staff would seemingly mark those involved as dangerous cranks, fanatics not unlike the extremists of ISIS, rather than serious participants in modern civil society.

But the truth is that those who are anti-choice are far from monolithic. As a professional journalist, pro-choice activist, and clinic escort, I have had ongoing face-to-face dealings with them for decades, and I have found them to be as varied as the patients who come to our clinic. Certainly, some are angry, intolerant fanatics. But many, and I would argue most, of those who call themselves "pro-life" have far more nuanced beliefs than we generally give them credit for.

First, we have to understand what motivates them. No doubt the Randall Terrys of this world are primarily motivated by misogyny and personal ambition. But for most of the rank-and-file, church-going couples and families in a conservative milieu, going to a "pro-life prayer vigil" is seen as a way of doing good in the world, surely a powerful motivator.

We must also acknowledge that there *are* ethical issues around human reproduction and abortion. I don't need anti-choice activists to tell me this; it is clear to me that abortion is ethically complex just from the range of opinion that I've heard from patients at at the clinic where I work as a patient escort. While some arrive and leave feeling fairly light-hearted, many struggle with their decision. At the least, it is a sad day for them. At worst, they experience abortion as a terrible loss, a cause for weeping and sorrow. As staff, we can only be supportive and comfort patients who are obviously unhappy. Evidence shows that most of them will come to terms with their decision to terminate a pregnancy, but a small minority will probably always suffer from various degrees of guilt and self-recrimination.[2]

I don't think anyone in the pro-choice movement would in any way condemn a woman receiving an abortion for feeling this way. We would commiserate and respect the personal ethics of a woman who feels that abortion is wrong. Indeed, it is hardly unusual for people to reach that conclusion; virtually all religious and philosophical traditions have taboos against the taking of life. We don't begrudge Hindus or Buddhists their beliefs, so we can hardly turn around and tell Christians that their concerns about the value of human life are crazy. These are legitimate and widespread beliefs, and those who are anti-choice have every right to feel the way they do about abortion.

I'm making a point of defending the right of anti-choicers to an ethical framework different from my own because I've noticed that progressive people have, in recent years, tended to become quite apoplectic about the beliefs of our opponents, often claiming that opposing beliefs are offensive and, more worryingly, shouldn't be aired in public. To counter that view, I could easily raise some familiar arguments illustrating how calls for censorship of others' views can backfire on us all. But I'd rather respond with some ideas about the relative importance of beliefs versus actions.

A couple of years ago, I discovered that a Roman Catholic order of nuns, the Sisters of Life (founded in New York in 1991), had established its Toronto mission in a closed up church five minutes from my home. I'd seen their pamphlets being circulated in front of our clinic and had noted that the literature contained no alarmist or nonsense medical misinformation, or shocking pictures. Rather, it conveyed the simple message that the nuns were there for any woman who needed help raising an unplanned child. The text was straightforward and nonjudgmental. When I met the sisters, I discovered that they were as well.

The Sisters of Life, being Catholic nuns, are hardly pro-choice. In fact, as a religious order, they represent a fairly conservative outlook in the Roman Catholic Church. I'm sure I could spend a lifetime disagreeing with the sisters about the ethics of abortion. But unlike many in the anti-choice movement, their outward expression of their internal ethics has not been to shame or condemn anyone. They strongly disapprove of aggressive behaviour against clinic patients and, of course, of violence directed at abortion providers. Instead, and this is key, what they do is support women regardless of their choices.

What does "support" mean in this case? It means giving new mothers material goods such as diapers, strollers, food, and furniture. It means providing shelter if the woman is fleeing an abusive relationship. It means advocating for women at immigration hearings. It means getting pro bono legal and medical help. Above all, it means offering genuine love, kindness, and emotional support. All of this is unconditional and independent of religious belief; the sisters' Toronto mission is in a heavily Muslim area, and their clientele reflects that.

For many pro-choice advocates, this probably doesn't sound like enough. After all, how is a woman supposed to get by raising an unplanned child with a few free diapers? But having been so poor that I didn't know where my next meal was coming from, I can tell you that a few free items can make a very big difference in one's life. Moreover, it is not up to us to judge what a young mother considers enough support. Poor women are as entitled to raise children as anyone else and are capable of making decisions regarding what is "enough" for their child. The nuns merely facilitate those decisions.

This point is worth elaborating. As pro-choice advocates, we often talk about women whose economic circumstances are so dire that they have been left with "no choice" but to terminate their pregnancy. For most women in this situation, choosing an abortion is the right decision. They know it and act accordingly. They are making choices and taking control of their lives. But what about those who believe that abortion is wrong or who really do want a child at this time? Faced with poverty, these women have no choice, and compelling a woman into having an abortion she doesn't want is at the very least an outrage. We usually imagine that the agent behind such an event is a controlling boyfriend or parent. But far more often the culprit is neoliberal economics. Either way, the end result is the same: a woman undergoing a procedure to which she hasn't really consented. And she has to live the rest of her life with this fact. Women such as these can turn to the nuns, who provide them with the means to make a different choice. And the undeniable reality is that these anti-choice nuns are helping women to make choices freely.

Few people have ever heard about the Sisters of Life. Since 1991, they have established a number of missions across North America, providing long-term support to women who need it. It's not glamorous or controversial—it's hard work and a heavy responsibility. The anti-choice proponents we usually hear about are the angry misogynists, the cruel lunatics who

scream at patients entering clinics, the doctor-stalkers, and the elected officials who keep suggesting that the state should investigate every uterus in
the land. These zealots demand that women "take responsibility," but, unlike
the nuns, they won't lift a finger to help young families. Unfortunately, such
extremists drive the agenda simply by being so out there. They grab all the
media attention and force pro-choice advocates to react constantly to their
mean-spirited nonsense.

But this is just not good enough. Decent people who have ethical concerns
about abortion should not be led by absolutist fanatics. And pro-choicers
should not have to be constantly fighting against intrusive legislation and
abusive, threatening behaviour in the streets. Both sides claim to be concerned about women and their families. Perhaps it's time we all stopped
focusing on how bad the other side is and started looking at how we can all
support women and their children by putting actions before rhetoric.

Trying to talk about this to those who are anti-choice will be quite a challenge for our side. Their rhetoric is often provocative and difficult to ignore,
and most anti-choice leaders will do everything in their power to thwart a
constructive dialogue. Over the years, we've tended to reduce the opposition
to angry caricatures, and their leaders' words often reinforce our cartoonish
view of them. But I think opening the door to anti-choicers who are willing
to talk can only be rewarding. I have already found it so.

By far the greater challenge lies squarely on the anti-choice side, whose
characterization of pro-choicers as minions of Satan has aroused fear of
pro-choice proponents. Considerable resources have been spent on promoting a view of the world in which the abortion issue is a biblical struggle
between heaven and hell, with the universe hanging in the balance. But it
doesn't. The lives of actual women and their children, real human beings
whose personhood is beyond all doubt, are what matters, and both atheists
and people of faith can see this simple truth.

It will be difficult for anti-choice proponents, but I think that many of them
are up to the challenge. Now seems like an opportune time to pursue this
approach, since Pope Francis has made it clear that while he may be against
abortion, he has no time for judgmental rhetoric.[3] The Sisters of Life are
the Church's own example of how those who are anti-choice can conduct
themselves in the future. If Francis is prepared to embrace this example,
the Church can rise to the challenge by officially denouncing anti-choice
harassment at clinics and devoting its considerable resources to genuinely

helping the women who want its support. This is the only principled way to be against abortion, and one can only hope that Pope Francis has the vision to make it happen. If he is hesitant to make such a radical change and challenge the more conservative powers within the Church, he need only ask himself what a certain humble Galilean would have done.

Notes

1   Angus Reid Global, "Canadians Express Little Desire to Re-introduce Abortion Laws in Their Country," news release, 21 July 2014, http://angusreidglobal.com/wp-content/uploads/2014/07/ARG-Abortion-2014.pdf.
2   Corinne H. Rocca, Katrina Kimport, Heather Gould, and Diana G. Foster, "Women's Emotions One Week After Receiving or Being Denied an Abortion in the United States," *Perspectives on Sexual and Reproductive Health* 45, no. 3 (2013): 122–31.
3   David Willey, "Pope Francis Strikes an Unusual New Tone," *BBC News*, 29 July 2013, http://www.bbc.com/news/world-europe-23493038.

part four

Practitioners and Clinic Support

Dissolving Fear, Fostering Trust

Lessons from Life in Abortion Care

Peggy Cooke

The first time I put on an escort pinny and stood outside of my local abortion clinic was in February 2007, on one of the coldest days of that Fredericton winter. At the time, I didn't know anyone who had had an abortion (at least none who had told me). As for me, I had never even had a pregnancy scare. I was driven more by my rage at the Catholic protesters than by any understanding of the movement or the struggles of the women I was escorting.

It wasn't long before abortion became my whole life—at least, it seemed that way. A part-time job at the clinic, along with a blog and a media training workshop, catapulted me into becoming the go-to person for pro-choice opinion in that small city. I became involved with bigger pro-choice organizations and began going to conferences and even giving workshops on abortion activism.

I have never felt more fulfilled, however, than I did during those first few months of volunteering as a patient escort, stuffing toe warmers into my boots, stomping and jumping in the howling wind to keep my blood flowing, and always watching the movements of the ten or twelve old folks who marched back and forth in front of the clinic with their asinine signs. My mother once told me that religion is something men do to women, with other women's help. I didn't understand that until I saw those women out there.

There were men, too, of course—the surly priest we nicknamed Father Grim; the Knight of Columbus who had written more than seventy screeds against abortion on his personal website; the tall, burly fellow who used to stare into the windows at the staff. But the women were the most hateful and vocal. The Holy Ghost, as we called her, who patrolled the boundaries of the clinic unencumbered by a sign, entreating the patients in her wispy voice. Crazy Legs, the "counsellor" whose arms and legs flailed every which way like a giraffe as she chased women down the sidewalk, sometimes throwing herself on their moving cars. Glare-y Mary, dressed monochromatically (usually in red) and holding aloft a bloody crucifix whose Jesus was continually losing limbs until it was just a gruesome torso clutched in her hands.

These women seemed to find purpose in passing judgment on our patients, a way to channel their own insecurities and fears into condemnation of other people. Their church appeared to encourage this projection. I saw them gather in prayer before setting out, huddled in the parking lot next door at their so-called crisis pregnancy centre. Although they called out to the patients, they rarely entreated or even addressed us; perhaps they believed us to be beyond redemption.

What must it be like to work in a clinic that doesn't have to deal with this, I often wondered. An eye doctor's or a dentist's practice. How nice it must be to book an appointment with a patient who is not crying, how pleasant to sit at the front desk without having to move a plant in front of the window to block the stares of the scary man outside. How lovely it would be for our counsellor to have to simply inform a patient of the risks of the procedure and obtain her consent without having to wade through twenty minutes of traumatized sobbing caused by her experience with the bullies outside. How convenient to not have to padlock our dumpster. What must it be like to work or volunteer in a place that is free from harassment?

By necessity, I eventually had to prioritize activism in the movement over work in the movement. It is a relief that my life as an activist makes me less fearful than did my life as clinic staff, and that it brings less stress to the people who love me. But mostly, my heart aches for the people who don't

Without Apology

have that choice—for those women who need abortions, who have to walk the gauntlet of judgment to reach the safe space of the clinic. I worry about them and their safety, and their emotional well-being. I worry about a country that allows this to go on.

My working life in abortion services taught me many things, but the main lesson was to trust other people as the experts on their own lives. There were some patients whom I couldn't stand, some who I thought were making the wrong decision—but whenever I needed a reminder of the consequences of going down that road of judgment, I had only to look out the window and see the bitter old people staring back at me, shivering in the cold and sacrificing their mornings—time that would have been better spent with grandchildren or a cup of tea—in order to stand in the snow and register their contempt of the choices of strangers. May that never, ever be me, I would think to myself, and then turn to meet each person with love.

What separates those who work for universal access to health care and those who oppose it is not a political difference of opinion or even a religious or ethical one. It is the ability to take responsibility for our own fears and insecurities, to resist the urge to push them onto others. From there, we learn to trust other people. The actions of the people who stood outside our clinic had nothing to do with babies or abortion. They had to do with the inability to trust women with their own bodies. For men, that comes from a desire to control women; for women, it comes from an inability to trust themselves.

When I think about the possibility of becoming pregnant, I am not afraid, because I trust myself to make the right decision for myself at that time, just like I trust myself to know when to go to the dentist or the eye doctor. In the four years I spent working in abortion care, I came to trust hundreds of patients, and through that, I learned that I, too, am worthy of trust. And that is something that no judgmental stranger with a sign and a crucifix can ever take away.

"Do you think I will go to hell for this?"

RUTH MILLER

"Do you think I will go to hell for this?"

The young woman sitting across from me asks this question half in jest, but her eyes show me she is worried. We are in a counselling room at the Morgentaler Clinic in Toronto. She has come for an abortion, and it is my job to counsel her about the procedure, to calm her if she is nervous, and to make sure she is certain about her decision.

I have worked as a part-time counsellor at the clinic for seven years, after retiring from twenty years at Toronto Public Health, where I was a sexual health educator and counsellor. Each time I mount the steps of the clinic, I enter another world.

Shoppers, families, people young and old go about their business on the street outside, oblivious to the human drama playing out on

This essay was originally published in the Globe and Mail, 26 January 2011, under the title "The Human Drama of Abortion Counselling." It is reprinted here with minor revisions.

the second floor of the office building on the corner. Each day when I have finished my work, I re-emerge into what I think of as the real world, but the women I've met that day stay in my mind: the fifteen-year-old who has come with her mother from Barrie, Ontario; the twenty-year-old student who, when the condom broke, took the morning-after pill but it didn't work; the forty-three-year-old mother of three with an unemployed husband who, after using the rhythm method as she always has, knows she can't welcome another child at this point in her life.

Women of all ages come. Women of every colour and every religion come. Sometimes they come more than once. They come alone or with partners, with mothers or aunts or sisters or friends. They are often astonished to see how many others like them are in the waiting room.

Some days are difficult. Many women enter my office on the verge of tears. They try not to cry but inevitably they do, and that is a good thing. The tension leaves, and they are able to begin the journey to calmness. Some women's lives are so complicated—so much has happened to them, most of it not good, that I can only admire their strength. "You are a strong woman," I say, or, "You are a smart woman," or, "You are a loving mother, who wants to care for the family you have." I am not dissembling; I am truly in awe.

In the world outside the clinic, everyone has an opinion on abortion. In our society, in spite of a long struggle to make it legal and safe, abortion is still viewed by many as a selfish and damnable act. Women are supposed to feel guilty. And many women do. Others feel guilty for not feeling guilty. The world outside is quick to judge. How often I have heard well-meaning people say that no one needs to get pregnant these days if they don't want to. "Why don't they just use contraception?" people ask. If they were sitting in my chair, they would understand why.

They would understand that not every woman can use the pill safely or even afford it. They would know that there are men who won't use a condom, even though it puts their partner at risk of a pregnancy neither of them wants; that because there is so much ignorance about fertility among both men and women, couples are often playing Russian roulette every time they have sex.

Most women have no idea when they are fertile, so it is hard for them to figure out what kind of contraception to use and how to use it effectively. And when I explain to women how to determine when they can conceive (which has little to do with using the calendar and much to do with recognizing the fertile mucus they see in their underpants), their eyes widen. "I didn't know that," they say. "No one ever taught me."

As a counsellor, I try not to judge the women I see. I admit that I get frustrated sometimes. And then I remind myself that human beings don't always act rationally where sex is concerned. That's part of being human.

In the early 1970s, when I became interested in the reproductive rights of women, my mother was firmly on my side. "Abortion is a woman's decision, and it should be legal," she said. Perhaps her unwavering belief came from the knowledge that, when abortion was illegal, her friend had had two abortions on the kitchen table.

A friend told me, when we were both young mothers, that she'd had two illegal abortions before she was married. Twice she had to seek that questionable help, frightened and alone. "You are not to blame," I told her. "You knew nothing about fertility, nothing about sex. We can blame a society that denies girls and women information about their bodies, a society that shames women about sexuality. But you are not to blame."

At least three of my married friends had abortions after bearing children. I knew their marriages were rocky, and later they divorced. We all know women who have had abortions, although we may not know that we do. That may be why it is easy for some people to condemn women for making the abortion decision, labelling them irresponsible or selfish. Even women who have had an abortion themselves sometimes condemn other women for having had one, in the belief that another woman's reasons are not as compelling as their own.

I remember a young intern who was doing a practicum at our public health clinic insisting that he would never refer someone for an abortion or prescribe the morning-after pill. "If you want to tell people how to live," I said, in a moment of courage and anger, "be a priest or a minister, not a doctor!"

Our attitudes toward sex and women's sexuality cloud our thinking when it comes to women's health. A moral issue? Yes, of course. But is it moral to ask a woman to risk injury or death rather than be able to have a safe abortion? Or to force her to have a baby she never meant to conceive? It's complex, I admit. But when I am sitting with a woman who has found her way to our clinic, I am grateful that here she can have a safe procedure that is relatively simple and that can restore her peace of mind and her life.

"Do you think I will go to hell for this?" the young woman asks.

We smile at each other. "No," I say.

Countering Shame with Compassion

The Role of the Abortion Counsellor

Erin Mullan

"You look really familiar. Have we met before?"

The friendly young woman who is pouring for one of the wineries at the tasting event smiles as she tries to place me.

I smile back and say, "Yeah, I've got one of those faces that look really familiar. I hear that a lot." I shift the conversation back to the wine. This isn't the kind of world where I could say, "Have you had an abortion lately? I might have been your counsellor."

I was not sure whether she had been one of my clients. Once you've been an abortion clinic counsellor for many years, everyone old enough to get pregnant begins to look a bit familiar. During more than twenty-five years of working in abortion and reproductive health, I have seen more than twenty thousand clients. The ever-changing river of women that flows through my counselling office reflects all the diversity of the part of the world in which I work. The one generalization I can make is about their fertility: the kind of woman who has an abortion is one who is able to get pregnant.

There is something else that these women often hold in common—the values behind the abortion decision. The most important thing I have learned in my career is this: almost all of us make the decision to end a pregnancy because we love and value children; we want to be able to be good mothers. We take a long, hard look at our lives and we realize that we are not in the place we need to be to do the best we could. We know whether we are unable to provide properly for a child, for another child, or for the children we already have. This is a decision made in a profoundly ethical and moral framework, one that is based on valuing children.

Often, during the course of a counselling session, I share this observation with clients after they have talked to me about their situation. The discussion of the decision to have an abortion may be brief and straightforward or complex and emotionally fraught. Many come to the appointment fully certain in their decision, with strong support from their partner, friends, and/or family. Some make the decision to end a pregnancy in isolation, perhaps with only a single person in their lives in whom they can confide. Some have no one to talk to, and the people at the clinic are the only ones with whom they will fully discuss their decision and their feelings about having an abortion—the only ones who hear their stories or give them support.

In our work, we normalize the abortion experience for women by countering misinformation with knowledge and shame with compassion. We practice what Alissa Perucci calls "purposeful normalization":

> When abortion care becomes normalized, we model how the experi-
> ence—both for staff and patients—can be lived as a normal part of
> women's reproductive health life span. In a purposefully normalizing
> approach, abortions and abortion work are lived as destigmatized
> events in women's lives. Staff are encouraged to be proud of their
> work and mentored to grow and change. Patients are welcomed into
> the clinic and are *met where they are.* . . . In this approach, we live as if
> abortion care were completely mainstreamed, routinely available, and
> non-compartmentalized. This attitudinal and behavioral shift is part
> and parcel of the teaching of destigmatization.[1]

The clinic counsellor (and other staff) can play a pivotal role in a woman's abortion experience, but relatively little has been written about what we do.[2] Our work as abortion counsellors includes decision assessment, emotional support, the obtaining of informed consent, health education, and contraceptive teaching. Perhaps the most important aspects of our work, though, involve normalization, destigmatization, and ethical reframing. About one-third of Canadian women will have at least one abortion over the course of their reproductive life, but few talk about this very common experience.[3] How women feel when they end a pregnancy varies tremendously. Every emotion is within the range of normal with an abortion, but the stigma that surrounds abortion increases the likelihood that a woman will feel shame or guilt or that she is somehow "bad."

The dominant narratives in society about abortion often have little to do with women's lived experience and too much to do with shaming women. Despite the fact that Canadians are, in the majority, pro-choice, negative and unfair attitudes toward the subject are rife in the popular discourse.[4] Abortion stigma has been defined as "a negative attribute ascribed to women who seek to terminate a pregnancy that marks them, internally or externally, as inferior to ideals of womanhood."[5] The fact that abortion is a common event in women's reproductive lives does not lessen the stigma associated with it—a phenomenon that the same authors describe as "the prevalence paradox: the social construction of deviance despite the high incidence of abortion."[6]

Women can be silenced and harmed by stigma, and abortion stigma is increased by silence. Among the factors that the American Psychological Association's 2008 Task Force on Mental Health and Abortion identified as being "predictive of more negative psychological responses following first-trimester abortion among women in the United States" are "perceptions of stigma, need for secrecy, and low or anticipated social support for the abortion decision."[7] In my experience, in addition to a woman's confidence in her decision, having good support makes a pivotal difference in how well she copes afterwards.

Not all women feel shame about having an abortion, and some are less affected than others by abortion stigma. Cultural differences can mean that some women are outside of the influence of stigma. Women who are recent immigrants often answer the counselling session question as to how they will feel afterwards with "better," "happy," or "free." Some women do not feel shame because they do not know they are "supposed to" feel bad. Abortion stigma, rather than being a universal truth, is "a social phenomenon that is constructed and reproduced locally through various pathways."[8] There are women who only feel shame when they are introduced to negative messages or judgment about abortion. Stigma is a social construct, something that is made by others. I use the metaphor of a coat when talking with clients about others' attitudes about abortion shame. The shaming is like a coat; it is something outside of us. On the inside are the good values women use to make the decision. The coat is not theirs. It is too heavy and does not fit. Someone else is trying to get them to wear it.

I am never sure where things are going to go once I close the door to my counselling office. The women's stories often contain similar themes, but the focus of our conversation can vary wildly. As counsellors, we see women who have no issue with their decision and our time together is spent addressing contraception and the informed consent. Much of our work involves education, answering questions about all aspects of reproductive and sexual health. We spend a tremendous amount of time correcting misinformation about abortion and contraception. Our role is to provide the most accurate information possible, so we are constantly updating our own knowledge. One of the things I love about my profession is being able to learn new things every day I work.

The context in which an abortion takes place often shapes a woman's experience much more than the event itself.[9] Having an abortion often puts a bright spotlight on everything that is good in our lives and everything that is not. For many women, this experience is a catalyst for making positive changes in their lives.

One of the hardest parts of the work is bearing witness to the horrific circumstances of some women's lives. Hearing stories of rape or abuse is nothing compared to having lived them, but repeated exposure to others' pain puts us at risk for vicarious trauma. Just as support is crucial for women when going through an abortion, having good support both in and outside of the workplace is key to being able to survive and thrive in this extraordinary profession.

An abortion counsellor also needs to possess a genuine and openhearted curiosity about others. In our work, we meet women of every race, language, culture, and class; few people have the opportunity that we do to meet such a wide cross-section of the population. Our clients teach us so much about their cultures and perspectives, which is a rare privilege for us. Our work teaches us how important it is to not make assumptions. I once saw a sixteen-year-old who, two years earlier, had been protesting outside our clinic, having been bussed in from her Catholic school. She told me she felt very guilty, not about having an abortion but about having been a protestor.

Without Apology

She was absolutely certain that at age sixteen she was not ready to parent and her decision was not the issue. She felt bad about having judged others. Stories like hers underline how incredibly helpful forgiving ourselves for being human and fallible can be in moving on emotionally.

We wrestle with judgment and stigma in our counselling sessions, and we frequently encounter women's fears about having an abortion. Our clients are often feeling hormonal, nauseous, exhausted, and terrified. They are afraid of terrible pain during the procedure and of harm to their future fertility. The two most common questions are, will it hurt and will this affect my ability to get pregnant again? As counsellors, we fight fear with knowledge and education, just as we try to reduce shame with compassion.

Some women are even afraid for their lives, like the client from Brazil whose sister back home had died from an unsafe and illegal abortion. This client fully believed that she might die in our clinic but was so determined in her decision to have an abortion that she came to her appointment anyway. Fortunately for her, abortion is incredibly safe when taken out of the backstreet. As we frequently explain to our clients, everything about this situation can be complicated, but the medical part is not. When it is done in a safe setting like the one where I work, abortion, particularly first-trimester abortion, is one of the safest medical procedures there is.

In much of the world, women are much less safe. When I think of the tens of thousands of women who die unnecessarily each year from unsafe abortions, and the millions more who are injured, it is not just an appalling abstraction. I hear those numbers and I see the faces of the women who sit across from me every day in my counselling office. Those of us who work in abortion provision are truly pro-life in that we save women's lives and their fertility by providing access to safe abortion. We also prevent unwanted pregnancies—and future abortions—by helping women find contraceptive methods and strategies that will work for them. In the words of one woman who wrote in after her abortion to express her gratitude to the clinic she attended, "Thank you for accepting me and my choice, thank you for not judging me, thank you for listening to me and foremost thank you for protecting me."[10]

Abortion counsellors prevent more abortions than anti-abortion protesters ever do. We are often the ones who recognize when the woman sitting across from us is not done with her decision and is not ready to have an abortion. We send women home when they are uncertain, saying, "This doesn't mean that you can't have an abortion. It just means that today isn't the day to do it." Often they come back; sometimes they do not. We do not have an agenda as to whether a woman should have an abortion; we are just there to be on her side. I am ever more certain that I have no idea what the woman facing me in my counselling office should do about her pregnancy. I know that I do not know. The decision is hers to make.

An unwanted pregnancy is, by its nature, an out-of-control experience, and our focus as counsellors is to give back as much control as possible to the women we see. Our form of counselling is nondirective and client-centred. I think of our role as that of a navigator: we know the terrain and have been down these roads before. The woman is in the driver's seat, and she sets the destination.

We are often spiritual advisors. Although most of us are not conventionally religious, many of our clients are, so we talk about issues of faith every day with some of the women we see. We aid them in working through the theological and spiritual questions that arise during the decision process. I put conventional religiosity aside a very long time ago, but I have more conversations about matters of faith over the course of my work week than do most devotedly religious folk.

When people I meet ask me what I do for a living, I exercise a degree of caution. It is not that I am ashamed about what I do—far from it. I feel very fortunate to be part of this work and am proud of what we do to aid women. There is deep satisfaction in being able to help someone get through what is often a turning point in her life. It has been exciting to participate in the creation and evolution of a profession, one that evolved from the work of the women's movement.[11] But there are times when I am not at work when I would rather discuss anything else. I have little patience with people who want to tell me, often at length, their ill-informed opinions. The other reason for reticence in talking about my work is security. We know more about suspicious packages, bomb sweeps, and anthrax than most police officers do, although it is crazy that health care workers need to know about these things. Abortion providers have been injured and even killed for the work they do, and that is heartbreaking.

In the debates that rage about abortion, the counsellor's voice is one that is seldom heard. This may be in part because of how we work—in a very private sphere. Our workdays are spent sitting across from women who come to our clinics to have abortions. For some women, the only time in their entire life that they will talk with another person about their abortion experience is during their time in the clinic. Our work carries with it the exquisite privilege of access to the interior of these women's lives and the profound responsibility of bearing witness to their stories. By reframing the abortion decision as one that stems from ethical values, we help women lighten the weight of the abortion stigma they may be carrying. The bigger challenge is the much-needed wider societal reframing that could reduce, and someday eliminate, abortion stigma here and unsafe abortion everywhere.

Notes

1   Alissa Perucci, *Decision Assessment and Counseling in Abortion Care: Philosophy and Practice* (New York: Rowman and Littlefield, 2010), xxii–xxiii.

2   There are two excellent texts about abortion counselling: Alissa Perucci's definitive work, cited above, and Anne Baker, *Abortion and Options Counseling: A Comprehensive Reference* (Rochester, NY: Hope Clinic for Women, 1995).

3   Wendy V. Norman, "Induced Abortion in Canada, 1974–2005: Trends over the First Generation with Legal Access," *Contraception* 85 (2012): 185–191. This study found that 31 percent of Canadian women who turned forty-five in 2005 had had at least one abortion.

4   According to a survey conducted by Ipsos in late January and early February 2016, 57 percent of Canadians feel that "abortion should be permitted whenever a woman decides she wants." The survey canvassed opinion in twenty-three countries: at 57 percent, Canada ranked seventh. See Andrew Russell, "6 in 10 Canadians Support Abortion Under Any Circumstances: Ipsos Poll," *Global News*, 23 February 2016, http://globalnews.ca/news/2535846/6-in-10-canadians-support-abortion-under-any-circumstances-ipsos-poll/.

5   Anuradha Kumar, Leila Hessini, and Ellen M. H. Mitchell, "Conceptualising Abortion Stigma," *Culture, Health and Sexuality* 11, no. 6 (2009): 628.

6   Ibid., 629.

7   American Psychological Association, *Report of the APA Task Force on Mental Health and Abortion* (Washington, DC: APA, 2008), http://www.apa.org/pi/women/programs/abortion/mental-health.pdf, 4.

8   Kumar, Hessini, and Mitchell, "Conceptualising Abortion Stigma," 628.

9   The APA Task Force on Mental Health and Abortion noted that factors such as "poverty, prior exposure to violence, a history of emotional

problems, a history of drug or alcohol use, and prior unwanted births place women at risk of experiencing both unwanted pregnancies and mental health problems after a pregnancy, irrespective of how the pregnancy is resolved." American Psychological Association, "Mental Health and Abortion," n.d., http://www.apa.org/about/gr/issues/women/mental-health-and-abortion.aspx.

10 Every Woman's Health Centre, "Client Comments," 2014–16, http://everywomanshealthcentre.ca/client-comments/, comment dated August 2014.

11 For a fascinating account of the evolution of abortion counselling, see Carole Joffe, "The Politicization of Abortion and the Evolution of Abortion Counseling," *American Journal of Public Health* 103, no. 1 (2013): 57–65.

Women Judging Women

Whose Reasons Are "Good Enough"?
Whose Choice Is OK?

Ellen Wiebe

I love being an abortion provider. I performed my first abortions and delivered my first babies as a medical student, and I knew then that my career would focus on women's health. Now, at the age of sixty-four, I no longer deliver babies, but I still see women every day who struggle with the issues of whether to have children, when to have children, how many children to have and with whom, and what to do with an unplanned pregnancy. Naturally, some of these women are easier to empathize with than others.

One of the most challenging cases is the woman who is anti-choice, even though she is coming for an abortion herself. One such client referring to the others in the waiting room said, "Those women shouldn't be allowed to have abortions. They are just using it for birth control." I thought this attitude was uncommon until 2004 when I conducted a study along with my colleagues about anxiety levels and attitudes toward abortion. Then in 2005, we gave questionnaires to women having abortions and discovered that over half of the respondents (54 of 102) thought there were some reasons why women should not be allowed to have abortions. We then interviewed twenty-six anti-choice women having abortions. The most common reasons these women gave for why other women should not be allowed to have an abortion was "wants no more children," "not married," and "cannot afford." The two most common themes were that one needed "enough" reasons to have an abortion and that women should take better precautions to prevent conception.

In the forty years I have been doing abortions, the climate surrounding the procedure has changed. In the 1970s, I was only dimly aware of the activism for and against access to legal abortions. I really thought that everything was fine, because my patients and other women in Vancouver could get safe abortions in the hospital within a couple of weeks. The three-member hospital abortion committee approved all properly completed forms. A woman needed to see a doctor, who would refer her to an abortion provider, who then submitted forms to the hospital committee and scheduled the procedure. That sounds cumbersome, but we made it into an efficient system. I never felt harassed or in danger. During the 1980s, I certainly became aware of the harassment of other providers, but I never felt it affected my own life and work. That all changed on 8 November 1994, when my colleague, Gary Romalis, was shot. That day I had a police escort to work. Over the next years, I wore a bullet-proof vest to work, faced protestors, and received death threats: "Dr. Wiebe is a murderer," "You are next," "God will get you for what you are doing." I received "presents" such as bullets of increasing sizes. One of my colleagues quit after a death threat, leaving more work for me. Since 9/11, there has been less violence against abortion providers, and my vest stays in a drawer.

If I start wondering why we are still having trouble maintaining access for women seeking abortion in Canada and why abortion providers still face harassment, I only have to think of my anti-choice patients. If women who choose abortion for themselves continue to judge other women for making the same choice and to believe that others should not be allowed to have an abortion unless their reasons are good enough, we will probably never have free access for all women in Canada. I feel so lucky to have been able to help so many women make the best choice for themselves about having babies or having abortions. I also feel lucky that I could choose to have my three children, not eleven, like my grandmother.

Therapeutic Abortion

A Nonnegotiable Women's Right

STERLING HAYNES

When I first began practicing medicine, in 1960 in Williams Lake, British Columbia, I encountered cases of botched illegal abortions with serious long-term complications. The hotel-room abortionist's usual method was the insertion of a small piece of slippery elm, a wooden stem, into the cervical canal and the pregnant uterus. The slippery elm was full of spores and bacteria, and when in contact with the woman's blood, it would expand and dilate the cervix with disastrous results. A woman bleeding profusely with septic abortion would appear in the emergency ward of the Cariboo Memorial Hospital. The specialists in Kamloops always answered my phone calls regarding gynecological and obstetrical emergencies, and thanks to their help and the dedicated Williams Lake nursing staff, there were no fatalities.

On one occasion in 1965, in the town of 100 Mile House, a male hotel-room abortionist shoved lye pellets up the young woman's cervical canal into her pregnant uterus. In this case, the young woman began bleeding heavily, became septic, and sustained a badly burned vagina, cervix, and uterus. This horrific injury gradually healed, taking months, but the woman would remain sterile for the rest of her life.

The certified gynecologists in Kamloops were beacons to whom I could turn and they helped me and my colleagues during difficult maternity and gynecological situations in isolated communities. When I moved to Kamloops in 1966, I got to know them well.

When therapeutic abortions became legal, the Kamloops "Obs and Gyne" group performed many abortions in BC's central interior. They did their own surgery as well as a large number of therapeutic abortions on a weekly basis, making themselves available to these mostly young women despite the risks to their own safety and reputation in the community. Some of the Kamloops-based gynecologists were picketed by pro-lifers on the streets in front of the gynecologists' personal residences, where the protesters displayed their anti-abortion placards as they marched back and forth in confrontation seven days a week, fifty-two weeks a year. Many of my pro-life medical colleagues were also opposed to the local gynecologists who performed therapeutic legal abortions.

In 1969, the Canadian Parliament amended section 237 (now section 287) of the Criminal Code. Following the amendment, the existing criminal sanctions against a doctor who performs an abortion and a woman who procures one would no longer apply, provided the abortion was approved in writing by a therapeutic abortion committee consisting of three medical doctors and was carried out in an accredited or approved hospital.[1] For many years, I served on the committee at the Royal Inland Hospital, in Kamloops, with other general practitioners and my friend Doug, the local psychiatrist. In twelve years, we never rejected an application for abortion by a pregnant patient under twenty weeks' gestation.

The many disastrous cases resulting from backroom abortions that I encountered proved to me how important it is to have safe therapeutic abortions available to all women. Each woman must have complete control of her reproductive rights and must be uninfluenced by men or religious zealots. Pro-lifers, whether politicians or ordinary citizens, have a different agenda for Canadian women's reproductive rights. The pro-choice decision by the Supreme Court of Canada must be maintained. Canadian laws must not be changed.

Note

1   See Molly Dunsmuir, "Abortion: Constitutional and Legal Developments"
     (Ottawa: Library of Parliament, Research Branch, 1990 [1989]), http://
     www.publications.gc.ca/Collection-R/LoPBdP/CIR/8910-e.htm:
     "Background and Analysis," section C, "The 1969 Law." For the text of the
     law, see *Criminal Code*, R.S.C., 1985, c. C-46, http://laws-lois.justice.gc.ca/
     PDF/C-46.pdf, section 287, esp. subsections (1), (2), and (4).

On Becoming
an Abortion Provider

An Interview

Shannon Stettner and "Dr. James"

In October 2012, when I was gathering contributions to this collection, I interviewed an abortion provider whom I had first met more
than a decade earlier through our mutual activism—his with Medical
Students for Choice and mine with the Ontario Coalition for Abortion Clinics. For reasons of safety—both his own and his family's—he
has chosen to use a pseudonym, "Dr. James." The original interview,
which was conducted via email, has since been updated slightly, but
it is for the most part unchanged.

SS: How and why did you make the decision to be an abortion provider?

Dr. J.: I don't remember the exact moment that I decided to become
an abortion provider. I have always been pro-choice, and, growing up,
I was somewhat insulated from the anti-choice movement. I say this
because I helped two friends contact abortion clinics but didn't really
consider the fact that there was so much opposition or difficulty in

obtaining the procedure. When I moved away for my undergraduate studies, I became heavily involved in the LGBTQ movement, and the reproductive aspect of my "sexual rights" work took a back seat. It wasn't until a few years later that I realized that Guelph, a city of a hundred thousand, did not have an abortion clinic!

I decided to apply to medical school during my time at the University of Guelph. I was sitting in a philosophy of feminism class, and we were discussing systems of oppression and equality-seeking movements, and it became clear to me that medicine could be both a tool of oppression, through unequal access to health care, and a tool of social justice, by working with equality-seeking groups. Women's health became the key reason I chose to pursue medical studies.

Early in medical school, I became involved with Medical Students for Choice, and, after my first conference, I was determined that this was something that I had to do. I could not simply be a pro-choice feminist physician. I could not stand up for women and not provide abortions. It was simply a matter of principle.

But I realized that it takes more than just principle to become an abortion provider. As I matured through my medical training (from the lectures to the first days on the ward as a student, through my internship, residency and fellowship, and in early practice), it became clear that no one ever "just" becomes an abortion provider. At each step in the process, one must consider the practical aspects: obtaining training, finding mentors, establishing a practice, and seeking support from other colleagues. This is often done under a cloak of secrecy for fear of reprimand. In addition, I was taking this journey along with my partner, who has been unwavering in his support for me and my decision. I concede that the "difficult ethical challenges" have never really bothered me—most of them are back-door excuses for justifying restricting access to abortion—but staying the course was harder than I expected.

There is no one reason why I am proud to provide abortions. Having daughters helps, and I care very deeply for my patients, even the ones whom I meet only for a few minutes. Knowing that I play a part in what will nearly always be an important moment in a woman's life is something that I consider a privilege.

SS: What does "choice" mean to you? Is it still an adequate term to describe the movement for reproductive autonomy?

Dr. J.: Choice means having the opportunity to achieve greatness on one's own terms. Choice also reinforces the fact that women who choose abortion are making a maternal choice in doing so—it's the best option for both her and the pregnancy.

I think there are three problems with "choice," the term. First, simplifying the abortion issue to one of choice and autonomy minimizes the complexity and depth that women explore when making a decision about their pregnancy. Choice implies a proactive decision ("If I get pregnant, I'm having an abortion"), whereas, for many women, the choice to have an abortion is reactive—many factors go into the abortion decision. I have yet to see a woman who is completely cavalier about having an abortion or is choosing to have an abortion "just because."

Second, most women I see who choose abortion do so with the best interests of the potential child in mind, not because they like the idea of having an abortion. So, even though the abortion is her choice, a woman may be choosing to undergo a medical procedure that she does not especially want because it is the right thing to do in the circumstances.

Third, "choice" implies the ability to follow through on that choice. But the barriers that exist for women who need access to reproductive health services have little to do with the demand for these services—with women's choice to seek them out. Our greatest challenge as health care providers is that we are unable to adequately provide for the members of our community.

I do believe in the paradigm of "choice," but it could be insulting to suggest that one need only choose, and the abortion happens. These issues are complex and extend beyond reproductive rights, and to fix them as medical professionals and community builders will require us to examine our own power and privilege carefully—a process that is slow moving.

SS: How does performing abortions affect you professionally?

Dr. J.: Every abortion provider whom I know, myself included, cares deeply about each and every patient—whether I have cared for them for other reasons and have an ongoing relationship, whether I have just met them in the office, or whether I am just asked to be the technician to carry out the procedure. I sometimes wish that I had more time to convey this emotion to the patient. For me, professionally, I am able to say unequivocally that I provide the full spectrum of reproductive care to my patients, which is something that gives me great pride.

I have also had the privilege of providing abortion care to women with complex medical issues, women who are at very high risk if the pregnancy continues, as well as in special circumstances such as fetal anomalies and fetal deaths beyond the first trimester that require emergency care. Having the skills to manage these patients, particularly when few others will, is very rewarding.

SS: How does performing abortions affect you personally?

Dr. J.: Personally, I am affected by abortion in different ways. I am an adoptive parent, and as such, I belong to a community of families that have not historically been very pro-choice, if for no other reason than that of supply and demand: more abortions mean fewer potential children to be placed for adoption.

I empathize with those who want to become parents through adoption, and I see adoption support as being a part of reproductive health and social justice. I also cannot imagine my life without my children. I recognize that they were born of unintended pregnancies, and I'm not sure if, when the time comes for them to form their own identities, they will take exception to the fact that other pregnancies conceived in a similar circumstance will end in abortion.

That said, I have had women tell me they feel guilty about choosing abortion when couples are waiting for children. And I have patients who are experiencing infertility express frustration that their treatments are not funded when "abortion is free." To be clear—even when my partner and I were unsure whether our desire to become parents would ever be fulfilled, I would *never* ask a woman facing an unintended pregnancy to carry a pregnancy to term simply because of my desire to become a parent. No woman owes me this. She must come to that decision on her own and not be coerced by an external party.

I think that being an adoptive parent, an obstetrician, and an abortion provider allows me to stand proudly in support of all pregnancy options. I know that each option can be the right one for the right patient, and I will do my very best to support whatever decision is made.

SS: Can you reflect more on your thoughts about adoption in relation to your experiences as an adoptive parent?

Dr. J.: I think adoption is a wonderful thing, and, like abortion, many people who haven't experienced it seem to have strong and varied opinions about it. I have seen adoption being thrown around by both anti-choice groups (many so-called crisis pregnancy centres are affiliated with adoption agencies) and pro-choice groups (some of whom see it as an unacceptable alternative to abortion).

My observation is that many prospective families—adoptive parents in waiting—are not fond of abortion. I wouldn't go as far as to say they are anti-choice. I think many couples are hurting and come to adoption because of infertility. They struggle with the fact that abortion services are covered in most provinces whereas infertility services are not. Adoption is their Plan B, and their fate as parents rests in the hands of women with unintended pregnancies, many of whom go on to choose abortion.

My other observation is that a lot of birth mothers are pro-choice. Many were late in diagnosing their pregnancy, and others are pro-choice but feel that abortion isn't the right choice right now. Some prospective birth mothers consider adoption before moving to abortion. This observation, of course, is limited to a few patients and women whom I have met who have placed children into adoptive homes. It reminds us not to presume we know what someone else is thinking or where they stand on an issue.

Not being infertile, I can't really relate to the concerns I have mentioned. Adoption has always been my Plan A, as I believe that biology does not a family make. Above all else, though, I wanted my children to be raised knowing that adoption is what their birth parents wanted for them. The thought of a woman being coerced into adoption over abortion is as unacceptable as being forced into parenthood, and I could never ask that of a woman. So I continued to provide abortions while we waited to become parents. Oddly enough, I specifically remember my lack of an emotional response to the first abortion I performed after becoming a parent. I was worried that I would feel different or would struggle—but the case went on without hesitation. Perhaps being a parent has made me realize just how ready one should be before embarking on such a life-changing event.

SS: I know from the work of Medical Students for Choice, among others, that there is concern over the availability of training for abortion procedures in Canadian medical schools. Can you reflect on your experiences as someone who has gone through the process recently?

Dr. J.: The challenge in recruiting physicians to become abortion providers lies in the apathy and lack of coverage of family planning in most medical school curricula. In an attempt to avoid a "hot topic" for fear of offending students (usually those who are anti-choice), medical schools have removed the social responsibility of physicians as community advocates and removed the medical aspect from what is, at the end of the day, a medical procedure. If students don't know how prevalent abortion is, how to counsel patients appropriately, and how much work some women must do to access one of the most common medical procedures in North America, how are they supposed to make a difference?

There is a second challenge: once medical students develop an interest in abortion, much of their education on the subject and the procedure itself is self-directed. I know of no other area of medical education where students have to work so hard just to get trained. It does not get easier in residency. Many programs have an opt-in approach, so the default position is that you do not learn about abortions.

I will say that my experience in seeking training was largely positive. Organizations like Medical Students for Choice allow students to network in a safe space, and students always leave conferences energized to further their skill set and knowledge. Many OB-GYN faculty members support a woman's right to choose, even if they don't provide abortions (a bit hypocritical, yes), so there is support to get training; the hard part is sticking it out. It is certainly unnecessarily hard, and I am hopeful that more MSFC alumni will find ways to make it easier for new learners to acquire these important skills.

SS: Although there is no abortion law at present, doctors continue to be the "gatekeepers" to abortion. Some pro-choice advocates argue that abortion should be a decision a woman makes "in consultation with" her doctor, while others would have the physician be more of a "rubber stamp," for lack of a better term. As an abortion provider, what do you perceive as your role in the abortion decision?

Dr. J.: I really see my role as a facilitator. Very few women come to an abortion clinic or request a referral for an abortion without having done most of the decision making themselves. I think there is a role for counselling, but we border on paternalism by requiring all women to speak with a counsellor first. I recognize that I am a gatekeeper, and I take that role seriously—I hope

I never inadvertently abuse that power. I see the pendulum swinging away from comprehensive counselling to "informed choice."

One hot topic for "gatekeepers" currently is gender-selection abortion (particularly with patients being able to determine fetal sex very early in the pregnancy), as well as other "less socially desirable" reasons to choose abortion. There certainly are many physicians, and also clinic workers, including counsellors and nurses, who will restrict access to an abortion if they don't agree with the reason. I worry that any blanket restriction is a slippery slope. I have not faced an overt example of this in my own practice, which leads me to believe that its prevalence has been exaggerated.

Allow me to meander slightly. There have been media reports recently about gender imbalances in certain areas—in particular, areas where there are large immigrant populations. The media allows viewers to draw their own conclusions about where the girls are going, but we have no idea whether (a) sex-selective abortion occurs with significant regularity, or (b) the gender imbalance isn't also affected by other practices (cessation of child-bearing once a male is born, pre-implantation sex selection at the time of IVF). These also contribute significantly to imbalances.

SS: Dr. Ellen Wiebe has contributed a piece to this collection, in which she discusses providing abortion services to patients who are anti-choice. She surveyed women having abortions and discovered that just over half (54 out of 102) thought that there were some reasons why women should not be allowed to have abortions. It's interesting that such an apparent lack of empathy can exist among women who are going through the same experience. It's also interesting that women feel a need to justify their own abortions as somehow having a level of "merit" that they don't allow to other women. Do you have any thoughts on that? Or on the idea that women need to have "good enough" reasons to have an abortion?

Dr. J.: I'm always cautious about separating the women who are quietly against all or some aspects of abortion but who go on to have abortions (probably most of the women in Dr. Wiebe's study) from those who are vociferous opponents of abortion, who use fear and inaccurate information to trick women, and who then go on to have an abortion for their "superior" reason. The reality is that all women, pro-choice or not, those who have had abortions and those who have not, have been bombarded with messages about their bodies, their reproduction, and abortion their entire lives. It is extremely hard to ignore all of the baggage we bring with us on the ride. And few women expect to be having an abortion, even though one out of three will. If a woman must justify her own abortion as being for a better reason than the woman beside her, so be it—but she should keep her opinion to herself.

I always wonder how those same women would answer six months after their abortion, or after they become parents, if they were not already parents when they had an abortion. I suspect that these women were asked before their abortions occurred, a time when many women experience feelings of shame and guilt. (Post-procedure, these are generally replaced with relief and positive thoughts.) Asking them when they may still be in that "apprehensive" phase may not accurately represent their true feelings. I bet you would see less anti-choice sentiment over time.

SS: Judgments of women who have had an unplanned pregnancy can be pretty harsh. It's not uncommon to hear criticisms of women for failing to use birth control at all or for not using it properly. Yet birth control fails, and human beings are flawed—sometimes bad decisions get made, especially in the "heat of the moment." Women speak of being pressured to go on birth control after an abortion, as if the assumption is that they've been irresponsible. While I understand wanting to provide women with contraception, pushing birth control pills on a woman who has just aborted seems to contain an implicit judgment of her. What are your thoughts on this? How do we address the stigmatizing of women as irresponsible?

Dr. J.: I think that the stigmatization of patients as being irresponsible is a common paternalistic view within medicine. It cannot possibly be us, because we have birth control options to offer—we have pills and IUDs and public health nurses who can say the names of body parts without blushing and doctors who can write prescriptions. Surely, it is her fault. The reality is that unintended pregnancy is a problem for both women and their health care providers. Half of all unintended pregnancies occur as a result of contraceptive failure.[1] Contraceptive failure happens because of multiple factors, and I cannot tell you which one specific aspect causes it for each specific woman.

We use many colloquialisms to describe unplanned pregnancy: in trouble, knocked up, up the duff, with child. We sexualize women and yet judge them when they get pregnant without planning to. I see no short-term solution to that problem other than to acknowledge that none of us is immune to our exposure to such terms.

I am sorry that women sometimes feel insulted when doctors talk to them about birth control. In practice, most women who have chosen abortion or who are postpartum are quite motivated to prevent pregnancy, and my recommendation to start birth control is not meant to be punitive. I actually think we tend to underprovide birth control to women who are post-abortion and postpartum.

SS: Reading the stories of women's abortions submitted for this collection, I was struck by the differences in the attitude of their partners. Two of the women were well supported by the men in their lives, but several others weren't, which really underlines the truth that the responsibility for conception, maternity, and fertility falls unevenly on the women. As a physician and a provider, do you have any thoughts or reflections on this observation?

Dr. J.: My views on this issue have evolved. At first, my initial feeling was that some of the burden is self-imposed. For example, we did a study on couples and found that most women made the decision to have an abortion before involving their partners, which means they had to journey that decision-making process alone. I think the way in which we have developed the abortion clinic model, in an attempt to empower women, further segregates her burden of choice from his deference to her decision. The more I see women in my practice, even though many of the partners I see are supportive, I agree, the burden does fall on women. As a physician and a provider, I fear I have little more to offer, though there is a recognition in the family planning community of a need for more male-led contraceptive options.

As a man and a father in a nontraditional family, I struggle with society's privileging of maternity over paternity. I'm just the dumb dad. I'm not expected to be openly affectionate to my children, or to share in parental roles, or to know when my baby is mad because she hates her car seat and not because she's hungry. But I also see how my family—a two-male-led household—is threatening to some. The only solution to this inequality is for society to encourage men to take on a greater parental role and allow women to delegate without shame. But, as men's roles change, we will have to engage in a greater discussion about how we allow men to have opinions (I'm not saying they should have a vote) about their partners' pregnancy decisions.

SS: I think what you're saying here is really important, and there's a lot to unpack in your answer. As a woman who is resolutely pro-choice, unquestionably I see women as the final arbiters. As a movement, we have largely avoided the issue of men's place in the decision—generally denying the existence of a place—because there is a fear of creating an opening whereby a man can compel a woman to continue an unwanted pregnancy. But, as you indicate, by so doing, we also cement the "burden of choice" as something a woman too often faces alone.

Dr. J.: Exactly. The choice to have an abortion is directly related to one's reproductive autonomy. I believe that it is not only a woman's choice but often a maternal decision. I agree that men are not entitled to the final say, though I think it's healthy for couples to communicate and share in stressful life events—it's what you sign up for when you enter a relationship. I guess my conundrum is that I'm not sure whether it's a "burden" when a woman chooses to make the decision without consulting a partner (which I absolutely support) and whether it is "empowerment" or "burden" when a male partner defers to the decision to the pregnant woman. If there is an element of burden being placed, then I think we have to spend some time teaching men that it is very "manly" to be a supportive partner.

SS: In a couple of the narratives in this collection, the women make comments to the effect that they didn't want to become "women who have had abortions." Much is implicit in those statements—the stigma that is still associated with abortion, the secrecy, the shame, as well as the recognition that the procedure ends a potential life. It's odd that there's so much shame associated with a procedure that approximately one-third of Canadian women have undergone. One contributor to this volume, an abortion counsellor, wrote: "We all know women who have had abortions, although we may not know that we do." Why does the shame, silence, and secrecy continue to surround abortion? Why don't we talk about abortion? How do we go about ending the secrecy? Can or should we be talking about and understanding abortion differently?

Dr. J.: As long as clinic workers feel unsafe or are murdered (and, like me, stay silent publicly about the work we do), as long as women lack complete control over their bodies, as long as our society oppresses women, and as long as the media tiptoes around the issue or only covers it as an ethical issue, I don't see this improving. I think there are some wonderful grassroots movements afoot to increase the conversation about abortion, but I also think women have a right to privacy, and this must be respected.

SS: Do you have concerns for your safety? If so, how does that affect your practice and life?

Dr. J.: My first priority is the safety of my family—my partner and my children. We do have some tactics that we employ to fly under the radar, but it is hard at times to be an advocate in public and still have a private life. While I am proud of what I do, I am not always forthcoming with the specifics of my job description.

I am fortunate to work in a city with very little protest activity, but the city also has a history of anti-choice violence, including an attempted murder, so there is an institutional memory that commands additional safety measures. I sometimes park a little further away and walk. I check to see if people are following me to my car. I work in locked clinics. I always worry what kind of message we send to patients when we tell them that this is their right and their choice, and we support them, but we are going to hide the clinic in the basement in this derelict area and we'll put security guards at the entrance. No wonder women keep it a secret!

Would I die for this cause? Yes. I think that most providers would agree with me on that. But I very much hope it doesn't come to that. We have already lost some very good doctors and clinic workers. I still can't wrap my head around how the anti-choice movement supports such violent murders.

SS: It's easy to see the outcome of that fear and secrecy. A number of contributors to this book express feeling isolated and unsupported through their abortion experiences. One woman wrote: "The worst part of this whole experience was the shame and isolation." I believe that we, as pro-choice advocates, need to better support women who require support. Some women don't need post-abortion support, but some do. My personal belief is that the Silent No More movement (and comparable movements) preys on women who were more emotionally vulnerable post-abortion and who didn't—for whatever reasons—get the support they needed. Do you have thoughts on the adequacy of pro-choice post-abortion support available to women who need it?

Dr. J.: We are terrible at this, and we have been since the beginning. I have a clipping from the *Ottawa Citizen* about Norma McCorvey, the woman behind *Roe v. Wade*. The reason she is no longer pro-choice is that the movement used her and then pushed her aside when they were done with her. From the very first patient, we got it wrong!

I think the clinic setting is not the right place for post-abortion support—it's too value-laden a place. I'm surprised there aren't more Web-based resources for this in the age of social media and message boards. Sometimes, I think that we as a profession and movement are afraid of the fact that some women regret their decision, and that's why we don't want to engage in post-procedure support.

SS: If you see the clinic as too value-laden, where is a more ideal setting for counselling?

Dr. J.: Hospital-based clinics and public health units could easily take the talking aspect out of the procedure room and move it elsewhere. I think that referring physicians and family health teams could make use of their spaces as well.

SS: I think your comment about how the lack of post-abortion support may reflect some sort of fear on our part is important. Many women make the decision to have an abortion while they're in a state of crisis—whether because becoming a parent would totally disrupt the planned trajectory of the woman's life or because the circumstances of her life (relationship problems, money issues, etc.) make the pregnancy a crisis. Then, when the pregnancy is terminated, the sense of desperation dissipates and the woman starts to second-guess herself. Either way, the lack of post-abortion support needs to be addressed.

Dr. J.: The analogy that comes to mind is from the LGBTQ community. When I came out and realized how supportive people could be and saw LGBTQ youth coming out younger and younger, I really felt a sense of regret about not coming out sooner. But I think it's easy to forget the context in which we make decisions once that life context changes. So, in that sense, I completely sympathize.

This is why it is so important that women feel supported in that time of need so that, when they look back, their memory of that challenging time is of a group of people who cared for them unconditionally and gave them the opportunity to find their power again.

SS: How do we go about changing the abortion experience for women so that it is neither shameful nor isolating?

Dr. J.: We need to slowly become visible again. We can have bubble zones and clinic protection and privacy without being completely anonymous. Go to five hospitals with abortion clinics and you'll see five different euphemisms for abortion: Family Planning Clinic, Women's Health, Surgical Centre, Procedure Clinic, and so on. Let's call it what it is.

Within the clinics themselves, we need to create a sense of community—comfortable seating, up-to-date colour schemes, tea in regular mugs, places for women to journal or draw or sit together or hold each other. A place for partners to be present and supportive and relieved and to be able to say, "Thank you for doing this." Doctors need to be willing to hold a patient's hand if she wants, and laugh if she wants, and tell her that she or he supports her and takes his or her role in this part of her life with honour. We get so bogged down with the procedure, and we don't stop to consider the experience. Yes, these women become "women who have had an abortion," but why does that have to be a negative? To me, it's a time of great courage and strength.

SS: Another theme that weaves through several of narratives I've read is that of forgiveness, of women needing to forgive themselves for their choice. One contributor, for example, wrote, "I know this is something I'll have to forgive myself for. . . . The pain isn't in the choice. It's in finding the peace in it." Do you have any reflections or thoughts on that?

Dr. J.: It will come with time. I believe that the decision to have an abortion is a maternal decision, one made with the potential child in mind first and foremost. Trust yourself and your decision, for only you will ever be in that exact moment and circumstance.

Note

1   Regarding the proportion of unintended pregnancies that result from contraceptive failure, Dr. James provided a reference: Kirsten I. Black, Sunanda Gupta, Angela Rassi, and Ali Kubba, "Why Do Women Experience Untimed Pregnancies? A Review of Contraceptive Failure Rates," *Best Practice and Research Clinical Obstetrics and Gynaecology* 24, no. 4 (2010): 443–55.

part five

Sites of Struggle

The Myth of Reproductive Choice

A Call for Radical Change

KAREN STOTE

I recently completed five years of research on the coercive sterilization of Aboriginal women in Canada.[1] In addition to the well-documented policy of residential schooling, the destructive effects of the Indian Act, and the many other ways in which Canada has failed to respect Indigenous peoples and their lands, resources, and ways of life, I had often been told that Aboriginal women were sometimes subject to sterilizations under coercive circumstances or without their consent. The paucity of research on this topic led me on a journey through government records to begin to formally document this practice. Although the full extent to which sterilizations were carried out and the complete circumstances under which these took place have yet to come fully to light, what I uncovered was consistent with the stories I had heard.

The federal documents I looked at reveal that approximately twelve hundred sterilizations were carried out in federally operated medical services hospitals and Indian hospitals from 1970 to 1976 on Aboriginal women from at least fifty-two northern settlements.[2] Documents indicate that linguistic barriers and the failure of health workers to use proper interpreters when providing medical services to often isolated communities led women to be sterilized without their informed consent.[3] In the 1970s, Brian Pearson, then a councillor for the Northwest Territories at Frobisher Bay, stated that it was generally known that a number of women had been sterilized without their full knowledge of what the procedure entailed.[4] Granting that perhaps this was not an intentional policy, he noted a general climate of paternalism that led doctors to perform the procedure on women "for their own good" in the face of their "enormous" families.[5]

As my research progressed, it became clear that Aboriginal women had experienced injustices in the provision of other reproductive services as well. The documents I reviewed tell us that prior to the 1969 amendment to the Criminal Code decriminalizing contraceptives, the first controversial birth control pill was distributed to Indigenous women in many areas across Canada and that health workers sometimes persuaded women to take it as a matter of a "departmentally directed course of instruction."[6] At least some officials hoped that this measure would prove effective in reducing the Indigenous birth rate, thus enabling a reduction in the size of the homes government would need to provide.[7] Federal discussions around this time demonstrate that this fiscal concern influenced its decision to decriminalize contraceptives; it was anticipated that making contraceptives available to the whole population would have an effect on certain groups with high birth rates—in particular, Aboriginal peoples.[8] The Criminal Law Amendment Act, 1968–69, also granted women the ability to procure an abortion if a committee comprising three medical doctors agreed that an additional pregnancy would endanger her mental, emotional, or physical health.[9] While some continued to be denied access to abortions—namely, those in better financial situations and whose "health" was unlikely to be negatively affected by another child—others were subject to the procedure for economic reasons.[10] The Badgley Committee, formed in 1975 to study the equitable operation of abortion law in Canada, also found that some women were pressured to consent to sterilization when they were in the vulnerable position of being an applicant for abortion and that sterilization was sometimes a prerequisite to obtaining the service.[11]

An investigation into abortion in the North began as a result of one Indigenous woman claiming she was forced to undergo an abortion without

Without Apology

anaesthesia at the Stanton Territorial Hospital in Yellowknife. Her revelation led to more than one hundred additional complaints from women who had had similar experiences.[12] The hospital, which serves primarily Indigenous women, responded that it provided Aspirin for pain relief during abortion procedures. A subsequent medical audit in 1992 confirmed these and other instances of abuse.[13] This type of situation also existed elsewhere. For instance, a 1994 British Columbia Task Force on Access to Contraception and Abortion found that because of their poverty, many Aboriginal women were pressured by health care providers to have abortions, consent to sterilization, or submit to long-acting contraceptives and that because of these practices, they were being denied the right to make genuine choices about their reproduction.[14] As recently as the early 2000s, Aboriginal women were being encouraged to use the long-acting, provider-dependent, and potentially dangerous contraceptive Depo-Provera as a first-choice option in what appears to be an attempt to alleviate the strain on inadequately funded public health and social services.[15]

The above examples demonstrate that reproductive services have been imposed on Aboriginal women in unequal, coercive, and abusive ways. In all of these instances, however, these injustices, which are not part of Canadians' common knowledge, took place at the same time that other women struggled for increased access to these very same services. Why do these contradictions consistently arise? What is missing from our struggle that allows so-called gains for some to be employed coercively on others? Many thoughtful people have pointed out that we make choices in different contexts and that many factors constrain the options available to us. The prominent focus on individualized choice in Western society denies the contextual nature of decision making and obfuscates the existence of any systematic abuse directed toward certain populations. As Marlene Gerber Fried and Loretta Ross write,

> Individual freedom of choice is a privilege not enjoyed by those whose reproductive lives are shaped primarily by poverty and discrimination.
> . . .
> There are common threads in public policies that restrict abortion, coerce birth control, advance population control and criminalize pregnant women. In each area the government uses the ideology of individual choice to escape responsibility for the conditions of people's lives. It locates the cause and the blame of poverty in women's

individual choices—women are poor because they have too many children. This mentality also legitimizes state control when individual decisions are not to the liking of those in power.[16]

Unequal relations exist between the Indigenous peoples of Canada and non-Indigenous Canadians and between Western medical practitioners and Indigenous women. The context in which Indigenous women make choices continues to be one characterized by colonialism and assimilation. The reproductive violence experienced by Indigenous women cannot be separated from the larger systemic violence perpetrated as a result of the past and current colonization of Indigenous peoples and their lands.[17] Nor can the lack of control that non-Indigenous women experience over their reproductive lives be separated from the larger capitalist and patriarchal society in which we live.[18] The reproductive rights movement must move beyond reformist strategies and single-issue struggles and work to transform this larger context, both to avoid reproductive options from being wielded coercively on Indigenous and other marginalized women and to ensure real choice for all women.[19]

This transformation must involve the reproductive rights movement critically assessing the types of choice that women are being offered. If women are, in any way, denied control over our reproduction, how does increased access to state-provided services work to affect this reality? Are those services that are offered truly gains, or do they pale in comparison to the control and understanding that we could hold and have held, historically, over our bodies under different modes of social organization?[20] Our enforced dependence on state-provided services in the absence of a transformation of the very system that has been built on the exploitation of women results in our "choices" sometimes being manipulated in ways that further perpetuate exploitive and oppressive relations. We also need to consider that many reproductive services have been developed at the expense of women's well-being and are often harmful to our bodies and that instances of their coercive use are now increasingly concealed behind doctor-patient privilege and the rhetoric of individual choice.

Maria Mies argues that only by revolutionizing the relations upon which exploitation and oppression are based can the reproductive abuses experienced by women be overcome.[21] Nearly thirty years ago, Betsy Hartman also argued that two basic sets of rights are at issue in attempts to gain reproductive freedom for women. Women have a fundamental right to control our

Without Apology

own reproduction, but to achieve this, the relationship between the provider and recipient of reproductive services must be transformed: control must be taken out of the hands of the medical profession and placed back into the hands of women. Yet, as Hartman points out, reproductive freedom is predicated on women having greater control over our economic and social lives. This brings us to the second set of rights: everyone on earth today has the right to a decent standard of living through access to food, shelter, health care, education, employment, and social security.[22] Notwithstanding the birth rate in any community, it is possible to create such a society. The question we need to ask is whether this can be achieved from within a system based on values and principles that are antithetical to this vision.

To this we must add another crucial point. The abuses experienced by Indigenous women have been perpetrated by a foreign government with the help of Western institutions, including Western medicine. Aboriginal women have the right, as members of their own peoples, to decide what types of reproductive options to employ, whether these originate in Western or Indigenous ways.[23] To create a context in which choice becomes a meaningful concept, Aboriginal peoples must have their lands, resources, and freedom returned to them. Then they can choose to provide subsistence without stipulations. As Justine Smith writes,

> In the Native context, where women often find the only contraceptives available to them are dangerous . . . where they live in communities in which unemployment rates can run as high as 80 percent, and where their life expectancy can be as low as 47 years, reproductive "choice" defined so narrowly is a meaningless concept. Instead, Native women and men must fight for community self-determination and sovereignty over their health care.[24]

This is indeed where the struggle must be differentiated for non-Indigenous Canadian women and the Indigenous peoples on whose lands all non-Indigenous Canadians now depend. Indigenous voices have consistently challenged the relevance of a feminist movement that has often found itself on the wrong side of history, especially when it comes to the lived realities of Aboriginal women.[25] If social justice advocates are to pursue goals that are good for all women, we must acknowledge, and prioritize active resistance to, the long-standing colonial relations between Indigenous peoples and settlers. We need to enlarge our view of what control over our bodies truly looks like and what steps are needed to achieve this. But we must also envision what type of world we want to live in and what the fundamental requirements are to get us there. Justice will never be achieved by settling for only those rights that an oppressive and exploitive system is willing to grant. What is given too often falls short of what is truly needed and is constantly under threat of being taken away. As Linda Gordon pointed out three decades ago, to win real justice for all women is to ask for profound societal change, and it is best to recognize the radical implications of this type of project.[26]

Notes

1   Karen Stote, "An Act of Genocide: Eugenics, Indian Policy, and the Sterilization of Aboriginal Women in Canada."

2   For a more in-depth discussion of the information included in this chapter, see Karen Stote, *An Act of Genocide: Colonialism and the Sterilization of Aboriginal Women*. For a general overview of some of these findings, see Karen Stote, "The Coercive Sterilization of Aboriginal Women in Canada." These sterilizations are in addition to those we already know about. Under legislation in effect in Alberta from 1928 to 1972, Aboriginal women were disproportionately targeted relative to their numerical significance in the general population. They were also the most likely to be defined as mentally incompetent: hence, their consent was not required. In British Columbia, similar legislation was in effect from 1933 to 1973. Although records are said to be lost or destroyed, Aboriginal people were institutionalized in facilities where sterilizations took place, and at least two out of nine women involved in a class action lawsuit in 2005 were of Aboriginal descent. There is also evidence of sterilizations occurring in other provinces, including Ontario, Manitoba, and Québec. See Jana Grekul, Harvey Krahn, and Dave Odynak, "Sterilizing the 'Feeble-Minded': Eugenics in Alberta, Canada, 1929–1972"; Gail Van Heeswijk, "'An Act Respecting Sexual Sterilization': Reasons for Enacting and Repealing the Act"; Kathleen McConnachie, "Science and Ideology: The Mental Hygiene and Eugenics Movements in the Inter-war Years, 1919–1939"; and Angus McLaren, *Our Own Master Race: Eugenics in Canada, 1885–1945*.

3   LAC (Library and Archives Canada), RG 29, "Birth Control," vol. 2870, file 851-1-5, pt. 3A; Jim Eayrs, "Sterilization of Eskimos," *Weekend Northerly News Program*, 1 April 1973, Canadian Broadcasting Corporation, NWT.

4   LAC, RG 29, "Birth Control," vol. 2870, file 851-1-5, pt. 3A, correspondence from Marc Lalonde to Laurent Picard, president, Canadian Broadcasting

Corporation, 6 April 1973; reprinted in *The MacKenzie Pilot*, 3 May 1973, 29–30.

5 LAC, RG 29, "Birth Control," vol. 2870, file 851-1-5, pt. 3A; *News of the North*, Yellowknife, NWT, 11 April 1973.

6 Enovid, the first hormonal contraceptive on the market, was controversial because of its high hormone levels and because it had been tested on Puerto Rican women in unregulated clinical trials during the late 1950s and early 1960s. See LAC, RG 29, "Birth Control," vol. 2869, file 851-1-5, pt. 2, correspondence from J. H. Wiebe, MD, director, Medical Services, to regional directors, 8 October 1971; and Annette B. Ramírez de Arellano and Conrad Seipp, *Colonialism, Catholicism, and Contraception: A History of Birth Control in Puerto Rico*.

7 LAC, RG 29, "Birth Control," vol. 2869, file 851-1-5, pt. 1A, correspondence from H. A. Proctor to zone superintendents, 27 August 1965.

8 LAC, RG 29, "Birth Control," vol. 2869, file 851-1-5, pt. 1A, memorandum from minister of Health to Dr. J. N. Crawford, deputy minister of Health, 12 February 1969.

9 The Criminal Law Amendment Act, 1968–69 (S.C., 1968–69, c. 38), which originated as Bill C-150, received royal assent on 27 June 1969. The section of the law dealing with abortion was eventually overturned in 1988 with the *R. v. Morgentaler* ruling, which left abortion governed only by provincial and medical regulations.

10 The rationale was that an additional child born to an impoverished woman would cause a strain on her mental or emotional health. See Geoffrey Stevens, "Warning on Abortion," *Globe and Mail*, 23 October 1974, and "A Strange View of Law," *Globe and Mail*, 24 October 1974.

11 See Robin F. Badgley, *Report of the Committee on the Operation of the Abortion Law*, 360; Edward D. Boldt, Lance W. Roberts, and Abdel H. Latif, "The Provision of Birth Control Services to Unwed Minors: A National Survey of Physician Attitudes and Practices"; and Bernard M. Dickens, "Reproduction Law and Medical Consent." The Canadian Civil Liberties Association also made this claim, as reported in John Gray, "The Oddity of Canada's Abortion Law," *Ottawa Citizen*, 24 October 1974, 5. Charges of alleged unnecessary hysterectomies being performed on Indian patients were also forthcoming, and at least some of these were substantiated in the House of Commons. "Staff Squabbling Hurt Patient Care, Stony Plains Doctor Tells Inquiry," *Globe and Mail*, 16 November 1974, 13. See also the section headed "Operations Performed at Whitehorse Hospital" in *House of Commons Debates*, 28th Parliament, 3rd session, vol. 9 (20 October 1971 to 26 November 1971), 9194 (1 November 1971).

12 These complaints were received by the Northwest Territories Status of Women Council. One woman quoted her doctor as stating, after the abortion was completed: "This really hurt, didn't it? But let that be a lesson before you get yourself into this situation again." See Mary Williams Walsh, "Abortion Horror Stories Spur Inquiry—Canada: Questions Raised After Women Allege Hospital Denied Them Anesthesia as Punishment," *Los Angeles Times*, 3 April 1992; and JoAnn Lowell, "NWT Abortion Review Puts Spotlight on the Politics of Medicine," 27.

13 Northwest Territories, Abortion Services Review Committee, *Report of the Abortion Services Review Committee*, 30–32.

14 British Columbia Task Force on Access to Contraception and Abortion Services, *Realizing Choices: The Report of the British Columbia Task Force on Access to Contraception and Abortion Services*, 10, 14.

15 Two examples of articles encouraging the use of Depo-Provera by Aboriginal women are Madeline Cole, "The Shot Is Where It's At," *Nunatsiaq News*, 23 November 2001, http://www.nunatsiaqonline. ca/archives/nunavut011130/news/editorial/columns.html; and Jane George, "Babies Having Babies: An Explosion of Infants Born to Teenage Mothers," *Nunatsiaq News*, 19 May 2000, www.nunatsiaqonline.ca/ archives/nunavut000531/nvt20519_01.html. At the same time, other writers were raising questions about the disproportionate use of the drug among Aboriginal women. See, for example, Mary R. Hampton and Barb McWatters, "Process Model of Depo-Provera Use in Canadian Women"; Danylo Hawaleshka, "A Shot in the Dark?" *Maclean's*, 24 November 2005, 46; Andrea Smith, *Conquest: Sexual Violence and American Indian Genocide*; and Carolyn Tait, *A Study of Service Needs of Pregnant Addicted Women in Manitoba*, esp. 14–15.

16 Marlene Gerber Fried and Loretta Ross, "'Our Bodies, Our Lives: Our Right to Decide': The Struggle for Abortion Rights and Reproductive Freedom," 36–37.

17 See Smith, *Conquest*; Leanne Simpson, "Not Murdered and Not Missing"; and Amnesty International, *Stolen Sisters: A Human Rights Response to Discrimination and Violence Against Indigenous Women in Canada*.

18 For a historical understanding of the connections between capitalism and patriarchy in Western European society, how these relations were imposed, and the consequences for women and their knowledge of and ability to control their reproductive lives, see Silvia Federici, *Caliban and the Witch*; and Maria Mies, *Patriarchy and Accumulation on a World Scale: Women in the International Division of Labour*.

Without Apology

19 Andrea Smith, "Beyond Pro-choice Versus Pro-life: Women of Color and Reproductive Justice," 133, 135.

20 For an outline of some of the knowledge historically held by Western women and how it was undermined, see Barbara Ehrenreich and Deirdre English, *Witches, Midwives, and Nurses: A History of Women Healers*; and John Riddle, *Contraception and Abortion from the Ancient World to the Renaissance*, and *Eve's Herbs: A History of Contraception and Abortion in the West.*

21 Maria Mies, "'Why Do We Need All of This?' A Call Against Genetic Engineering and Reproductive Technology," 553.

22 Betsy Hartman, *Reproductive Rights and Wrongs: The Global Politics of Population Control and Contraceptive Choice*, 32–34.

23 See Kim Anderson, *Life Stages and Native Women: Memory, Teachings, and Story Medicine*; Yvonne Boyer, *First Nations, Métis, and Inuit Health Care: The Crown's Fiduciary Obligation*; Jessica Yee, "Reproductive Justice: For Real, For Me, For You, For Now," 6 November 2010, http://jolocas. blogspot.ca/2011/11/reproductive-justice.html; and Lesley Malloch, "Indian Medicine, Indian Health: Study Between Red and White Medicine."

24 Justine Smith, "Native Sovereignty and Social Justice: Moving Toward an Inclusive Social Justice Framework," 211.

25 For some examples of these voices, see Maile Arvin, Eve Tuck, and Angie Morrill. "Decolonizing Feminism: Challenging Connections Between Settler Colonialism and Heteropatriarchy"; Sandy Grande, "Whitestream Feminism and the Colonialist Project: A Review of Contemporary Feminist Pedagogy and Praxis"; Patricia Monture-Angus, *Thunder in My Soul: A Mohawk Woman Speaks*; Jessica Yee, ed., *Feminism for Real: Deconstructing the Academic Industrial Complex of Feminism*; Yee, "Reproductive Justice"; and Sally Roesch Wagner, *Sisters in Spirit: Haudenosaunee (Iroquois) Influence on Early American Feminists.*

26 Linda Gordon,"Who Is Frightened of Reproductive Freedom for Women and Why? Some Historical Answers," 23.

References

Amnesty International. *Stolen Sisters: A Human Rights Response to Discrimination and Violence Against Indigenous Women in Canada.* October 2004. http://www.amnesty.ca/sites/default/files/ amr200032004enstolensisters.pdf.

Anderson, Kim. *Life Stages and Native Women: Memory, Teachings, and Story Medicine.* Winnipeg: University of Manitoba Press, 2011.

Arvin, Maile, Eve Tuck, and Angie Morrill. "Decolonizing Feminism: Challenging Connections Between Settler Colonialism and Heteropatriarchy." *Feminist Formations* 25, no. 1 (2013): 8–34.

Badgley, Robin F. *Report of the Committee on the Operation of the Abortion Law*. Ottawa: Supply and Services Canada, 1977.

Boldt, Edward D., Lance W. Roberts, and Abdel H. Latif. "The Provision of Birth Control Services to Unwed Minors: A National Survey of Physician Attitudes and Practices." *Canadian Journal of Public Health* 73, no. 6 (1982): 392–95.

Boyer, Yvonne. *First Nations, Métis, and Inuit Health Care: The Crown's Fiduciary Obligation*. Discussion Paper Series in Aboriginal Health: Legal Issues, no. 2. Ottawa: National Aboriginal Health Organization, and Saskatoon: Native Law Centre, University of Saskatchewan, 2004.

British Columbia Task Force on Access to Contraception and Abortion Services. *Realizing Choices: The Report of the British Columbia Task Force on Access to Contraception and Abortion Services*. Victoria: Province of British Columbia, 1994.

Dickens, Bernard M. "Reproduction Law and Medical Consent." *University of Toronto Law Journal* 35, no. 3 (1985): 265–78.

Ehrenreich, Barbara, and Deirdre English. *Witches, Midwives, and Nurses: A History of Women Healers*. New York: Feminist Press, 1973.

Federici, Silvia. *Caliban and the Witch*. Brooklyn, NY: Autonomedia, 2004.

Fried, Marlene Gerber, and Loretta Ross. "'Our Bodies, Our Lives: Our Right to Decide': The Struggle for Abortion Rights and Reproductive Freedom." *Radical America* 24, no. 2 (1992): 31–37.

Gordon, Linda. "Who Is Frightened of Reproductive Freedom for Women and Why? Some Historical Answers." *Frontiers* 9, no. 1 (1986): 22–26.

Grande, Sandy. "Whitestream Feminism and the Colonialist Project: A Review of Contemporary Feminist Pedagogy and Praxis." *Educational Theory* 53, no. 3 (2003): 329–46.

Grekul, Jana, Harvey Krahn, and Dave Odynak. "Sterilizing the 'Feeble-Minded': Eugenics in Alberta, Canada, 1929–1972." *Journal of Historical Sociology* 17, no. 4 (2004): 358–84.

Hampton, Mary R., and Barb McWatters, "Process Model of Depo-Provera Use in Canadian Women." *Health Care for Women International* 24, no. 3 (2003): 193–208.

Hartman, Betsy. *Reproductive Rights and Wrongs: The Global Politics of Population Control and Contraceptive Choice*. New York: Harper and Row, 1987.

Lowell, JoAnn. "NWT Abortion Review Puts Spotlight on the Politics of Medicine." *Herizons* 9, no. 1 (1995): 27–28.

Malloch, Lesley. "Indian Medicine, Indian Health: Study Between Red and White Medicine." *Canadian Woman Studies* 10, nos. 2–3 (1989): 105–13.

McConnachie, Kathleen. "Science and Ideology: The Mental Hygiene and Eugenics Movements in the Inter-war Years, 1919–1939." PhD diss., University of Toronto, 1987.

McLaren, Angus. *Our Own Master Race: Eugenics in Canada, 1885–1945.* Toronto: McClelland and Stewart, 1990.

Mies, Maria. *Patriarchy and Accumulation on a World Scale: Women in the International Division of Labour.* London: Zed Books, 1986.

———. "'Why Do We Need All of This?' A Call Against Genetic Engineering and Reproductive Technology." *Women's Studies International Forum* 8, no. 6 (1985): 553–60.

Monture-Angus, Patricia. *Thunder in My Soul: A Mohawk Woman Speaks.* Halifax: Fernwood Publishing, 1995.

Northwest Territories. Abortion Services Review Committee. *Report of the Abortion Services Review Committee.* Yellowknife, NT: Abortion Services Review Committee, 1992.

Ramírez de Arellano, Annette B., and Conrad Seipp. *Colonialism, Catholicism, and Contraception: A History of Birth Control in Puerto Rico.* Chapel Hill: University of North Carolina Press, 1983.

Riddle, John. *Contraception and Abortion from the Ancient World to the Renaissance.* Cambridge, MA: Harvard University Press, 1994.

———. *Eve's Herbs: A History of Contraception and Abortion in the West.* Cambridge, MA: Harvard University Press, 1997.

Simpson, Leanne. "Not Murdered and Not Missing," *NB Media Co-op*, 17 March 2014, http://nbmediacoop.org/2014/03/17/not-murdered-and-not-missing/.

Smith, Andrea. *Conquest: Sexual Violence and American Indian Genocide.* Boston: South End Press, 2005.

———. "Beyond Pro-choice Versus Pro-life: Women of Color and Reproductive Justice." *NSWA Journal* 17, no. 1 (2005): 119–40.

Smith, Justine. "Native Sovereignty and Social Justice: Moving Toward an Inclusive Social Justice Framework." In *Dangerous Intersections: Feminist Perspectives on Population, Environment, and Development*, edited by Jael Silliman and Ynestra King, 202–41. Boston: South End Press, 1999.

Stote, Karen. *An Act of Genocide: Colonialism and the Sterilization of Aboriginal Women.* Halifax: Fernwood Publishing, 2015.

———. "An Act of Genocide: Eugenics, Indian Policy, and the Sterilization of Aboriginal Women in Canada." PhD diss., University of New Brunswick, 2012.

———. "The Coercive Sterilization of Aboriginal Women in Canada." *American Indian Culture and Research Journal* 36, no. 3 (2012): 117–50.

Tait, Carolyn. *A Study of Service Needs of Pregnant Addicted Women in Manitoba*. Winnipeg: Prairie Women's Health Centre of Excellence, 2000.

Wagner, Sally Roesch. *Sisters in Spirit: Haudenosaunee (Iroquois) Influence on Early American Feminists*. Summertown, TN: Native Voices, 2001.

Van Heeswijk, Gail. "'An Act Respecting Sexual Sterilization': Reasons for Enacting and Repealing the Act." Master's thesis, University of British Columbia, 1994.

Yee, Jessica, ed. *Feminism for Real: Deconstructing the Academic Industrial Complex of Feminism*. Ottawa: Canadian Centre for Policy Alternatives, 2011.

Sex-Selective Abortion and the Politics of Race in Multicultural Canada

H. Bindy K. Kang

During my pregnancy a few years ago, I collided with the assumption that I, as a woman of South Asian ancestry, might opt to abort my unborn daughter. Racial categorization—which collapses all individuals who share a particular ethnic heritage into a single, homogeneous group—has a long history in race politics in many countries, including Canada. While Canadians publicly espouse multiculturalism, the country is still imbued with a white settler identity, redolent of the early-twentieth-century ballad "White Canada Forever."[1]

Both as a Canadian woman of South Asian ancestry and as a feminist, one who has strongly supported the pro-choice movement in hopes that all women will someday have control over their own bodies, I have struggled with the issue of sex-selective abortion. Advocating for women's rights, particularly their right to exercise control over their bodies, while at the same time acknowledging that some women may choose to terminate a future body precisely because that body is female, poses an ethical dilemma. How do we decide when an abortion is "ethical"? Who decides this? Is it up to Canadians as a whole or to individual women?

My ethnic identity positions me as an insider, as someone who can pull back the curtain and reveal the hidden truths of "my people." Yet, while I share cultural roots with other Canadians of South Asian ancestry, we are not one monolithic community marching to the same drum, and no one person can be "our" collective voice. I enter this discussion with caution, since my words, the words of a "native informant," could be used to confirm practices of racial profiling—in this case, the profiling of pregnant South Asian women and South Asian communities as "baby girl killers." As someone who has faced race-based profiling, I offer my thoughts regarding the racial politics that surround the issue of sex-selective abortion.

———◆———

Like many couples, my partner and I wanted to know the sex of our baby so that we could make preparations for her or his arrival. I shared our desire with my family physician, who is also an obstetrician, and she agreed to schedule an ultrasound. When I arrived back at the front desk, however, one of the receptionists interrogated me with questions: "Why do you need to know this? Why do you care? What does it matter?" I was taken aback by this line of questioning, as it is not uncommon to wish to know a baby's sex, and I was certain that many patients before me had made this request. I explained that we were planning to purchase many baby items prior to the baby's arrival and also wanted to finalize the baby's name. The receptionist looked at me with suspicion and continued shaking her head. Despite all the polite exchanges we had had over the years, my South Asian ancestry suddenly took precedence: I was reduced to a stereotype, according to which I might be likely to abort a daughter.

Over the past decade or so, concerns have been raised about the possible practice of sex selection in Asian and South Asian immigrant communities. An analysis of census data from 2003, for example, revealed a disproportionate number of male births in areas of British Columbia and Ontario where large South Asian populations reside. While natural births occur at a rate of about 105 males to 100 females, in these communities the ratio ranged from 107 to 110 boys for every 100 girls.[2] Moreover, if the previous two children had been girls, the ratio was even further off balance: the odds were nearly two to one that the third child of an Indian-born Canadian woman would be a boy.[3] While researchers cannot confirm that the skewed ratio results from the use of sex-selective abortion or sex-selective embryo implantation, they acknowledge that such a ratio is not a naturally occurring phenomenon.

Various tactics have been adopted in an effort to avert sex selection. In British Columbia, as elsewhere in Canada, doctors are generally unwilling to order an ultrasound prior to week 20 simply for the purpose of determining a child's sex.[4] In the case of ultrasound examinations conducted as a routine part of prenatal care, clinics may also choose not to record information about the baby's sex in the report returned to the doctor.[5] Informing parents of the sex of the fetus only after week 20 is another option, given that, in Canada, abortions are rarely performed after week 20 unless the mother's life or health is at risk or the fetus is seriously impaired.[6] Theoretically, these measures should prevent abortions based solely on a preference for male children. In practice, however, it is not difficult to circumvent such policies. Private commercial clinics, both in Canada and the United States, offer ultrasound imaging prior to week 20, for a fee.[7]

Canada's Assisted Human Reproduction Act (2004) explicitly prohibits the sex-selective use of reproductive technologies, although this regulation applies only to technologies used to create an embryo.[8] However, Canadians can access sex-selective reproductive services simply by crossing the border. In fact, American clinics have advertised their provision of sex-selective embryo implantation in South Asian and Asian newspapers in British Columbia, on the assumption that members of these communities prefer boy children and will be prepared to spend substantial sums of money to choose a baby's sex.[9] "Reproductive tourism" has become increasingly popular, and Canadians can easily travel next door to access reproductive services and procedures that are not legal in Canada.[10]

Like many others of South Asian ancestry, I do not have a preference for a male child. My partner and I celebrated our daughter's birth, and we would welcome a future child (or children) of any sex. Our sense of honour in being our daughter's parents is woven from our Sikh philosophical beliefs regarding gender equality, my strong feminist standpoint, and our personal ethics and values around equality, as well as our relative freedom from the patriarchal pressure to bear sons. This freedom is anchored in our many sites of privilege that have sheltered us from dependence on traditional patriarchal structures to fulfil our needs, including a need for male children to support us financially in our elder years. Female infanticide and sex-selective embryo implantations and abortions have been traced to patriarchal mores that prevail in many South Asian communities. While patriarchy is not the only operating hierarchy, it incessantly informs both explicit and implicit social, economic, cultural, and political practices surrounding the preference for sons.[11]

Alongside the economics of raising and marrying daughters, social factors such as the perpetuation of the family name and the perceived prestige of having sons have been well documented in South Asian communities, although these values are not universally shared. Given the persistence of dowry customs, some families consider girl children to be a financial liability. Additionally, because girls are traditionally raised as "guests" in their parents' home until they are married, at which point they are given over to their husband's family, investing in a daughter does not ultimately contribute to her family's financial situation.[12] Sons, however, are traditionally raised to remain with their natal families and to care for their parents in their later years and carry out the last rites.[13]

North Americans of South Asian ancestry do not necessarily need to rely on their sons to care for them in their elder years. However, a recent study of Indian-born immigrants in the United States reveals that some families of South Asian ancestry continue to uphold this ideal, even while acknowledging that elder care is primarily carried out by daughters.[14] In India, pensions and social support are not universally available, and this lack perpetuates the ongoing preference for male children. The preference for male children persists, however, even in relatively well-educated, higher-income groups, as the ratio of male to female births reveals.[15]

In 1992, in an editorial published in the *British Medical Journal*, Amartya Sen estimated that 37 million women were "missing" in India as a result of inequities in care, which contributed to a much higher female mortality rate. In a follow-up editorial written in 2003, Sen reported that although the "female disadvantage in mortality" had been substantially reduced, "this has been counterbalanced by a new female disadvantage—that in natality—through sex specific abortions aimed against the female fetus."[16] Researchers have indeed postulated an increase in sex-selective abortions of female fetuses in India from 2001 to 2011; their findings are based in part on the growing imbalance in the number of boys versus girls revealed in the 2011

Indian census, which counted 7.1 million fewer girls than boys in the age range from birth to six years.[17]

In an effort to combat the preference for male children, India banned the use of sex-selective technologies in 1994 with the enactment of the Pre-Natal Diagnostic Techniques (PNDT) Act. The Indian government has also launched campaigns to support the education of girls from elementary school through to university or college in an effort to offset gender inequities. In addition, during my last visit to India, in 2009, I saw billboards throughout Punjab advertising programs and charitable organizations that provide support to poor families to help with wedding expenses. While, in the long run, these measures may work in unison to improve the status of women, their impact on the sex imbalance so far seems limited.[18] After all, policing the practice of sex-selective abortion and embryo implantation is difficult. As Sen suggests, as access to new reproductive technologies becomes easier, the use of sex-selective procedures will probably increase, further enlarging the gap between the number of boys and girls in India.[19]

◆

The issue of sex selection is bound up with a complicated web of ethical concerns and, understandably, provokes strong emotional reactions. All the same, I am troubled by the shadow of apparent racism in media and scholarly articles when sex selection is discussed. In "Sex Selection Migrates to Canada," Lauren Vogel calls attention to the view—expressed by a number of economists and bioethicists—that "easy access to abortion and advances in prenatal sex determination have combined to make Canada a haven for parents who would terminate female fetuses in favour of having sons."[20] Like the contention that Canada has become a safe haven for terrorist organizations, such a view implies that immigrants are now bringing another social evil into our country: their alleged preference for boy children and female infanticide. The opinions she goes on to quote implicitly blame the South Asian diaspora for disrupting the Canadian value system. Such arguments quickly evoke concerns about Canada's claim to support "the accommodation of different religious values and practices," in accordance with a policy of "peaceful pluralism," and to expect its institutions to be "both respectful and inclusive of Canada's multicultural character."[21]

Vogel goes on to quote Canadian bioethicist Kerry Bowman: "It really works against everything we believe in Canada in terms of equality. It works against our Charter [of Rights and Freedoms]."[22] The idea that there is a unified "Canadian" belief regarding equality is puzzling, given the numerous issues pertaining to gender inequality in Canada, including institutionalized barriers restricting women's movements away from violent intimate partnerships, women's health, and the ongoing wage gap between women and men.[23] Indeed, Amartya Sen's warning to Western nations not to be "smug" about gender inequality applies to Canada as well: "Gender equality exists in most parts of the world, from Japan to Morocco, from Uzbekistan to the United States. Yet inequality between women and men is not everywhere the same. It can take many different forms. Gender inequality is not one homogeneous phenomenon, but a collection of disparate and inter-linked problems."[24] Without acknowledging that other forms of gender inequality exist in Canada, Bowman situates the cause of sex-selective abortion, which she cites as a violation of the Canadian Charter of Rights and Freedom and Canadian values, as immigration and the concomitant importation of non-Canadian cultural and political values.

With regard to sex selection, Lena Edlund, an associate professor of economics at Columbia University, is quoted as saying: "We don't expect immigrants, let alone their children, to continue doing it once they've settled in North America."[25] The statement that "immigrants" and their subsequent offspring are not "expected" to carry on cultural practices reveals how cultural intolerance for immigrants' less palatable cultural practices is reformulated and perpetuated. The world of the Other is divided into two hemispheres—one is considered exotic, voyeuristic, and fun, such as our clothing, bangles, food, music, weddings, and Bollywood films; the other marks our culture as dark, potentially dangerous, backward, immoral, and violent. Unravelling the discourse allows us to trace how race, class, and gender are constituted in Canadian society, thus exposing processes of racialization that are highly dependent on maintaining the binary of us versus them, the Other versus the norm. When the discourse specifies racialized communities, it draws on colonial beliefs that Europeans are inherently superior and needed to "save" the misguided Other.[26] It is the role of Canadians of European ancestry to identify and police these unwanted cultural practices—the "snakes and scorpions" that were never invited into Canada's multicultural immigration and settlement process.[27]

Without Apology

In "'It's a Girl!'—Could Be a Death Sentence," Rajendra Kale articulates similar notions regarding the by-products of Asian migration to the West, commenting that, even as these immigrants "brought welcome recipes for curries and dim sum," they "also imported their preference for having sons and aborting daughters." Kale acknowledges that the tendency to abort daughters "is a small problem localized to minority ethnic groups," but it is a problem that cannot be ignored: sex-selective abortion is, he says, an "evil" that "devalues women." His solution is to prohibit doctors from disclosing the sex of a baby until "after about 30 weeks of pregnancy"—an "ethical compromise" that Kale describes as "reasonable."[28] However, his suggestion merely contributes to the ongoing colonial surveillance project, whereby the Other is monitored and regulated. "Compared with the situation in India and China," Kale writes, "the problem of female feticide in Canada is small, circumscribed and manageable. If Canada cannot control this repugnant practice, what hope do India and China have of saving millions of women?"[29] The requirement that Canadian authorities "control this repugnant prac-tice" highlights the need for the presumably civilized white settler nation to intervene in the moral habits of the backward Other. Such proposals echo the sentiments expressed in a June 1914 article in *The Vancouver World*, according to which

> it is the universal opinion of all citizens resident upon the Pacific Coast of the Dominion of Canada, that the influx of Asiatics is detrimental and hurtful to the best interests of the Dominion, from the standpoint of citizenship, public morals and labor conditions.
>
> All good British subjects respect the law, even though they may not approve of it. There is a species of anarchy in the attitude of these Hindoos which, if white people were the offenders would be vigorously suppressed. We are all alike in wishing our own working people to have food and enough to live upon, and we do not want any sort of immi-gration that, by cutting wages and lowering the standard of living tends to degrade our people to Asiatic standards.[30]

Articles in the *Canadian Medical Association Journal* and contempor-ary Canadian media continue to echo this early-twentieth-century call for surveillance, monitoring, and managing of the "Hindoo" population. These sentiments—that "Hindoos" cannot assimilate into Canadian cul-ture because our beliefs, customs, values, and practices are so dramatically different, that making allowances for our "special" practices would negatively impact the "white" Canadian identity—haunt contemporary discussions.[31]

While these historically rooted opinions identify the "Asiatic" as "detrimental and hurtful" to Canadian citizenship and morals, these sentiments resounded in responses to the media articles about sex-selective abortion in 2012. Three articles published in the *Canadian Medical Association Journal* regarding sex-selective abortion within the span of a month were taken up by Canadian media.[32] The Canadian Broadcasting Corporation (CBC), the *National Post*, the *Globe and Mail*, and the *Toronto Star* were among the media organizations to report on this issue, specifically implicating Canadian communities comprising individuals with South Asian and Asian ancestry, as the scholarly articles had. One CBC News article quotes Roger Pierson, a director of research at the University of Saskatchewan, as saying that he isn't "surprised" that an American reproductive clinic is targeting the South Asian community, because "from the American perspective this is business, and you are not only creating, you are working to expand your market." Pierson also argues that "Canada has a very strict law respecting gender equity and the difficulty is that they have no way to enforce it due to the extremely porous nature of the border."[33] This contention situates the Canadian South Asian community as deviating from Canadian laws, eager to accept alternative options presented by Canada's "porous borders" that allow these immigrants to slip into the United States and procure these "repugnant" procedures. The assertion that the American company is simply creating and expanding their market removes any "repugnancy" from their service offerings.

The media's presentation of sex-selective abortions as a South Asian and Asian cultural practice that has "migrated" along with the South Asian and Asian bodies offers those who question Canada's immigration policies another reason to "keep them out." The well-established rhetoric of "keeping them out" or "sending them back to where they came from" is apparent in the comments left by readers of the online media articles.

> When multiculturalism was invisioned [*sic*], I think the idea was only that we would be sharing the best of each other's cultures . . . we end up mostly sharing the worst. . . . The people that come to Canada from India are pretty much the 1/100th of the 1% in India who have lots of money and little respect for human life in the way westerners view life. Their caste system is simply not compatible with our western ways. . . .

I think we have to be selective on who comes and it shouldn't be just those that can write a check. I see no value in bringing in 50 year old + people from India as they will bring us nothing but outdated ways of thinking.[34]

Here is another case where the problem is imported and remains restricted to culturally alien minorities, but the measures to alleviate it would be extended to the completely innocent majority . . . If the term Minority-Run Canada (MRC) has not been copyrighted yet, I'm claiming it. Diversity, the gift that keeps on giving.[35]

gender selective pregnancies are here to stay . . . we have a morally decaying society when things like this are allowed to happen, but time and again we are told to be tolerant of other's choices . . . no warm fuzzy feeling here . . . some choice, eh?[36]

Who would have guessed that 3rd world immigration would bring 3rd world cultural problems to Canada? . . . The same idiots who insist on even more immigration now, insisting there's no danger, even though they've been dead wrong.[37]

These comments illustrate the racism that many visible-minority individuals and communities face in multicultural Canada. While the language has changed, the early-twentieth-century newspaper articles and the contemporary online responses express similar sentiments. Immigrants of South Asian ancestry are conflated with the "Hindoos"—"a species of anarchy" who degrade Canada to their "Asiatic standards." Drawing on the legacy of white settler identity, authors writing in *CMAJ* and in popular media alike choose to racialize sex-selective abortion, presenting it as a cultural practice of the non-white, one that violates the fundamental norms of Canadian society.

Is it possible to discuss this issue without naming specific communities? Yes. The Abortion Rights Coalition of Canada (ARCC) released a position paper on sex-selective abortion and was careful not to focus on a racial or ethnic community. Naming ethnic-ancestry communities first and foremost as "South Asians" or "Indian immigrants" and not as Canadians operates to differentiate those communities as Other. This practice perpetuates the surveillance and policing of these brown bodies, especially when they do not conform to "good" Canadian standards. ARCC acknowledged cultural practices and poignantly identified the vulnerability that women may experience, without further marginalizing these women and the communities with which they identify:

> Being pro-choice means supporting a woman's right to decide whether or not to continue a pregnancy for whatever reason, even if one personally does not agree with her reason. . . .
>
> . . . If a woman is in a dependent and vulnerable position within her family, where she feels obligated to abort a female fetus or suffer serious personal consequences, these complex issues are dealt with in a compassionate and safe way. . . .
>
> . . . The root issue is the value and respect—or lack of value and respect—that society and certain cultures give to girls and women. The answer lies in education and raising the status of girls and women over the long-term, not in restricting abortion.[38]

Tackling gender inequality and challenging ongoing patriarchal privilege is a holistic and global project that is not fixed within a particular location or particular culture. It is a broader issue of social justice for girls and women.

Notes

1 "White Canada Forever" was one of many racist responses to the influx of immigrants to Canada during the early decades of the twentieth century, a period in which race-based theories of eugenics also became popular. On racialization, especially in the context of Canadian multiculturalism, see Himani Bannerji, *The Dark Side of the Nation: Essays on Multiculturalism, Nationalism, and Gender*; Sunera Thobani, *Exalted Subjects: Studies in the Making of Race and Nation in Canada*; and Sherene Razack, Malinda Smith, and Sunera Thobani, eds., *States of Race: Critical Race Feminism for the Twenty-First Century*. See also Homi Bhabha's analysis of cultural hybridity in *The Location of Culture*; and, for depictions of the East in the context of Western imperialism, Edward Said, *Orientalism*.

2 Andrea Mrozek, "Canada's Lost Daughters," *Western Standard*, 5 June 2006, 34–35. Similar ratios were observed in Chinese immigrant communities.

3 Lauren Vogel, "Sex Selection Migrates to Canada." The male-female ratio for the third child was 1.9 to 1—that is, 190 boys for every 100 girls.

4 Health Canada advises against the use of ultrasound for nonmedical purposes, including determining the child's sex, as does the Society of Obstetricians and Gynaecologists of Canada. BC's College of Physicians and Surgeons has a similar guideline: "Physicians should only perform or

provide ultrasound examinations, including obstetrical ultrasounds, for valid medical indications and not solely for non-medical reasons." See Shia Salem, Kenneth Lim, and Michiel Van den Hof, "Joint SOGC/CAR Policy Statement on Mon-medical Use of Fetal Ultrasound"; College of Physicians and Surgeons of British Columbia, "Non-medical Use of Ultrasound."

5 For discussion, see Allison T. Thiele and Brendan Leier, "Towards an Ethical Policy for the Prevention of Fetal Sex Selection in Canada." ·

6 Abortion Rights Coalition of Canada, "Late Term Abortions (After 20 Weeks)."

7 See Timothy Sawa and Annie Burns-Pieper, "Fetal Gender Testing Offered at Private Clinics," *CBC News*, 12 June 2012, http://www.cbc.ca/news/canada/fetal-gender-testing-offered-at-private-clinics-1.1183673; Sam Solomon, "Sex-Selective Abortion Comes to Canada: Recent BC Dispute Sparks Ethical Debate over Abortion Practice."

8 Assisted Human Reproduction Act (S.C. 2004, c. 2), Justice Laws Website, 2015, http://laws-lois.justice.gc.ca/eng/acts/a-13.4/. Section 5(1)(e) prohibits any action that "would ensure or increase the probability that an embryo will be of a particular sex, or that would identify the sex of an *in vitro* embryo, except to prevent, diagnose or treat a sex-linked disorder or disease."

9 See, for example, Annie Burns-Pieper, "Baby Sex Selection Ad Targets Indo-Canadians," *CBC News*, 17 April 2012, http://www.cbc.ca/news/canada/story/2012/04/16/sex-selection-advertisement-child.html. See also National Post, "Canadians Go South to Choose Baby's Sex," *Canada.com*, 4 July 2006, http://www.canada.com/story.html?id=e13b3886-2f10-4e9f-a26c-850bbf212d53. According to this report, the fee for embryo selection at one set of clinics was roughly US$18,000 (in 2006). The doctor in charge of these clinics readily acknowledged that "we've had a ton of Canadian patients."

10 On Canadian reproductive tourism, see Christabelle Sethna and Marion Doull, "Accidental Tourists: Women, Abortion Tourism, and Travel."

11 On the structural marginalization of daughters within strongly patrilineal family systems, see Monica Das Gupta, "Selective Discrimination Against Female Children in Rural Punjab, India."

12 Ravinder Kaur, "Missing Women and Brides from Faraway: Social Consequences of the Skewed Ratio in India," 6.

13 Ibid., 3.

14 See Sunita Puri et al., "'There Is Such a Thing as Too Many Daughters, but Not Too Many Sons': A Qualitative Study of Son Preference and Fetal Sex Selection Among Indian Immigrants in the United States."

15 S. V. Subramanian and S. Selvaraj, "Social Analysis of Sex Imbalance in India: Before and After the Implementation of the Pre-Natal Diagnostic Techniques (PNDT) Act."

16 Amartya Sen, "Missing Women—Revisited: Reduction in Female Mortality Has Been Counterbalanced by Sex Selective Abortions," 1297. Sen's original findings were presented in "Missing Women: Social Inequality Outweighs Women's Survival Advantage in Asia and North Africa," as well as in a 1990 essay in the *New York Review of Books*, "More Than 100 Million Women Are Missing." For an analysis of the structural inequities that underlie such imbalances, see Sen, *Inequality Reexamined*.

17 Prabhat Jha et al., "Trends in Selective Abortions of Girls in India: Analysis of Nationally Representative Birth Histories from 1990 to 2005 and Census Data from 1991 to 2011."

18 See S. Sudha and S. Irudaya Rajan, "Female Demographic Disadvantage in India: Sex Selective Abortions and Female Infanticide"; Subramanian and Selvaraj, "Social Analysis of Sex Imbalance in India." As the findings of these studies indicate, attempts such as the PNDT Act (http://pndt. gov.in/writereaddata/mainlinkFile/File50.pdf) to legislate new social norms have had little effect on the skewed birth ratio, nor does improved socioeconomic status seem to make a significant difference.

19 Sen, "Missing Women—Revisited."

20 Vogel, "Sex Selection Migrates to Canada."

21 *Promoting Integration: Annual Report on the Operation of the Canadian Multiculturalism Act, 2011–2012*, 9, 20.

22 Quoted in Vogel, "Sex Selection Migrates to Canada," E163.

23 See Natasha Jategaonkar and Pamela Ponic, "Unsafe and Unacceptable Housing: Health and Policy Implications for Women Leaving Violent Relationships"; Marina Morrow, Olena Hankivsky, and Colleen Varcoe, eds., *Women's Health in Canada: Critical Perspectives on Theory and Policy*; Krishna Murthy Pendakur and Ravi Pendakur, "Colour My World: Has the Majority-Minority Earnings Gap Changed over Time?"

24 Amartya Sen, "The Many Faces of Gender Inequality," 35.

25 Quoted in Vogel, "Sex Selection Migrates to Canada," E163.

26 Linda Carty, "The Discourse of Empire and the Social Construction of Gender."

27 Uma Narayan, "Eating Cultures: Incorporation, Identity and *Indian Food*," 67.

28 Rajendra Kale, "'It's a Girl!'—Could Be a Death Sentence," 387. As Kale notes, his solution is very similar to that proposed by Thiele and Leier in "Towards an Ethical Policy for the Prevention of Fetal Sex Selection in

Canada." For similar debates in a different postcolonial context, see Sawitri Saharso, "Sex-Selective Abortion: Gender, Culture, and Dutch Public Policy."

29 Ibid.

30 "Great Mass Meeting Says Hindoo Ship Must Return: Vancouver People Determined That East Indians Shall Not Be Permitted to Land (Huge Building Packed: Overflow Meeting Held: Approaches to Auditorium Jammed by Masses of Indignant Citizens)," *Vancouver World*, 24 June 1914. This article appeared during the *Komagata Maru* "incident," as it is sometimes called. In 1914, the *Komagata Maru* arrived in Vancouver carrying 376 passengers from British India, many of them Sikhs from the Punjab region, who were seeking to immigrate to Canada, in deliberate defiance of regulations that effectively barred South Asians from entry. The ship was denied permission to land, and its passengers—all of them British subjects—were held offshore for more than two months without adequate provisions for food and water. Eventually, the ship was ordered to turn around and transport them back to their place of origin. The fate of the *Komagata Maru* is chronicled in Ali Kazimi's documentary *Continuous Journey* (2004), which includes a sound clip of Vancouver locals singing "White Canada Forever." See also Hugh Johnston, "Komagata Maru," *Canadian Encyclopedia*, 2006 (updated 2014), http://www. thecanadianencyclopedia.ca/en/article/komagata-maru/.

31 See, for example, Enakshi Dua, "The Hindu Woman's Question"; Harminder Bindy Kaur Kang, "A Post-colonial Reading of Vaisakhi: Unveiling the Indo-Canadian Sikh Identity Through Canadian Media."

32 The articles were Rajendra Kale's "'It's a Girl!'" and Lauren Vogel's "Sex-Selective Abortions," and "Sex Selection Migrates to Canada."

33 Quoted in Burns-Pieper, "Baby Sex Selection Ad Targets Indo-Canadians."

34 Lipper2000 [pseud.], comment on Carly Weeks, "Study: Is Sex Selection to Blame for Birth Trends in Ontario?" *Globe and Mail*, 16 April 2012, comment posted 17 April 2012, http://www. theglobeandmail.com/life/health-and-fitness/sex-selection-may-be-at-pla y-among-indian-south-korean-families-in-ontario-study/article4223491/.

35 Sonofkaz [pseud.], comment on Michel Viatteau, "Keep Sex of Fetuses a Secret to Prevent Selective Abortion of Girls: Journal," *National Post*, 16 January 2012, comment posted February 2012, http://news. nationalpost.com/2012/01/16/canada-is-haven-for-parents-seekin g-sex-selective-abortions-medical-journal/.

36 Thornylius [pseud.], comment on Burns-Pieper, "Baby Sex Selection Ad Targets Indo-Canadians," comment posted 17 April 2012.

37 Fast Frankie [pseud.], comment on Weeks, "Study: Is Sex Selection to Blame for Birth Trends in Ontario?" *Globe and Mail*, comment posted 17 April 2012.
38 Abortion Rights Coalition of Canada, "Sex Selection Abortions."

References

Abortion Rights Coalition of Canada. "Late Term Abortions (After Week 20)." Position Paper # 22, July 2005. http://www.arcc-cdac.ca/postionpapers/22-Late-term-Abortions.PDF.

———. "Sex Selection Abortions." Position Paper #24, January 2006. http://www.arcc-cdac.ca/postionpapers/24-Sex-Selection-Abortions.pdf.

Bannerji, Himani. *The Dark Side of the Nation: Essays on Multiculturalism, Nationalism, and Gender.* Toronto: Canadian Scholar's Press, 2000.

Bhabha, Homi. *The Location of Culture.* New York: Routledge, 2003. First published 1994.

Carty, Linda. "The Discourse of Empire and the Social Construction of Gender." In *Scratching the Surface: Canadian, Anti-racist, Feminist Thought*, edited by Enakshi Dua and Angela Robertson, 35–48. Toronto: Women's Press, 1999.

Citizenship and Immigration Canada. *Promoting Integration: Annual Report on the Operation of the Canadian Multiculturalism Act, 2011–2012.* Ottawa: Citizenship and Immigration Canada, 2013. http://www.cic.gc.ca/english/pdf/pub/multi-report2012.pdf.

College of Physicians and Surgeons of British Columbia. "Non-medical Use of Ultrasound." January 2012. https://www.cpsbc.ca/files/pdf/PSG-Non-medical-Use-of-Ultrasound.pdf.

Das Gupta, Monica. "Selective Discrimination Against Female Children in Rural Punjab, India." *Population and Development Review* 13, no. 1 (1987): 77–100.

Dua, Enakshi. "The Hindu Woman's Question." *Canadian Woman Studies* 20, no. 2 (2000): 108–16.

Jategaonkar, Natasha, and Pamela Ponic. "Unsafe and Unacceptable Housing: Health and Policy Implications for Women Leaving Violent Relationships." *Women's Health and Urban Life* 10, no. 1 (2011): 32–58.

Jha, Prabhat, Maya A. Kesler, Rajesh Kumar, Faujdar Ram, Usha Ram, Lukasz Aleksandrowicz, Diego G. Bassani, Shailaja Chandra, and Jayant K. Banthia. "Trends in Selective Abortions of Girls in India: Analysis of Nationally Representative Birth Histories from 1990 to 2005 and Census Data from 1991 to 2011." *The Lancet* 377, no. 9781 (4 June 2011): 1921–28.

Kale, Rajendra. "'It's a Girl!'—Could Be a Death Sentence." *Canadian Medical Association Journal* 184, no. 3 (2012): 387–88.

Kang, Harminder Bindy Kaur. "A Post-colonial Reading of Vaisakhi: Unveiling the Indo-Canadian Sikh Identity Through Canadian Media." Master's thesis, Simon Fraser University, Burnaby, BC, 2007.

Kaur, Ravinder. "Missing Women and Brides from Faraway: Social Consequences of the Skewed Ratio in India." In *AAS Working Papers in Social Anthropology / ÖAW Arbeitspapiere zur Sozialanthropologie*, edited by Andre Gingrich and Helmut Lukas. Wien: Österreichische Akademie der Wissenschaften, 2008. http://hw.oeaw.ac.at/0xc1aa500d_0x001a819c.

Kazimi, Ali. *Continuous Journey*. Toronto: Peripheral Visions Film and Video, 2004.

Morrow, Marina, Olena Hankivsky, and Colleen Varcoe, eds. *Women's Health in Canada: Critical Perspectives on Theory and Policy*. Toronto: University of Toronto Press, 2007.

Narayan, Uma. "Eating Cultures: Incorporation, Identity and *Indian Food*." *Social Identities* 1, no. 1 (1995): 63–86.

Pendakur, Krishna Murthy, and Ravi Pendakur. "Colour My World: Has the Majority-Minority Earnings Gap Changed over Time?" *Canadian Public Policy* 28, no. 4 (2002): 489–12.

Puri, Sunita, Vincanne Adams, Susan Ivey, and Robert D. Nachtigall. "'There Is Such a Thing as Too Many Daughters, but Not Too Many Sons': A Qualitative Study of Son Preference and Fetal Sex Selection Among Indian Immigrants in the United States." *Social Science and Medicine* 72, no. 7 (2011): 1169–76.

Razack, Sherene, Malinda Smith, and Sunera Thobani, eds. *States of Race: Critical Race Feminism for the Twenty-First Century*. Toronto: Between the Lines, 2010.

Saharso, Sawitri. "Sex-Selective Abortion: Gender, Culture, and Dutch Public Policy." *Ethnicities* 5, no. 2 (2005): 248–66.

Said, Edward. Orientalism. 25th anniversary ed. New York: Vintage Books, 2003. First published 1978.

Salem, Shia, Kenneth Lim, and Michiel C. Van den Hof. "Joint SOGC/ CAR Policy Statement on Mon-medical Use of Fetal Ultrasound." SOGC Policy Statement no. 304. Society of Obstetricians and Gynaecologists of Canada, February 2014. http://sogc.org/wp-content/uploads/2014/02/gui304PS1402Erev.pdf.

Sen, Amartya. *Inequality Reexamined*. Oxford: Oxford University Press, 1992.

———. "The Many Faces of Gender Inequality." *New Republic* 225, no. 12 (2001): 35–41.

———. "Missing Women: Social Inequality Outweighs Women's Survival Advantage in Asia and North Africa." *British Medical Journal* 304 (7 March 1992): 587–88.

———. "Missing Women—Revisited: Reduction in Female Mortality Has Been Counterbalanced by Sex Selective Abortions." *British Medical Journal* 327 (6 December 2003): 1297–98.

———. "More Than 100 Million Women Are Missing." *New York Review of Books*, 20 December 1990. http://www.nybooks.com/articles/1990/12/20/more-than-100-million-women-are-missing/.

Sethna, Christabelle, and Marion Doull. "Accidental Tourists: Canadian Women, Abortion Tourism, and Travel." *Women's Studies: An Interdisciplinary Journal* 41, no. 4 (2012): 457–75.

Solomon, Sam. "Sex-Selective Abortion Comes to Canada: Recent BC Dispute Sparks Ethical Debate over Abortion Practice." *National Review of Medicine* 4, no. 15 (2007). http://www.nationalreviewofmedicine.com/issue/2007/09_15/4_policy_politics02_15.html.

Subramanian, S. V., and S. Selvaraj. "Social Analysis of Sex Imbalance in India: Before and After the Implementation of the Pre-Natal Diagnostic Techniques (PNDT) Act." *Journal of Epidemiology Community Health* 63, no. 3 (2009): 245–52.

Sudha, S., and S. Irudaya Rajan. "Female Demographic Disadvantage in India, 1981–1991: Sex Selective Abortions and Female Infanticide." *Developmental Change* 30 (1999): 585–618.

Thiele, Allison T., and Brendan Leier. "Towards an Ethical Policy for the Prevention of Fetal Sex Selection in Canada." *Journal of Obstetrics and Gynaecology Canada* 32, no. 1 (2011): 54–57.

Thobani, Sunera. *Exalted Subjects: Studies in the Making of Race and Nation in Canada*. Toronto: University of Toronto Press, 2007.

Vogel, Lauren. "Sex-Selective Abortions: No Simple Solution." *Canadian Medical Association Journal* 184, no. 3 (2012): 286–88.

———. "Sex Selection Migrates to Canada." *Canadian Medical Association Journal* 184, no. 3 (2012): E163–64.

The Public Pregnancy

How the Fetal Debut and the Public Health Paradigm Affect Pregnancy Practice

Jen Rinaldi

The routinized, ritualized use of ultrasound technology during pregnancy produces imagery that has affected cultural understandings of
the fetus such that pressure to preserve and to terminate pregnancy
alike may be framed as obligatory, in either instance carried out for
the purpose of maximizing public health. In this chapter, I investigate
the cultural effect of the ultrasound ritual and its product, "baby's
first photograph." I go on to discuss the association of ultrasound
visuals with normalcy and health, and the implications of that association: that women are the gatekeepers of public health, such that
abortion, often opposed by those making use of fetal imagery as a
political tool, comes to be the logical, inevitable conclusion to an
ultrasound appointment gone wrong, in the same way that absten-
tion from caffeine comes to be framed as good pregnancy practice.
My interest is in exploring the range of maternal responsibilities
that functions as a consequence to the social and political work fetal
imagery accomplishes.

In reproductive contexts, ultrasounds employ sound waves to produce images of what is interior to the body—the contents of the uterus.[1] Originally a military and industrial tool used to detect underwater phenomena, the technology was discovered to have medical application in the 1950s.[2] Use of ultrasound has become such a prominent pregnancy ritual that it is assumed to be standard, even compulsory, and often desired by the prospective parent(s). Indeed, Susan Sontag describes the ultrasound as an example of "an aesthetic consumerism to which everyone is now addicted."[3] But Gordon Fyfe and John Law caution against the power of fixed visuals: "A depiction is never just an illustration. It is a material representation, the apparently stabilized product of social difference. To understand a visualization is thus to inquire into its provenance and into the social work that it does."[4] We turn, then, to the social work accomplished: the mandate built into the fetal imagery produced via technological intercourse, and how that mandate may be internalized.

Ultrasound imagery has been used to frame fetal-maternal identities and relationships.[5] The technology affords the opportunity to, according to common cultural understandings, "see the baby," and accessing this visual representation is thought to facilitate bonding. Having a window into the interior of the womb has come to be understood as a medically mediated quickening, a confirmation of the experience of pregnancy and a chance to forge a more personal connection with the fetus.[6] But this intimate peering into the uterus renders public that which is private, and this publicization of the fetus has an individuating effect: "the technological removal of the fetus from the 'secrecy of the womb' through ultrasound . . . gives the fetus social recognition as an individual separate from the mother."[7] The relationship that the prospective mother forges with the fetus is cultivated through the technological medium that makes it possible for mother to meet fetus, for one individual entity to encounter another, because it sharpens the focus between the two.

Although in the early days of ultrasound use, the images produced were difficult to decipher—little more than static and snow—the idea that the interior of the womb could be explored by technological means came to be an enticing prospect and an engrossing preoccupation. Technologically produced fetal imagery first became public—to much fanfare—thanks to a 1965 *Life Magazine* cover and photo spread featuring Scandinavian artist Lennart Nilsson's pictures of fetuses in utero. Described at length in the magazine feature are the art pieces' dark backgrounds, sometimes depicting outer space, replacing the uterus in which the fetus is actually situated.[8] Carol Stabile argues that this background, together with the captions discussing the thriving child, has the effect of disappearing the mother: "both visually and textually, the embryo-fetus enjoys a thoroughly autonomous status."[9] Images like these have functioned as tools used to "personify" the fetus and to render the female body invisible at best, and often even as hostile terrain.[10] Tongue in cheek, Shelley A. M. Gavigan describes the picture painted: "the virtually autonomous foetus [is] trapped in its mother's womb, begrudgingly serving a nine-month sentence of confinement."[11] The pregnant woman's role is erased and reshaped through the production of fetal identity such that she, far from facilitating fetal development, is regarded as potentially standing in its way.

This effort to individuate the fetus for the purpose of protecting the fetus does not require technological mediation, but the materiality of the ultrasound image furthers the project of individuation. Indeed, according to Barbara Katz Rothman, "the sense of separation of the fetus and mother was already there as a concept; the new technology allows the separation to be reified."[12] Normalization of ultrasound, along with the power of the image, is compatible with long-standing anti-abortion politics. And opponents of abortion have recognized this compatibility, evidenced by their wielding visual imagery as political strategy. Organizations have fundraised to provide counselling and crisis pregnancy centres with ultrasound machinery and have lobbied in the United States and Canada to pass laws that would render ultrasounds legally mandatory when women express an interest in having an abortion.[13] The *Windsor Star*, a Canadian publication, reported that the American evangelical group Focus on the Family spent $4.2 million in the 2005 fiscal year to equip crisis centres with ultrasound machines and to provide training for their use, and the Canadian-based Christian Association of Pregnancy Support Services points to the persuasiveness of fetal imagery: "anti-abortion advocates say an ultrasound image makes a far more effective case against abortion than any legal or bioethical argument."[14] Rosalind Petchesky argues that anti-abortion advocates have sought "to make foetal personhood a self-fulfilling prophecy by making the foetus a *public presence*" in "a visually oriented culture."[15] While activists against abortion have used imagery of the mutilated, aborted fetuses of *Silent Scream* fame, far more common is the "friendly fetus" or "the familiar and well-articulated fetus who is already a member of the family."[16] This cultural icon has proven to be a powerfully influential device in political activism waged against reproductive rights, one that manifests personal vulnerability, calls for legal protection, and inspires maternal shame.

So far, though, a piece of the picture is missing: while this political history has fallen away from collective memory and the ultrasound appointment has been taken up as a banality, even a cause for celebration in cases of wanted pregnancies, there are times when the diagnosis rendered via ultrasound radically changes the appointment's tone. Ultrasounds are only effective as ritual to the extent that they produce imagery that is universal and publicly recognizable. The canonical experience of pregnancy includes obtaining the same picture every other pregnant woman has received of her fetus: as Rebecca Kukla notes, "our pleasure in these first 'encounters' with our 'baby' is inextricably bound up with our pleasure in the conformation of our experience to the shared norm."[17] This can only happen when the fetus lives up to health expectations, where health is understood to be the absence of disease and disability.[18]

Often overlooked in the ritual of obtaining that first family photo is what happens when the visuals are not recognizable, when deviations to canon are detected. While ultrasound carries a social meaning that "dominates its medical uses," the tool was originally used in the 1950s to detect not merely the innocuous fetal positioning and the presence of twins but also anencephaly, or the absence of a fetal skull and upper brain.[19] Currently, ultrasounds are employed "to detect increasingly subtle structural and functional abnormalities such as gastrointestinal tract anomalies, urinary tract anomalies, congenital heart defects and skeletal dysplasia."[20] The Society of Obstetricians and Gynaecologists of Canada (SOGC) developed guidelines specifically recommending the use of ultrasound to detect chromosomal anomalies that result in intellectual disability.[21] The social work of the ultrasound appointment abruptly shifts because the fetus can no longer be personified, for its identity comes to be entirely constituted by impairment.[22]

When the fetus cannot be idealized or regarded as friendly, the social purpose of the ultrasound ritual deviates, for the experience is no longer about facilitating the relationship between mother and child. The responsibilities of the woman change such that she is socially—perhaps even medically, morally, and civically—expected not to nurture and protect her offspring, not to ensure that it is healthy, but to abandon the pregnancy. That is, responsibilities shift to disability deselection, which, in the absence of cures for many fetal conditions or effective and safe surgeries performed on the fetus in utero, equates to termination of the pregnancy. Abortion has come to be the "logical follow-up" and "action imperative" to diagnoses of fetal impairment.[23] Here, I would stress the difference between abortion as reproductive right and abortion as reproductive responsibility. Although I would not advocate for limiting a woman's reproductive access even if it meant the termination of a pregnancy where fetal impairments have been detected, I nevertheless hold that the social work of the ultrasound image includes expectations and imperatives around termination.

Some scholars have gone so far as to consider whether it is morally wrong to reproduce or to refuse to access reproductive technologies when the risks for a disease or disability are high.[24] Women who refuse ultrasound run the risk of being considered irresponsible for not doing everything within their power to promote fetal health.[25] Susan Sherwin argues that while women are not legally coerced into consenting to ultrasounds, "it is so commonly used and so generally valued that it is difficult for anyone to resist its use without being judged irrational and irresponsible."[26]

Has the analysis gone too far? Fetal imagery has been taken up by opponents of abortion, after all; must they, too, be wary of cultural appropriations getting away from them, of the picture meaning more than they had intended? I would wager as much: the friendly fetus promoted in anti-abortion campaigns is also the healthy fetus and thus is only effective when in compliance with our current health paradigm. Health as absence of disability is understood to be, at least in part, pictorially representable. The social meaning of ultrasound is built on the condition that health can be seen and disability can be marked. That the image is normalized, that there is a universal, ideal image sought at ultrasound appointments, carries the (perhaps unintended) implication that there is such a thing as abnormality, and the presence of abnormality in an ultrasound picture precludes women from the social conventions of pregnancy. Abortion comes to be an obligation in the interest of public health, for the fetus as a public figure—one that makes its social debut with the help of sonographic waves—must be familiar.[27]

Through ultrasound, then, we have seen the woman disappeared, cast in an adversarial role, and consigned to the gate, responsible for not only bringing persons into but also "barring the entry of disabled persons" from a community.[28] Women as gatekeepers safeguard and maximize public health, the health of a polity, by denying passage to identifiable impairments, to deviations from the ideal. They are responsible for preventing, and thus at fault for reproducing, disability. There are myriad ways in which they are obliged to manage pregnancy or to have pregnancy managed in order to avoid health complications, ranging from regimenting caffeine and fish, to taking folic acid and iron supplements, to avoiding too much or too little weight gain, to forgoing alcohol and cigarettes.[29] Fetal health is such a pressing public concern that women are little trusted with its preservation and promotion: "they are constantly judged by family, friends, and strangers, in the transformation of pregnant bodies into objects of public concern."[30] Social compliance is framed as personal responsibility: women are to blame for not maintaining a proper diet; for not submitting to medical scrutiny; and for not terminating when the fetus is marked, abnormal, and unhealthy. This range may seem to admit contradictions, but I mean to defend a woman's right both to terminate and to carry through with a pregnancy, for I am interested in the way in which neither reproductive choice is entirely hers when her womb and the contents of it become public theatre and when her decisions and activities come to be measured according to standards like the needs of the fetus or the demands of the social good. In either case, our preoccupation with the imagery that the ultrasound yields perpetually casts women to the background.

So in sum, the evocative and voyeuristic ultrasound picture has factored into social efforts to draw attention away from women's needs, interests, and entitlements. The fetus as a political figure has accomplished much since its appearance on the public scene sixty years ago, for it has served to reify reproductive control and to reframe that control as maternal responsibility. This is not to say that a woman should not derive pleasure from a technologically derived sneak peek or that she should decline folic acid or opt out of exercising a hard-fought legal right to terminate pregnancy. I mean only to claim that social context—replete with so many pressures around good pregnancy practice—does not make authentic choice easy and that fetal imagery has been used to further muddy the waters. If we ever hope to disentangle ourselves from the problematics of pregnancy maintenance, even of pregnancy termination, more work needs to be done to consider how ultrasound has been culturally taken up—that is, how visual representations are interpreted and in turn embedded within our valuing systems.

Notes

1 Society of Obstetrician and Gynaecologists of Canada, "Ultrasound in Pregnancy," n.d., http://sogc.org/publications/ultrasound-in-pregnancy/.

2 Carol Sanger, "Seeing and Believing: Mandatory Ultrasound and the Path to a Protected Choice."

3 Susan Sontag, *On Photography*, 24.

4 Gordon Fyfe and John Law, *Picturing Power: Visual Depiction and Social Relations*, 1.

5 See Isabel Karpin, "Legislating the Female Body: Reproductive Technology and the Reconstructed Woman"; Lisa Mitchell, "The Routinization of the Other: Ultrasound, Women, and the Fetus," and *Baby's First Picture: Ultrasound and the Politics of the Fetal Subjects*; and Rosalind Pollack Petchesky, *Abortion and Woman's Choice*, and "Fetal Images: The Power of Visual Culture in the Politics of Reproduction."

6 Mitchell, *Baby's First Picture*, 6; Sanger, "Seeing and Believing," 355.

7 Robert H. Blank, "Maternal-Fetal Relationship: The Courts and Social Policy," 73.

8 Barbara Duden, *Disembodying Women: Perspectives on Pregnancy and the Unborn*, 14; Barbara Katz Rothman, *The Tentative Pregnancy: Prenatal Diagnosis and the Future of Motherhood*, 108; Mitchell, *Baby's First Picture*, 91; and Carol Stabile, "Shooting the Mother: Fetal Photography and the Politics of Disappearance," 187.

9 Stabile, "Shooting the Mother," 187.

10 Rebecca Kukla, *Mass Hysteria: Medicine, Culture, and Mothers' Bodies*, 122.

11 Shelley A. M. Gavigan, "*Morgentaler* and Beyond: Abortion, Reproduction, and the Courts," 131.

12 Barbara Katz Rothman, *Recreating Motherhood: Ideology and Technology in a Patriarchal Society*, 158.

13 Sanger, "Seeing and Believing," 372.

14 Joanne Laucius, "Anti-Abortion Groups Seek Ultrasound Access," *Windsor Star*, 19 February 2005.

15 Petchesky, "Fetal Images," 263.

16 Sanger, "Seeing and Believing," 356. Produced with support from the National Right to Life Committee, *The Silent Scream* (1984) was directed by Jack Duane Dabner and narrated by Dr. Bernard Nathanson.

17 Kukla, *Mass Hysteria*, 116.

18 Roxanne Mykitiuk and Jeff Nisker, "Social Determinants of 'Health' of Embryos," 116; Shelley Tremain, "Reproductive Freedom, Self-Regulation, and the Government of Impairment in Utero."

19 Quoted in Linda Layne, "'Your Child Deserves a Name': Possessive Individualism and the Politics of Memory in Pregnancy Loss," 31. For the history of ultrasound as a prenatal diagnostic tool, see Margaret B. McNay and John E. E. Fleming, "Forty Years of Obstetric Ultrasound, 1957–1997: From A-Scope to Three Dimensions," 28; Mitchell, *Baby's First Picture*, 32; and Sanger, "Seeing and Believing," 365.

20 Ian Ferguson MacKay and F. Clarke Fraser, "The History and Evolution of Prenatal Diagnosis," 15.

21 Michiel C. Van den Hof and R. Douglas Wilson, "Fetal Soft Markers in Obstetric Ultrasound."

22 Rayba Rapp, Testing Women, *Testing the Fetus: The Social Impact of Amniocentesis in America*, 129; Susan Sherwin, "Normalizing Reproductive Technologies and the Implications for Autonomy."

23 See Erik Parens and Adrienne Asch, "The Disability Rights Critique of Prenatal Genetic Testing: Reflections and Recommendations"; and Melissa Masden, "Pre-Natal Testing and Selective Abortion: The Development of a Feminist Disability Rights Perspective."

24 See Jeff McMahan, *The Ethics of Killing: Problems at the Margins of Life*; Laura Martha Purdy, *Reproducing Persons: Issues in Feminist Bioethics*; and Rosamond Rhodes, "Abortion and Assent," and "Why Test Children for Adult-Onset Genetic Diseases?"

25 Blank, "Maternal-Fetal Relationship"; Thomas Lemke, "Genetic Testing, Eugenics, and Risk."

26 Sherwin, "Normalizing Reproductive Technologies," 369.

27 Abby Lippman, "Prenatal Genetic Testing and Screening: Constructing Needs and Reinforcing Inequities," 23.

28 Yvonne Peters and Karen K. Lawson, *The Ethical and Human Rights Implications of Prenatal Technologies: The Need for Federal Leadership and Regulation*, 3.

29 On caffeine and fish, see Marty Munson and Greg Gutfield, "Baby and Java Don't Jive: To Get Pregnant or Stay that Way, Try Putting the Cap on Caffeine," 26; Health Canada, *Prenatal Nutrition Guidelines for Health Professionals: Fish and Omega-3 Fatty Acids*; and Lisa Murphy, "The Healthiest Catch," *Chatelaine*, July 2002. On folic acid and iron supplements, see Health Canada, *Prenatal Nutrition Guidelines for Health Professionals: Folate*, and *Prenatal Nutrition Guidelines for Health Professionals: Iron*. On managing weight, see Health Canada, *Prenatal*

*Nutrition Guidelines for Health Professionals: Gestational Weight
Gain*; and Jenny Wright, "'You Selfish Cow!': One of the Insults Hurled
at Me by Other Mothers as I Jogged . . . Because I'm Pregnant," *Daily
Mail*, 5 May 2012, http://www.dailymail.co.uk/health/article-2139955/
You-selfish-cow--One-insults-hurled-I-jogged-Im-pregnant.html. On
alcohol and cigarettes, see March of Dimes, "Is It Safe?" 2015, http://www.
marchofdimes.org/pregnancy/is-it-safe.aspx.

30 Roxanne Mykitiuk and Dayna Nadine Scott, "Risky Pregnancy: Liability,
Blame, and Insurance in the Governance of Prenatal Harm," 311.

References

Blank, Robert H. "Maternal-Fetal Relationship: The Courts and Social Policy."
Journal of Legal Medicine 14 (1993): 73–92.

Duden, Barbara. *Disembodying Women: Perspectives on Pregnancy and the
Unborn*. Cambridge, MA: Harvard University Press, 1993.

Fyfe, Gordon, and John Law. *Picturing Power: Visual Depiction and Social
Relations*. London: Routledge, 1988.

Gavigan, Shelley A. M. "*Morgentaler* and Beyond: Abortion, Reproduction,
and the Courts." In *The Politics of Abortion*, edited by Janine Brody, Shelley
A. M. Gavigan, and Jane Jensen, 117–46. Toronto: Oxford University Press,
1992.

Health Canada. *Prenatal Nutrition Guidelines for Health Professionals: Fish
and Omega-3 Fatty Acids*. Ottawa: Health Canada, 2009. http://www.hc-sc.
gc.ca/fn-an/alt_formats/hpfb-dgpsa/pdf/pubs/omega3-eng.pdf.

———. *Prenatal Nutrition Guidelines for Health Professionals: Folate*. Ottawa:
Health Canada, 2009. http://www.hc-sc.gc.ca/fn-an/alt_formats/hpfb-
dgpsa/pdf/pubs/folate-eng.pdf.

———. *Prenatal Nutrition Guidelines for Health Professionals: Gestational
Weight Gain*. Ottawa: Health Canada, 2010. http://www.hc-sc.gc.ca/fn-an/
alt_formats/pdf/nutrition/prenatal/ewba-mbsa-eng.pdf.

———. *Prenatal Nutrition Guidelines for Health Professionals: Iron*. Ottawa:
Health Canada, 2009. http://www.hc-sc.gc.ca/fn-an/alt_formats/hpfb-
dgpsa/pdf/pubs/iron-fer-eng.pdf.

Karpin, Isabel. "Legislating the Female Body: Reproductive Technology and
the Reconstructed Woman." *Columbia Journal of Gender Law* 3, no. 1
(1992–93): 325–49.

Kukla, Rebecca. *Mass Hysteria: Medicine, Culture, and Mothers' Bodies*.
Lanham, MD: Rowman and Littlefield, 2005.

Layne, Linda. "'Your Child Deserves a Name': Possessive Individualism and the Politics of Memory in Pregnancy Loss." In *The Anthropology of Names and Naming*, edited by Gabriele vom Bruck and Barbara Bodenhorn, 31–50. Cambridge: Cambridge University Press, 2006.

Lemke, Thomas. "Genetic Testing, Eugenics, and Risk." *Critical Public Health* 12, no. 3 (2002): 283–90.

Lippman, Abby. "Prenatal Genetic Testing and Screening: Constructing Needs and Reinforcing Inequities." *American Journal of Law and Medicine* 17, no. 1–2 (1993): 15–50.

MacKay, Ian Ferguson, and F. Clarke Fraser. "The History and Evolution of Prenatal Diagnosis." In *Prenatal Diagnosis: Background and Impact on Individuals: Research Studies of the Royal Commission on New Reproductive Technologies*, vol. 12 of Commission on New Reproductive Technologies Research Studies, 1–30. Ottawa: Minister of Supply and Services, 1993.

Masden, Melissa. "Pre-natal Testing and Selective Abortion: The Development of a Feminist Disability Rights Perspective." Women with Disabilities Australia, 1992. http://www.wwda.org.au/masden1.htm.

McMahan, Jeff. *The Ethics of Killing: Problems at the Margins of Life*. New York: Oxford University Press, 2002.

McNay, Margaret B., and John E. E. Fleming. "Forty Years of Obstetric Ultrasound, 1957–1997: From A-Scope to Three Dimensions." *Ultrasound Medicine and Biology* 25, no. 3 (1999): 3–56.

Mitchell, Lisa M. *Baby's First Picture: Ultrasound and the Politics of the Fetal Subjects*. Toronto: University of Toronto Press, 2001.

———. "The Routinization of the Other: Ultrasound, Women, and the Fetus." In *Misconceptions: The Social Construction of Choice and the New Reproductive and Genetic Technologies*, vol. 2, edited by Gwynne Basin, Margrit Eichler, and Abby Lippman, 146–60. Hull, QC: Prescott Voyageur, 1994.

Munson, Marty, and Greg Gutfield. "Baby and Java Don't Jive: To Get Pregnant or Stay that Way, Try Putting the Cap on Caffeine." *Prevention* 46 (1994): 26–27.

Mykitiuk, Roxanne, and Jeff Nisker. "Social Determinants of 'Health' of Embryos." In *The "Healthy" Embryo: Social, Biomedical, Legal, and Philosophical Perspectives*, edited by Jeff Nisker, Françoise Baylis, Isabel Karpin, Carolyn McLeod, and Roxanne Mykitiuk, 116–35. Cambridge: Cambridge University Press, 2010.

Mykitiuk, Roxanne, and Dayna Nadine Scott. "Risky Pregnancy: Liability, Blame, and Insurance in the Governance of Prenatal Harm." *UBC Law Review* 43, no. 2 (2011): 311–60.

Without Apology

Parens, Erik, and Adrienne Asch. "The Disability Rights Critique of Prenatal Genetic Testing: Reflections and Recommendations." In *Prenatal Testing and Disability Rights*, edited by Erik Parens and Adrienne Asch, 3–43. Washington, DC: Georgetown University Press, 2000.

Petchesky, Rosalind Pollack. *Abortion and Woman's Choice*. Boston: Northeastern University Press, 1986.

———. "Fetal Images: The Power of Visual Culture in the Politics of Reproduction." *Feminist Studies* 13, no. 2 (1987): 263–92.

Peters, Yvonne, and Karen K. Lawson. *The Ethical and Human Rights Implications of Prenatal Technologies: The Need for Federal Leadership and Regulation*. Winnipeg: Prairie Women's Health Centre of Excellence, 2002.

Purdy, Laura Martha. *Reproducing Persons: Issues in Feminist Bioethics*. Ithaca, NY: Cornell University Press, 1996.

Rapp, Rayna. *Testing Women, Testing the Fetus: The Social Impact of Amniocentesis in America*. London: Routledge, 1999.

Rhodes, Rosamond. "Abortion and Assent." *Cambridge Quarterly of Healthcare Ethics* 8, no. 4 (1999): 416–27.

———. "Why Test Children for Adult-Onset Genetic Diseases?" *Mount Sinai Journal of Medicine* 73, no. 3 (2006): 609–16.

Rothman, Barbara Katz. *Recreating Motherhood: Ideology and Technology in a Patriarchal Society*. New York: W. W. Norton, 1990.

———. *The Tentative Pregnancy: Prenatal Diagnosis and the Future of Motherhood*. New York: Penguin, 1987.

Sanger, Carol. "Seeing and Believing: Mandatory Ultrasound and the Path to a Protected Choice." *UCLA Law Review* 56 (2008): 351–408.

Sherwin, Susan. "Normalizing Reproductive Technologies and the Implications for Autonomy." In *Globalizing Feminist Bioethics*, edited by Rosemarie Tong, Gwen Anderson, and Aida Santos, 96–113. Boulder, CO: Westview Press, 2001.

Sontag, Susan. On Photography. New York: New York Review of Books, 1977.

Stabile, Carol. "Shooting the Mother: Fetal Photography and the Politics of Disappearance." *Camera Obscura* 10 (1992): 178–205.

Tremain, Shelley. "Reproductive Freedom, Self-Regulation, and the Government of Impairment in Utero." *Hypatia* 21 (2006): 35–53.

Van den Hof, Michiel C., and R. Douglas Wilson. "Fetal Soft Markers in Obstetric Ultrasound." SOGC Clinical Practice Guidelines no. 162. Society of Obstetricians and Gynaecologists of Canada, June 2005. http://www.sogc.org/guidelines/public/162E-CPG-June2005.pdf.

A Harm-Reduction
Approach to Abortion

SHANNON DEA

As I began to write this chapter, Canadian MP Stephen Woodworth's Motion 312 (henceforth M-312) had just been defeated in a 203-91 parliamentary vote. M-312 proposed "that a special committee of the House be appointed and directed to review the declaration in Subsection 223(1) of the Criminal Code of Canada which states that a child becomes a human being only at the moment of complete birth."[1] Since that vote, Canada has undergone a change in government that will likely keep the abortion debate off the legislative radar for the foreseeable future. However, the M-312 debate did not occur in a vacuum: it was part of a systematic effort by North American pro-life advocates to extend to fetuses the legislated rights and privileges accorded to persons. While Woodworth's motion failed, pro-life forces have had too much success with this method in other jurisdictions to abandon the approach any time soon. Thus, it is worth examining the positions at play in the M-312 debate, and considering their merits.

In what follows, I begin with a brief sketch of the rights-based dialectic that emerged over the course of the M-312 debates. I then contend that the arguments that were advanced on both sides were precisely the wrong ones to have. In any competition between fetal rights and women's autonomy, a loser is inevitable.[2] It is a zero-sum game. I argue that shifting the discussion to a focus on harms is less polarizing and hence more conducive to compromise and agreement, and that such a shift could actually accomplish the most important goals for both sides. Indeed, characterizing the abortion issue as one with two opposing sides may be counterproductive for all concerned.

Whose Rights?

The Rights of the Child

Subsection 223(1) of the Criminal Code of Canada, to which M-312 refers, is situated in a portion of the code concerned with homicide. Subsection 223(1) stipulates at what stage a child legally becomes a human being and hence the kind of legal entity who could be a victim of homicide:[3]

> A child becomes a human being within the meaning of this Act when it has completely proceeded, in a living state, from the body of its mother, whether or not
>
> *(a)* it has breathed;
> *(b)* it has an independent circulation; or
> *(c)* the navel string is severed.

Subsection 223(2) goes on to say that "a person commits homicide when he causes injury to a child before or during its birth as a result of which the child dies after becoming a human being."

In a December 2011 press release about M-312, Woodworth described subsection 223(1) as "an unusual Canadian statute which defines a human being as a child who has completely proceeded in a living state from the mother's body, whether or not the child has breathed." It follows from this, argued Woodworth, that in Canada, "a child is legally considered to be sub-human while his or her little toe remains in the birth canal, even if he or she is breathing."[4]

According to Woodworth, subsection 223(1) is outdated, in that it does not reflect contemporary scientific evidence about when someone becomes a human being. In his view, if science shows that a baby is actually a human being at some point before birth, then the law ought to extend human rights to the baby after that point. In various interviews, Woodworth mocked the idea that the event of birth could magically confer humanity upon a baby.[5] It is, after all, counterintuitive to suppose that a baby delivered at thirty-nine gestational weeks is a human being while an overdue baby, still unborn at forty-one weeks, is not. When we examine our ideas of what makes an entity a human being, we tend to think in terms of such things as cognitive development and ability to survive outside of the womb. The forty-one-week undelivered baby surely satisfies these criteria just as well as—or better than—the thirty-nine-week delivered baby. So why should the law treat the former differently than the latter?

Woodworth insisted that subsection 223(1), which has its origins in seventeenth-century English common law, wrongly fails to attribute humanity to the forty-one-week undelivered baby because of the now outdated science of the period.[6] This is mistaken on two counts. First, seventeenth-century science was more advanced than Woodworth implies. The period saw enormous progress in all areas of science, not least medicine, in which sophisticated anatomical and physiological research swiftly eclipsed the Aristotelian and Galenic medicine of the Middle Ages. Woodworth's suggestion that seventeenth-century scientists were ignorant of the character of fetal development is simply mistaken. Second, and just as crucially, no science is necessary to underwrite our strongly held intuitions that the forty-one-week undelivered baby is worthy of moral consideration. Most of us, regardless of our views on the abortion debate, regard such a child as a human being worthy of protection and sympathy. This was as much the case in seventeenth-century England as it is in twenty-first-century Canada. In other words, even if seventeenth-century scientists were ignorant of the stages of fetal development that might be relevant to the question of a child's humanity, it wouldn't matter. Our sympathy with the third-trimester fetus is rooted in human nature and common sense. And this sympathy is powerfully motivating.

So why does subsection 223(1) (and the older law from which it descends) fail to accord humanity to such children? In brief, section 223 is intended neither to deny human fetuses membership in the human species nor to make any claim about when life begins or at what developmental stage a fetus is the appropriate object of sympathy and moral concern. The question addressed in subsection 223(1) is a purely legal one: At what point does one become a legal agent, the kind of entity who can (*inter alia*) be the victim of a crime? Subsection 223(1) answers this question by stipulating the condition that legal human beings must have been born.[7]

Ought we to value, respect, and seek to protect third-trimester fetuses? I think that we should. It seems clear to me that at this developmental stage, babies have the kind of cognitive complexity and capacity for independent existence that makes them worthy of moral consideration.[8] So why not extend legal consideration to them as well? Why not amend the Criminal Code to recognize third-trimester fetuses as legal human beings?

One obvious answer (but not the one that I will ultimately endorse) is that such an amendment would create the legally untenable position of recognizing the existence of legal, rights-bearing human beings who reside inside of other legal rights-bearing human beings. Such an amendment would thus potentially conflict with the rights of pregnant women.

The Rights of the Mother

In 1988, in *R. v. Morgentaler*, the Supreme Court of Canada struck down Canada's abortion law on the grounds that it violated women's rights to "life, liberty and security of the person," rights encoded in section 7 of the Canadian Charter of Rights and Freedoms. The Court ruled that the law, in limiting access to abortion, put both women's health and safety and women's aspirations at risk. It is worth noting that the Court did not rule that *any* abortion law would necessarily conflict with women's section 7 Charter rights, only that the particular abortion law then on the books did so. (In fact, that law is still on the books, even though it has been unenforceable since the 1988 decision.) In principle, any new abortion law that did not threaten women's life, liberty, or security of the person would be unaffected by the 1988 decision. However, it is difficult to conceive of a law limiting access to abortion that would not, in so doing, compromise one or more of these rights.

However important section 7 rights are in the history of abortion in Canada, even Canadian pro-choice proponents do not discuss women's rights to life, liberty, and security of the person as frequently or as centrally as they do the alleged "right to choose" whether or not to have an abortion. Since *Roe v. Wade*, pro-choice advocates in the United States have sometimes located the right to choose in the Ninth Amendment of the US Constitution, but it is arguably more plausible to regard the phrase "right to choose" as a corollary of the "pro-choice" appellation, itself a rhetorical move to avoid the label "pro-abortion." Unlike "pro-abortion," the "pro-choice" label and the corresponding assertion of women's right to choose emphasize that abortion rights supporters are motivated by a desire to support women's autonomy, not by a desire to promote abortion for its own sake. While the right to choose may have had rhetorical rather than constitutional origins, it is sometimes invoked as a basic human right. Debating M-312 in Parliament on 26 April 2012, MP Niki Ashton, of the New Democratic Party, averred: "A woman's right to reproductive choice is a human right. In Canada, in 2012, a woman's right to choose is not up for negotiation."[9]

Toward a Harm-Reduction Approach to Abortion

The Harm-Reduction Landscape

Ultimately, the debate about whose rights matter most—those of the fetus or those of the pregnant woman—is probably intractable. Moreover, pursuing this polarizing debate has gotten in the way of addressing the abortion issue in a sensible way that addresses the chief concerns of both sides. Indeed, I suggest that the very notion that the issue has two sides is a mistake. The pro-life/pro-choice distinction is, quite simply, a false dichotomy. If we bracket pro-life and pro-choice dogmas, we can see that most interlocutors in the abortion debate are primarily concerned not with rights but with abortion-related harms and how best to avoid them. While both sides deploy the language of rights for rhetorical reasons, most individuals actively involved in the abortion debate are motivated less by in-principle support of particular rights than by the very practical desire to reduce harms—with pro-life advocates focusing on harms to fetuses and pro-choice proponents focusing on harms to pregnant women. When we consider the abortion debate through the lens of harm, we can see that there are actually three, not two, broad positions in the abortion debate. These three positions are distinguished by their views on whether abortion causes harms and on whether and how to reduce those harms. I will argue that logic dictates that proponents of two of the three positions ought to agree on abortion law, policy, and practice, since they ought to agree to support those approaches that reduce abortion-related harms. Adherents to the third position ought to disagree, but their views should be of no concern to jurists, legislators, voters, or policy makers.

At the heart of this way of thinking about abortion is the concept of "harm reduction," a notion that is perhaps most familiar in such contexts as sex work and drug addiction. Here is the definition of *harm reduction* used by the Centre for Addiction and Mental Health (CAMH) in the context of substance abuse: "Harm reduction is any program or policy designed to reduce drug-related harm without requiring the cessation of drug use. Interventions may be targeted at the individual, the family, community or society."[10] Needle exchanges and safe injection sites are familiar examples of the harm-reduction approach to substance abuse. Neither is designed to cure addiction; instead, both services seek to mitigate the risks to addicts. Crucially, both types of service are premised on the belief that substance abuse causes direct or indirect harm.

Adapting the CAMH definition, I consider a harm-reduction approach to abortion as *any program or policy designed to reduce abortion-related harm without requiring the prohibition of abortions. Interventions may be targeted at the individual, the family, community, or society.* Any policy, program, or set of programs that seeks to reduce harms directly or indirectly caused by abortion would count as abortion-related harm reduction. Of course, this conception is premised on the belief that abortions cause harm.

What might count as an abortion-related harm? The most obvious candidate is death to embryos and fetuses in general. Additionally, many people regard death to gestationally older fetuses—in particular, those potentially capable of experiencing pain—as a more serious harm than death to embryos.[11] Injury or death to women who undergo abortions is also an abortion-related harm. Likewise, being left motherless, with all that entails emotionally and financially, is a harm for the surviving children of women who die because of abortions. Other alleged harms resulting from abortion include depression, increased risk of breast cancer, and difficulty conceiving or bearing children in the future.

Two things are noteworthy about the above list of potential abortion-related harms. First, it is manifestly a matter of opinion whether or not any of the potential harms listed above actually constitutes a harm. Many pro-choice advocates, for instance, do not consider embryonic death in itself a harm. By contrast, pro-life supporters typically do consider it a harm. On this matter, it is unlikely that either side could adduce evidence that might change the other side's mind. However, the second noteworthy feature of the above list of potential harms is that while the question of what counts as a harm may be a matter of opinion, the question of which of the potential harms actually results from abortion is an empirical question that must be decided by evidence. If I say that abortion causes injury to women, I must provide evidence to support this claim. It is not enough to insist that it is my opinion. While the likelihood that we will all agree on which potential abortion-related harms actually count as harms is slim, there is good reason to hope that we can agree on the incidence of the alleged harms. All that is required for such agreement is evidence—and sensitivity to evidence.

So do abortions cause the death of fetuses? Manifestly. Do they cause the death of gestationally older fetuses? While such deaths are considerably less common than those of embryos, yes, abortions cause such deaths. Is injury or death to women undergoing an abortion sometimes the result of the procedure? Again, yes. Do children whose mother dies as a result of an abortion suffer harm? Yes. On all of these questions, pro-choice and pro-life proponents can agree. And evidence is plainly available to support all of the foregoing claims, although it is unlikely to be required to persuade anyone since all of the alleged harms just discussed are uncontroversially the direct results of abortions.

What about the last three possible abortion-related harms—depression, breast cancer, and infertility? Are they caused by abortions, as is alleged by some pro-life supporters? Since, in all three cases, the causation (if such there is) is indirect, independent evidence is needed to establish that abortions actually produce such effects. At present, there is no good evidence connecting abortion with either depression or breast cancer.[12] And most researchers agree that abortions—whether surgical or medical—do not affect future reproductive outcomes so long as they are performed using modern techniques and infection does not occur.[13] It seems that, for now, these particular harms do not number among those that should concern supporters of a harm-reduction approach to abortion. However, it bears repeating that in an evidence-based approach, if new evidence emerged that abortion causes any of these harms, we would have to expand any harm-reduction approach to address them.

Three Positions

We have seen that a variety of effects clearly follow from abortions and that some of these effects, to some people, constitute harms. Moreover, on some accounts, abortion in itself constitutes a harm. How do we get from these observations to my claim that there are three, not two, positions in the abortion debate? We need only ask two questions: Are there abortion-related harms? If so, ought we to try to reduce them? At first, this seems to produce four positions based on the four possible pairs of responses to the foregoing questions: yes/yes; no/no; yes/no; no/yes. However, we can remove the final pair, since it is unintelligible to hold at once that abortions do not cause harms and that we ought to try to reduce these harms. This leaves us with three positions. The first affirms that there are abortion-related harms and that we should seek to reduce them. The second position denies that there are abortion-related harms and affirms that nonexistent harms need not be reduced. According to the third position, abortions cause harms but there is no need to reduce those harms.

I propose that most self-described pro-lifers fall into the first category, which I refer to as the harm-reduction position. They regard abortion as constituting a harm and/or as causing harms, and they wish to see such harms reduced. That this is so is apparent in this group's frequent opposition to abortion on the grounds that it causes fetal suffering and subsequent remorse and health problems for the woman undergoing the procedure—hence, the pro-life chant "One dead, one wounded."[14] What is striking is that most pro-choice advocates also fall into this category, typically arguing in favour of access to safe abortions precisely because they regard such a policy as reducing harms such as maternal morbidity and death.[15]

Notice that even though both pro-life advocates and pro-choice supporters populate this category, they can (and do) disagree on which aspects of abortion or its effects constitute or cause harms and on how to reduce the harms associated with abortion. However, this is true *within* both camps as well. That is, there is room within each of the pro-life and pro-choice camps to disagree on which aspects of abortion are harmful and on how best to reduce harm.

The harm-reduction position with respect to abortion is also attractive to many people who do not identify as either pro-life or pro-choice. Many people, for instance, claim that they are not opposed to first-trimester abortions but that they believe in prohibiting abortions of gestationally older

Without Apology

fetuses who could potentially feel pain. For these individuals, legal prohibitions are seen as a mechanism to reduce harms to third-trimester fetuses. Again, people who take this, shall we say, *neutral* harm-reduction position (neutral in the sense that it is neither pro-life or pro-choice) may disagree both among themselves and with pro-life or pro-choice advocates about what aspects of abortion actually constitute or cause harms and how best to reduce those harms. However, they agree with the basic position that there are harms associated with abortion and that we ought to reduce those harms.

Some pro-choice supporters fall outside the broad harm-reduction category I have just described because they claim that abortion does no harm and that hence there are no harms associated with abortion to be reduced. Against the long list of purported abortion-related harms that are adduced in pro-life materials, these pro-choicers respond by denying that abortion causes or constitutes harm. Thus, for instance, Richard Carrier explicitly maintains that "abortion does no harm" and hence ought to be legal.[16] One line of argument in this vein became particularly pronounced in response to former US president Bill Clinton's famous dictum that abortions should be "safe, legal, and rare." This prescription, argue some pro-choice advocates, wrongly casts abortion, unlike other medical procedures, as generally undesirable and hence gives too much away to the pro-life side. Some critics of Clinton's coinage maintain that it is unrealistic to suppose that abortion ever could be rare. Thus, for instance, in an October 2007 letter to *The Lancet*, Marge Berer wrote: "Abortion could only become rare in a world in which contraceptives never failed, women and men having sex together never failed to use them, and sex between them was only ever preplanned and consensual. None of that is realistic, and there seems little point in calling for something that is totally unfeasible."[17]

There is thus good reason to suppose that pro-choicers who deny the harmfulness of abortion do so for rhetorical reasons, in order to avoid contributing to the vilification of abortion. While they deny that abortion constitutes a harm, or remain silent on the question of harm, we shall see below that they nonetheless support those programs and policies that are most effective in reducing those effects of abortion that are often regarded as harms by others. While their refusal to treat abortion as harmful separates them, in principle, from harm-reduction pro-choicers, in practice they support the same or similar programs.

Adherents of the final conceptual position we identified above regard abortion as either constituting a harm or as directly or indirectly causing harms, and yet they do not wish to support mechanisms that reduce the harms associated with abortion. Someone falls into this category if she opposes the mechanisms that reduce the incidence of abortion-related harms even if she knows that these mechanisms effect such reductions. Could anyone really hold such an irresponsible position? We will return to this question below.

Reducing Abortion-Related Harms

We have seen that there are three broad positions in the abortion-related harm-reduction landscape—(1) abortion constitutes or causes harms that should be reduced; (2) abortion does not constitute or cause harms, but mechanisms that reduce alleged abortion-related harms should be supported; and (3) abortion constitutes or causes harms, but mechanisms that reduce those harms should be opposed. So those adhering to either of the first two positions wish to reduce the harms associated with abortion. Which harms are on the table, and how best do we reduce them?

Above, we identified as the main alleged harms associated with abortion: fetal death, including the death of gestationally older fetuses, morbidity and death among women who undergo abortions, and the trauma experienced by children of women who die from unsafe abortions. In order to reduce all of these harms, it is necessary both to reduce the incidence of abortion and to improve the safety of abortions that are performed.

The data shows that, internationally, the lowest abortion rates generally correlate with the most liberal abortion laws. A 2012 study concluded that, worldwide, "the proportion of women living under liberal abortion laws is inversely associated with the abortion rate."[18] The same study found sharp drops in abortion-related mortality and morbidity in South Africa and Nepal after the procedure was legalized in those countries.[19] However, the authors argue that legalization alone cannot explain either lower abortion incidence or lower rates of morbidity associated with abortion. Just as crucial is access to quality abortion aftercare and availability of contraception and adequate sexual health education: "Other necessary steps include the dissemination of knowledge about the law to providers and women, the development of health service guidelines for abortion provision, the willingness of providers to obtain training and provide abortion services, and government commitment to provide the resources needed to ensure access to abortion services, including in remote areas."[20] In short, the best approach to reducing harm is a systemic one that combines safe, legal, accessible abortion services with a wider array of sexual health and education services. Moreover, access to abortion earlier in the pregnancy prevents both the abortion of gestationally older fetuses and the increased risk of injury or death to the mother associated with late-term abortions. While there is a paucity of research on gestational age at the time of abortion, Sedgh et al. suggest that "women might delay seeking an abortion where abortion laws are restrictive or abortion is widely stigmatised."[21]

The authors conclude that several measures in addition to providing access to safe abortions are needed to ensure a decrease in unwanted pregnancies and unsafe abortions:

> Abortions continue to occur in measurable numbers in all regions of the world, regardless of the status of abortion laws. Unintended pregnancies occur in all societies, and some women who are determined to avoid an unplanned birth will resort to unsafe abortions if safe abortion is not readily available, some will suffer complications as a result, and some will die.[22]

What is striking is that a unified approach—one that involves good-quality, comprehensive sexual health services, both clinical and educational; good social services; and legal access to abortions—reduces all of the harms we have been considering. It is, I suppose, obvious that such an approach reduces abortion-related harms to women and, consequently, to their existing children. What is less obvious is that such an approach strongly correlates to a reduction in the incidence of abortion itself. That is, for those who regard abortion as itself constituting a harm and who therefore wish to reduce the incidence of abortion, the most effective mechanism combines liberal abortion laws, access to safe abortions, and a broad suite of sexual health and social services.

For this reason, I think we can characterize those pro-choicers who deny the harmfulness of abortion as de facto supporters of a harm-reduction approach to abortion. Despite their refusal to link abortions with harm, these individuals overwhelmingly support the very mechanisms that correlate with the reduction of abortions, and hence those effects of abortion that are deemed to be harmful by others. Clearly, as well, harm-reduction proponents—those individuals who, whether they identify as pro-life, pro-choice or neither, think that abortions cause harm and who seek to reduce those harms—ought to favour the approach that is shown to correlate most highly to reductions in abortion-related harms. Logic dictates, then, that all those who seriously seek to reduce the harms associated with abortions, whatever their affiliation in the abortion debate, should agree to support legal, accessible abortions within a broader system of sexual health and social services.

This will be a difficult pill for pro-lifers to swallow, if only because it is counterintuitive to say that the best way to reduce the incidence of abortion is to make abortion legal and accessible. However, any pro-life advocate who is genuinely motivated by a wish to reduce the incidence of abortion and abortion-related harms must, to be effective, approach the reduction of those harms using the best evidence available, even if that evidence turns out to be counterintuitive.

But what should we make of those pro-life advocates who decry the harmfulness of abortions but oppose the very mechanism associated with a reduction in the incidence of abortion? Perhaps they just do not understand the evidence yet, in which case we should seek to persuade with the best evidence, and they should, in principle, be open to such suasion. Other pro-lifers, however, not only reject abortion-reducing mechanisms but champion practices associated with higher abortion rates—for example, abstinence-only sex education and reduced access to contraceptives. Moreover, as we have seen in much of the United States in recent years, they actively promote legislative and clinical delays to abortion seekers, thereby increasing the incidence of harms related to late-term abortion. Why might a pro-life advocate who understands the evidence oppose mechanisms that reduce abortion-related harms and support those that increase them? Most plausibly, this is because they are not primarily concerned with the harms associated with abortion. Rather, they are motivated by their deeply held moral or religious conviction that abortion is always wrong, regardless of its consequences.

Given this landscape, who should opt for a harm-reduction approach to abortion? The answer is everyone—pro-life, pro-choice, and neither—who genuinely wishes to reduce the incidence of abortion and the harms that result from abortion, as well as those pro-choicers who deny the harmfulness of abortion but nonetheless champion the mechanisms shown to reduce abortion-related harms. The only people who should oppose a harm-reduction approach are those who privilege adherence to personal ethics and/or religious convictions over the reduction of abortion-related harms. However, since law and public policy should be based on the public good rather than on people's individual moral or religious commitments, the views of such individuals should be of no concern to courts or governments.

Notes

1 The full text of M-312 is in the Sixteenth Report of the Standing Committee on Procedure and House Affairs, Parliament of Canada, 41st Parliament, 1st session, n.d., http://www.parl.gc.ca/HousePublications/Publication.aspx?DocId=5437818.

2 Not all persons with uteruses identify as women. Increasingly, for instance, trans men are choosing to give birth. I use "woman" and "women" throughout as a term of convenience. Clearly, however, our approach to abortion affects anyone who might become pregnant, whether or not that person is a woman.

3 The question of what terminology to use for the unborn child is perhaps even more fraught than that of what terminology to apply to the competing camps in the abortion debate. Unlike terms like *pro-choice* and *pro-life*, which make very explicit one's philosophical and political commitments, terms like *child*, *fetus*, *embryo*, and *baby* can influence readers and interlocutors in subtle, implicit ways. Pro-choice proponents tend to favour *embryo* and *fetus* in order to sound clinical and avoid arousing the reader's or listener's sympathy for the child. Pro-life supporters prefer *baby* and *child* for converse reasons. Throughout, I alternate among these terms, but in general, I use *baby* or *child* for the third trimester and *embryo* or *fetus* for the first or second trimester.

4 Quoted in "When Are We Human? MP Woodworth Wants Canadians to Review Law with 400-Year-Old Roots," *The Record*, 21 December 2011, http://www.therecord.com/news-story/2604105-when-are-we-human-mp-woodworth-wants-canadians-to-review-law-with-400-year-old-roots/.

5 See, for example, "Stephen Woodworth on Talk Local Kitchener/Waterloo," *Talk Local*, hosted by Hayley Zimak, Rogers Cable Kitchener, 11 January 2012, https://www.youtube.com/watch?v=bW-QRzIpv7s.

6 "When Are We Human?" and "Stephen Woodworth on Talk Local."

7 Having said this, it bears note that the next subsection, 223(2), is explicit that if a (fully born) human being dies because of an act performed upon it in utero, that death constitutes a homicide. This is to say that section

223 actually does provide some legal protection to unborn children, even though *qua* unborn they do not yet count as legal human beings.

8 I will not defend that view here, but see Laurie Schrage, *Abortion and Social Responsibility*, 72, for a discussion of the moral status of late-term fetuses.

9 Niki Ashton, "Private Members' Business: Special Committee on Subsection 223(1) of the Criminal Code." Ashton has represented the riding of Churchill, Manitoba, since 2008.

10 Centre for Addiction and Mental Health, "CAMH Position on Harm Reduction: Its Meaning and Applications for Substance Use Issues," June 2002, http://www.camh.ca/en/hospital/about_camh/influencing_public_policy/public_policy_submissions/Pages/publicpolicy_harmreduc2002.aspx.

11 Such abortions are extremely rare. Of the 27,576 abortions reported by Canadian hospital (excluding Québec) in 2010, only 537, or 1.9 percent, were performed on fetuses at twenty-one gestational weeks or later. Canadian Institute for Health Information, *Therapeutic Abortion: Data Tables, 2010*, Table 4: Number and Percentage Distribution of Induced Abortions Reported by Canadian Hospitals (Excluding Quebec) in 2010, by Gestational Age. This proportion is skewed, however, by the fact that in Canada, late-term abortions are performed only at hospitals, not in clinics. If we include in our total 2010 abortion count the 37,065 abortions performed at clinics (excluding Québec), the total number swells to 64,641, meaning that late-term abortions constitute a mere 0.83 percent of all abortions performed in Canada outside of Québec. Ibid., Table 1: Number Induced Abortions Reported in Canada in 2010, by Province/Territory of Hospital or Clinic.

12 On the possible link to depression, see Trine Munk-Olsen et al., "Induced First-Trimester Abortion and Risk of Mental Disorder"; and Brenda Major et al., "Abortion and Mental Health: Evaluating the Evidence." On breast cancer, see National Cancer Institute, *Summary Report: Early Reproductive Events and Breast Cancer Workshop*; and Robert Lea et al., "Breast Cancer and Abortion," 491.

13 Royal College of Obstetricians and Gynaecologists, "Induced Termination of Pregnancy and Future Reproductive Outcomes—Current Evidence." A report on complications associated with Canadian abortions performed in 2010 found that, of the 27,576 abortions for which detailed reports were available, infections occurred in only 107 cases, or 0.38 percent. Canadian Institute for Health Information, *Therapeutic Abortion Data Tables, 2010*, Table 8: Number and Percentage Distribution of Induced

Abortions Reported by Canadian Hospitals (Excluding Quebec) in 2010, by Complication Within 28 Days of Initial Induced Abortion.

14 See Dave Daubenmire, "Abortion Harms Women," Pass the Salt Ministries, 14 January 2010, http://www.newswithviews.com/Daubenmire/dave180. htm. Pro-life arguments for prohibiting abortion because of presumed harm to women are ubiquitous. See, for instance, Erika Bachiochi, "How Abortion Hurts Women: The Hard Proof," *Crisis Magazine*, June 2005; and Ellie Dillon, "Legalized Abortion Harms Women and Children," n.d., *Casey's Critical Thinking* (blog), http://www.hoshuha.com/articles/harm. html.

15 See, for instance, Joyce Arthur, "Yes, Legalizing Abortion Does Save Women's Lives."

16 Richard Carrier, "Abortion Is Not Immoral and Should Not Be Illegal," n.d., The Secular Web, http://www.infidels.org/library/modern/debates/ secularist/abortion/carrier1.html. However, in the next paragraph, Carrier admits that, like any medical procedure, abortion can cause indirect harm.

17 Marge Berer, "Legal, Safe, and Rare?"

18 Gilda Sedgh et al., "Induced Abortion: Incidence and Trends Worldwide from 1995 to 2008," 631. See also Marge Berer, "Making Abortions Safe: A Matter of Good Public Health Policy and Practice," 580; and World Health Organization, *Safe Abortion: Technical and Policy Guidance for Health Systems.*

19 Sedgh et al., "Induced Abortion," 631.

20 Ibid., 631.

21 Ibid., 630.

22 Ibid., 631.

References

Arthur, Joyce. "Yes, Legalizing Abortion Does Save Women's Lives." 4 March 2010. Abortion Rights Coalition of Canada. http://www.arcc-cdac.ca/ action/legalizing-abortion-saves-lives.html.

Ashton, Niki. "Private Members' Business: Special Committee on Subsection 223(1) of the Criminal Code." *Hansard*, 26 April 2012. http://www.parl.gc.ca/HousePublications/Publication. aspx?DocId=5524696&Language=E&Mode=1.

Berer, Marge. "Legal, Safe, and Rare?" Letter to *The Lancet* 370, no. 9595 (13 October 2007): 1309. http://www.thelancet.com/pdfs/journals/lancet/ PIIS0140-6736(07)61567-0.pdf.

———. "Making Abortions Safe: A Matter of Good Public Health Policy and Practice." *Bulletin of the World Health Organization* 78, no. 5 (2000): 580–92. http://www.who.int/bulletin/archives/78%285%295 80.pdf.

Canadian Institute for Health Information. *Therapeutic Abortion: Data Tables, 2010*. Ottawa: CIHI, 2014. http://www.cihi.ca/CIHI-ext-portal/pdf/internet/TA_10_ALLDATATABLES20120417_EN.

Lea, Robert, Diane Provencher, John F. Jeffrey, Amit Oza, Robert Reid, and Kenneth Swenerton. "Breast Cancer and Abortion." SOGC/GOC Joint Committee Opinion. *Journal of Obstetrics and Gynaecology Canada* 27, no. 5 (2005): 491.

Major, Brenda, Mark Appelbaum, Linda Beckman, Mary Ann Dutton, Nancy Felipe, and Carolyn West. "Abortion and Mental Health: Evaluating the Evidence." *American Psychologist* 64, no. 9 (2009): 863–90.

Munk-Olsen, Trine, Thomas Munk Laursen, Carsten B. Pedersen, Øjvind Lidegaard, and Preben Bo Mortensen. "Induced First-Trimester Abortion and Risk of Mental Disorder." *New England Journal of Medicine* 364, no. 4 (2011): 332–39.

National Cancer Institute. *Summary Report: Early Reproductive Events and Breast Cancer Workshop*. March 2003, updated March 2010. http://www.cancer.gov/cancertopics/causes/ere/workshop-report.

Royal College of Obstetricians and Gynaecologists. "Induced Termination of Pregnancy and Future Reproductive Outcomes—Current Evidence." 16 September 2009. London: RCOG. https://www.rcog.org.uk/en/news/rcog-statement-on-the-paper-on-termination-of-pregnancy-and-birth-outcomes-published-in-bjog/.

Schrage, Laurie. *Abortion and Social Responsibility: Depolarizing the Debate*. New York: Oxford University Press, 2003.

Sedgh, Gilda, Susheela Singh, Iqbal H. Shah, Elisabeth Åhman, Stanley K. Henshaw, and Akinrinola Bankole. "Induced Abortion: Incidence and Trends Worldwide from 1995 to 2008." *The Lancet* 379, no. 9816 (18 February 2012): 625–32.

World Health Organization. *Safe Abortion: Technical and Policy Guidance for Health Systems*. 2nd ed. Geneva: WHO, 2012. http://apps.who.int/iris/bitstream/10665/70914/1/9789241548434_eng.pdf?ua=1.

The Unfinished Revolution

Shannon Stettner

I did choose life—mine.

Sonya Renee Taylor

In August 2014, Colleen MacQuarrie and I hosted an interdisciplinary conference called "Abortion: The Unfinished Revolution," at the University of Prince Edward Island.[1] The decision to hold the conference in Charlottetown was political. As pieces in this collection indicate, anti-abortion activists in PEI had, over the years, done a tremendous job of eliminating abortion from the island's hospitals, keeping the service inaccessible to women in need.[2] Anti-abortion activists in Canada, proud to have eliminated access to abortions in PEI, referred to the province as a "life sanctuary." In response, by holding the conference in Charlottetown, we symbolically brought abortion to the island. In addition to academics who travelled from around the globe, contingents of activists came from nearby provinces, especially New Brunswick, where, only a few weeks earlier, Fredericton's Morgentaler Clinic had announced its impending closure. This gathering of academics, long-time activists, and individuals newly committed to the cause was, and still is, an encouraging sign for women in Canada. So, of course, was Premier Wade MacLauchlan's announcement, on 31 March 2016, that the province of Prince Edward Island would make abortion services available by the end of that year. This victory reflects the work of a dedicated contingent of pro-choice and reproductive justice advocates in the Maritimes, who have been motivated by the continued lack of access and by women's abortion experiences, such as those described in the research of Colleen MacQuarrie and her colleagues.[3]

In the weeks following the conference, pro-choice and reproductive justice activists in New Brunswick responded to the closure of the Morgentaler Clinic by forcing provincial politicians to accept abortion access as a major issue in the September 2014 provincial election. Through an intense social media campaign, pickets and protests, and petitions, activists forced abortion onto the agenda and ultimately contributed to the defeat of the incumbent anti-abortion premier, David Alward, of the Progressive Conservative Party.[4] In November, the new Liberal premier, Brian Gallant, announced the demise of regulation 84-20, the long-standing "two-doctor" rule, according to which provincially funded abortions could be performed only by an OB-GYN specialist and only after the abortion had been certified as medically necessary by two medical doctors.[5] New Brunswick serves as an exemplar of the importance of women's voices and activism supporting reproductive rights: safe and accessible abortion can be an election issue, and more and more we see women around the world making it one.

The political climate in New Brunswick and Prince Edward Island, as elsewhere, shows us that women's voices count and that the language we employ when discussing abortion matters. Talking about abortion is not easy. Abortion is more than a word. It operates as a concept, an action, and a set of knowledges that must be situated within its broader social, economic, and political contexts. Abortion requires us to make choices. The authors in this collection have commented on the idea of "choice," explicitly and implicitly, and on its meanings in women's lives, as well as on the strategic choices we make as activists, as academics, as women, and as allies.

Some authors in this collection envision choice more narrowly, as referring specifically to the decision to terminate a pregnancy. As noted in the introduction, the language of choice is often inadequate when used to explain women's experiences, because it suggests that all women operate within the same structural and cultural frameworks when making their decisions. In this collection, both Clarissa Hurley and "Dr. James," for example, see problems with the term. As Hurley observes, "'Choice' implies that desire trumps circumstance, while I believe the opposite is frequently true." She continues, "Unfettered choice cannot exist in a world that remains judgmental, unaccommodating, and punitive to unpartnered pregnant women and mothers." James, meanwhile, highlights other limits to the term *choice*, noting that simplifying the abortion issue to one of choice and autonomy minimizes the complexity and depth that many women explore when making a decision about their pregnancy. Significantly, he also observes, "Choice implies a proactive decision ('If I get pregnant, I'm having an abortion'), whereas, for many women, the choice to have an abortion is reactive." We must continue to struggle with the language we use when talking about abortion because that process of struggle, in and of itself, is transformative.

Here, alternative framings—like those offered by reproductive justice advocates and socialist feminists, among others—hold value, for they allow us to conceive of choice more broadly. Carolyn Egan and Linda Gardner, for example, explain that, in the view of the Ontario Coalition for Abortion Clinics, which adopted a socialist feminist framework when it formed in 1982, to have a genuine choice women must also have "safe and effective birth control services in their own languages and their own communities, decent jobs, paid parental leave, child care, the right to live freely and openly regardless of their sexuality, an end to forced or coerced sterilization, employment equity, and, of course, full access to free abortion." Although socialist feminism and the movement for reproductive justice differ in certain respects, their adherents share a revolutionary perspective, according to which achieving equity for women presupposes a fundamental transformation of the social, economic, and political structures on which the culture of patriarchy rests. I would thus argue that our understanding of the history of reproductive rights in Canada would benefit from a more detailed exploration of the relationship between these two movements.

As Jessica Danforth has observed, the concept of reproductive justice, which evolved in the United States, initially met with some resistance in this country. Danforth was extremely critical of the pro-choice movement in Canada and what she experienced as an apparent reluctance to fully adopt a reproductive justice (RJ) framework, arguing that "actualizing RJ beyond a hot, new buzz word still has a long way to go and it has to start with being honest about where we are at and what's really going on in terms of racism, sexism, classism, white supremacy, homophobia, transphobia, ableism and more—not just systemically, but what we ourselves are complicit in as well."[6] Since Danforth wrote, in 2010, the movement for reproductive justice has gained ground in Canada, but hers is a criticism that we must ponder as we move forward, especially now that RJ has gained increased prominence among Canadians organizing around the abortion issue. As is clear from Karen Stote's chapter in this volume, the movement for reproductive justice is fundamental to improving the lives of women in Canada, especially those who have been racialized and marginalized..

Advocates of RJ consider access to abortion essential to achieving reproductive justice, seeing the issue as linked to matters of racial inequity, economic justice, youth issues, violence, religious intolerance, immigrants' rights, disability rights, and imperialism.[7] Although the issue of abortion access may not be the central or most important component of reproductive justice, RJ advocates acknowledge that it is appropriate to focus on a particular aspect of RJ, provided that such work is undertaken within an RJ framework: "We may not be able to work on every issue, but we can ask ourselves: How does my work support or undermine the work of others in this movement?"[8] As I indicated in the introduction, what a RJ framework means and how that materializes is something that many of us who are new to RJ are only beginning to envisage as a possibility, much less comprehend. What we do know is that reproductive justice necessitates a reorientation of how we conceptualize and discuss abortion.

The main goals of this collection were to provide a space for voices speaking out on abortion to be heard and to explore questions about abortion and the issues of choice (the abortion decision, language choices, and movement strategy choices) with the hope that these conversations will continue beyond the covers of this book. To survive and to be relevant, the movements for reproductive autonomy, reproductive justice, and abortion rights—however these are labelled and conceptualized—must continue to evolve. This collection raises a number of important areas of discussion, but many additional issues and conversations await exploration. I hope to persist in encouraging dialogue around the shame, silence, stigma, and secrecy that continues to surround abortion. Not only do we need to speak openly about abortion, but as Danforth and others argue, we must also talk about the oppressions that continue to frame women's lives and determine the choices they can or cannot make. I believe that overcoming the shame and stigma surrounding abortion is essential in the fight to overcome reproductive oppression. As I and others in this volume have expressed, if we eliminate the shame and stigma of abortion, if we reach a point where women can talk openly about their abortion experiences without fear of being judged or harassed, the anti-abortion movement will lose much of the power that it currently possesses.[9] RJ activists work on the premise that incorporating abortion within the social, economic, and environmental contexts in which women live will help to better connect abortion to women's lives, reducing the isolation, shame, and stigma often associated with it.[10] Abortion, then, is not a dramatic or defining reproductive moment, but one life decision among many that women make over the course of their lives.

Eliminating the isolation of abortion as a single issue and overcoming the silence that surrounds abortion will destabilize opponents. I want to be clear, though, that the onus is not on women to stop anti-abortion harassment and violence. The anti-abortion movement maintains strength and relevancy in part because a few powerful elements (such as media and government) permit it. As Jane Cawthorne notes in her contribution to this collection, the media insist on giving equal weight and equal time to both sides of the issue despite the fact that those opposed to abortion are a minority in Canada and have been for decades. More importantly, those opposed to abortion access for women often employ misogynist materials and messages. Their use of words and images constitute hate speech and should not be tolerated.[11] There are extreme elements in the anti-abortion movement that engage in violence and terrorism and as long as they are given equal space, women will continue to receive the message that their health care choices are shameful, selfish, and immoral.

Allowing these harmful and hateful voices to continue has other effects, including contributing to the decline in abortion providers. As a consequence, we need to encourage medical students to become providers. Historically, we know that physicians performed abortions prior to legalization because of the risks women faced when they either attempted to self-abort or sought help from untrained individuals. We also know that since abortion has been legally available, we have moved away from the generation(s) of physicians who could spot the consequences of attempted abortions.[12] Additionally, health care professionals who engage in abortion work confront the stigma of that work, stigma that makes them targets both at an individual level and within a health care system that keeps abortion care separate from other forms of health care delivery; sufficient provider support, then, becomes a part of addressing the provider shortage.[13] In this volume, Dr. James highlights the effort it took on his part to opt into provider training given that most medical schools provide minimal abortion-related training. Activists need to collaborate with and support organizations like Medical Students for Choice in their efforts to ensure sufficient physician training. The failure of medical schools to provide adequate abortion education is an issue that deserves more attention. Not only are doctors ill-equipped to recognize the signs of illegal abortion attempts, but the fact that medical students need to opt into abortion training suggests that it is not a medically necessary service, which sets the stage for what is often labelled "conscientious objection." Few other professions would allow members to refuse to perform key components of their job. There should be no exception for abortion, which is not to say that all doctors need to provide abortions, but if they cannot recognize the signs of incomplete abortions, if they cannot offer their patients a full spectrum of care, and if they choose not to refer their patients to pro-choice providers in their stead, they are inflicting their personal beliefs on their patients—and that is intolerable.

As long as women's bodies—and abortion—remain medicalized, as long as physicians remain the gatekeepers to abortion procedures, women will continue to endure reproductive oppression. Here the question of the involvement of others in the provision of abortion services is relevant. Can physicians be supplemented (and in some cases replaced) by nurses, abortion doulas, midwives, or others?[14] Ultimately, anti-abortion ideologies have no place in the health care practices related to abortion.[15] The need to address these issues—provider shortage and insufficient training, provider stigma, so-called conscientious objection, and the potential role of other technicians—takes on a certain urgency when one considers the statistics put forth by Canadians for Choice to illuminate the provider shortage in stark terms—in spring 2012, the total number of providers in Canada was 134, with the provincial and territorial breakdown as follows: Nunavut, 1; Yukon, 1, Northwest Territories, 2; British Columbia, 23; Alberta, 4; Saskatchewan, 3; Manitoba, 4; Ontario, 36; Québec, 54; New Brunswick, 3; Prince Edward Island, 0; and Newfoundland and Labrador, 3.[16] These numbers take on increased significance when one considers that, according to 2015 data from Statistics Canada, women account for 18.1 million (or 50.4%) of Canada's population.[17] What these numbers mean, then, is that there are 134 abortion providers for 18.1 million women who will all experience roughly thirty years of fertility during the course of their lifetime.

In addition to rethinking who can provide abortions, the imbalance in fertility responsibility needs to be addressed. Currently, the responsibility for fertility falls unevenly on women's shoulders. But how do we incorporate men into discussions (and decisions), honouring their voices and feelings, without ceding control? Women must retain control of the final decisions, yet, as Dr. James notes, until we figure out how to involve men effectively, women will continue to bear the brunt of fertility responsibilities and decisions—which includes the emotional and financial costs, as well as the shame and stigma, associated with abortion.

Issues of fertility play out in other ways, too. There is an enormous disconnect between the advertised effectiveness of birth control and the level of contraception failure. Moreover, the people overwhelmingly responsible for using contraception, women, feel disconnected and alienated from it. Women of colour have a long history of being critical of various hormonal contraceptives.[18] Increasingly, studies suggest that young women are disenchanted with hormonal birth control (whether because of side effects or lifestyle choices) and that this dissatisfaction leads to a reliance on less effective forms of contraception.[19] Rather than push hormonal contraception on women, especially at the time of termination, the medical profession and those who care about lowering the abortion rate need to think carefully about why women increasingly do not like using hormonal contraceptives and look for alternatives that better resonate with them. Shannon Dea's harm-reduction model can be applied to this issue. It is neither productive nor accurate to label women as contraceptively irresponsible: not only does it relieve men of responsibility for birth control, but such energies would be better directed to actualizing more effective and safer forms of birth control.

Understanding women's fertility needs will ultimately help us to improve women's abortion experiences. Where, when, and how abortions take place impact a woman's experience, often negatively.[20] Medical technology like RU-486 allows for early abortion to occur at home, which is, for many women, more comfortable than a clinic or hospital. In July 2015, Health Canada approved the sale of RU-486, which should be available late in

2016; theoretically, this will alleviate some of the barriers to access faced by women in the Maritimes, the North, and rural Canada.[21] But medical abortions do not eliminate the need for surgical interventions or solve the lack of support for women who choose abortion. Several narratives in this collection highlight the isolation experienced by women who undergo abortions; often partners, friends, and family members are not allowed to accompany patients because of safety concerns or privacy issues. If we are looking for the best abortion experience, the option of having a supportive person with them throughout the procedure should be available to women. Furthermore, certain practical measures, like better enforcement of injunctions against clinic harassers, would also go a long way to improving abortion experiences.

It is important to remember that abortion experiences do not end with the procedure. As abortion rights advocates, we have often failed to support women post-abortion. Along with and as part of the process of reducing shame and stigma surrounding abortion, we need to provide better support to those women who require it. Some advocates argue that women only need support because of the anti-abortion messages that have bombarded us for decades.[22] Certainly women would experience less guilt or stress or sadness if they stopped receiving messages that they are horrible human beings for having an abortion, but, as shown by several pieces in this collection, abortion is a complicated issue for many people, and sometimes women have abortions when, under different circumstances, they would have preferred to continue the pregnancy. Ultimately, working within an RJ framework, we hope to reach a point where women can decide on abortion without feelings of regret or shame. Until then, we need to accept—and honour—that some women struggle with abortion and need to be supported, regardless of the underlying cause(s) of their struggles.

Changing abortion experiences also necessitates changing the way we talk about abortion. Laura Gillespie's essay challenges us to better control how abortion is framed. She calls on us to move from a reactive position to a defining one. Similarly, Katha Pollitt, in 2014, issued a call to redefine abortion as a positive social good.[23] Ultimately, we need to stop apologizing for abortion. As Erin Mullan and Dr. James contend in this volume, abortion is most often a parental decision made out of love and consideration. It is also a remarkably common, even ordinary, reproductive decision that women make every day.

Becoming more aware of language has far-reaching consequences. Activists, the media, and others often use the term *pro-choice* in reference to those who advocate for safe and legal abortion. As we have seen repeatedly in this collection and as is abundantly clear in external criticisms of the concept, the notion of "choice" is problematic. We need to be more conscious, moving forward, of the costs and limitations of the word. As noted, a number of organizations and activists are abandoning the "pro-choice" label, but should we do so entirely? There is a generation of activists who very much identify with the term and spent their lives fighting to see the decriminalization of abortion, and we need to recognize their contributions while at the same time acknowledging the need for continued activism, especially in the United States.[24] *Pro-choice* is also a term that resonates publicly; especially within the larger general public who are not inclined toward activism, the "pro-choice" label is an easy and comfortable, if problematic, shorthand. Speaking from the perspective of a historian, I propose that retaining the term makes sense because it has historical resonance—at least when discussing almost half a century of abortion rights activism. But for those of us concerned with the implications of language choices, it becomes increasingly difficult to use *pro-choice* because historically, the pro-choice movement has excluded the experiences and concerns of racialized women. We need, then, to continue the conversation about the term—what it means and how it is, and is not, applicable.

Connected to this issue of terminology is the need to build better linkages between generations of activists; between academic and front-line activists; between the different groups advocating for reproductive choice, freedom, and justice; and between the resolutely pro-choice and those not quite as comfortable with abortion. Many segments of the population feel alienated from the pro-choice movement because of its largely white, middle-class nature and its overwhelming failure to articulate demands for broader structural changes in Canadian society. Indeed, it is the very middle-class and white nature of the pro-choice movement that makes it so resistant to change or self-reflection. Looking inward and questioning our positions is extremely difficult, especially when it reveals that we are complicit, tacitly or not, in the perpetuation of privilege and power. For those of us who choose to involve ourselves in struggles to ensure that women have access to abortion, the suggestion that we are complicit in undermining the rights of racialized women to make choices is incredibly difficult to face and hard to comprehend.[25] But in order to move forward and to make real change, we have to acknowledge that "the regulation of reproduction and exploitation of women's bodies is both a tool and a result of systems of oppression based on race, class, gender, nation and sexuality."[26] So building linkages and partnerships necessitates engaging in self-reflection and self-awareness, educating ourselves on what it means to be an ally, and truly listening to the needs of other people.

The pieces in this collection have addressed different perspectives (choice, reproductive justice, harm reduction) that might provide useful arguments at different times. Debate on reproductive rights occurs at different levels— interpersonal, familial, social, and institutional (e.g., university, church, the media, and government). At stake in all these debates are views of women and their roles. In Canada, many of us have come to see the promise of reproductive justice as an organizing framework, although many of us still have much to learn from the powerful examples of women of colour in the United States, Canada, and elsewhere. We need to adopt more fully the RJ framework, which situates abortion in the broader context of human rights, thus combatting reproductive oppression by framing abortion as a social justice issue.[27] As well, many of the pieces in this collection point to the need to continue to listen to women's stories about their abortion experiences; only by talking openly and often about abortion will we move to a place where abortion is normalized, removed from the shame, secrecy, and silence that has, for too long, characterized abortion in Canada. To that end, the voices in this collection are transformative, and they will be made more powerful as they are supplemented by additional voices. Muriel Rukeyser, a poet, once asked, "What would happen if one woman told the truth about her life?" and offered an answer: "The world would split open." Now is the time for us to tell the truth about our abortions—without apology.

Notes

1   On the conference, see Shannon Stettner, "Abortion: The Unfinished Revolution Conference, 7–8 August 2014, Charlottetown, PEI." *ActiveHistory.ca*, 21 July 2014, http://activehistory.ca/2014/07/ abortion-the-unfinished-revolution-conference-augus t-7-8-2014-charlottetown-pei/.

2   See, for example, Sara Fraser and Jesara Sinclair, "Abortion Services Coming to PEI, Province Announces," *CBC News*, 31 March 2016, http://www.cbc.ca/news/canada/prince-edward-island/

pei-abortion-reproductive-rights-1.3514334. For a historical account of abortion access in PEI, see Katrina Ackerman, "In Defence of Reason: Religion, Science, and the Prince Edward Island Anti-Abortion Movement, 1969–1988."

3   See Colleen MacQuarrie, Jo-Ann MacDonald, and Cathrine Chambers, *Trials and Trails of Accessing Abortion in PEI: Reporting on the Impact of PEI's Abortion Policies on Women.*

4   Sarah Boesveld, "Abortion Thrust into Spotlight in New Brunswick Election After 'Strategic' Blitz by Activists," *National Post*, 17 September 2014.

5   See, for example, "New Brunswick Abortion Restriction Lifted by Premier Brian Gallant," *CBC News*, 26 November 2014, http://www.cbc.ca/news/canada/new-brunswick/new-brunswick-abortion-restriction-lifted-by-premier-brian-gallant-1.2850474. Under the new regulation, however, which took effect on 1 January 2015, abortions must still be performed in a hospital.

6   Jessica Yee (now Danforth), "Reproductive Justice—for Real, for Me, for You, for Now," 6 November 2010, http://jolocas.blogspot.ca/2011/11/reproductive-justice.html.

7   Leila Hessini, Lonna Hays, Emily Turner, and Sarah Packer, "Abortion Matters to Reproductive Justice," Pro-Choice Public Education Project, n.d., http://www.protectchoice.org/article.php?id=144.

8   Ibid.

9   We are not alone in the belief that tackling abortion stigma should be a key focus. In addition to a number of academic articles on the issue, this topic is receiving considerable attention in online media. See, for example, Steph Herold and Kate Cockrill, "Imagining a World Without Abortion Stigma," *RH Reality Check*, 26 September 2014, http://rhrealitycheck.org/article/2014/09/26/imagining-world-without-abortion-stigma/.

10 See, for example, Hessini et al., "Abortion Matters to Reproductive Justice."

11 For a critique of the images used by anti-abortionists, see Carol Williams and Don Gill, "Visual Spectacle as Propaganda," *The Meliorist*, 7 November 2013, http://themeliorist.ca/2013/11/visual-spectacle-as-propaganda/.

12 On greying physicians, see Anne Mullens, "7:10 am, Nov. 8, 1994." On provider training, see Pat Smith, "The New Generation: Abortion in Medical Schools"; Laura Eggertson, "Abortion Services in Canada: A Patchwork Quilt with Many Holes"; Erika Bennett, "Barriers to Access to Abortion Services in Ontario"; Abortion Rights Coalition of Canada, "The Canadian Abortion Provider Shortage: Now and Tomorrow"; and Atsuko Koyama and Robin Williams, "Abortion in Medical School Curricula."

13 See Jenny O'Donnell, Tracy A. Weitz, and Lori Freedman, "Resistance and Vulnerability to Stigmatization in Abortion Work."

14 Noël Patten argues that midwives could easily be used to expand the provision of abortion services given the extensive training they already receive. Patten, "Pro-choice or No-choice? Midwifery Led Abortion Care in Canada." Midwives, as well as nurse practitioners and physician assistants, have been trained in pilot projects in the United States to provide first-trimester abortions. See Susan Yanow, "It Is Time to Integrate Abortion into Primary Care," 15.

15 See Yanow, "It Is Time to Integrate Abortion," 15.

16 Canadians for Choice, "Access at a Glance: Abortion Services in Canada [Spring 2012]," http://www.sexualhealthandrights.ca/wp-content/uploads/2015/09/Access-at-a-Glance-Abortion-Services-in-Canada.pdf. For more on access issues, see Melissa Haussman, *Abortion Politics in North America*, 87–97.

17 See Statistics Canada, "Population by Sex and Age Group," last modified 29 September 2015, http://www.statcan.gc.ca/tables-tableaux/sum-som/l01/cst01/demo10a-eng.htm.

18 For accounts of this criticism, see, for example, Betsy Hartmann, *Reproductive Rights and Wrongs: The Global Politics of Population Control*; Jael Silliman et al., *Undivided Rights: Women of Color Organizing for Reproductive Justice*, 12–13; Dorothy Roberts, *Killing the Black Body: Race, Reproduction, and the Meaning of Liberty*, 104–49; and Andrea Smith, "Beyond Pro-choice Versus Pro-life: Women of Color and Reproductive Justice," 130–32.

19 See Hadley Freeman, "Why Young Women Are Going off the Pill and on to Contraception Voodoo," *The Guardian*, 29 October 2013; Ann Friedman, "No Pill? No Prob. Meet the Pullout Generation," *The Cut*, 5 September 2013, http://nymag.com/thecut/2013/09/pill-no-prob-meet-the-pullout-generation.html; Katie Gilbert, "The New Old-School Birth Control," *The Atlantic*, 26 September 2013; and Lori Frohwirth, Ann M. Moore, and Renata Maniaci, "Perceptions of Susceptibility to Pregnancy Among U.S. Women Obtaining Abortions."

20 For one study on the negative impact of the clinic setting, see Katrina Kimport, Kate Cockrill, and Tracy A. Weitz, "Analyzing the Impacts of Abortion Clinic Structures and Processes: A Qualitative Analysis of Women's Negative Experience of Abortion Clinics."

21 "RU-486 Abortion Pill Approved by Health Canada," *CBC News*, 30 July 2015, http://www.cbc.ca/news/health/ru-486-abortion-pill-approved-by-health-canada-1.3173515.

22 See, for example, Kate Cockrill and Adina Nack, "'I'm Not That Type of Person': Managing the Stigma of Having an Abortion."

23 Katha Pollitt, *Pro: Reclaiming Abortion Rights*. As noted in the introduction to this collection, Dr. Henry Morgentaler viewed abortion as having positive social consequences.

24 For an assessment on the limitations of legal victories in the US context, see Marlene Gerber Fried, "Reproductive Rights Activism in the Post-Roe Era."

25 For a thought-provoking blog post on the reaction of settler Canadians to this suggestion, see Lynn Gehl, "Unhinging Settler Consciousness," *Black Face Blogging*, 24 September 2014, http://www.lynngehl.com/black-face-blogging/unhinging-settler-consciousness. Gehl's website includes a list of readings for settlers wishing to learn how to be allies.

26 Eveline Shen, "Asian Communities for Reproductive Justice Answers the Question: What Is Reproductive Justice?" 6. As Loretta Ross argues, "What we see is the failure of the pro-choice movement to analyze how white supremacy has affected them. You cannot do RJ without analyzing white supremacy—you just can't." Quoted in Yee, "Reproductive Justice."

27 Jessica Shaw, in "Abortion as a Social Justice Issue in Contemporary Canada," makes a compelling argument for viewing abortion from the perspective of social justice.

References

Abortion Rights Coalition of Canada. "The Canadian Abortion Provider Shortage: Now and Tomorrow." Position Paper No. 5. October 2005. http://www.arcc-cdac.ca/postionpapers/05-Abortion-Provider-Shortage.PDF.

Ackerman, Katrina. "In Defence of Reason: Religion, Science, and the Prince Edward Island Anti-Abortion Movement, 1969–1988." *Canadian Bulletin of Medical History* 31, no. 2 (2014): 117–38.

Bennett, Erika. "Barriers to Access to Abortion Services in Ontario." Graduate School of Public and International Affairs, University of Ottawa, 2014. https://www.ruor.uottawa.ca/bitstream/10393/31472/1/BENNETT,%20Erika%2020145.pdf.

Cockrill, Kate, and Adina Nack. "'I'm Not That Type of Person': Managing the Stigma of Having an Abortion." *Deviant Behavior* 34, no. 12 (2013): 973–90.

Eggertson, Laura. "Abortion Services in Canada: A Patchwork Quilt with Many Holes." *Canadian Medical Association Journal* 164, no. 6 (2001): 847–49. www.cmaj.ca/cgi/reprint/164/6/847.pdf.

Fried, Marlene Gerber. "Reproductive Rights Activism in the Post-Roe Era." *American Journal of Public Health* 103, no. 1 (2013): 10–14.

Frohwirth, Lori, Ann M. Moore, and Renata Maniaci, "Perceptions of Susceptibility to Pregnancy Among U.S. Women Obtaining Abortions." *Social Science and Medicine* 99 (December 2013): 18–26.

Hartmann, Betsy. *Reproductive Rights and Wrongs: The Global Politics of Population Control.* Boston: South End Press, 1995.

Haussman, Melissa. *Abortion Politics in North America.* Boulder, CO: Lynne Rienner, 2005.

Kimport, Katrina, Kate Cockrill, and Tracy A. Weitz. "Analyzing the Impacts of Abortion Clinic Structures and Processes: A Qualitative Analysis of Women's Negative Experience of Abortion Clinics." *Contraception* 85, no. 2 (2012): 204–10.

Koyama, Atsuko, and Robin Williams. "Abortion in Medical School Curricula." *McGill Journal of Medicine* 8, no. 2 (2005): 157–60.

MacQuarrie, Colleen, Jo-Ann MacDonald, and Cathrine Chambers. *Trials and Trails of Accessing Abortion in PEI: Reporting on the Impact of PEI's Abortion Policies on Women.* January 2014. http://projects.upei.ca/cmacquarrie/files/2014/01/trials_and_trails_final.pdf.

Mullens, Anne. "7:10 am, Nov. 8, 1994." *Canadian Medical Association Journal* 158, no. 4 (1998): 528–31.

O'Donnell, Jenny, Tracy A. Weitz, and Lori Freedman. "Resistance and Vulnerability to Stigmatization in Abortion Work." *Social Science and Medicine* 73 (2011): 1357–64.

Patten, Noël. "Pro-choice or No-choice? Midwifery Led Abortion Care in Canada." *Canadian Journal of Midwifery Research and Practice* 8, no. 2 (2009): 29–30, 37.

Pollitt, Katha. *Pro: Reclaiming Abortion Rights.* New York: Picador, 2014.

Roberts, Dorothy. *Killing the Black Body: Race, Reproduction, and the Meaning of Liberty.* New York: Vintage, 1999. First published in 1997 by Pantheon Books.

Shaw, Jessica. "Abortion as a Social Justice Issue in Contemporary Canada." *Critical Social Work* 14, no. 2 (2013): 1–17.

Shen, Eveline. "Asian Communities for Reproductive Justice Answers the Question: What Is Reproductive Justice?" *Collective Voices* 1, no. 2 (2005): 6.

Silliman, Jael, Marlene Gerber Fried, Loretta Ross, and Elena Gutierrez. *Undivided Rights: Women of Color Organizing for Reproductive Justice.* Boston: South End Press, 2004.

Smith, Andrea. "Beyond Pro-choice Versus Pro-life: Women of Color and Reproductive Justice." *NWSA Journal* 17, no. 1 (2005): 119–40.

Smith, Pat. "The New Generation: Abortion in Medical Schools." In *Of What Difference? Reflections on the Judgment and Abortion in Canada Today*, 49–53. Proceedings of the Twentieth Anniversary *Regina v. Morgentaler* Symposium, 25 January 2008, Toronto. http://www.prochoice.org/pubs_research/publications/downloads/canada/ofwhatdifference.pdf.

Yanow, Susan. "It Is Time to Integrate Abortion into Primary Care." *American Journal of Public Health* 103, no. 1 (2013): 14–16.

Contributors

Aalya Ahmad is a community and labour activist and a member of the Radical Handmaids. She teaches at the Pauline Jewett Institute of Women's and Gender Studies at Carleton University, in Ottawa. Her interests include feminism activism and cultural production in diaspora, as well as the politics and poetics of horror film and fiction. Her essay "Feminist Spaces in Horrific Places" appeared in the July 2014 issue of *Offscreen*.

Tracey L. Anderson taught English as a second language in China, Macedonia, Morocco, and the United Arab Emirates. Currently, she's a freelance writer and editor based in Edmonton, Alberta, where she lives with her husband, Roland. When she's not working with words, Tracey enjoys travel, movies, reading, and fine dining.

Jane Cawthorne is the author of the play *The Abortion Monologues*. She has been active in the reproductive rights movement for over twenty-five years, has taught women's studies at Mount Royal

College, in Calgary, and has been a volunteer with organizations such as Planned Parenthood Alberta, the Calgary Sexual Health Centre, and the Abortion Rights Coalition of Canada. She is the co-editor, with Elaine Morin, of a literary anthology titled *Writing Menopause*, forthcoming in spring 2017 from Inanna Publications.

Peggy Cooke is a nonprofit staffer by day and a reproductive justice activist by . . . later that same day. In addition to her three years as a volunteer coordinator at the Fredericton Morgentaler Clinic, she has served as a board member and media spokesperson for the Abortion Rights Coalition of Canada and as a fundraiser and administrator for ACORN Canada. She wants to burn prisons, although she always crosses at the lights. Founder of the blog *Anti-Choice Is Anti-Awesome*, she is an active commentator on the Internet.

Shannon Dea is an associate professor of philosophy at the University of Waterloo. Her areas of specialization are the history of philosophy, gender issues, and pedagogy. She is the author of *Beyond the Binary: Thinking About Sex and Gender*, as well as of numerous articles. An advocate of gender equity, LGBTQ inclusivity, and improved sexual health, Dea contributes many volunteer hours to academic committees and community agencies dedicated to these goals. In this capacity, she devotes much of her time to public outreach, discussion panels, media interviews, and public speaking engagements. She is the former director of the Women's Studies program at the University of Waterloo and past president of Planned Parenthood Waterloo Region.

Carolyn Egan is a member of the Ontario Coalition for Abortion Clinics. She is president of the community board of the Immigrant Women's Health Centre and president of the United Steelworkers Toronto Area Council. She has worked with Women Working with Immigrant Women and the International Women's Day Committee in Toronto and has been a long-time activist in the women's and reproductive rights movements.

Linda Gardner has served on the boards of the Canadian AIDS Treatment Information Exchange, Maggie's: The Toronto Sex Workers Action Project, and the Gay Asians AIDS Project Toronto. A leader with the Ontario Coalition for Abortion Clinics during the campaign to overturn the federal abortion law, she has worked for many years in the area of sexual health and was the Diversity and Community Access Coordinator at Women's College Hospital.

Laura Gillespie graduated from the University of Victoria in 2013 with a bachelor's degree in sociology. As a burgeoning reproductive rights activist, Laura is particularly interested in examining the socially constructed meaning behind the language used in reproductive justice discourse.

Sterling Haynes is a retired GP and an octogenarian writer of stories, zany poetry, and haiku. He is the author of two collections of stories, *Bloody Practice* and *Wake-Up Call: Tales from a Frontier Doctor*, both published by Caitlin Press. He loved doing obstetrics and, over the course of his practice, delivered about three thousand babies.

E.K. Hornbeck is a feminist, doula, and radio lover living in Halifax, Nova Scotia. She has written for the *Dalhousie Gazette* and has been featured on CBC Radio, CKDU, and Anglican Video in Halifax. Her interests include reproductive justice, the history of science, a cup of tea, and a good book.

Clarissa Hurley is completing a PhD at the Centre for Drama, Theatre, and Performance Studies at the University of Toronto and lives in Fredericton, New Brunswick, where she works with NotaBle Acts Theatre Company. She has lectured in English, theatre, and women's studies at universities in Ontario and New Brunswick and is currently co-authoring *Roughing It in the Sacred Grove*, an examination of campus-based fiction and life writing by Canadian women academics.

"Dr. James" is an obstetrician and gynaecologist based in Ontario. He has been involved in the pro-choice movement in many ways, first as a member of Medical Students for Choice and then as an abortion provider and a board member for several national pro-choice organizations.

H. Bindy K. Kang received her bachelor's and master's degrees at Simon Fraser University. After eleven years of social science research and three years in community health outreach, she returned to school and is currently completing a PhD in the University of British Columbia's Interdisciplinary Studies Graduate Program. Her research interests include the intersectional influence of gender, ethnicity, and culture on health, barriers to and facilitators of health care access and delivery, and culture and identity constructions.

Kristen has a Bachelor of Social Work from Ryerson University and a background in early childhood education. A feminist and mental health advocate, she identifies as Mad and currently works for a peer-led Toronto-based mental health organization that supports individuals experiencing borderline personality disorder. She lives in Toronto with her partner and their child.

Natalie Lochwin is an activist and artist based in Toronto, where she raises her three children. A graduate of the Ontario College of Art and Design, she is a member of the Socialist Party of Ontario, serving as the party's spokesperson and candidate in Etobicoke-Lakeshore riding in the 2014 provincial election.

Mackenzie lives in southern Ontario. Having completed an MSW degree, she currently works to support adults with co-occurring addiction and mental health concerns.

Colleen MacQuarrie, an associate professor in and currently chair of the Department of Psychology at the University of Prince Edward Island, is an academic activist and developmental health researcher who has been working in feminist community organizations for more than twenty years. Critical perspectives on social justice are central to her research, teaching, and community actions.

Ruth Miller began her career in the field of women's reproductive rights early in the 1970s, working for the repeal of section 251 of the Criminal Code. She was for many years a board member of the Canadian Association for Repeal of the Abortion Law (CARAL) and a trustee of the Childbirth by Choice Trust. In these capacities, she created and edited material on abortion and contraception, including the 1989 publication *No Choice: Canadian Women Tell Their Stories of Illegal Abortion*. She served for two decades as a sexual health educator for Toronto Public Health and, since retirement, has been counselling part time at the Morgentaler Clinic.

Judith Mintz is a PhD candidate in the Gender, Feminist, and Women's Studies program at York University, in Toronto. Her doctoral research, in which she adopts a feminist ethnographic approach, focuses on yoga and the intersections of social location and health. Her essay "Empowering Women to Become Mothers," an examination of modern midwifery in Ontario, appeared in *The 21st Century Motherhood Movement*, a collection edited by Andrea O'Reilly and published by Demeter Press.

Erin Mullan is an abortion counsellor and sexual health educator with more than twenty-five years of experience in the field of reproductive health. She works from a social justice perspective and has a special interest in reducing the stigma surrounding abortion. She is also an organic master gardener who believes that helping plants grow is excellent therapy.

Jen Rinaldi is an assistant professor in the Legal Studies program at the University of Ontario Institute of Technology and holds a PhD in critical disability studies from York University. In her dissertation, she employed a postmodern feminist framework to analyze the impact of medical technologies on reproductive decision making. Rinaldi earned her master's degree in philosophy at the University of Guelph, where her research focused on constitutional protections of same-sex marriage legislation. In her current academic work, she uses narrative and arts-based methodologies to deconstruct eating disorder recovery in relation to queer community. Rinaldi works in collaboration with Recounting Huronia, a SSHRC-funded arts-based collective that explores and documents traumatic histories of institutionalization.

Sadie Roberts holds a master's degree in community psychology from Wilfrid Laurier University and a master's in counselling from Acadia University. She completed her undergraduate degree at the University of Prince Edward Island, where she majored in psychology. Her research interests include reproductive justice, LGBTQ issues, and liberation psychology, as well as local food movements. She has been the recipient of grants from the Canadian Institute of Health Research and the Ontario Graduate Scholarship Program.

Martha Solomon, a British Columbia–based educator, activist, and writer, holds a master's degree in women's studies and history from the University of Toronto and has taught philosophy and women's studies at the postsecondary level in both Canada and the United States. Passionate about social justice and equity, she is especially drawn to the intersection between art and activism. She is the cofounder, with photographer Kathryn Palmateer, of the award-winning Arts4Choice project, dedicated to ending the silence and stigma surrounding abortion through narrative and image. Exhibits based on the project have travelled to Toronto, Ottawa, Calgary, and Portland, and a book, *One Kind Word: Women Share Their Abortion Stories*, appeared in 2014 from Three O'Clock Press.

Shannon Stettner is an activist-academic who has been involved in the abortion rights movement for many years. She holds a PhD in history from York University and presently lectures on gender history in the Department of Women's Studies at the University of Waterloo. She was active on the planning committee for Abortion: The Unfinished Revolution, an international interdisciplinary conference held in Charlottetown, Prince Edward Island, in August 2014. The author of numerous publications, she also served as the Canadian Manuscripts editor at the *Canadian Bulletin of Medical History*.

Karen Stote is assistant professor of women and gender studies at Wilfrid Laurier University, where she teaches courses on the history of Indian policy and Indigenous-settler relations, feminism and the politics of decolonization, and issues of environmental and reproductive justice. She is the author of *An Act of Genocide: Colonialism and the Sterilization of Aboriginal Women* and has collaborated on various public education projects on issues surrounding Indigenous-settler relations.

Nick Van der Graaf is a journalist and long-time pro-choice activist with the Ontario Coalition for Abortion Clinics. He works as a patient escort at an abortion clinic and is a board member of the BCVD sexual health clinic in Toronto. He has written on women's rights and abortion politics for the *Huffington Post* and for magazines such as *On the Issues* and *NOW*.

Bernadette Wagner is a writer, a mother, and a community educator and organizer who lives in Regina, Saskatchewan. Her work has been featured on radio and television, in film and on the Web, in schools, on stages, and in the streets, as well as in journals, anthologies, newspapers, and magazines. *This Hot Place*, her first collection of poetry, appeared from Thistledown Press in 2010. She maintains a multi-author blog, *The Regina Mom*, devoted to women's issues and political activism.

Laura Wershler is a Calgary-based sexual and reproductive health advocate, writer, and speaker. She has been involved with pro-choice organizations at the local, provincial, and national levels for more than twenty-five years, serving on the board of the Planned Parenthood Federation of Canada and as the executive director of Sexual Health Access Alberta. She writes about a wide range of sexual and reproductive health issues from a sociopolitical perspective and is presently an active member of the Society for Menstrual Cycle Research, an interdisciplinary organization that supports research into the role of menstruation in women's health and well-being.

Shannon West lives the adventurous life of stay-at-home mom to three kids on the autism spectrum and an incontinent dog. She's married to a wonderful man who bakes scones and lets her sleep in on weekends. She has a master's degree in linguistics that she feels she should mention because it was expensive. She's a feminist, a Christian, and a socialist, although not necessarily in that order. She blogs under the name Luna at feministchristian. blogspot.com and @heading_west on Twitter.

Ellen Wiebe, a clinical professor in the Department of Family Medicine at the University of British Columbia and the medical director of Willow Women's Clinic, has been an abortion provider in Vancouver since 1977. The author of more than sixty research papers on abortion and contraception, she was the first to provide medical abortions in Canada, spearheading clinical trials of RU-486 long before the drug was approved by Health Canada. She has also assumed a pioneering role with regard to the right to die. In February 2016, she secured judicial authorization to assist in the death of a Calgary woman suffering from late-stage ALS.

Jess Woolford is an essayist, memoirist, and prize-winning poet whose reflections on abortion and reproductive anxiety have appeared in *Social Politics, Prairie Fire,* and *Contemporary Verse 2.* Her work has also been featured in anthologies, including *A/Cross Sections: New Manitoba Writing* and *In the Company of Animals: Stories of Extraordinary Encounters.* Although she grew up in Vermont, Woolford now calls Winnipeg home.